Damned Souls in a Tobacco Colony

Damned Souls in a Tobacco Colony:
Religion in Seventeenth-Century Virginia

Edward L. Bond

Mercer
University
Press
2000

ISBN 0-86554-708-4
MUP/H526

∞The paper used in this publication meets the minimum
requirements of American National Standard for Information
Sciences—Permanence of Paper for Printed Library Materials,
ANSI Z39.48-1992.

Library of Congress Cataloging-in-Publication Data
Bond, Edward L.
Damned Souls in a tobacco colony: religion in seventeenth-century
Virginia / Edward L. Bond.
p. cm.
Includes bibliographical references and index.
ISBN 0-86554-708-4 (alk. paper)
1. Virginia—Church history—17th century. 2. Church of
England—Virginia—History—17th century. I. Title.

BR555.V* B66 2001
277.55'06—dc21

00-067569

Contents

To Kathleen

"*Souls!* Damn your Souls! Make Tobacco."

Attributed to Sir Edward Seymour, one of His Majesty's
Lords of the Treasury

PREFACE

When I was researching and writing my book, people often asked me what I was writing about. When I told them I was writing about religion in seventeenth-century Virginia, I was frequently confronted by several different reactions. One group of people were quite certain that there was no religion, at least not enough of one to write a book about, in Virginia until the Great Awakening. Another group of people were willing to grant that there was a topic here worth pursuing, but were nonetheless confused by the word "religion." Some people thought I meant that I was writing an institutional history of Virginia's established Anglican Church. Others thought I had told them I was writing about theology, devotion, and piety. Yet others believed the book was going to be about the place of religion in the colonial polity. Some people thought that when I said religion I meant popular religion—magic and witchcraft. With the exception of popular religion, which I have chosen to address elsewhere,[1] this book encompasses all of those understandings of religion, for to English people of the seventeenth century, there was simply no means of separating questions about the divine, about which form of religious polity was the best, about how God should best be worshipped, or about theology—to mention just a few issues having to do with religion—from the rest of one's life.

I have tried, first and foremost, to understand religion as a relationship with God, finding this a far more successful way of investigating the host of questions associated with religion than the interpretive model of the institutional church, which historians often use when writing about polities that have established churches. Focusing on religion as a relationship with the divine forces us to emphasize an end rather than a means.

---

[1]Edward L. Bond, "Source of Knowledge, Source of Power: The Supernatural World of English Virginia, 1607-1624," *Virginia Magazine of History and Biography* 108 (2000): 105-38.

The end of religion for the faithful Christian in the early modern era was a relationship with a personal deity; one the believer hoped would culminate in the glories of eternal salvation. An institutional church, established or not, is but a means to achieving this end. But the relational quality must come first. This approach has been particularly useful in my study of early Virginia, for it has allowed me to see clearly both the conservative and dynamic elements in the way Virginians, as individuals and as corporate members of the polity, defined their individual and corporate relationships with the divine. They were not only transplanters of institutions, but also creators of new ones, or, more accurately, ones they later came to realize were new and different from the traditional English models.

So, to answer the question of what this book is about, it is about institutional facets of Virginia's established church, it is about theology, personal piety, and the ways in which people showed their devotion. It is about the place of institutional religion in the good polity, and it is about how a people from different religious parties could organize a corporate relationship with God despite their enduring differences about theology and devotional practice. In addressing these issues, it became obvious that by the end of the seventeenth century, Virginians had created their own religious identity separate from that of the mother country. It is this story that my book seeks to tell.

The chapters are organized to address more particular issues as the book progresses. The first chapter sets the Virginia colony in the context of the English relationship with God and the origins of the English empire. The second chapter then explores the religious polity the Virginia Company and colonial leaders created and the forces that shaped their decisions. Chapter 3 then focuses on the growth of religious devotion in the colony, the colonist's desire for a greater presence of institutional religion in Virginia, the origins in the colony of both a colonial version of the Church of England, and a broadly tolerant religious polity (noting, however, the difficulties of creating the latter). Chapter 4 picks up the many threads touching upon the issue of religious identity in the previous chapters and demonstrates how Virginians by the end of the seventeenth century believed themselves to be Anglicans, but were nonetheless defending an ecclesiastical institution of a different model. The fifth chapter provides an analysis of theology and devotional practices within Virginia's Anglican Church from the 1680s to the 1740s. The last chapter uses the story of Devereaux Jarratt not only to look towards the mid-eighteenth century but also to suggest that Anglicans and dissenters had far more in common than they may have cared to admit and reiterates the emergence of a distinct colonial identity in Virginia.

At all points, I have been guided in this study by the available sources. Most historians of Virginia are familiar with just how maddening these materials can be. Tremendous gaps exist in the extant sources, making it far easier to address theology between 1680 and 1740 than between 1607 and 1640, a period from which there are virtually no sources that can be used to establish a coherent theology among Virginians beyond the simple fact that they were overwhelmingly Christians. The converse is true about Virginia's ecclesiastical polity. It is far easier to describe this polity early in the century than it is between the years of 1685 and 1710. With that being said, the extant materials, given their spottiness, still allow us to gain a fairly solid understanding of religion in colonial Virginia and its place in the lives of the people who lived there.

There are many people to thank for the assistance they have offered me during the years I worked on this project. I benefited from the assistance of archivists and reference librarians at the Virginia Historical Society, the Library of Virginia, and the Earl Gregg Swem Library at the College of William and Mary. Most of the research was done at the Colonial Williamsburg Foundation's John D. Rockefeller, Jr. Library. I owe special thanks to Susan Berg and her staff there, especially to John Ingram, who taught me how to make my way through the labyrinth of the Virginia Colonial Records Project. Gail Greve and Del Moore graciously answered numerous questions about sources and gave the project their support. At Alabama A & M University,

Sebastian Nwaneri, the interlibrary loan librarian, filled my numerous requests for materials quickly and with good humor.

I am indebted to Warren Billings, Thad Tate, Anne Loveland, Brent Tarter, Gaines Foster, James Morris, and, especially, Charles Royster, for their comments and criticisms on earlier drafts of the manuscript. Charles Royster and James Morris taught me what it is to be a historian.

I am grateful to the *Virginia Magazine of History and Biography* for permission to reprint portions of "Anglican Theology and Devotion in James Blair's Virginia, 1685-1743: Private Piety in the Public Church"; and to *Anglican and Episcopal History* for permission to reprint portions of "England's Soteriology of Empire and the Roots of Colonial Identity in Early Virginia."

Lastly, I owe more to Kathleen for this project and my life than I can put into words. Each day, I am filled with joy and gratitude that we met. This book is dedicated to her.

Edward L. Bond
1 December 1999
Natchez, Mississippi

CHAPTER ONE

GET THEE OUT OF THY LAND

William Crashaw mounted the pulpit of Paules Crosse in London in February 1609/10. He had come to the church at the behest of fellow members of the Virginia Company of London, an English trading company interested in establishing and profiting from overseas colonies. They had asked the young Church of England minister to preach a sermon to the group before Lord De la Warr, Virginia's new governor and captain-general, set sail for the colony. These were not auspicious times for supporters of English colonial grandeur, and the company hoped that la Warr, a veteran of fighting in the Low Countries, would make Virginia a success. Not only had England begun colonizing long after her Spanish and Portuguese rivals had established New World empires, but England's few attempts at planting permanent settlements had so far failed miserably. And the situation in Virginia was not looking good. In the three years since the colony's founding in 1607, little had been accomplished. No one had reaped any profits, the colony tottered on the verge of collapse, and Virginia had gained a reputation as a deathtrap. English settlers went to Virginia; English settlers died in Virginia. Foreign intrigue threatened the settlement as well. Not content to let the colony fail as a result of English ineptitude, Spanish diplomats in London sent dispatches to King Philip III outlining what they would do to remove England's outpost in North American if only they, rather than Philip, were king of Spain. The outlook for Virginia's success in the early months of 1610 was, in fact, even more distressing than anyone in England may have realized.

Even as the adventurers in Crashaw's London audience listened to his sermon, the few colonists remaining in Virginia were seriously considering packing up and abandoning the settlement.[1]

Crashaw preached that February day from Luke's Gospel: "I have prayed for thee, that thy faith fail not." He gave the oft-repeated advice of putting religion first, acting from the inspiration of religious motives rather than greed, and especially urged the conversion of Virginia's native peoples—these were typical sentiments expressed by most ministers who supported colonization. For a colonial effort beset with crises, he also offered hope, implying that an Anglophile deity had fore-ordained English success in Virginia. The venture's "principall friend and defender," Crashaw declared, "is the Lord our God."[2] This was no insignificant claim. By the early seventeenth century, the phrase "friend of God" had a long and evocative history.

---

[1] William Crashaw, *A Sermon Preached in London before the right honorable the Lord Laware, Lord Governour and Captaine Generall of Virginea* (London, 1610); Richard Beale Davis, *Intellectual Life in the Colonial South, 1585-1763*, 3 vols. (Knoxville: University of Tennessee Press, 1978) 2:706-707; Pedro de Zuñiga to Philip III, 5 March 1609/1610, in Alexander Brown, ed. *The Genesis of the United States*, 2 vols. (New York: Russell & Russell, 1964) 1:246; Richard L. Morton, *Colonial Virginia*, 2 vols. (Chapel Hill: University of North Carolina Press, 1960) 1:22-26. For background on the animosities between Spain and England, see Louis B. Wright, "Elizabethan Politics and Colonial Enterprise," *North Carolina Historical Review* 32 (1955): 254-69. For accounts of English exploration before the Virginia venture, see David Beers Quinn, *Set Fair for Roanoke: Voyages and Colonies, 1584-1606* (Chapel Hill: University of North Carolina Press, 1985) and Karen Ordahl Kupperman, *Roanoke: The Abandoned Colony* (Totowa NJ: Rowman & Allanheld, 1984). Adventurers were people who invested or "adventured" their funds in the Virginia venture. People who actually came to Virginia as colonists were known as planters.

[2] Crashaw, *Sermon Preached in London*, title page, I-2, A-3, C-3; Edmund S. Morgan, *American Slavery, American Freedom: The Ordeal of Colonial Virginia* (New York: W. W. Norton, 1975) 45-48; Patricia Seed, "Taking Possession and Reading Texts: Establishing the Authority of English Overseas Empires," *William and Mary Quarterly* 3rd ser. 49 (1992): 188, n. 16.

Plato had referred to the just man in this fashion; Christians in the third and fourth centuries had employed the term to describe holy men ranging from martyrs and bishops to ascetics like the hermit Antony; during the Middle Ages churchmen had often used it when they alluded to extraordinarily pious believers or those possessed of saintly qualities such as Meister Eckhart or Bernard of Clairvaux. The Old Testament also referred to God's friends, which was the likely source of Crashaw's reference. The book of Exodus endowed the lawgiver Moses with this intimate relationship to the God of the fathers: "And the Lord spake unto Moses, face to face, as a man speaketh unto his friend." Yet Moses was not the only Old Testament hero described in this manner. God had also spoken directly to the patriarch Abraham, who had left his homeland at God's command armed with the deity's promise that he would found a great nation, a model that English colonizers associated with Virginia found particularly appealing during the first years of successful overseas expansion in the early seventeenth century.[3]

Describing an individual as one of God's friends implied a relationship with the deity closer than that between God and ordinary believers. Perhaps God protected his friends from their enemies, or perhaps he placed greater responsibilities on them. "A friend of God," according to one modern political theorist, "wishing to please God, does what he thinks God wishes him to do, and therefore the presumption might be that God reciprocates the friendship." Crashaw intensified the relationship further, calling God a "principall friend and defender," then expanded it into a communal definition: "our God." In short, he described to the Virginia Company a special relationship between an expanding nation and a God in the practice of choosing favorites, thereby tying friendship with God to English national identity. Crashaw was not alone. Anglican, Puritan, and

[3] Sebastian de Grazia, *Machiavelli in Hell* (Princeton: Princeton University Press, 1989) 50-51; Perry Miller, "Religion and Society in the Early Literature of Virginia," in *Errand Into the Wilderness* (Cambridge: Harvard University Press, 1956) 119.

Roman Catholic authors in England who otherwise quarreled with each other about religious doctrines and practices nonetheless accepted this construction of English nationhood and agreed that the end result of this friendship would be an English North America.[4] On that, at least, most Englishmen could agree; it formed part of the nation's collective mood on the eve of colonization.

Of the Christian deity and his friendship the English were certain, even if they disagreed about how he should be worshipped or what theology his scriptures advocated. Other aspects of English identity, however, were more ambiguous than the general belief in the nation's relationship with God. Late Elizabethan and Jacobean England lacked a stable concept of nationhood, experiencing instead what has been termed a "growing and widespread anxiety...concerning England's cultural identity." The roots of this crisis lay in the changing understanding of politics and administration taking place in the sixteenth century. The transformations were profound and had immense implications, bringing about in England the death of medieval forms of government and the birth of something recognizable to modern sensibilities. The Tudor "revolution," as it has been called, transformed the nature of sovereignty by shifting its focus from the king and his household to the nation as a whole. No longer did government consist of the private management of the king's estate by the king and his household as it had in the past, but rather it came to mean something national in scope, support, and administration that existed separately from the king and his household. One could say that England as a state began to have interests of its own which transcended regnal concerns. Summarizing the changes, historian G. R. Elton wrote: "[T]he duality of state and church was destroyed by the victory of the state, the crown triumphed over its rivals,

---

[4]de Grazia, *Machiavelli in Hell*, 51; Karen Ordahl Kupperman, *Settling With the Indians: The Meeting of English and Indian Cultures in America, 1580-1640* (Totowa NJ: Rowman and Littlefield, 1980) 159-68, esp. 159-63.

parliamentary statute triumphed over the abstract law of Christianity, and a self-contained national unit came to be, not the tacitly accepted necessity it had been for some time, but the consciously desired goal." England was moving toward a polity in which the status and abilities of the king and those close to him did not determine whether or not government existed within a territory. The pivotal decisions in England had occurred in the 1530s. In that decade Parliament had declared England an empire, the nation had severed its ties with the Church of Rome, establishing in its place a Church of England, and the monarch had become the supreme head of both church and state. While these events helped shape the new political world, King Henry VIII's administration was in the process of creating a national governmental apparatus. A new concept of sovereignty demanded a new sense of national self-definition, elevating as a result national issues rather than dynastic identity. England, things English, and England's deeds at once became issues of greater importance than in the past, for England now mattered more and traditional dynastic sources of identity mattered less.[5]

In the years between 1530 and 1600, England's Tudor monarchs oversaw the gradual consolidation of a recognizable nation-state. Largely feudal when Parliament had declared the nation an empire in the 1530s, England had taken the shape of a modern state by the time James I ascended to the throne in 1603. Bureaucratizing the state, however, was one thing, constructing an identity another. The issue of identity was an important one, for the new sovereignty and the new politics raised questions foreign to the past. If national identity rather than regnal identity was what mattered, then which English people counted as English? Despite the development of an English state, on the eve of colonization no accompanying source of national identity had yet emerged to articulate an un-

---

[5] Richard Helgerson, *Forms of Nationhood: The Elizabethan Writing of England* (Chicago: University of Chicago Press, 1992) 4; G. R. Elton, *The Tudor Revolution in Government: Administrative Changes in the Reign of Henry VIII* (Cambridge: Cambridge University Press, 1969) 4.

ambiguous English self-understanding. England in the late sixteenth and early seventeenth centuries remained a jumble of
cultural remnants and competing groups, still in the process of
completing the movement from dynastic to nation-state politics.
Numerous cultural and political rifts divided the nation. A
variety of Protestant religious parties squabbled for control of
the English Church, while a sizable minority of English
Catholics prayed that the nation would recognize its errors and
return to the Church of Rome. Crown and Parliament guarded
their powers jealously, each trying when it could, to expand its
control at the expense of the other. Even the lines of dissension
between court and country familiar to historians of the American
Revolution were already being drawn and a growing number of
merchants increasingly challenged the traditional powers of the
nobles. Class divisions further muddled the question of English
identity. Although springing from very different facets of English
culture, both aristocrats and members of the lower classes
considered themselves English. Was English culture based on the
"folk" or on an English version of aristocratic society like that of
other European nations—on the high culture of the elite or the
revels of the mob? On this important question of national
identity there was no agreement. Jacobean poet Michael Drayton
poked fun at his nation's lack of an identity, suggesting that
given the nature of his countrymen any identity they found
would be transitory at best: "My muse is rightly of the English
strain,/That cannot long one fashion entertain." English people
shared little more than a sense of their own superiority over
Frenchmen and Spaniards and the members of other less
fortunate nations, by which they meant everyone who was not
English. Arrogant and confident, the English looked down upon
other people, believing themselves to be especially blessed, a
pridefulness well captured by William Shakespeare's John of
Gaunt in *Richard II*: "This happy breed of men, this little world,
This precious stone set in the silver sea...the envy of less happier
lands." But just which English people constituted this "Happy
breed of men" depended upon who answered the question. At a
time when the nation began more and more to think of planting

overseas colonies, who was English and what was England remained vexing issues.[6]

Englishmen sought solutions to this problem in many places. Elizabethan and Jacobean intellectuals—including Francis Bacon, William Shakespeare, John Speed, and Herbert Spencer—became obsessed with the question, participating in what has been called a "generational project" to define their nation. They offered answers to the question of England's cultural identity in religion, law, rhyme, and mission, prescribing in their own ways an idealized England they wanted to exist rather than describing the real England that existed. Sensitive to the charges of foreigners who ridiculed English law and verse as vulgar remnants of a barbarous past, Edward Coke and Herbert Spencer, respectively, constructed suitable English versions of both. Other authors addressed more tangible facets of nationhood. Richard Hakluyt, a minister more devoted to England than the Church, urged his countrymen to take up as a national mission the colonization of North America, transforming in the process the voyage literature of the day. Rather than recounting the wonders of newly discovered worlds or the accomplishments of European explorers in general, as similar

---

[6] Peter Lake, *Anglicans and Puritans? Presbyterian and English Conformist Thought from Whitgift to Hooker* (London: Unwin Hyman, 1988); Peter Holmes, *Resistance and Compromise: The Political Thought of the Elizabethan Catholics* (Cambridge: Cambridge University Press, 1982); John Bossy, *The English Catholic Community, 1570-1850* (New York: Oxford University Press, 1976) especially 182-94; Helgerson, *Forms of Nationhood*, 14; G. R. Elton, "Contentment and Discontentment on the Eve of Colonization," in G. R. Elton, *Studies in Tudor and Stuart Politics and Government*, 3 vols. (Cambridge: Cambridge University Press, 1983) 3:338; Warren M. Billings, John E. Selby, and Thad W. Tate, *Colonial Virginia: A History* (White Plains NY: KTO Press, 1986) 7-8; William Shakespeare, *The Tragedy of King Richard the Second*, Act II, scene ii, lines 40-64; Kathleen M. Brown has noted that this unsettled notion of English identity transcended politics and included gender issues as well. For this argument, see her *Good Wives, Nasty Wenches, and Anxious Patriarchs: Gender, Race, and Power in Colonial Virginia* (Chapel Hill: University of North Carolina Press, 1996) especially 13-41.

continental works had done, his *Principal Navigations, Voyages, and Traffics of the English Nation*, first published in 1589, celebrated instead the triumph of English navigation alone and advocated the nation's economic expansion. The volume's thesis was unmistakable: England had an identity separate from the rest of Europe. Exclusive in his narrow and polemical focus on one nation, Hakluyt defined England and England's mission in terms equally broad and inclusive. He believed that for a nation like his, which he perceived as overpopulated and teeming with vagrants unable to find work, overseas colonies would benefit all segments of the population. Colonies would bring empire, commercial rewards, and the spread of "true" English religion, although the latter did not rate prominently on the minister's list of reasons for adventuring abroad. Colonies might also help the numerous English poor by giving them work abroad, thus saving them from the jailhouse or the gallows. Anyone could participate in this venture. From the queen and courtiers to merchants and the idle poor, all comprised part of Hakluyt's England. Not everyone, however, constructed national identity as broadly as Hakluyt. Many intellectuals defined England more narrowly, often excluding portions of the English population from their forms of nationhood, and thus limiting English identity to only a certain segment of the nation. The churchman Richard Hooker, for example, offered a brilliant construction of the English Church, designed at once to include true English Christians while excluding both Roman Catholics and Puritans, at one point equating followers of Calvin with swindlers who knowingly peddled religious error.[7]

The young Elizabethans who "wrote" England helped to define their nation for later generations. Hakluyt, Coke, Shakespeare, Hooker: their names still stand as monuments of English intellectual and cultural accomplishments, standards against whom all intellectuals who came after them would be compared

---

[7] Helgerson, *Forms of Nationhood*, 1-10, 21-104, 151-91, 249-94; Morgan, *American Slavery, American Freedom*, 14-18, 28-31; Richard Hooker, *Of the Laws of Ecclesiastical Polity*, Preface, 3.4-3.14.

and against whose genius they would be found wanting. Their works provided the intellectual foundations that would shape the English nation. Hindsight makes that evaluation easier than it was at the time, for their efforts then lacked the general authority future generations have granted their words. As confused as the rest of their countrymen, intellectuals offered prescriptions for the English nation, mythic constructions of what England might become and about whom they considered English. Yet the question remained unsettled: Who was English? Those who accepted a certain form of law? People who adhered to a particular type of Protestant religion? Anyone sent on English ships to spread the English nation abroad? On this crucial issue there existed no consensus. Intellectuals thought and pondered, wrote and argued, constructed and prescribed. The more they did those things, the more they demonstrated their own and their nation's anxiety about its cultural identity. "Who are we?" Perry Miller claimed the Puritans asked of themselves after they had been "left alone" with the North American wilderness.[8] The question was neither particularly novel nor peculiar to those who fled to Leyden and then to America. It was a broader facet of sixteenth- and early seventeenth-century English culture, an issue raised and answered in contradictory ways for the better part of a century.

Many English people, and many historians, found a partial answer to the question of national self-understanding by interpreting recent events in light of the post-Reformation political world. Begun earlier in the sixteenth century by Martin Luther, a German monk, the Reformation had shattered the political and theological unity of Western Christendom. It did so at a time when throughout Europe emerging nation-states had begun to replace the traditional medieval dynasties as sources of national identity and administration. As the Roman Catholic Church lost its monopoly over the people and nations of Europe, the idea of a European Christendom faded and a new political reality took

---

[8] Miller, "Errand Into the Wilderness," in *Errand Into the Wilderness*, 10.

hold. Reduced to the status of a religious party among others rather than the universal church, the Church of Rome competed with new Protestant churches for favor in the developing nation-states of Europe. European leaders constructed various "state-church system[s]" that associated particular religions with particular nations, thereby adding the passion of religious convictions to the pride and ambition of emergent nationalisms. England, Holland, and parts of Germany embraced Protestantism; Spain and France defended the traditional Roman Catholic religion. Thus people did—and historians still do—refer to Roman Catholic Spain and Protestant England, identifying nations in terms of the religion their state policy favored, regardless of its distortion of the truth, essentially associating identity with the ephemeral whims of leaders' wishes. If one did not think about the matter too hard, and if one were willing to accept the fictional goals of "state-church systems" as reality rather than prescriptions of what powerful people may have wanted to exist, and if one willingly denied the internal incoherence of the link between theory and facts, then heresy was a political issue—an extremely dangerous form of treason. Such fictions made for a simple world divided clearly between good and evil, truth and error. In the case of England, to do so required discounting the existence of a sizable and loyal Catholic minority who, much as the fiercest Protestant, believed England blessed by God and themselves truly English. Such fictions also marginalized the more tolerant views of intellectuals such as Sir Edwin Sandys who eight years prior to Virginia's colonization had already begun to advocate the "peaceful coexistence" of England's various religious groups.[9]

---

[9] On the Reformation in general, see Steven E. Ozment, *The Age of Reform, 1250-1550: An Intellectual and Religious History of Late Medieval and Reformation Europe* (New Haven: Yale University Press, 1980) and Owen Chadwick, *The Reformation* (Baltimore: Penguin Books, 1964); Bossy, *English Catholic Community, 1570-1850*, 77-107, 182-94; Theodore K. Rabb, *Jacobean Gentleman: Sir Edwin Sandys, 1561-1629* (Princeton: Princeton University Press, 1998) 36-38. For a sense of religious animosity mixed with the political goals of rising nation states, see Garrett Mattingly,

Despite contrary realities, many English people accepted the myth of a united and Protestant England, or at least believed the existence of such a nation would please both themselves and God. To those in the early seventeenth century who thought this way, a series of significant moments, or "hinge-point[s]" in time, filled the history of the previous seventy-five years, occasions when they believed the course of English history could have shifted irrevocably in another direction had not a providential deity intervened to save the nation. Time and again England's existence had hung in the balance between utter destruction and a future filled with divine purpose, and at each crisis God had delivered his blessed England. One "hinge-point" occurred in 1588 as a result of an international threat. Philip II of Spain ordered an Armada of Spanish ships to spearhead an invasion of England, fully expecting the English people, especially Catholic English people, to rise up against Queen Elizabeth's government. News of the planned assault traveled quickly, and panic spread throughout the land. Militia companies gathered weapons and prepared to defend their England. Bonfires up and down the English coast announced the Spaniards' approach. English arms, fortuitous weather, faulty Spanish gunnery, luck, and confusion all conspired to foil the invasion. Neither among English Catholics nor the rest of the English population did the popular revolt Spaniards had hoped for develop. Yet the nation's official prayer of thanksgiving—and many Englishmen—took a different view of the nation's deliverance from Spanish arms, interpreting it as an act of God.[10]

The Armada, and Wright, "Elizabethan Politics and Colonial Enterprise," 254-69. Jon Butler, *Awash in a Sea of Faith: Christianizing the American People* (Cambridge: Harvard University Press, 1990) 261. See also Richard Hooker, *Of the Laws of Ecclesiastical Polity*, 8:1.2.

[10] David Cressy, *Bonfires and Bells: National Memory and the Protestant Calendar in Elizabethan and Stuart England* (Los Angeles: University of California Press, 1989) 109, 117-25, 141-42; Mattingly, *Armada*. Cressy defined a hinge point as "a resolution of critically dangerous uncertainty, a moment when English history was fatefully determined."

Another "hinge-point" came as a result of a political threat from within the nation rather than from foreign arms. In November 1605, just over a year before the Jamestown voyage would leave London, a group of Roman Catholic agitators plotted to blow up King James I and his government at the opening of Parliament. Fortunately, English authorities discovered the conspiracy in time to avert the tragedy. Yet, as with the Armada, credit for delivering the nation went not to the individual detective work of human agents or to the guilty conscience of a co-conspirator turned traitor to his own cause, but to a merciful deity. In both instances English people mentally crafted a passive England unable to defend itself against an aggressive Roman Catholicism, spared only by the timely intervention of a Protestant deity. By attributing to God's providence rather than to human skill or ingenuity the defeat of the Spanish Armada and the revelation of the Gunpowder Plot, Englishmen could argue that their friend, God, had preserved the nation. Not only had he preserved the nation, but perhaps the deliverances offered evidence that he had done so for a purpose. Apocalyptic interpretations of recent events did not provide the English with a positive identity, but they reinforced the idea reaching back at least as far as John Foxe's *Book of Martyrs* that God had reserved a special destiny for his Englishmen.[11]

Yet ambiguity about the nation's identity remained. Although English people celebrated their escapes from popery in typical sixteenth- and seventeenth-century fashion by lighting bonfires and ringing bells, popular anti-Catholic displays and rhetoric were tempered by more conciliatory elements within English society. Many people, for instance, often chose not to enforce the recusancy laws against their Roman Catholic neighbors, and despite the attempt on his life by the Gunpowder plotters, James I tried throughout his reign to accommodate the spiritual dimensions of Roman Catholicism. In addition, one of

---

[11] Cressy, *Bonfires and Bells*, ch. 5. For an analysis of Foxe's *Book of Martyrs* see Helgerson, ch. 6, especially 254-56.

the greatest English composers of the age and the co-owner along with Thomas Tallis of the monopoly on print music sales, William Byrd, was a Roman Catholic.[12] Roman Catholic English-men loved their nation as much as Protestants—so much so that some of them were willing to kill the king and Parliament in order to return the nation to the religion they believed God favored. Public displays of anti-Catholicism pointed in one direction, private actions in another. Together they revealed England's unsettled religious identity. The lessons of history may have suggested anti-Catholic sentiment, but the abiding truth had less to do with extremists and foreign powers than with the shared understanding that God had saved England from destruction and had reserved a special purpose for the nation.

Parliament's actions of the 1530s had implied that a national church and a national empire would emerge to provide England with a clear identity. They had not. As the sixteenth century drew to a close, there was no empire, no clearly defined English Church, and no national accomplishment deserving of the nation's imperial pretensions. After seven decades, English people were still trying to prove England worthy of being termed an empire and still trying to define just who they were as a nation. Ambitious of empire, England held not an inch of territory outside the home islands when Richard Hakluyt sat down in the 1580s to write of the triumph of English navigation. Smooth words about empire remained a comforting myth with which to assuage English arrogance. Nor did the English Church offer a distinct identity to the nation's people. Generally interpreted by historians as one of the more stable facets of English identity, the Church of England—beyond being a

---

[12] Kenneth Fincham and Peter Lake, "The Ecclesiastical Policies of James I and Charles I," in Kenneth Fincham, ed., *The Early Stuart Church, 1603-1642* (Stanford: Stanford University Press, 1993) 31. On recusancy, see Leo F. Solt, *Church and State in Early Modern England, 1509-1640* (New York: Oxford University Press, 1990) 148-52; Edward Norman, *Roman Catholicism in England from the Elizabethan Settlement to the Second Vatican Council* (New York: Oxford University Press, 1985) 11, 33-34. On William Byrd, see *Dictionary of National Biography*, 3:575.

church and English—actually offered no clearer understanding of English self-definition. Since the English Reformation had begun under Henry VIII, the national church had lurched from Catholicism to Calvinism and back again several times. Protestants by law in the 1580s, England nonetheless harbored a significant number of English Catholics who often went unpersecuted for practicing their religion. Richard Hooker, the great theorist of the Elizabethan Church, clouded the matter further. Although he worried about the possible contamination of the Church of England by Roman Catholicism, he still counted the Church of Rome as a true church, marked with the seal of "one Lord, one faith, one baptism." Nor was the Church of England's Protestantism exactly clear. Hooker's was but one voice among many, and groups historians would later call Puritans and Anglicans wrangled with each other for control of the national religion. One sect, the Brownists, had already forsaken the national church and separated from it.[13]

Confronted by so many contradictions within their culture, English people often denied their own internal ambiguities and tried to find an identity in national differences. They knew they were not Spaniards or Frenchmen and they knew as well that the English were superior to other peoples, a conviction once termed a "visible hallmark of the [sixteenth] century." More importantly, these views were not the ignorant chauvinism of men confined to England; many people who thought this way had traveled abroad and returned from France and other lands with tales of foreign inferiority with which to prove the point. Frenchmen, the sixteenth-century author Richard Morrison had written, survived on a diet of vegetables and broth while English people feasted on beef—clear evidence to Morrison of English superiority. In short, England and things English were good;

---

[13] Lake, *Anglicans and Puritans?*, quotation on 155. See also Christopher Haigh, ed., *The English Reformation Revisited* (Cambridge: Cambridge University Press, 1987); Patrick Collinson, *The Religion of Protestants* (Oxford: Oxford University Press, 1982); A. G. Dickens, *The English Reformation* (London: B. T. Batsford, LTD, 1964).

other people and places were inferior.[14] But chauvinism and arrogance failed to provide the English with a positive identity. It told them who they were not, not who they were. What was this England that would become an empire and who was English (or to set the matter in Crashaw's words, which English people had God befriended), remained open questions.

The simplest answer and the one easiest to accept was Crashaw's: the English were God's friends. When he said this in 1610 Crashaw said nothing English people had not thought of themselves for nearly a century. Claiming friendship with God embodied the English people's confidence and arrogance as well as the conviction that God loved them more than others. It was also another means of claiming superiority, asserting it in such a way that English people had to do nothing to prove the proposition of England as chosen, special, set apart, and an elect nation. Broad and vague in its definition, God's friendship offered a construction of English identity nearly anyone could accept, thus allowing people to believe at the same time both that England was specially favored and that their own view of what constituted England was somehow more true than that of other people and might someday prevail. It had the virtue, in other words, of offering a definition that all could agree upon while avoiding the question. By starting with Englishness itself, the inescapable fact of an ethnic birth, rather than with the theology of a religious faction or a particular manifestation of nationhood such as class, the English people could deny the ambiguities of their identity and unite as an elect nation. Conceived of not as a Church but in Old Testament terms as a relationship between a chosen people and their deity, religion gave the English people a common faith. Wrote Crashaw: "He that was *the God of Israel* is still *the God of England*."[15]

---

[14] Elton, "Contentment and Discontentment on the Eve of Colonization," 338.

[15] Kupperman, *Settling with the Indians*, 64; Crashaw, *Sermon Preached in London*, L-1.

Virginia's history began with this conviction. English belief that God had chosen to befriend them reflected not only confidence in the nation's relationship with God but also the importance of religion to the era. Only with difficulty, and perhaps a leap of faith, can people at the end of the twentieth century understand the "God-centered" men and women of Tudor-Stuart England who believed in an active, immanent deity concerned at every moment with even the smallest events of life. Men and women doubted neither the reality of God nor his relational quality. They lived in a dangerous and mysterious world permeated with a sense of cosmic vulnerability. Their God was one certainty in an otherwise uncertain and transitory universe, and the starting point for their understanding of the world was his providence. According to their essentially medieval cosmology the deity was ever present, although he spoke less directly to his English friends than he had to Moses and Abraham. They received no "plaine and personall charge" in speech, but discerned God's will metaphorically through human history and the elements of creation. A fire or storm might manifest the deity's anger, while battles won and seasonable rains revealed his favor. Floods, tempests, and fair weather all indicated signs of God's will. Even the breezes that filled the sails of ocean-going vessels carried with them divine significance. Bound for Virginia aboard the *Bonny Bess* in 1623 one young man wrote to his mother about God's role in the first stages of his trip: "Wee hauinge the wynd faire (that messenger of God) hoised vp saile this daye and sailed some part of our Journeye."[16]

---

[16] Stuart E. Prall, *Church and State in Tudor and Stuart England* (Arlington Heights IL: Harland Davidson, 1993) 1; Perry Miller, "Religion and Society in the Early Literature of Virginia," 110-15; Keith Thomas, *Religion and the Decline of Magic: Studies in Popular Beliefs in Sixteenth and Seventeenth Century England* (London: Weidenfeld and Nicolson, 1971) chap. 4, esp pp. 79-82, 107; Robert Gray, *A Good Speed to Virginia*, ed. Wesley Frank Craven (orig. London, 1609; rpt. New York: Scholars' Facsimiles & Reprints, 1937) C-1; Anthony Hilton to his mother, 4 May 1623, Susan Myra Kingsbury, ed. *The Records of the Virginia Company of*

The natural world became a stage on which to discern the will of God.

Yet how one interpreted the deity's actions depended upon the observer's perspective. When writing of their journeys to Virginia, travelers typically emphasized their own fears and frailties and their personal reliance on God. Familiar with the poor condition of the ship on which he would cross the Atlantic, William Tracy realized he would have to rely upon divine aid: "god is abel in ye gretest wekness to helpe be yond hope." Frightened people offered prayers of praise and supplication. When all hope seemed to evaporate into the oblivion of a raging storm, a traveler could, with confidence, entreat the favor of a merciful God. After danger passed, prayers of thanks and praise arose. That of Michael Lapworth was typical: "thankes be to god I have escaped sickness at sea."[17]

Others viewed the voyages from a different perspective and cared little about the potential terror of those aboard ship. They spoke for England and interpreted the voyages within a national context rather than personal religion. England's relationship with God was their concern. They did not dwell upon the hardships of a voyage to the colony—the fetid air below deck, the storms that could snap a mast and cripple a ship—but rejoiced in how easy the passage had become. One minister converted the dangerous voyage to the colony into a simple undertaking: "This passage into *Virginea* is in true temper so faire, so safe, so secure, so easie, as though God himselfe had built a bridge for men to passe from *England* to *Virginea*."[18]

London, 4 vols. (Washington, DC: United States Government Printing Office, 1906-1935) 4:164.

[17] William Weldon to Edwin Sandys, 6 March 1619-1620, *Records of the Virginia Company of London*, 3:262; Michael Lapworth to John Ferrar, 26 June, 1621, Ferrar Papers, f. 268, Magdalene College, Cambridge University.

[18] Crashaw, *Sermon Preached in London*, E-1; John Donne, *A Sermon upon the viii. verse of the i. chapter of the Acts of the Apostles. Preached to the Honourable Company of the Virginia Plantations*, (London, 1622) 44; Patrick Copeland, *Virginia's God Be Thanked*, (London, 1622) 9.

Those who spoke for the nation believed God wanted
England to colonize North America, and they proclaimed again
and again the ease of settling the continent, confident that God
had made it so. They pointed out that neither Spaniards nor
Frenchmen controlled the seas between England and the colony,
thus eliminating the military might of rival nations as a potential
threat to English vessels sailing to Virginia. Just as he had used
the rocks and seas and winds to defeat the Armada in 1588,
colonizers believed God showed his favor through the elements
of creation by easing the way to Virginia: "Our course and
passage is through the great ocean, where is no fear of rocks or
flats...and most winds that blow are fit for us....When we come
to the coast there is continual depth enough." Not only was the
journey safe from storms and privateers, but the land also
harbored no frightening enemies to threaten settlers. John Rolfe
assured people back in England, in an allusion to the land of
Canaan, that rumors of fierce giants who inhabited the continent
were false accusations spread by designing men who hoped the
venture would fail. God's friends of the seventeenth century, his
early modern Israel, would apparently have an easier time
gaining their promised land than had the children of Israel. Yet
even if the God whom propagandists evoked wanted England to
possess North America, saying that the task was easy, did not
make it any less dangerous in reality. Travelers could not wish
away threats from bad weather and foreign powers with a few
lines of rhetoric. Even if no giants lived in Virginia, its native
inhabitants presented dangers enough. Armed conflict with the
Native Virginians erupted within hours of an English landing
party coming ashore at Cape Henry, initiating intermittent
warfare that would continue throughout the century. Despite
their own arguments to the contrary, the authors of the
literature of colonization recognized the difficulties associated
with establishing a settlement in North America. They were of
two minds when they wrote of the Virginia venture, proclaiming
both the simplicity of the venture and the necessity of courage
to fulfill a daunting mission. John Smith posed the issue starkly,
accusing his countrymen of cowardice and a lack of faith: "Had

the seed of Abraham, our Saviour Christ Jesus and his Apostles, exposed themselves to no more dangers to plant the Gospell wee so much professe, than we, even our selves had at this present been as Salvages."[19]

Although English theorists may have wanted to spread Christianity to the New World, they urged their countrymen whom they expected to take up the task to emulate not Jesus the gentle savior but Abraham, Moses, and other Old Testament figures known for military prowess, statecraft, and treachery in foreign affairs. Moses, Abraham, Joshua and Deborah were not meek contemplatives who had withdrawn from the world in order to pray, but men and women of action willing to risk their lives to further ends they believed their God desired. Moses was the great archetype of a lawgiver, but he was also a military leader who had commanded the Israelites on their way to the promised land of Canaan. On his orders countless men died. One Hebrew tribe alone, the Levites, killed several thousand relatives, friends, and neighbors because Moses told them to do so.[20] Nor was Abraham innocent in the use of force or diplomatic guile. Not only had he left his homeland at God's command, thereby becoming the model for those who ventured into the unknown out of faith, but he had also willingly offered the son whom he loved as a sacrifice to God. To protect himself, he had more than once opened his wife Sarah to potential sexual exploitation by passing her off as his sister rather than as his wife.[21] There is no doubt these were men of faith, and so the English believed. Yet

---

[19]Robert Johnson, *Nova Britannia. Offering Most Excellent Fruits By Planting in Virginia* (London, 1609; reprint, Rochester, 1897) 9; John Rolfe, *A True Relation of the State of Virginia lefte by Sir Thomas Dale Knight in May last 1616* (New Haven: Yale University Press, 1951) 41; Morgan, *American Slavery, American Freedom*, 71-72; John Smith, *Advertisements for the Planters of New-England*, Philip L. Barbour, ed., *The Complete Works of Captain John Smith*, 3 vols. (Chapel Hill: University of North Carolina Press, 1986) 3:277. Rolfe's biblical reference is to Numbers 14:6-8.

[20] The reference is to Exodus 32:27-29.

[21] See Genesis 12:1-3, 10-20; 20:1-18; 22:1-19.

they were also wily men capable of and willing to employ brutality and deception to further the epic drama of Israel's history that rested upon God's promise to Abraham that he would become a great nation. Put simply, they were men at once both holy and heroic. Despite their historical distance from early modern England, Old Testament leaders were not perceived by the English as musty figures from the ancient Near East. Known first-hand in sermons, scripture readings, and the religious press, they may have been more immediate to many English people than some of their contemporaries who lived down the street or in another part of the village.[22] Comparing English colonizers to such Biblical heroes did not imply that Virginia would be easily won. Colonization demanded action not contemplation. It demanded men possessed of military expertise, skilled in the shadowy arts of foreign affairs and willing to cooperate with God. It demanded in addition to faith, valor, fortitude, and courage—what Renaissance authors called "virtú."[23]

The contradictory appeals of propagandists to expand the English nation abroad spoke a similar language, belying a growing anxiety over what its authors believed was the English people's unwillingness to act upon their nation's relationship with God. English people believed God had chosen them as his friends and set them aside for a special mission. Yet as a source of identity, God's friendship carried with it a certain passive quality, differing little in this respect from claims that the English were neither Frenchmen nor Spaniards. England had accomplished nothing that might indicate that God had befriended the nation. When they referred to their chosen status or to how they knew this truth, the English relied upon passive descriptions detailing the deity's repeated defenses of England—Elizabeth's accession to the throne in 1558, the destruction of the Spanish Armada in 1588, the revelation of the Gunpowder Treason in 1605.

---

[22] Christopher Hill, *The English Bible and the Seventeenth-Century Revolution* (New York: Penguin Books, 1994) 3-44.

[23] Quentin Skinner, *Foundations of Modern Political Thought*, 2 vols. (New York: Cambridge University Press, 1978) 1:126.

England, the elect nation, had done nothing in this relationship except exist. To hear some voices from the era tell the tale, the nation's survival was more the work of God than Englishmen.[24]

Colonization literature urged Englishmen to demonstrate their faith in the nation's relationship with God through action, to trust the deity, to leave their homeland, and to participate in the work of colonization abroad. The fact that the majority of English people in the early seventeenth century were happy with their condition only made the task more difficult. As one historian has observed of the English population on the eve of colonization: "They might dislike one another, trouble one another, and be discontented with one another, but relative to the foreigner, relative to the poor and depressed subjects of supposedly despotic powers, they knew themselves specially favoured."[25] Englishmen were not particularly inclined to leave England, and those who did were the exceptions rather than the rule, "freaks" in the words of G. R. Elton. Content with their own feelings of superiority and their happy lot as Englishmen, they had stayed at home while the Spaniards had established one of the grandest empires in the history of the world. English pirates, to be sure, had plundered a bit of New World treasure from foreign powers and, acting as statesmen rather than pirates, the same men had liberated a few Indians from Spanish oppression, but most Englishmen were happy to remain in England.[26] This unwillingness to leave the land troubled those who spoke for the nation. Might God withdraw his favor? Might he choose another nation as his favorite? Through tracts, sermons, and propaganda supporters of colonization encouraged Britons to leave their native shores, suggesting in arguments that were not always internally consistent that they do so for God, for their nation, and for themselves.

---

[24] Cressy, *Bonfires and Bells*, 142.

[25] Elton, "Contentment and Discontentment on the Eve of Colonization," 332-43, quotation on 338.

[26] Morgan, *American Slavery, American Freedom*, 9-14, 27-28.

Spreading Christianity to the natives of North America was the "most obvious" motive in the literature of colonization. Who better than God's friends to act upon the great commission at the end of Matthew's Gospel: "Go ye into all the world, & preache the Gospel to euerie creature." Ministers preached of this duty, they collected money for schools in the North American wilderness to train native children in the ways of proper religion, and members of the laity donated funds for books and buildings. Alluding to the familiar image of a bridge or passageway created by God linking England and Virginia, William Crashaw proclaimed as others did, only more eloquently, that the journey's ease proved Englishmen ought to spread Christianity to North America. The "faire, easie, and short" passage to the colony revealed God's providence, "as though he had seated us here and them there for such an entercourse." Having seen God's revealed counsel in the wonders of the natural world, how could his friends not cooperate with the deity and move into the world to act upon Matthew's evangelical imperative? Some colonial leaders took seriously the charge to Christianize the natives, but a three-month journey across the Atlantic to offer the Gospel to a people largely disinterested in England's spiritual gifts inspired few Englishmen to leave their native shores. Pure spiritual motives did not give many people a compelling reason to leave behind the comforts of home.[27]

---

[27] Miller, "Religion and Society in the Early Literature of Virginia," 101; Morgan, *American Slavery, American Freedom*, 47-48; Kupperman, *Settling With the Indians*, 160-66; George MacLaren Brydon, *Virginia's Mother Church and the Political Conditions Under Which it Grew*, 2 vols. (Richmond: Virginia Historical Society, 1947-1952), 1:53-56; Crashaw, *Sermon Preached in London*, C-3. See also Johnson, *Nova Britannia*, 13; William Symonds, *Virginia, A Sermon Preached at White-Chapel* (New York: Da Capo Press, 1964) 52; Donne, *Sermon upon the...Acts of the Apostles*, 24-41; George Benson, *A Sermon preached at Paules Crosse*, (London, 1609) 92. Robert Tynley, *Two Learned Sermons Preached, the one at Paules Crosse, the other at the Spittle* (London, 1609) 67. The biblical citation is from the Geneva Bible then popular in England, Matthew 28:19. Conversion as a motive for colonization has been vastly overrated by

If English people would not advance into the world to spread the Gospel, perhaps reasons of state could persuade them to journey overseas. By 1590 England's traditional Spanish rivals had established an immense empire in North and South America stretching from Peru to Florida. They had explored large portions of North America, but north of Mexico discovered little of the gold and silver they sought. Ultimately they decided that the rest of the continent was not worth their while, and chose to occupy only Florida, and that sparsely. Had they wanted it, the Spanish could likely have taken the entire continent. Occasionally they proved this by destroying settlements established by other European powers, as they did the Atlantic coast colonies founded by French Huguenots in Florida and South Carolina.[28] To English ways of thinking, however, what Spain could have done was not the point. Knowing that Spain had an empire and England did not galled them enough. Proponents of overseas colonization hoped to challenge Spain's presence in the New World by planting settlements along the North Atlantic coast and filling them with Englishmen. Samuel Purchas, perhaps the greatest of the English authors associated with the vast literature of colonization, portrayed the entire venture as a contest between Protestant England and Roman Catholic Spain. For Purchas, successful English colonies would prove the Spanish "Adultresse" had erred in thinking she was the "only Darling of God and Nature."[29]

English theorists not only wished to establish an English presence in North America, but they also hoped to use the new colonies as bases from which to plunder Spanish treasure fleets

---

historians. See Seed, "Taking Possession and Reading Texts: Establishing the Authority of English Overseas Empires," 188n16.

[28] Kupperman, *Roanoke: The Abandoned Colony*, 135.

[29] Loren E. Pennington, "Hakluytas Posthumous: Samuel Purchas and the Promotion of English Overseas Expansion," *Emporia State Research Studies* 14 (1966): 7; Daniel Price, *Sauls Prohibition Staid* (London, 1609) F-2; A Justification for Planting Virginia, Kingsbury, *Records of the Virginia Company of London*, 3:2. For a survey of Purchas see Pennington, 5-39; Miller, "Religion and Society in the Early Literature of Virginia," 115-19.

carrying home cargoes of gold and silver mined by enslaved natives in Peru and Mexico. Richard Hakluyt and Walter Ralegh, a young courtier who had planted the ill-fated Roanoke Island settlement, were among those who wished to damage Spain's material interests by promoting English ones. Hakluyt's plan, however, went further, envisioning the salvation of the English state as well. Acquiring wealth, challenging Spain, and projecting an English presence into the world were not enough. Overseas colonies would save both his country and his countrymen from what Hakluyt assumed was an impending disaster. He believed England was overpopulated; its roads crowded with poor, idle, out-of-work men in search of food that was scarce and jobs that were scarcer. It was a volatile combination: hungry men with neither jobs nor prospects. One did not need much of an imagination to see this could potentially result in riots and rebellions. The problem could be solved, he believed, by sending the poor to North America where they could find work in English settlements that incidentally would also establish a national presence in the New World's wilderness. As time passed, more and more people came to accept Hakluyt's diagnosis. Nearly two decades after first publication of *The Principal Voyages*, the Reverend Robert Gray asserted in words that could easily have come from Hakluyt's pen: "our land hath not milke sufficient in the breasts thereof to nourish all those children which it hath brought forth....we might justly be accounted as in former times, both imprudent and improuident, if we will yet sit with our armes foulded in our bosomes, and not rather seeke after such aduentures whereby the glory of God may be aduanced, the territories of our kingdome inlarged, our people both preferred and employed abroad."[30] The key, of course, to effecting any national goals abroad lay in getting English people to leave their "sceptred isle." Regardless of the incentives—spreading the Gospel, acquiring wealth, projecting national glory, or saving the English poor and thus

---

[30] Morgan, *American Slavery, American Freedom*, 9-10, 28-31; Gray, *Good Speed to Virginia*, B2-B3.

the nation—the underlying concern remained how best to encourage the people of England to leave their homeland and advance into the world. For that purpose, any motive would do.

If members of the nation could not be inspired to depart England for the glory of God or country, the literature of colonization suggested that perhaps Virginia's bounty and the rewards to be gained there could attract them to North America. Daniel Price, a Church of England minister who preached about the Virginia venture in 1609 on Rogation Sunday (a date in the spring of the year devoted to prayers for the success of the fall's harvest), made explicit the reference only alluded to by others in the twelfth chapter of the book of Daniel, assuring those who helped spread God's word that they would "recieue an vnspeakeable blessing, for they that turn manie to righteousness, shall shine as the starres for euer and euer."[31] Although fame, whether for reasons of religion or reasons of state, may have appealed to a few Renaissance Englishmen concerned with these matters, those interested in colonization did not rest their appeals on such transitory things as honor and fame. Adventuring abroad promised more tangible rewards as well. If one only had enough courage and character to sail to North America from London, Bristol, or some other English port, he could leave England and return much richer than before. Accounts of Virginia praised the colony's bounty and hinted at the likely profits the country offered. People who had seen the land marveled at the abundance of fish in its rivers and game in its forests, a land in the words of one sea captain who had piloted voyages to the colony "very fruytfull and apt to pduce any thinge wch England affords."[32] Potential cargoes of lumber, sassafras, and tobacco made men giddy with dreams of wealth. "Timber, Masts, Crystall (if not better stones) Wine, Copper, Iron, Pitch,

---

[31] Price, *Sauls Prohibition Staid*, F-3. The biblical reference is to Daniel 12:3.

[32] Captain Nuce to Sir Edwin Sandys, 27 May 1621, Kingsbury, *Records of the Virginia Company of London*, 3:455.

Tar, Sassafras, Sopeashes" all awaited an English harvest.[33] And in a round-about way, if Englishmen would only leave their homeland to exploit North America's resources, the search for wealth might eventually introduce religion to the Native Americans. From his parish in Henrico near present-day Richmond, the Reverend Alexander Whitaker offered a mercantilist reading of Paul's first letter to the Corinthians when he claimed God had "inriched the bowells of the Country with the riches and bewty of Nature that we wantinge them might in search of them communicate the most excellent merchandize and treasure of the Gospell" to Virginia's "Naturalls."[34]

Virginia beckoned, offering God's friends a wide array of opportunities if they would only cooperate with the deity. English proponents of overseas colonies portrayed Virginia in many ways: an opportunity to save souls, a source of untold wealth, an avenue to fame, a means of challenging national rivals, and a safety valve for England's excess population. A jumble of conflicting ideas, the various descriptions shared one common factor. From the most devout hope of spreading God's holy word to the basest search for booty, each goal required a space for English people. Each goal demanded land in the New World and that English people live on it. Although many of the planters who journeyed to Virginia may have planned to make their fortunes quickly and then return to a life of luxury in England, those who spoke for the nation took a longer view. They envisioned the establishment of a permanent English presence in North America, an overseas empire populated by English settlers projecting English might into the world. Even the most ardent proponents of christianizing natives, William Crashaw and John Donne, then dean of St. Paul's Cathedral, conceded that an English commonwealth in North America

---

[33] Crashaw, *Sermon Preached in London*, E-1.

[34] Alexander Whitaker to Mr. Crashaw, 9 August 1611, Brown, *Genesis of the United States*, 1:499; Crashaw, Sermon Preached in London, D-3, E-1. The biblical reference is to 1 Cor. 9:11—"If we communicate unto them our spirituall things, it is but a small thing if they impart vnto vs their temporall."

must precede the harvest of souls. The "high and principall end" of the venture was the "*plantation*, of an English Church and Common-wealth, and consequently the *conuersion* of heathen."[35]

Tracts and sermons urging colonization called the nation to action, implicitly challenging the courage, character, and faith of Englishmen. "Where is our force and ancient vigor," one author asked, implying that the present generation of Englishmen did not possess the character of preceding ones.[36] Christianity demanded action, personal and national wealth demanded action, and perhaps England's very existence demanded action. English people had rested content too long in their homeland, timid, seemingly unwilling to cooperate with a deity who had befriended them and chosen them for a purpose. If the exact nature of the purpose lacked the clarity of the New England Puritans' "city upon a hill" or if the various descriptions of the purpose often seemed at odds with each other, it simply reflected the nation's own confusion about itself. Imperial anxiety and unsettled ideas of English nationhood formed part of the intellectual context of Virginia's founding. Understood against this background, Virginia was not merely a mercantile venture, a religious mission to spread the Gospel, an outpost to rival the Spaniards, or even all of these together. The first permanent colony offered proponents of expansion tangible evidence of empire and thus became a vivid assertion of the nation's imperial identity.

Yet English anxiety did not end with word that settlers in three small ships had successfully reached a river they named the James and established a settlement there. A few settlers struggling to survive on a swampy peninsula on the edge of the North American continent hardly constituted an empire. Beset with famine, disease, native massacres, and ultimately, the failure of the Virginia Company of London, the colony's existence for nearly two decades remained perilous at best, thus rendering

---

[35] Crashaw, *Sermon Preached in London*, G-3; Donne, *Sermon upon the...Acts of the Apostles*, 25-26.

[36] Johnson, *Nova Britannia*, 6; Crashaw, *Sermon Preached in London*, F4; Kupperman, *Settling With the Indians*, 149.

England's imperial identity as tenuous as Virginia's survival.[37] Much of the vast literature of colonization, when not urging Englishmen to depart their homeland, seems designed to reassure English people that imperial beginnings existed. Allusions to Rome and the kingdom of Israel were common. Preaching from the book of Genesis, William Symonds made the familiar comparison of the English to Abraham: "Get thee out of thy Countrey, and from thy kindred, and from thy fathers house, unto the land that I will shew thee. And I will make of thee a great nation."[38] Others adopted the ancient Roman term for England, Britannia, and applied it to their descriptions of the colony, calling the settlement "Nova Britannia" or "Virginea Britannia."[39] Some people even placed the cause of God within an imperial framework. Converting Native Americans not only added names to the roles of heaven, but also helped English people emulate the ancient Romans who had carried civilization and Christianity to the British Isle. Robert Johnson wrote: "we may verily believe that God has reserved in this last age of the world an infinite number of those lost and scattered sheep, to be won and recovered by our means...how much good we shall

---

[37] There are numerous accounts of the colony's early difficulties. See Billings, Selby, and Tate, *Colonial Virginia*, 32-39; Morgan, *American Slavery, American Freedom*, 72-74, 98-102, 158-59; Carville V. Earle, "Environment, Disease, and Mortality in Early Virginia," in Thad W. Tate and David L. Ammerman, eds., *The Chesapeake in the Seventeenth Century: Essays on Anglo-American Society* (Chapel Hill: University of North Carolina Press, 1979) 96-125; Wesley Frank Craven, *The Dissolution of the Virginia Company of London: The Failure of a Colonial Experiment* (New York: Oxford University Press, 1932).

[38] Symonds, *Virginea Britannia*, 1.

[39] Johnson, *Nova Britannia*, 3; Symonds, *Virginea Britannia*, 1; *For the Colony in Virginea Britannia. Lawes Diuine, Morall and Martiall, &c.*, in Peter Force, ed., *Tracts and Other Papers, Relating Principally to the Origin, Settlement, and Progress of the Colonies in North America*, 4 vols. (Gloucester MA: Peter Smith, 1963) 3: number 2, title page; Gray, *Good Speed to Virginia*, D-1; William Strachey, *Historie of Travell into Virginia Britania*, ed. Louis B. Wright (orig. London, 1609; London: Hakluyt Society, 1953), title page; Helgerson, *Forms of Nationhood*, 8.

perform to those that be good, and how little injury to any, will easily appear by comparing our present happiness with our former ancient miseries, wherein we had continued brutish, poor, naked Britons to this day if Julius Caesar, with his Roman Legions...had not laid the ground to make us tame and civil."[40] Examples from history provided colonial leaders and promoters with reasons for confidence despite contrary appearances. They took comfort from knowledge that great states had been built from "base and disordered" human materials like those who peopled Virginia: "Remember who and what they were that came to *Romulus* and *Remus*, and were the founders of the Romane Citie & State, euen such as no man can without impudencie compare ours with them." Despite these base origins Rome had become "*the Mistresse of the world*." Those "who kept with *Dauid*, and were the beginners of the kingdom of Iudah," were little better, a collection of malcontents, debtors, and men in trouble with the law—an apt description as well of many of Virginia's earliest settlers.[41]

The allusions and models used to define the venture were telling. The English had national heroes of their own by this time, among them King Alfred, Henry V, and the Black Prince. In more recent memory there was Queen Elizabeth I, whose heroic qualities English people began to tout nearly as soon as she had been laid to rest in Westminster Abbey.[42] National heroes, however, do not dominate the literature of the Virginia venture. They rarely appear. Occasionally one finds a reference to Henry V, and a few authors alluded to Elizabeth, usually

[40] Johnson, *Nova Britannia*, 13; Crashaw, *Sermon Preached in London*, C-3; Alexander Whitaker, *Good Newes From Virginia*, ed. Wesley Frank Craven (London, 1613; rpt. New York: Scholars' Facsimiles and Reprints, 1937) 24-25; Robert Johnson, *The New Life of Virginia* (London, 1612; rpt Rochester: 1897) 1-2, 18; Strachey, *History of Travell into Virginia Britania*, 24; Morgan, *American Slavery, American Freedom*, 46.

[41] Crashaw, *Sermon Preached in London*, E2-F1; Miller, "Religion and Society in the Early Literature of Virginia," 124-26.

[42] Wallace Notestein, *The English People on the Eve of Colonization, 1603-1630* (New York: Harper & Row, 1954) 6-7.

comparing her to the biblical judge, Deborah.[43] More often than not, however, those who wrote about colonizing the New World chose as prototypes classical and biblical heroes, especially those associated with empire or the promised land. It suggests on their part a deliberate rejection of English heroes prior to empire. Authors could easily have tried to rally the English people around the great leaders of a common past, but they chose another course. People who thought this way did not see Virginia emerging out of a common history as much as they saw it creating a future very different from the immediate past. They skipped England's recent history for a distant antiquity filled with glory, and, in so doing, located models of what their nation could become if its people could only break free from the constraints of a past spent at home.

These were not millenialist dreams of a world grown old awaiting only England's conversion of the native peoples of North America before the age could hasten to a close as some historians have suggested.[44] The various descriptions of Virginia pointed to empire, to the hope that England would fulfill God's promise to his friend Abraham, that English men and women would leave their homeland, cooperate with the deity, and become a great nation with colonial possessions. Frequent comparisons to Israel and Rome helped give English people a form of positive identity, reinforcing the belief that they shared a special relationship with a God who encouraged the nation's imperial designs. Maps could prove this truth as easily as references to antiquity, and many people saw in the natural world signs indicating that England's possession of the continent was foreordained. Had not God placed North America, in the words of one Roman Catholic author, so that it seemed to "stretche out it selfe towardes England onelie"?[45]

---

[43] Johnson, *New Life of Virginia*, 12.

[44] For a good statement of this view see Kupperman, *Settling With the Indians*, 159-60.

[45] George Peckham quoted in Kupperman, *Settling With the Indians*, 161.

Other English people went beyond the geographic proofs made visible through cartography and tried to demonstrate that God wanted North America to become England's empire by linking events in Virginia to providential moments in national history. Such people believed that with Elizabeth's accession to the English throne, the defeat of the Spanish Armada, and the revelation of the Gunpowder Treason, an Anglophile deity had intervened in human affairs to prevent England's history from swinging irrevocably in another direction. Throughout the seventeenth century, almanacs marked these dates in red letters, designating the events as some of the most important occurrences since the creation of the world, the great flood in biblical times, and the birth of Christ. English people annually celebrated these deliverances by ringing bells and lighting bonfires, their celebrations invoking a process of "anamnesis," a term used by theologians to describe the Eucharist and its recollection of Christian salvation history: Christ's passion, resurrection, and ascension. More generally, it can refer simply to recollection. By setting certain providential national days apart, the English recalled their national salvation history in a manner not unlike some Israelite festivals. Lancelot Andrewes, then bishop of Winchester, wrote of the Gunpowder Plot: "the destroyer passed over our dwellings this day. It is our Passover, it is our Purim."[46] People interested in colonization were not content to find evidence of national salvation solely in England's past. They believed Virginia had a place in England's salvation history as well, especially Lord De la Warr's "miraculous" arrival at Jamestown in 1610 just in time to save the colony.

The winter of 1609–1610 was difficult for the colonists. The arrival in August of nearly four hundred new settlers portended trouble. Crops planted in the spring of the year were ready for harvest, and it was too late in the year to plant more for the new arrivals. Autumn faded into winter; bitter cold froze the colony.

---

[46] F. L. Cross and E. A. Livingstone, eds., *The Oxford Dictionary of the Christian Church* (New York: Oxford University Press, 1993) 49; Cressy, *Bonfires and Bells*, 123, 144, 67-92, quotation on 142.

Sick and weak men ate from meager supplies of food. An expedition sent to beg food from the local natives was attacked and the men killed or executed by torture. At least one man resorted to cannibalism. Another blasphemed and cried out that there was no God. Starvation, dysentery, and typhoid claimed hundreds of lives. Five hundred people in the fall were but sixty by springtime. Adopting the words of one of the survivors, historians have called this period "the starving time." The few settlers still alive in the spring had not heard William Crashaw's words earlier in the year urging faith and hope. Hungry, exhausted, and frightened, men in Jamestown were out of hope and out of faith. They decided to abandon the settlement. The small group of survivors packed up what supplies remained and set out for Newfoundland where they hoped to meet up with the English fishing fleet and then continue their journey home in the fall. Some men were not content merely to leave Virginia. They were out of charity as well and wanted to demonstrate their anger by burning to the ground what was left of Jamestown. But they did not get their way. Having boarded four small pinnaces, the colonists started toward the Atlantic, searching for the fair winds that this time would return them to England. Before reaching the mouth of the Chesapeake Bay, however, the settlers received word that Lord De la Warr, the colony's new governor, had arrived in the bay with men and supplies.[47] The colony was spared: another "hinge-point" in English history. Had the remaining settlers been unable to endure their condition that one additional day or had the winds that brought De la Warr to the colony been any less favorable, England's experiment in empire would have ended, its lands in North America left like those at the failed settlement on Roanoke Island to be reclaimed by the wilderness.

But God had intervened. To men like the Reverend Alexander Whitaker and Captain John Smith, Lord De la Warr's arrival was more than a coincidence. It betokened nothing less

---

[47] For a narrative of these events, see Billings, Selby, and Tate, *Colonial Virginia*, 38; Morton, *Colonial Virginia*, 1:25-27.

than the justice of England's imperial actions. God had "opened the doore of *Virginia*, to our countrey of England," and he would not allow the colony to fail.[48] William Crashaw agreed: "If euer the hand of God appeared in action of men, it was heere most euident: for when man had forsaken this businesse, God tooke it in hand."[49] Recounting in 1622 what he called England's "dangers and deliverances," Patrick Copeland compared events in Virginia in 1610 with God's preservation of "our whole Land in eightie-eight; and in the *Gun powder Treason.*"[50] Linking Virginia's colonization to these "moments" united the colony to England's salvation history in ways that implied empire. Prior deliverances in England had gained salvation from Roman Catholicism and national enemies. Yet Virginia's danger and deliverance came neither from popery nor foreign arms. No Spanish vessels carrying an invasion force had entered the James River. No Roman faction attempted to overthrow the settlement from within. Virginia tottered on the verge of collapse because of poor government and the colonists' own idleness. Yet God would not have it so wrote John Smith. He "would not this Countrie should be unplanted...this was the arme of the Lord of Hosts, who would have his people passe the red Sea and Wildernesse, and then to possesse the land of Canaan."[51] When Smith wrote of the "Lord of Hosts" he used language that has lost much of its meaning to people in the modern world but which likely evoked clear images to those who read his works in the seventeenth century. By using this term Smith referred to the God of battles or of armies, a God who went to war with his people. In Smith's usage it implied that God approved of England's invasion of the continent and desired its success. His rhetoric was that of a military man and he

---

[48] Whitaker, *Good Newes From Virginia*, 21.

[49] Cited in Miller, "Religion and Society in the Early Literature of Virginia," 111.

[50] Copeland, *Virginia's God Be Thanked*, 11, 14.

[51] John Smith, *The Generall History of Virginia, New-England, and the Sumer Isles* (London, 1624), Barbour, *The Complete Works of Captain John Smith*, 2:233-35.

therefore may have relied upon martial imagery more than other authors, but it nevertheless conveyed the same message. God approved of what England was doing in the business of planting colonies. Virginia's deliverance was not about the salvation of a passive nation under siege. It was an endorsement of English action and encouraged the nation to build upon its imperial beginnings. Old Testament prototypes implied as much. Abraham, Moses, and Joshua demonstrated their faith through action not prayer. Devoted to God, they praised him by furthering the ends of the state and a people. If only the English had the courage, and if only they had the faith, God's promise to Abraham was theirs to inherit.

Many English people were more ambivalent than Captain Smith and the Reverend Whitaker and did not share their confidence. Plays on the London stage openly lampooned the Virginia venture.[52] Some people, in fact, traveled to the colony intent on returning home so that they could mock the land and the colonization attempt. Speaking before the House of Commons in 1621, Francis Bacon, the Lord Chancellor, addressed the imperial hopes and anxieties Virginia stirred in an allusion to a parable: "Sometimes a grain of mustard-*seed* proves *a great tree*. Who can tell?"[53] When Jesus taught of the mustard seed his lesson had been about the importance of faith. But English people associated with overseas expansion wanted assurances firmer than faith or the smooth words of propagandists. They wanted "to tell" that Virginia would be their empire. Towards that end, colonial and Company leaders, ministers and propagandists alike, tried to cooperate with God by constructing a polity—a combination of land, laws, and people—that would establish England's uninterrupted presence in North America. A successful polity might guarantee the

---

[52] John Parker, "Religion and the Virginia Colony 1609-10," in K. R. Andrews, N. P. Canny, and P. E. H. Hair, eds., *The Westward Enterprise: English Activities in Ireland, the Atlantic, and America, 1480-1650* (Detroit: Wayne State University Press, 1979) 262, 267.

[53] Francis Bacon, Speech to the House of Commons, 30 January 1621, Brown, *Genesis of the United States*, 2:637

salvation of the English state abroad, thus clinching the nation's imperial desires and, just maybe, contributing to an English identity at home. But that left a troubling question: what sort of polity and what sort of people would please God? And that was the problem. Given their own unsettled identity, English people could not agree on just what specifics would please the deity they believed was their friend. The existence of a New World the English thought God wanted them to possess only made the issue more troubling. The greater question was whether or not people two thousand miles from England would care about English answers to questions about the colony's relationship with God. Perhaps they would forge their own.

CHAPTER TWO

CONSTRUCTING A POLITY: ENGLAND'S SOTERIOLOGY OF EMPIRE

The first voyage to Jamestown lasted eighteen weeks. On 20 December 1606, a fleet of three small ships under the command of Captain Christopher Newport departed London and beat down the Thames to await the fair winds that would speed the journey to North America and show evidence of God's favor upon the enterprise of colonization. The liturgical calendar of the Church of England observed the day as the eve of the feast of St. Thomas, the disciple who would not believe Christ's resurrection until he could touch his risen Lord's wounds. It is one of the ironies of history that the English often described their understanding of Virginia in similar terms, occasionally pointing to this tendency as a failing endemic to the nature of English people. "And this I do but mention," wrote Robert Johnson, an alderman for the city of London and supporter of colonization, "to note the blind diffidence of our English natures, which laugh to scorn the name of Virginia, and all other new projects, be they never so probable, and will not believe till we see the effects."

Englishmen may have been skeptical in the eyes of the nation's leaders, but nevertheless, about 140 planters had boarded the vessels bound for Virginia. They were a contentious lot, no more united as shipmates than England was as a nation. Even before England fell below the horizon to the east, they had taken to quarreling with one another. John Smith made the trip in chains, imprisoned for alleged conspiracy. Many "discontents" broke out, forcing Robert Hunt, the minister who accompanied the first settlers, to spend much of his time quenching a series of petty disputes. Conditions aboard the ship neither alleviated the harried minister's work nor made difficulties between individuals any easier to deal with. Oceangoing vessels in the sixteenth and seventeenth centuries did not provide comfort. Passengers shared space with cattle and chickens; provisions often consisted of "mustie bred...and stinckinge beere"; excrement filled the bilges and fouled the air. In the cramped spaces allotted them below deck, many men and women suffered seasickness. Others died. One survivor of an Atlantic crossing to Jamestown described the difficult conditions that voyagers typically endured: "Betwixt the decks there can hardlie a man fetch his breath by reason there ariseth such a ffunke in the night that it causeth putrification of bloud & breedeth a disease much like the plague." Little wonder that Patrick Copeland, one of the few ministers who mentioned the dangers of a voyage to Virginia in his sermons compared sea travelers to the three young men in the book of Daniel whom God had delivered from the fiery furnace.

The three vessels in England's colonization venture sailed to Virginia by way of the West Indies, where they arrived in late March 1607. There the colonists went ashore, explored the islands, and refilled their ships' casks with fresh water for the remainder of the journey. They did not know it, but already King Philip of Spain had asked his ambassadors in England to report on this "matter of Virginia" so he could consider "what steps had best be taken to prevent it." The first group of settlers passed Easter Day in the West Indies as well, still three weeks from their destination. As the voyagers approached the North American coast, the lessons appointed by the Church of England to be read on the Sundays after Easter may well have held special meaning to a people who considered themselves God's special friends. One lesson spoke of Israel as a nation unlike other nations; another recounted the Israelites' murmurings against Moses during their sojourn to the promised land and warned about the dangers of faction to a community. On 26 April 1607, sailors dropped anchor off the Virginia coast, and the initial landing parties went ashore at Cape Henry. In the Church of England's liturgical calendar it was the Third Sunday after Easter. The Old Testament reading appointed for the day came from the fourth chapter of Deuteronomy: "Now therefore hearken, O Israel, vnto the ordinances

and to the lawes wc I teache you to do, that ye may liue and go in,
& possesse the land, which the Lord God of your fathers giueth you.[1]

Virginia's polity emerged out of England's relationship
with God, and it began with the land, for without the
land there could be no polity. But before there could be a polity,
English people had to believe the land promised to them was

---

[1] My account comes from Richard L. Morton, *Colonial Virginia*, 2
vols. (Chapel Hill: University of North Carolina Press, 1960) 1:7-8; Robert
Johnson, *Nova Britannia. Offering Most Excellent Fruits By Planting in
Virginia* (London, 1609; rpt., Rochester, 1897) 8; John Rolfe, *A True
Relation of the State of Virginia lefte by Sir Thomas Dale Knight in May last
1616* (New Haven: Yale University Press, 1951) 33; Robert Gray, *A Good
Speed to Virginia*, ed. Wesley Frank Craven (London, 1609; rpt. New York:
Scholars' Facsimiles & Reprints, 1937) B1; Warren M. Billings, John E.
Selby, and Thad W. Tate, *Colonial Virginia: A History* (White Plains NY:
KTO Press, 1986) 24, 27; John Smith, *Proceedings of the English Colonie in
Virginia* [1606-1612], in Philip L. Barbour, ed. *The Complete Works of
Captain John Smith*, 3 vols. (Chapel Hill: University of North Carolina
Press, 1986), 1:204-205; Council in Virginia to the Virginia Company, 30
January 1623/24, in Susan Myra Kingsbury, ed. *The Records of the Virginia
Company of London*, 4 vols. (Washington, DC: United States Government
Printing Office, 1906-1935) 4:451; William Capps to John Ferrar, *Records
of the Virginia Company of London*, 4:77; Patrick Copeland, *Virginia's God
Be Thanked* (London, 1622) 18, 3-4; Philip III to Pedro de Zuñiga, 26
February 1606/1607, in Alexander Brown, *Genesis of the United States*, 2
vols. (New York: Russell & Russell, Inc., 1964) 1:91; George MacLaren
Brydon, *Virginia's Mother Church and the Political Conditions Under Which
it Grew*, 2 vols. (Richmond: Virginia Historical Society) 1:12; "Proper
Lessons to be Read at Morning and Evening Prayer on the Sundays, and
other Holy-days throughout the year," "A Table of Moveable Feasts," *The
Book of Common Prayer and Administration of the Sacraments, and Other
Rites and Ceremonies of the Church, According to the Use of the Church of
England,* (London, 1559) The passage from Deuteronomy is from the
version then preferred in England, *The Geneva Bible*, a facsimile of the 1560
edition (Madison: University of Wisconsin Press, 1969). The other
appointed readings were from Numbers 16 and Numbers 23-24. For more
on the Reverend Mr. Hunt, see Lewis Wright and Brenda Gardner, "Robert
Hunt, Vicar of Jamestown," *Anglican and Episcopal History* 66 (1997): 500-
519.

worth the effort of sending ships and men across the Atlantic. Virginia did not disappoint them.

The land they named Virginia was everything England was not, and it made a great impression upon the settlers. Their homeland was a small island nearly deforested. For men accustomed to living in England, Virginia was a source of wonder. It seemed boundless, an immense tract filled with meadows, grasslands, flowers in bloom, and stand after stand of tall trees. George Percy, one of the colonists in the first voyage to Jamestown, marveled at "Woods full of Cedar and Cypresse trees, which issue out sweet Gummes like to Balsam. Wee kept on our way in this Paradise." Astonished, he wrote of "faire meddowes and goodly tall Trees, with such Fresh-waters running through the woods," concluding in words with connotations of sexuality or mystical ecstasy, "as I was almost ravished at the first sight thereof."[2] The theoretical framework of colonization had conditioned travelers to look upon Virginia as Canaan,[3] but the reality of the place transcended even their expectations of a promised land. It was not only Canaan but Eden as well. Interpreting Virginia as testimony to God's craftsmanship, John Smith described the land as "all overgrowne with trees and weedes[,] being a plaine wildernes as God first made it."[4] Settlers

---

[2]George Percy, "Observations Gathered out of a Discourse of the Plantation of the Southerne Colonie in Virginia by the English, 1606," Lyon Gardiner Tyler, ed., *Narratives of Early Virginia, 1606-1625* (New York: Barnes & Noble, 1952) 16, 9-11. See also Rolfe, *True Relation of the State of Virginia*, 33; Ralph Hamor, *A True Discourse of the Present [E]state of Virginia* (1615; Richmond: Virginia State Library, 1957) 20-22; Bernard W. Sheehan, *Savigism and Civility: Indians and Englishmen in Colonial Virginia* (New York: Cambridge University Press, 1980) 9-36.

[3] Karen Ordahl Kupperman, *Settling With the Indians: The Meeting of English and Indian Cultures in America, 1580-1640* (Totowa NJ: Rowman and Littlefield, 1980) 166-67; Sir William Cope to Lord Salisbury, 12-13 August 1607, in Phillip L. Barbour, ed., *The Jamestown Voyages Under the First Charter, 1606-1609*, 2 vols. (London: Cambridge University Press, 1969) 1:108, 111.

[4]John Smith, *A True Relation...till the last returne*, (London, 1608), Barbour, *Works of Captain John Smith*, 1:145; Perry Miller, "Religion and

were not the only ones who marveled at the land. Accounts written by colonists and read in England inspired poets. Perhaps consciously referring to William Shakespeare's description of England as a "demi-paradise," William Drayton proclaimed the colony's superiority to the home island: "VIRGINIA, Earth's only Paradise."[5] English people's conceptual framework left little place for such natural wonders, and words failed many who wished to describe the land. A sea captain who had piloted a voyage to the colony claimed that even if he had possessed the eloquence of Cicero, that great model of rhetoric for Renaissance authors, he could not justly have praised the country.[6] So impressive was the land that both those who saw it and those who heard of it secondhand could not keep their metaphors straight, some called it Canaan, some called it Eden, and some called it paradise.

Land, of course, had been the object all along, a space on which English people could live outside of their homeland. The early emphasis in the literature of colonization on Abraham as a model for the settlers to follow made clear England's desire for territory. The promise of a new land had come along with God's command to Abraham to "Get thee out of thy land." In this, the implications of propagandists' references to Abraham squared with inherited legal notions that defined the process by which states could establish overseas authority. The English right to

---

Society in the Literature of Early Virginia," in *Errand Into the Wilderness* (Cambridge: Harvard University Press, 1956) 113; William Simmonds, *The Proceedings of the English Colonie in Virginia Since their first beginning from England in the Yeare of our Lord, 1606 till this present 1612, with all their accidents that befell them in the Journies and Discoveries* (Oxford, 1612), in Warren M. Billings, ed., *The Old Dominion in the Seventeenth Century: A Documentary History of Virginia, 1606-1689* (Chapel Hill: University of North Carolina Press, 1975) 27; James Horn, *Adapting to a New World: English Society in the Seventeenth-Century Chesapeake* (Chapel Hill: University of North Carolina Press, 1994) 124-28.

[5] Michael Drayton, "Ode to the Virginian Voyage," Brown, *Genesis of the United States*, 1:86.

[6] Fernando Yates, "The Voyage," Kingsbury, *Records of the Virginia Company of London*, 3:114.

rule portions of the New World originated in letters patent, open letters from an individual in authority granting a right or title to another person. Unlike forms of establishing dominion employed by other European colonial powers which referred to people—and often to Christianizing them in order to legitimate European occupation—English letters patent consistently identified land as the object over which holders of the patent gained title. The earliest English overseas patents, those to Sir Walter Ralegh and his half-brother, Sir Humphrey Gilbert, specifically mentioned North America's "soyle." Peculiar to English legal culture, the idea of controlling space expanded as additional patents were granted. James I's charter to the Virginia Company of London, for instance, authorized title to "landes, soile, groundes, havens, ports, rivers, woodes, mines, mineralls, marishes, waters, fishings, commodities, and hereditaments."[7] English letters patent, however, did not address the native peoples of the land, in part because the object of English imperial authority was not people. Unlike their Spanish and Portuguese rivals, English colonizers primarily sought to extend imperial authority over the land itself. English people thus looked upon the native inhabitants of North America as a bother rather than as a blessing. Overpopulated to begin with, or so colonizers believed, England had all the labor it could use and more. Colonizers hoped English overseas settlements would create a greater demand for workers, not discover an additional supply of labor. More new people, especially ones unfamiliar with English customs and who did not speak the English language, presented greater problems. Additional territory, however, might open a space on which English people could labor and, coincidentally,

---

[7] Patricia Seed, "Taking Possession and Reading Texts: Establishing the Authority of Overseas Empires," *William and Mary Quarterly* 2nd ser. 49 (1992): 185-89; Patricia Seed, *Ceremonies of Possession in Europe's Conquest of the New World, 1492-1640* (New York: Cambridge University Press, 1995) 16-40; Samuel M. Bemiss, ed., *The Three Charters of the Virginia Company of London With Seven Related Documents: 1606-1621* (Williamsburg: Virginia 350th Anniversary Celebration Corporation, 1957) 4.

expand England's influence into the New World. Legal tradition and the English people's self-understanding as friends of God in the manner of Abraham combined to reinforce to colonizers the importance of territory. Their easy acceptance of the patriarch's model may, in fact, have helped justify a means of establishing authority unique in the European world.

The beauty, fertility, and immensity of Virginia served to heighten a pre-existing cultural imperative. English people seemed peculiarly suited to the land and this only reinforced their desire for this particular territory. Neither too hot nor too cold, neither too dry nor too rainy, Virginia was just what the English wanted. "The country itself is large and great assuredly," the promotional author Robert Johnson wrote of the colony, "it is commendable and hopeful every way; the air and climate most sweet and wholesome, much warmer than England and very agreeable to our natures."[8] Could anyone miss the obvious fact that God had implanted within the English a nature which found North America peculiarly attractive? Johnson pushed the argument further. Crafting environmental proof that only people predisposed to believe him might accept, he suggested that Virginia was the natural geographic extension of England, even implying in one pamphlet that the Thames ran from London into the Atlantic then reemerged in North America as the James River.[9]

Much of what planters did (or failed to accomplish) in the early years of the settlement's history can be viewed as efforts to establish English possession of the territory they had named Virginia. To English ways of thinking, the land would become England's only after the colonists had established dominion over it, and that required evidence of an intent to remain. Merely touching "here and there upon the Coasts" and building temporary structures did not exhibit the necessary intent to inhabit

---

[8]Kupperman, *Settling With the Indians*, 162-63; Robert Johnson, *Nova Britannia*, 10. See also Rolfe, *True Relation of the State of Virginia*, 33.

[9]Johnson, *Nova Britannia*, 10.

the land. Although letters patent "activated" English possession of territory overseas, this mental action remained an intention until someone showed evidence of taking up residence. Taking possession to the English implied constructing permanent buildings and actually inhabiting the territory.[10]

Once on Virginia's shores in 1607, English settlers began the process of establishing authority over the land by choosing a favorable place to plant a settlement. After two weeks of investigating potential sites at Kecoughtan and Old Point Comfort, they chose a peninsula about thirty miles up the James River. Far enough from the mouth of the river and nearly surrounded by water, the site seemed to offer protection both from Spanish mariners who may have wished to destroy the colony and from natives who may have wanted to run off the intruders. In addition to the military advantages the site offered, there was fresh water nearby, plenty of game in the woods, and a deep channel that made access to the settlement easy for ocean-going vessels. In honor of their king, the colonists named the rude settlement Jamestown, just as they had named their river the James.[11]

At Jamestown, settlers carved an English space out of the wilderness and built a fort to defend the Englishmen who resided therein, in the process taking steps in the direction of dominion. Yet no one was foolish enough to believe occupation would be permanent without the institutions of government and religion, and on the soil they occupied, English leaders went about establishing these necessary institutions. (Government, in fact, had been instituted aboard ship before the colonists chose a place to settle.) Constructing a polity demanded these acts. Religion was a fairly simple matter to address—not worshipping God would have been unthinkable to people then, just as it would have been unthinkable for most English people not to follow the rites of the Church of England. In order to better

---

[10]Seed, "Taking Possession and Reading Texts," 189-97.

[11]Billings, Selby, and Tate, *Colonial Virginia*, 29-30; Morton, *Colonial Virginia*, 1:9.

worship their friend God, the settlers constructed a makeshift church building in the open air by hanging an old sail from several trees to shield minister and congregation from sun and rain, and by nailing a block of wood between two neighboring trees to serve as a pulpit. There the colonists participated in the religious life of English people: "daily Common Prayer morning and evening, every Sunday two Sermons, and every three moneths the holy Communion."[12]

Government proved to be more problematic. The English had no successful precedent of effective colonial administration to serve as a model for those given the task of governing the colony. Lacking good models to base their instructions upon, the Virginia Company of London offered what advice it thought best, much of it either vague or contradictory. Before Captain Christopher Newport and the planters bound for Virginia left England in 1606, the company had advised them: "Lastly and chiefly the way to prosper and achieve good success is to make yourselves all of one mind for the good of your country...and to serve and fear God the Giver of all Goodness, for every plantation which our Heavenly Father hath not planted shall be rooted out." Although overly general, this was nonetheless good advice; English people of the early modern era who thought about polity doubted neither the importance of political unity nor of the good state pleasing God. Unfortunately, the company's specific directions violated their own general counsel to pursue unity. Contrary to nearly every idea of good government that English people had inherited, Company leaders ordered the colony to be ruled by a council (similar to a modern board of directors), or in Aristotle's typology of governments, an aristocracy—a form of government thought to be particularly prone to the enmities of faction. Schooled in Aristotelian political the-

---

[12] Morton, *Colonial Virginia*, 1:11; John Smith, *Advertisements for the Unexperienced Planters of New England, or Any-Where* (London: 1631), Barbour, *Works of Captain John Smith*, 3:6.

ory, English leaders should have known better. But aristocracy they wanted, so aristocracy they had.[13]

In theory, the efforts taken by the company and colonists to prove dominion over the land moved England closer towards the empire so many in the homeland coveted. Reality was another matter. For several years, English colonizers struggled to keep Jamestown populated with enough planters to prove the nation intended to make Virginia a permanent settlement. Men died at an alarming rate. Only thirty-eight out of the one hundred and forty four colonists survived the first winter. Native raids and disease killed hundreds of settlers. The settlers' inability to feed themselves helped neither the death rate nor individual tempers. Many had come to Virginia hoping to find gold and so spent much of their time searching for riches instead of planting the corn that could have fed them. Game roamed the forests and Virginia's rivers teemed with fish of various sorts, but the truth of the matter was that few of the colonists knew how to fish or to hunt. So in the midst of plenty, they starved. Virginia seemed to promise English planters little more than a short life and a painful death.[14]

Government and institutional religion enjoyed existences as precarious as those of the settlers. After completing their fort, the colonists had erected a sturdier church—a "homely thing like a barn," John Smith called it—but time and again it fell to ruins and was likely more often frequented by men searching for

---

[13] Jon Kukla, "Order and Chaos in Early America: Political and Social Stability in Pre-Restoration Virginia," *American Historical Review* 90 (1985): 282-83; Karen Ordahl Kupperman, *Roanoke: The Abandoned Colony* (Totowa NJ: Rowman & Allanheld, 1984) 164-71; Council for Virginia to Captain and Virginia Company going to Virginia, 10 December 1606, Brown, *Genesis of the United States*, 1:85; Morton, *Colonial Virginia*, 1:6-8.

[14] Billings, Selby, and Tate, *Colonial Virginia*, 32-33; Morton, *Colonial Virginia*, 1:14; Edmund S. Morgan, *American Slavery, American Freedom: The Ordeal of Colonial Virginia* (New York: W. W. Norton, 1975) 84-85; Irene D. Hecht, "The Virginia Colony, 1607-1640: A Study in Frontier Growth" (Ph.D. diss., University of Washington, 1969).

convenient sources of firewood than by men hoping to engage the deity in prayer. During periodic episodes of stability, able leaders ordered the edifice repaired, only to have it crumble once again during the next round of disasters.[15] Religious faction stalked the settlement as well. "There is an unhappie dissention fallen out amongst them," John Beaulieu, secretary to the English ambassador in Brussels, wrote in 1609, "by reason of their Minister, who being, as they say, somewhat a puritane, the most part refused to go to his service, or to heare his sermons, though by the other part he was supported & favored."[16]

Government in Virginia fared worse than religion. The aristocratic form of government proved just as factious as Aristotle had predicted and as colonial authorities should have expected. Given more to pettiness than leadership, most of the councilors could not get along with each other let alone those they were charged with governing. Hunger and sickness only increased their obvious contentiousness. Trouble began within weeks of landing in Virginia. Fellow councilors charged their first president, Edward Maria Wingfield, of doling out extra rations of the colony's meager supplies to his favorites and voted to remove him from the group. He had earlier been accused of atheism because he did not have a Bible readily available among his possessions. Another member of the council, George Kendall, was tried for conspiracy, found guilty, and executed as a Spanish spy. During his turn as president of the council, John Ratcliffe's leadership proved so inept that before his term ended the colony bordered on mutiny. John Smith proved a more capable leader than the others. A soldier by trade and familiar with the ways of command both in practice and in theory (he had read Machiavelli's treatise on military leadership, *The Art of War*),

---

[15] John Smith, *Advertisements for the Unexperienced Planters of New England,* Barbour, *Works of Captain John Smith,* 3:295; William Strachey, *A Voyage to Virginia in 1609,* ed. Louis B. Wright (Charlottesville: University Press of Virginia, 1967) 63-64, 79-80; John Smith, *Proceedings of the English Colonie in Virginia,* Barbour, *Works of Captain John Smith,* 1:219.

[16] John Beaulieu to William Trumbull, 30 November 1609, in Barbour, *The Jamestown Voyages Under the First Charter,* 2:287, 253.

Smith brought order and martial discipline to the colony and introduced a compelling element of necessity to government by following the injunction in II Thessalonians: "he that does not worke shall not eate." During Smith's brief tenure as president Virginia prospered and relations with the natives improved, but jealous councilors sought to overthrow the captain. Though they failed in their attempt, what they had not achieved a gunpowder accident accomplished. Severely injured, Smith left Jamestown for England, and the colony floundered once again.[17]

Demonstrating evidence neither of dominion nor empire, Virginia's early history nevertheless revealed an unyielding tenacity on the part of colonization supporters. Virginia had become a place of mutinies, intrigue, and bickering. Confronted by so many disappointments, people interested in colonization could easily have quit and cut their losses. Yet to those who wrote about the venture, real progress had been made. Virginia was no longer a promise. It was real and tangible: not a dream conjured up by theorists who hoped for empire, but a reality peopled by English colonists on a faraway soil expanding the nation by their presence, even if their existence on the land remained doubtful. This fact influenced those who wrote about the nation's imperial designs. Having seen the land, smelled its flowers, and felt the cool of its refreshing streams—sometimes in person, sometimes figuratively by reading pamphlets or listening to sermons—English people began to think differently of their relationship to Virginia. They set Abraham aside. By 1610, authors of colonization literature rarely mentioned the biblical

---

[17] Morton, *Colonial Virginia*, 1:13-15; Morgan, *American Slavery, American Freedom*, 75-79; Edward Maria Wingfield, "A Discourse of Virginia," in Edward Arber, ed. *Works of Captain John Smith* (Westminster: Archibald Constable and Co., 1895) lxxxviii; John Smith, *The True Travels, Adventures, and Observations of Captain John Smith, in Europe, Asia, Africke, and America: beginning about the yeere 1593, and continued to this present 1629*, Barbour, *Works of Captain John Smith*, 3:156; Smith, *Proceedings of the English Colonie in Virginia*, Barbour, *Works of Captain John Smith*, 1:259; Billings, Selby, and Tate, *Colonial Virginia*, 35. The Biblical reference is to II Thessalonians 3.10.

hero who had left his homeland to found a great nation and gain a land of promise. They knew their Bible, and they knew Abraham's usefulness as a prototype had come to an end. Metaphorically, the task was no longer one of getting to Canaan but of securing it. Their nation poised between promise and empire, writers of pamphlets and propaganda began alluding to the Israelites who had spied out the promised land. "Believe Caleb and Joshua," wrote Thomas Dale in 1613, referring to the book of Numbers and the spies who had returned an honest account of Canaan to Moses. In a command sermon preached to the Virginia Company, William Symonds made more explicit the message of Numbers: "The land, by the constant report of all who haue seene it, is a good land."[18]

In hyperbole, in hope, and in truth, English authors continued this refrain. "It is a good land," they wrote. Despite every disappointment and every failure Virginia had suffered, they could still refer to the colony as the Israelites had to Canaan, as a good land. In this at least they were honest—they did not blame the land or its native inhabitants for their many failures. Cataloging the mistakes committed by Englishmen in Virginia took no special gift or revelation. The land had not betrayed them; the English through idleness, avarice, and faction had betrayed the land. Using the vague, general language typical of them, Company leaders summed up the myriad discouragements when they wondered why the "plantation went rather backwards than forwards."[19] More specific assessments of the colony's problems often pointed to its faulty government. John Rolfe denounced the aristocratic council, citing its daily creation

---

[18] Sir Thomas Dale to Sir Thomas Smythe, June 1613, Brown, *Genesis of the United States*, 2:639; William Symonds, *A Sermon Preached at White-Chapel* (London, 1609; rpt. New York: Da Capo Press, 1964) 24. The Biblical reference is to Numbers 13-14.10. For a good overview of the Biblical culture of early modern England, see Christopher Hill, *The English Bible and the Seventeenth-Century Revolution* (New York: Penguin Books, 1994) 3-44.

[19] "A True and Sincere declaration of the purpose and ends of the Plantation...," Brown, *Genesis of the United States*, 1:344.

of greater "envie, dissentions, and jarrs."[20] John Smith broadened a similar analysis to include the deity. God, he believed, preferred certain forms of political organization to others, and Virginia's near failure between 1609 and 1610 was a sign to Smith of his judgment on the factions common to concilliar government.[21] Faulting colonists for the settlement's perilous existence rather than the land or its inhabitants as Smith, Rolfe, and other authors did meant that colonizers' ontological views retained validity. God remained England's friend and still wanted the English to have the territory and eventually an empire. But if that was the case it raised troubling questions. What had gone wrong? If English colonizers' theory about God's friendship was correct, then why had there been so much difficulty? One broad answer suggested itself: if their theory was sound, and they believed it was, then the practice must have been flawed. Supporters of the venture took heart at this realization. Those who wrote about what had gone awry and how it could be corrected focused their attention on Virginia's polity—that combination of land, laws, and people that might help the English demonstrate dominion over territory in North America.

Constructing a polity is an act of creation and therefore implies the existence of will or design, sometimes human in origin, sometimes divine, sometimes both. For English settlers in Virginia, a stable and orderly polity would demonstrate dominion over the land by projecting into the future the nation's intent to remain in North America. Yet questions of polity opened a host of other issues, the most important of which addressed religion. The early seventeenth century was a religious age in which ideas about God, the church, and religious devotion touched upon nearly all aspects of life, both public and private. Thus, questions of polity necessarily implied questions of religion. That "no policie can stand long without religion" was a

---

[20] John Rolfe, *True Relation of the State of Virginia*, 3-4.
[21] John Smith, *Advertisements for the Unexperienced Planters of New England*, Barbour, *Works of Captain John Smith*, 3:295-96.

common assumption,[22] and this belief shaped Virginia's polity as much as it did that of any other European state of the early modern period. Order depended on religion. Early modern thinkers presumed that all civil governments, even those of "savages" and willful idolaters, possessed divine sanction. Medieval schoolmen and Protestant reformers alike accepted the premise that God had ordained government to help maintain order in the world. States without religion were abominations, creatures the early-modern mind could hardly have conceived. In 1610/11 Company leaders applied to Virginia the generally accepted principle that although religion might exist on its own, a state without religion could expect, at best, a brief existence when they admonished the colony's resident governor: "First of all beinge to establish religion." Only later did they instruct him to "establish good government and discipline" as well.[23]

To "God-centered" men and women of early seventeenth-century Europe, the deity was a central figure in the lives of individuals as well as nations, hardly the withdrawn, watchmaker God of the Enlightenment, but a being with personality and emotions like human beings, ever present and concerned with human history. God took particular interest in world affairs, or at least English people believed that he seemed concerned about their national history. English men and women did not doubt that God had preserved the nation from the Spanish Armada and the treason of the Gunpowder Plot, just as he had encouraged the settlement of Virginia.[24] So concerned was God in day-to-day events that many English people collected examples of his providences or interventions in human affairs. Robert Lowder, a farmer in Berkshire noted: "This year in sowing too early I lost

---

[22] Sebastian de Grazia, *Machiavelli in Hell* (Princeton: Princeton University Press, 1989) 194; Gray, *Good Speed to Virginia*, D3.

[23] Remembrances to be sent to the lo: Delaware, [March 1610/11], f. 29, Ferrar Papers, Magdalene College, Cambridge University.

[24] Miller, "Religion and Society in the Literature of Early Virginia," 129; David Cressy, *Bonfires and Bells: National Memory and the Protestant Calendar in Elizabethan and Stuart England* (Los Angeles: University of California Press, 1989) 142.

(the Lord being the cause thereof, but that the instrument wherewith it pleased him to work)...the sum of £10 at least."[25] Such providences revealed what God liked and disliked, whom he judged, and the fate that awaited sinners. A similar logic applied to Virginia, although settlers there may have been quicker than their countrymen to recognize the relationship between sin and the polity.

Dominion required a polity, and polity meant constructing a system that pleased God so that the English could maintain the deity's friendship. A successful polity might guarantee the salvation of the English state abroad, thus proving Parliament's imperial claims and contributing to an English identity at home. Despite their nation's undoubted relationship with God, colonizers did not believe God had preordained the establishment of an English overseas empire. Although he had occasionally taken the venture in hand when human actors had lost faith or hope, God apparently had no intention of helping the English gain an empire unless they cooperated with him. If settlers in Virginia did not please the deity, he would judge them harshly. Given the personality with which they endowed him, pleasing their divine friend was no easy task. What English people knew most clearly about God was that he had an extraordinarily bad temper. When early modern English people thought about how the cosmos were ruled, they did not inhabit a Christocentric universe. When planters in Virginia or supporters in England referred to God, they meant the first person of the Trinity, the creator of heaven and earth who revealed his favor and indignation through nature. He was the Old Testament Jehovah, swift to anger and quick to reveal his displeasure. If favorable winds served as tokens of God's favor, then storms, famine, plagues, and troubles with the native peoples of the land indicated that something was amiss in the polity's relationship with the deity.

---

[25] Keith Thomas, *Religion and the Decline of Magic: Studies in Popular Beliefs in Sixteenth and Seventeenth Century England* (London: Weidenfeld and Nicolson, 1971) 78-112, quotation on 81.

During the colony's first few decades, a theology of the natural world that defined the link between sin and divine vengeance framed Virginia's relationship with God. By acting in ways that God approved, colonists might rally the deity to their side, thereby gaining his blessings. They might just as likely, however, anger the deity by acting in ways which God did not like and thus endanger England's experiment in empire. Sin separated the polity from God, and God responded to the colonists' transgressions by sending hardships upon the community. Sometimes he chastised planters in Virginia as he had the children of Israel, by allowing the people of the land to come upon them with military arms. Company leaders back in London saw this pattern at work when they thought about the causes of the Indian uprising in 1622 that resulted in the deaths of nearly a quarter of the settlers then in Virginia. Their worldview did not allow them to posit causes for the surprise attack such as English land greed, English mistreatment of the natives, or the Powhatans' defense of their territory. Rather, the uprising had been an act of God caused by "those two enormous excesses of apparell and drinkeing...and the neglect of Devine worship." A letter to resident authorities concluded, "It is the heavie hand of God for the punishment of ors and yor transgressions."[26] Members of the resident council also saw God's hand at work, although they were no more prescient in their analysis: they suspected that the avarice of Company members back in England rather than the colonists' moral failings had drawn down God's judgment.[27]

Despite the troubles God sent upon the colony, he was not so capricious as to destroy the settlement without giving his

---

[26] Treasurer and Council for Virginia to the Governor and Council in Virginia, 1 August 1622, Kingsbury, *Records of the Virginia Company of London*, 3:666. There are numerous additional examples. See *Records of the Virginia Company of London*, 3:275, 446, 612, 678, 698; 4:23, 162, 232, 235; Alexander Whitaker, *Good Newes from Virginia*, ed. Wesley Frank Craven (New York: Scholars' Facsimiles & Reprints, 1937) 11.

[27] Council in Virginia to the Virginia Company of London, 20 January 1622/23, Kingsbury, *Records of the Virginia Company of London*, 4:9.

friends an opportunity to change their ways. Although he had taken the first step by befriending the English nation, human actions still determined the type of relationship colonists shared with him. A not-so-subtle Arminian theology related the colony to a God who expected human cooperation in the enterprise of colonization. "In ye first place," the Virginia Company Governor George Yeardley admonished, "yu be carefull that Almighty God may be duly & daily served, both by yrselfe & all ye people undr yr charges, wch may draw down a Blessing upon all your endeavours."[28] The instructions speak the language of influence, a concept not without precedent in English religious practice. To "draw down" God's blessings, like drawing down his judgments, implied that God acted in response to human behavior. That the community gathered at church could influence God reflected the medieval idea that communal processions could "induce God to show his mercy."[29] It was an expression of influence rather than entreaty, and it framed the colonists' understanding of the relationship between God and the polity.

Whereas human actions could anger God, amendment could appease the deity. When a plague struck the colony in 1623 and killed large numbers of settlers, Samuel Sharpe, a burgess from Charles City, wondered what sin the colonists could have committed for God to treat them so violently. The remedy, however, was clear: "*God grant that the cause may be found out* and amended."[30] If the sin stopped, so too would the punishment. "Whence the evill therefore sprung the remedy must first begin," Company leaders advised the colonists on

---

[28] Instructions of the Privy Council to Sir George Yeardley, 19 April 1623, Public Records Office, Colonial Office, 5/1354, f. 207. See also "Instructions to Sir Francis Wyatt," *Virginia Magazine of History and Biography* 11 (1903): 54; Council for Virginia to Captain and Virginia Company going to Virginia, 10 December 1606, Brown, *Genesis of the United States*, 1:85.

[29] Thomas, *Religion and the Decline of Magic*, 40-41.

[30] Samuel Sharpe to [?], 24 March 1622/23, Kingsbury, *Records of the Virginia Company of London*, 4:233-34.

another occasion, "and an humble reconciliation be made wth the devine Matie by future conformitie unto his most just and holie lawes."[31] Their cosmology dominated by divine causality, sin resulted in divine chastisement. The wages of sin were clear: famine, sickness, faction, and military defeats at the hands of foreign enemies. In defining the relationship between God and Virginia's polity, religion began not from the theology or soteriology of England's established church, but from the premise that God existed and that he demanded certain actions from human beings. The immediacy and activity that English people who were associated with the Virginia venture attributed to God reveal a notion of the covenant, a relationship acknowledged far more readily by colonial leaders than by the lower classes.[32] Not as complex as the covenant that was later developed by the New England Puritans, it was a covenant nonetheless and resembled that of the ancient Israelites: follow the laws of God and prosper, but lapse, and die.

Yet God's personal qualities and the covenant theology they fostered were not the only factors shaping Virginia's polity. A body of widely accepted political theory contributed to this act of creation as well. For the polity, religion formulated a series of relationships, perhaps best understood as horizontal and vertical means of communication, which helped to define and sustain political society, with unity under God the paramount goal. The horizontal plane united people within a particular polity; the vertical plane linked a united people to God. Within the polity, or on the horizontal plane, religion knit people together by giving them a shared understanding of theological doctrine, religious practice, and ultimate reality, thus removing the ominous threat of religious factions. With the political danger

---

[31] Treasurer and Council for Virginia to the Governor and Council in Virginia, 1 August 1622, Kingsbury, *Records of the Virginia Company of London*, 3:666.

[32] I do not wish to suggest that none of the lower classes accepted this covenant. There is, however, very little evidence that indicates much religious sentiment at all among the rabble who populated Virginia in the colony's early days.

posed by theological divisions absent, religious unity helped craft political unity, organizing for action in the world a polity made strong not only by shared ethnic, cultural, and linguistic traditions, but also by a common religion. Religious unity thereby became a facet of national identity. A nation so organized could present a solid and united front against any potential enemies, its population made up of countrymen who were also brothers in the faith, linked in existential ways that transcended the earthly divisions of temporal states. European nations organized both planes of communication around an established church, giving state approval to one religion and in the process marking all other forms of worship or belief as impure and heretical, probably the suspect ideas of men damned by God. So prevailing was the belief that religion and state ought to be linked that it engendered admiration even for enemies who had the good sense to organize their polities in this manner. With this belief in mind, John Smith lauded the superiority of Turkish to European political society for encouraging action in the world: "He that will but truly consider the greatnesse of the Turks Empire and power here in Christendome, shall finde the naturall Turkes are generally of one religion, and the Christians in so many divisions and opinions, that they are among themselves worse enemies than the Turkes."[33]

Although they struggled to put their theories of church and state into practice, most early seventeenth century Englishmen were Aristotelians in religion as well as politics. They believed that monarchy, or government of the one, was preferable to aristocracy, or government of the few, because it was by nature less prone to factions and thus more likely to produce unity. The same logic meant that one religion within a state was better than two or three or many religions. At its very best, this preferred form of political organization collapsed into one the duality

---

[33] Jon Butler, *Awash in a Sea of Faith: Christianizing the American People* (Cambridge: Harvard University Press, 1990) 281; John Smith, *Advertisements for the Unexperienced Planters of New England,* Barbour, *Works of Captain John Smith,* 3:296.

between church and state, ensuring that these two methods of organizing one people were not at odds within a single polity. Beneath this construction of unity lay a legal fiction accepting the myth that church and state were formally but not substantially distinct institutions comprising a nation's entire populace. Richard Hooker offered the best explanation of this early-modern prescription:

> We hold that seeing there is not any man of the *Church* of *England*, but the same man is also a member of the *Commonwealth*, nor any man a member of the *Commonwealth* which is not also of the *Church* of *England*, therefore as in a figure *triangular* the base doth differ from the sides thereof, and yet one and the selfsame line, is both a base and a side; a side simply, a base if it chance to be bottom and underlie the rest: So albeit properties and actions of one kind do cause the name of a Commonwealth, qualities and functions of another sort the name of a *Church* to be given unto a multitude, yet one and the selfsame multitude may in such sort be both and is so with us, that no person appertaining to the one can be denied to be also of the other. [34]

Religious unity helped to create and maintain political unity, resulting in the mingling of church and state in a single national identity.

What made creating a viable polity in Virginia such a problem, and ultimately a source of contention among English backers of colonization, was the lack of any settled English identity around which to construct the desired unity, let alone the mystical union between church and state. The Church of England held neither a set body of doctrine nor a particular creed to help it establish a clear and lasting identity. Since Virginia was settled before competing definitions of the English Church

---

[34] Richard Hooker, *The Works of that Learned and Judicious Divine Mr. Richard Hooker, With an Account of His Life and Death by Isaac Walton*, 3 vols., ed. John Keble (Oxford: Clarendon Press, 1887) 3:330. The material cited is in Book 8: i.2.

erupted into party animosity and open warfare, there was no history of persecution that a religious sect or party might employ as a means of crafting identity. Moreso than most of England's other seventeenth-century colonies, the first permanent colony was founded as an extension of the nation as a whole. Unlike Puritans who settled Massachusetts Bay, Roman Catholics who sought refuge in Maryland, or Quakers who fled to Pennsylvania, Virginia's early settlers did not leave England to escape persecution or to create a more "godly" society. They did not feel compelled to leave their homeland in order either to avoid God's impending judgment upon the land or to save it as those who participated in the later Puritan migrations believed. Nor did they think of themselves as the chosen remnant of God's elect; *all* England was then God's elect. Virginia was not the creation of a party, but of a nation. The only faith that nation shared in the early seventeenth century was a belief that God intended North America for his English friends. "What need wee then to fear," John Rolfe asked in a reference to the English and North America, "but to *goe up at once* as a *peculiar people* marked and chosen by the *finger* of God, to *possess* it?"[35] Couched in the familiar Old Testament metaphor of a chosen people and a promised land, Rolfe's assertion nevertheless belied the chauvinistic arrogance of a people confident they were on the side of God and convinced of their superiority to people of other nations. Virginia's colonization was not a flight from England by people pushed to the political and religious margins of their homeland, but a celebration of things English they hoped would culminate in the nation's possession of a "good land." The religious framework of Virginia's founding was the nation's in-

---

[35]Richard Helgerson, *Forms of Nationhood: The Elizabethan Writing of England* (Chicago: University of Chicago Press, 1992); Rolfe, *True Relation of the State of Virginia*, 41; Hill, *The English Bible and the Seventeenth-Century Revolution*, 264-70. Rolfe's use of the term "peculiar people" suggests his reliance on the King James or "Authorized Version" of the Bible rather than on the Puritans' beloved Geneva Bible. The phrase appears four times in the King James version and once in the Geneva Bible. See Hill, *The English Bible and the Seventeenth-Century Revolution*, 269-70.

clusive relationship with God rather than the specific identity of a church.

Old Testament concepts of nationhood shaped the advice offered by English authors to Virginia's leaders. Company instructions and colonial laws implied that religion was a corporate and public enterprise, particularly concerned with encouraging behaviors that would maintain the colony's covenantal relationship and therefore influence God to bless Virginia. Thus, with God's blessing, ensuring the continued existence of an English settlement in North America and the creation of English imperial identity. As a part of the colony's political structure, religion did not mean personal relationships with God, although colonial leaders hoped that the settlers would craft relationships with the divine, just as they had. Religion for the polity was based on Old Testament concepts of nationhood and concerned not with individual salvation in the hereafter but with national salvation in time, a logical extension of Old Testament themes associated with the patriarch Abraham. When God had called Abraham and told him he would father children whose heirs would become a great nation, Yahweh was not promising the patriarch individual salvation. He would live on in death, of course, but through his children and his children's who children would populate a land promised their forbear by God. Likewise, only by constructing a polity pleasing to God would England maintain its empire in the New World and thus gain national salvation. Those people who wrote about colonial polity wanted to construct in Virginia a society and government acceptable to a God offended by certain beliefs and actions. Successfully establishing such a polity would guarantee both the colony's success as well as England's continued presence in North America, an approach that might be called a "soteriology of empire." Salvation would be achieved by ensuring the continued existence of the English settlement in Virginia.

English desire to possess the land set in motion a logical progression of theoretical imperatives linking dominion to unity that required practical solutions if England was indeed to gain salvation in time by establishing a lasting New World empire.

Colonists inherited from their homeland neither an established identity nor a stable system of religious or political organization, but a jumble of conflicting ideas and potential constructions of meaning and unity. One of the few positive intellectual or practical concepts settlers inherited was the broad conceptual belief that the good polity demanded both unity and religion, although that still left to Company and resident leaders the task of filling the general theory with specific applications. Dominion required a polity; a polity meant pleasing God; pleasing God demanded unity—and there was the problem. English people of the early seventeenth century lacked any meaningful identity and, beyond being friends of God, were far more confident of who they were not than of who they were. Although never clearly stated, a single question lay beneath the colonization literature of advice and exhortation: how could the English people maintain their friendship with God so that they could maintain the land? On the eve of colonization, faith in God's friendship alone united the diverse elements in the English community. Ambiguous at best, deceitful at worst, this con-viction crafted a semblance of unity, at the same time allowing a people who desired unity to avoid the very obvious mixtures within their society. Yet Virginia was not England, and some authors found solutions feasible in a settled state intolerable in this expansion of the nation abroad. Writings of colonization supporters expressed dissatisfaction with the vague unity divine friendship furnished and with the hope that their own desires for more specific constructions of English identity would someday reign. Their prescriptions projected onto Virginia their hopes for what England could become, carrying with them messages of reform as well as identity. A successful North American colony would enable English people to prove their nation's imperial identity. England would make Virginia, and Virginia, in turn, would make England the empire it hoped to become.

But was empire enough? Securing the "good land" may not have been the only goal colonizers aspired to achieve. Men being men and prone by self-interest to seek their nation's own good and to exalt their own ideas above those of others, the writings of some colonizers suggest that they worried about questions of identity that transcended empire. Prescribing how Virginia could best craft its relationship with God also depicted visions of England. A successful polity had to please God, else it would fail. Thus, a thriving Virginia provided *prima facia* evidence that a particular method of crafting the polity's relationship with God was sound. If acquiring an empire meant pleasing God, and if one's religious prescription for colonial polity succeeded, having therefore pleased the deity, did one need better evidence that England should be the same? Hesitant and cautious, writers associated with the Virginia venture may have looked upon the colony as a trial run in answering the question of English national identity, thus making the colony a mirror reflecting what England might become.

Company and resident leaders, ministers, and propagandists, all citizens of an England in quest of identity and empire, prescribed forms of colonial polity they thought would please God, often agreeing only that unity was important. Two central factors, sometimes appearing in the same pamphlets, figured in their advice: belief and behavior. Counsel regarding belief took several forms and frequently reflected the growing divisions within England's religious community. William Crashaw urged colonial leaders to construct a purer Church of England based on his own religious prejudices. "Suffer no Brownists, nor factious Separatists," he told the Virginia Company, "let them keepe their conuenticles elsewhere." Crashaw's religious prejudices did not end with separatists; he disliked Roman Catholics as well and warned Virginians: "Suffer no Papists; let them not nestle there; nay let the name of the Pope for Poperie be never heard of in *Virginea*."[36] Crashaw had not meant Roman Catholics when he referred to God's English friends. While—like Crashaw—defining Roman Catholics out of England's experiment in empire, other supporters crafted Protestant unity more

---

[36] William Crashaw, *A Sermon Preached in London before the right honorable the Lord Laware, Lord Governour and Captaine Generall of Virginea* (London, 1610) L-1.

broadly. William Symonds warned the Virginia Company to accept in the colony only people he termed "true hearted Protestant[s]," suggesting that God despised Roman Catholics as much as Symonds himself did and would destroy any settlement harboring people he hated. Symonds believed that Catholic English people posed a graver threat to the infant settlement than native enemies, and he advised casting this leaven out of their house lest Virginia court the divine wrath. He described a Protestant colony free of Roman Catholic impurities: "The onely perill," he wrote, "is in offending God, and taking of Papists in to your company."[37]

Appeals to religious party unity were potentially divisive, revealing nascent rifts within English Protestantism as well as a suspicion of Roman Catholics that rose and fell with political events in Europe. The endemic arrogance of English people in the early modern era only made the rising desire for religious unity potentially more destructive. Roman Catholics were a minority, sizable, but still a minority; the issue of Protestant unity therefore was of greater importance, for a Protestant party would likely end up controlling the English Church. Puritans at this time still remained within the Church of England, albeit with a passion for sermons and an exuberant delight in their Calvinist beliefs that other members of the Church did not share and, frankly, found a bit disturbing. Yet in the early 1600s one may not accurately speak of Puritans separate from Anglicans for Puritans were Anglicans, content to reform the Church of England as members of that institution. There were, however, visible breaches in this uneasy relationship. Alternative visions of Protestant truth abounded, and topics ranging from the nature of the sacraments to the place of images and the proper form of church polity were hotly debated, all demonstrating that England's Protestant garment was made of seams easily rent and that the Elizabethan Settlement may have lacked the finality politicians desired. Unhappy with the unholy religious melange of their homeland, some colonizers projected a better England

---

[37] Symonds, *Virginea Britannia*, 45-46.

abroad, one they were sure God would approve and bless with success. Nationalistic colonization incorporated partisan conflict regarding the transcendent ideals that defined nationality.[38]

If belief tended toward fragmentation, behavior, the second factor in the colonial advice literature, carried with it the potential to unify people otherwise separated by theology and devotional practices. It also tapped into early modern England's increasing preoccupation with moral behavior. In the years after 1600, growing numbers of Englishmen—and not only those whom historians would later call Puritans—worried that England's Christian people were falling far short of the ethical standards set in the Bible and had begun calling for stricter regulation of morality. Members of Parliament introduced, debated, and passed by wide margins bills governing drinking and sexual morality.[39] This rising emphasis on moral rather than theological purity led some commentators to suggest that the company and resident leaders create a unified colonial relationship with God by establishing good and severe laws and enforcing these with rigor. People who thought this way also tended to hold up as a model leader for Virginia the Old Testament prophet Moses. Such people believed the colony needed a leader who mixed religion with Renaissance notions of "virtu," a man possessed of "true humility, temperance, and justice, joined with confidence, valor, and noble courage, such as was in Moses, the man of God, whose justice exceeded and courage was incom-

[38] John Bossy, *The English Catholic Community, 1570-1850* (New York: Oxford University Press, 1976) 182-94; David Underdown, *Fire From Heaven: Life in an English Town in the Seventeenth Century* (New Haven: Yale University Press, 1992) 18-21; Peter Lake, *Anglicans and Puritans? Presbyterian and English Conformist Thought From Whitgift to Hooker* (London: Unwin & Hyman, 1988); Christopher Haigh, ed., *The English Reformation Revisited* (Cambridge: Cambridge University Press, 1987).

[39] David Underdown, *Revel, Riot, and Rebellion: Popular Politics and Culture in England, 1603-1660* (New York, 1985) 47-51; Thomas, *Religion and the Decline of Magic*, 92.

parable, and yet the meekest man that went upon the earth."[40]
As heirs of a promise the English people compared themselves to
Abraham; to secure it they pointed to God's other friend, the
lawgiver, Moses: "that first & great commander ouer the Colony
of the children of Israel, conducting them from AEgypt [sic] to
make their plantation in the land of Promise."[41] By giving God's
laws to the Israelites, Moses had helped to establish a covenant
between the deity and a people who identi-fied themselves as a
distinct ethnic group sharing a special rela-tionship with God. As
long as the Hebrews followed God's laws the promised land
would be theirs. Although shrouded in not so oblique allusions,
references to Moses elevated the Ten Com-mandments to a
central place as an element in the colony's relationship with
God.

Since Europeans made belief systems central to state
identity, it may be easy to miss that some prescriptions for the
Virginia polity downplayed theological purity and emphasized
certain kinds of behavior instead. European custom militated
against the latter practice, set as it was in a world rent by the
Protestant Reformation and the subsequent close identification
of different religions with particular nation states. Nearly one
hundred years of history had taught Europeans to organize their
states in this manner, and they had institutionalized the theory
by developing state-church systems.[42]

Intentionally or not, proponents of the colonization venture
offered settlers two competing views of English identity overseas,
giving Virginians different answers to the question, "Who are
God's friends?" and implicitly challenging traditional European
ideas about political organization. The religious party approach

---

[40] Johnson, *Nova Britannia*, 21; Quentin Skinner, *Foundations of
Modern Political Thought*, Vol 2. (New York: Cambridge University Press,
1978) 94-95, 126.

[41] *For the Colony in Virginea Britania. Lawes Diuine, Morall and
Martiall, &c.*, in Peter Force, ed., *Tracts and Other Papers Relating
Principally to the Origin, Settlement, and Progress of the Colonies in North
America*, 4 vols. (Gloucester MA: Peter Smith, 1963) 3: #2, 36.

[42] Butler, *Awash in a Sea of Faith*, 281.

implied unity through a shared faith, in effect excluding Roman Catholics and Separatists from this form of English nationhood. Hating these groups and claiming they were offensive to God also gave people who thought this way a convenient "other" whom God despised against which to define themselves. Such advice accepted and attempted to extend overseas mythic constructions of an England religiously pure and united by a particular form of Protestantism. By adhering to the proper religious beliefs people could thus retain God's friendship. The Mosaic solution epitomized by general agreement on the importance of the Ten Commandments, on the other hand, suggested that behavior among a group rather than belief determined the polity's relationship with God. To compound an already ambiguous matter, the advice literature did not indicate whether belief or behavior or both together provided the primary determinant of this relationship.

What is more, although established by Europeans, Virginia was not a settled state with decades of custom to help determine its political organization. It was an infant commonwealth, its existence already menaced by political and religious factions which threatened unity.[43] Authors of colonization literature recognized Virginia's special circumstances as well as the difficulties associated with creating new polities. Time and again they suggested that Company and resident leaders use as model state-builders ancient figures who had founded states or given new laws to a people: Moses and King David from the Old Testament, and Romulus and Remus, the mythic founders of Rome. Recommending these models made authors' advice the arrogant assertions of an arrogant people. It suggested that England's greatest glory lay in the future, not the past, and the nation's recent history offered no heroes worthy of the venture. So grand was the colony's potential that only men who had founded great empires or spoken with God could provide adequate examples for Virginia's leaders to emulate. The literature of colonization skipped English history for something better

---

[43] See page 46 for a brief discussion of the colony's religious factions.

on which to base a more glorious national future. Despite
reflecting their European political background, authors who
wrote about Virginia's polity offered tacit recognition that the
colony's setting was different from England's and that what
worked in a settled state might be less effective in a new one.

North America and its native peoples created a context for
empire-building far different from what Europe afforded,
opening physical and intellectual spaces that allowed—perhaps
forced—colonial authorities to define unity and faction in more
inclusive ways. The continent played a role in the decision, but
the early modern era was also a fertile period in the creative life
of the English nation. Great talents emerged in literature, music,
and political theory that remain unsurpassed as national
treasures, figures still possessed of international import. Coke,
Hooker, Shakespeare, and Byrd were but a few of the age's
greats. Within decades of Virginia's founding, English people
took the momentous and creative step of claiming for the people
the right to resist and execute monarchs, thus challenging the
limited resistance theories of the past.[44] It was an age of ferment
and ideas, a fluid era ripe with potential, and there was no reason
why such people could not have applied their genius to colonial
polity as well as to literature, law, or music. European forms of
governmental organization become normative for colonial polity
only if customary practices take on the status of Platonic forms
from which colonial deviation is evidence of decay and
imperfection.

By 1610 Virginia Company leaders broke with the
traditional pattern and established government in the colony
along the lines of behavior, institutionalizing their choice in the
Lawes Diuine, Morall and Martiall, a severe code of laws that
replaced the existing statutes and that the company hoped
would bring order and success to the colony.[45] By doing so, the
company redefined Virginia's relationship with God and, by

---

[44] Skinner, *Foundations of Modern Political Thought,* 2:302-348.
[45] Morgan, *American Slavery, American Freedom,* 79-80; Morton,
Colonial Virginia, 1:32.

implication, the role of religion in the good polity, for the *Lawes* made belief less important than behavior as a determinant of identity. Although the new law code was brutal and harsh and led to the creation of a military regime in the settlement, the statutes were nonetheless imbued with a deep sense of religion and held great religious significance for the colony.[46] In Virginia's setting, the *Lawes Diuine, Morall and Martiall* served to construct a religious identity suitable to the North American context. Building a polity is no trivial task, involving more than philosophical ideas about institutions. It must account for the physical and cultural environment of the new state as well as for the human matter on which the form of government will act. From the combination of inherited theories about political organization and human nature, the North American context, and the Englishmen who peopled Virginia, the *Lawes* were the logical outcome, the result of experience as much as theory.

Englishmen came to Virginia not only with theories about polity but with ideas about pedagogy and human nature—one of the building blocks of polity. Three interrelated factors inherited from English ways of thinking formed the intellectual basis of early Virginia's culture: the malleability of human nature, the potential of education to shape individuals, and the role of sight as a method of instruction. Human nature to the English was not a fixed quality, it was malleable and could change depending upon the particular cultural and environmental setting in which an individual lived. Robert Gray, a supporter of the venture, wrote: "it is not the nature of men, but the education of men, which makes them barbarous and uncivill, and therefore chaunge the education of men, and you shall see that their nature will be

---

[46] Contemporary military laws often referred to religion. See Robert Barret, *The Theorike and Practike of Moderne Warres* (London 1598) 26-27, 89, 129, 149; Barnaby Rich, *A Pathway to Military Practise* (London 1587) B3, D4, H4, G3; Niccolo Machiavelli, *The Art of War (1521)* in Allan Gilbert, trans., *Machiavelli: The Chief Works and Others*, 2 vols. (London: Cambridge University Press, 1958-1966), 2:563-64, 661, 689-91.

greatly rectified."[47] Other people did not say this as directly, but readily implied identical conclusions. With a "strict forme of government, and severe discipline," William Crashaw told the Virginia Company of London, individuals "doe often become new men, even as it were cast in a good mould."[48] Crafting new persons was an act of creation, in effect changing their natures to make of them something different. Certain that nurture outweighed nature in the social formation of individuals, Englishmen believed human nature could be guided by education.

English people of the seventeenth century also believed that much learning took place through sight. They commonly believed that what struck a man's eye could "peirce his heart the better." All sorts of people showed confidence in this means of transferring knowledge, often explicitly citing the superiority of sight to sound. Patrick Copeland summed up this common point of view in the preface to the published edition of a sermon he had previously delivered to Company members at Paules Crosse, in the process justifying his decision to print the discourse: "words spoken are soone come, soone gone; but those written withall, they make a deeper impression."[49] The impact of sight extended far beyond the written word; it was a force that could speak across linguistic divides as well as to illiterate men like many of those who peopled the colony. Writing at mid-century to Lady Berkeley, wife of the colony's Governor William Berkeley, Virginia Ferrar referred to the concept in a way typical of many others: "[I have] found that the sight of a thing brings menny times greate good Notice [to] a mans mind and understanding for the happy and more ready compliting of many

---

[47] Gray, *Good Speed to Virginia*, C-2. See also Treasurer and Council for Virginia to Governor and Council in Virginia, 1 August 1622, Kingsbury, *Records of the Virginia Company of London*, 3:672; Sheehan, *Savagism and Civility*, 123.

[48] Crashaw, *Sermon Preached in London*, F-1.

[49] Patrick Copeland, *Virginia's God Be Thanked* (London 1612) preface (no pagination in preface).

good designes; farr better than the hearring of it...alone."[50] Virginia may have known this first hand. Her father, John Ferrar, a colonization supporter, had named his daughter Virginia so that by seeing her each day he would better remember to pray daily for the colony.[51] Settlers in Virginia also accepted this theory of knowledge. John Smith set the idea to verse: "But yet I know this not affects the minde,/Which eares doth heare, as that which eyes doe finde."[52] What entered the mind through the eye left a more vivid impression than what entered through the ear.

For people who think this way, in the union between knower and known, the knower remains passive while the object that is integrated into the self takes the active role. The object or visual event thus "impresses itself upon the mind." Therefore, unless a person is weak of mind or willfully perverse, what an individual sees articulates the reality a particular event or object represents.[53] Demonstrated through actions, the customs and

---

[50] Virginia Ferrar to Lady Berkeley, 10 August 1650, Ferrar Papers, Magdalene College, Cambridge Universtiy, f. 692. There are numerous additional examples. See, for instance, Gray, *Good Speed to Virginia*, D2-D3; *Lawes Diuine, Morall and Martiall*, 30; Instructions to George Yeardley from His Majesty's Council for Virginia, 2 December 1618, f. 92, Ferrar Papers, Magdalene College, Cambridge University; William Waller Hening, ed., *The Statutes at Large: Being a Collection of All the Laws of Virginia...* 13 vols. (Richmond, 1809-1823) 1:158; John Donne, *A Sermon upon the viii. verse of the i. chapter of the Acts of the Apostles. Preached to the Honourable Company of the Virginia Plantations* (London, 1622) 32.

[51] Bernard Blackstone, ed. *The Ferrar Papers, Containing a Life of Nicholas Ferrar* (London: Cambridge University Press, 1938) 88.

[52] John Smith, *The Generall History of Virginia, New-England, and the Summer Isles* (London, 1624), Barbour, *Works of Captain John Smith*, 2:107.

[53] William J. Bouwsma, *John Calvin: A Sixteenth-Century Portrait* (New York: Oxford University Press, 1988) 69-71, 90; Paul H. Kocher, *Science and Religion in Elizabethan England* (San Marino: Huntington Library, 1953) 29-32, 44; Harry S. Stoudt, "Religion, Communication, and the Ideological Origins of the American Revolution," *William and Mary Quarterly* 3rd ser. 34 (1977): 529; Rhys Isaac, *The Transformation of Virginia, 1740-1790* (Chapel Hill: University of North Carolina Press, 1982) 52-57.

mores of a society play the central role in educating members of that society. Living among a particular people and learning their ways by observing their actions thus affects a person's nature.

For colonists, English theories of knowledge and human nature functioned in an environment very different from England. Several thousand miles of ocean from their homeland and its comforting symbols of civilization separated the North American context where they hoped to construct a polity. Yet the wilderness held few terrors for Virginia's early planters. John Smith, Thomas Dale, John Rolfe, and other early colonial leaders were not cringing men clinging to the edge of a continent, fearful of what existed on the interior. They were national chauvinists confident of their own and their nation's superiority. To men so confident and brash, the wilderness challenged neither their civility nor their Christianity.

Their Christianity, in fact, was portable. The very presence of Englishmen brought Christianity to the land, and they carried their spiritual regimen in their pockets or supplies. John Smith described the liturgical practice of explorers, one likely taken from the Church of England's *Book of Common Prayer*: "Our order was daily to have Prayer, with a Psalm."[54] Christianity shaped lives in the wilderness just as it did back in the more settled regions of Europe. It even shaped the land. Some men believed North America was the "place where Satan's throne is," and that Englishmen, by bringing Christianity to the land, participated in spiritual conquest because their presence liberated territory from the devil's "freehold."[55] The land itself was neutral and could be shaped by human culture. The land did not make people English according to the Reverend Richard Eburne, people made the land English: "imagine all that to be

---

[54] John Smith, *Generall History of Virginia*, Barbour, *Works of Captain John Smith*, 2:171. *The Book of Common Prayer* contained both services for Morning and Evening Prayer as well as the complete Psalter with tables indicating which Psalms were to be prayed each day.

[55] Crashaw, *Sermon Preached in London*, K-3, H-1. See also *Lawes Diuine, Morall and Martiall*, 67; On the devil in Bermuda, see Strachey, *A Voyage to Virginia in 1609*, 16.

England where Englishmen, where English people, you with them, and they with you, do dwell."[56]

North America as a whole, however, was not completely neutral and held significant threats to colonial polity. The land England wished to possess for its empire already lay under the dominion of another people, the Powhatan Indians, and they were not sure they wanted to share their ancestral lands with these invaders. Colonists learned quickly that the land could be an unwelcoming place. When the first landing party came ashore at Cape Henry in April 1607, nearby Indians engaged the settlers in a brief skirmish, forcing them to retreat to the safety of their ships. Shortly thereafter Powhatan's warriors attacked the recently constructed fort at Jamestown, with only fire from English vessels at anchor in the James River preventing the natives from destroying the settlement. The natives were powerful enemies who, had they chosen to do so, could easily have destroyed a settlement filled over the first few years of colonization with fewer and fewer people less and less able to feed themselves.[57]

Despite their martial skills, the natives presented less a military than a cultural threat to English settlers. Their first encounters with the natives taught English people that these creatures were men like themselves. They defended their territory by attacking the English intruders, and they did so with tools fashioned by human skills. Bows and arrows were no match for English arms, but they were human weaponry nonetheless. Virginia's native peoples presented such a tremendous cultural threat because they simply were not alien enough. Had they run together in herds as some European authors believed, or had they acted more like animals than human beings, English settlers could have dismissed them as beasts possessing no culture. But the natives were not beasts. Despite their differences, which were at once fascinating and frightening to Englishmen, colonists who

---

[56] Kupperman, *Settling With the Indians*, 162.

[57] Morgan, *American Slavery, American Freedom*, 71-73; Billings, Selby, and Tate, *Colonial Virginia*, 28.

saw the natives and observed their ways realized that they possessed the attributes of men. They walked erect like men (always an important indicator of humanness to people of the Renaissance); they spoke a language which, although strange, English people could learn; and they possessed identifiable social and political institutions, even government and religion. John Smith believed the Native Virginians best enslaved, but he still recognized the existence of another culture, recounting in detail in his various writings their music, religion, manner of making war, diet, and government. Using words similar to those of other colonists, Smith wrote: "There is yet in *Virginia* no place discovered to bee so *Savage* in which the *Savages* have not a religion."[58]

Native religion fascinated colonial observers. Convinced that native rites centered on worship of the devil who controlled them and demanded a variety of lengthy ceremonies, English settlers were both gripped and repelled by a religion so alien to their own. Often basing their reports more on hearsay and imagination than fact, they described in lurid and speculative detail rituals that they were certain involved human sacrifice and witchcraft, practices often linked in the English mind.[59] And not only did the natives worship Satan, but Englishmen were also certain that on important issues native "Priests haue conference and consult indeed with the Deuill and receaue verball an-

---

[58] Kupperman, *Settling With the Indians*, 33-106, 118-19; John Smith, *A Map of Virginia. With a Description of the Countrey, the Commodities, People, Government and Religion* (London, 1612), Barbour, *Works of Captain John Smith*, 1:168; William Strachey, *The Historie of Travell into Virginia Britania* (London 1612) ed. Louis B. Wright (London: Hakluyt Society, 1953) 88-89.

[59] Thomas, *Religion and the Decline of Magic*; Sheehan, *Savigism and Civility*, 39-48; Strachey, *Historie of Travell into Virginia Britania*, 98-100; Kupperman, *Settling With the Indians*, 65-68; Philip L. Barbour, "The Riddle of the Powhatan 'Black Boyes,'" *Virginia Magazine of History and Biography* 88 (1980): 148-54.

sweres," a relationship more intimate than English people shared with the God of the Old and New Testaments.[60]

Natives possessed civil government as well; moreover, to English eyes it resembled monarchy. The emperor, Powhatan, ruled over lesser kings who held their lands directly from him in a manner similar to the way James I ruled England. Colonists could find little wrong with this arrangement, noting on occasion that like English government it was neither despotic nor arbitrary. During the colony's first few years, when the settlement suffered from the factions of the councilliar form of government under which they labored, colonists used to the English monarchical system who understood native political society may have looked upon the latter with envy. Native work habits, however, were something else altogether and revealed disturbing patterns. Native men appeared to do little work, and much of the labor they engaged in seemed less like work to Englishmen than frivolous leisure. Men took part in "such manlike exercises" as hunting (a pursuit reserved back home to members of the English gentry), fishing, and warfare. Regardless of how fruitful the land may have been, natives did not live off of manna, and there was much work to be completed. Crops, of course, had to be planted, tended, and harvested; fruits and nuts were gathered to supplement the diet of squash, corn, and melons sown by native labor; dwellings needed to be constructed and furniture built. Women performed all of these tasks. This apparent inequitable division of labor and the obviously slothful lives of native men that it engendered gave the impression to colonial authorities of a culture beset with wanton idleness.[61]

The early modern English mind found few things as repulsive as idleness—a particularly damning vice and the first

---

[60] Strachey, *Historie of Travell*, 95, 89-90; Whitaker, *Good Newes from Virginia*, 24-26; Francis Magnel, "Francis Magnel's Relation of the First Voyage and the Beginnings of the Jamestown Colony," 1 July 1610, Barbour, *Jamestown Voyages Under the First Charter*, 1:154; Morgan, *American Slavery, American Freedom*, 56-57.

[61] Morgan, *American Slavery, American Freedom*, 50-52, 58, 60; Kupperman, *Settling With the Indians*, 48-51.

cause of other more serious violations of God's will for human beings. There is no separating this idea from early modern English Christian society. The English Church warned of its dangers, implying that idleness begat a veritable domino effect of sin: "Idleness is never alone, but hath always a long tail of other vices hanging on."[62] Labor was good, proof of a man's worth before God and his neighbors. It did not hurt that labor also inclined people to keep God's laws by inhibiting their opportunities to sin. In the New World, set against a rival culture that made a masculine virtue of this Christian vice, labor became an identifying feature of Christian culture, just as idleness marked "savagery."[63]

For one person to have worshipped Satan, lived a life of idle pleasure, or consulted with witches would have been an aberration, problems for which English society had created solutions: witches were executed, and Parliament had passed laws compelling individuals to work. A culture that lived this way, however, was another matter—especially a culture that actively chose to continue in this manner of life after being exposed to the truths of Christianity. To colonial leaders, native culture was an abomination marked by willful perversion. Indians were not Christians; they practiced witchcraft, worshipped Satan, and were given to habitual idleness. These traits in particular distinguished the people of the land from an English culture that possessed qualities antithetical to those of the natives: civility, Christianity, and an almost pathological obsession with putting people to work. Native culture, to colonial leaders, epitomized savagery. The general consensus among the company and resident leaders was that natives lived like beasts, offering a shocking vision to them of what happened to human nature absent the influence of Christianity. Yet as disturbing as colonial authorities found the natives' way of life, it was embraced by men

---

[62] *Sermons or Homilies, Appointed to be Read in Churches in the Time of Queen Elizabeth of Famous Memory* (New York, 1815) 441.

[63] Morgan, *American Slavery, American Freedom*, 61-62; add Sheehan.

like themselves, men "that with vs (infallibly) they had one, and the same discent and begynning from the vniversall Deluge, in the scattering of Noah his children and Nephewes."[64] Historian Karen Kupperman makes the point well: "Manner of life was the only thing, besides Christianity, which surely distinguished Indians from English colonists."[65] As a culture the natives were alien; as men they were not.

Colonial authorities found native culture far more frightening than the wilderness. Men could shape the wilderness,[66] but native culture could shape men, Englishmen as well as Indians. English notions of pedagogy and human nature only heightened the distinctions, thereby making the natives more dangerous and more frightening. If human nature was not a fixed quality, then civility and savagery were not absolute categories either, but unstable forms of existence intimately related to cultural environment. To paraphrase Robert Gray, change the cultural education of men and change their natures as well.

Wariness toward cultural rivals manifested itself in England's approach to converting the natives, an endeavor which rested upon the twin premises of the malleability of human nature and faith in the power of education. The English missionary impulse, to the extent that one existed, kept native peoples at a distance, reflecting a defensive effort designed to protect English manners from a dangerous foreign culture. Unlike Jesuits in New France or Maryland who traveled among indigenous populations to win converts, sometimes adopting their ways of

---

[64] Morgan, *American Slavery, American Freedom*, 50-52, 56-57, 63-69; Kupperman, *Settling With the Indians*, 106, 118-19; Sheehan, *Savigism and Civility*; Strachey, *Historie of Travell*, 53; Rolfe, *True Relation of the State of Virginia*, 40; Whitaker, *Good Newes from Virginia*, 24.

[65] Kupperman, *Settling With the Indians*, 119. See also John Smith, *Generall History of Virginia*, Barbour, *Works of Captain John Smith*, 2:125: "Religion 'tis that doth distinguish us,/From their brute humor, well we may it know."

[66] Kathleen M. Brown, *Good Wives, Nasty Wenches, and Anxious Patriarchs: Gender, Race, and Power in Colonial Virginia* (Chapel Hill: University of North Carolina Press, 1996) 19.

life and instructing natives as people at least partially integrated into Indian society, English settlers in Virginia attempted to "allure" natives to colonial society through a process of "cultural evangelism," thus encouraging Indians to give up their traditional lifestyle and come live among the colonists where they could learn English civility in preparation for becoming Christians. English communities embracing "peace and love as becometh xpians" would demonstrate the gentle Christian life, and natives impressed by what they had observed would forsake their own culture and ask to become both English and Christian.[67]

As early as 1609, the Virginia Company of London realized the failure of cultural evangelism and began to take a longer view, suggesting that the best means of destroying native ways and winning Indians to Christianity was by removing native children from their own cultural environment and raising them as Englishmen in the colony where they could learn "yor language and manners" in a proper English setting.[68] Still young and adaptable, "theire minds not overgrowne wth evill Custtomes"[69] that they no longer questioned, children were more

---

[67] Instructions to Thomas West Knight Lo: La Warr, 1609/10?, Kingsbury, *Records of the Virginia Company of London*, 3:26; Roy Harvey Pearce, *Savagism and Civilization: A Study of the Indian and the American Mind* (Berkeley: University of California Press, 1988) 17; James Axtell, *The Invasion Within: The Contest of Cultures in Colonial North America* (New York: Oxford University Press, 1985) ch. 5; John Fredrick Woolverton, *Colonial Anglicanism in North America* (Detroit: Wayne State University Press, 1984) 38-39, 59-67; Sheehan, *Savigism and Civility*, 125-26; Kupperman, *Settling With the Indians*, 164-65. For a similar approach to converting natives, but by the Spanish and using plays, see Ramon A. Gutierrez, *When Jesus Came the Corn Mothers Went Away: Marriage, Sexuality, and Power in New Mexico, 1500-1846* (Stanford: Stanford University Press, 1991) 83-86.

[68] Instructions to Sir Thomas Gates, Kingsbury, *Records of the Virginia Company of London*, 3:14. For a good statement regarding the "integration of culture and religion," see Kupperman, *Settling With the Indians*, 79.

[69] Treasurer and Council for Virginia to the Governor and Council in Virginia, 1 August 1622, Kingsbury, *Records of the Virginia Company of London*, 3:672; H. R. McIlwaine, ed., *Journals of the House of Burgesses of*

susceptible to education than their parents and thus made better potential converts. By immersion in English culture, which offered a visual feast of educational possibilities, native children could become civil, then move on and complete the transformation of their natures by becoming Christians. Less benign approaches to changing native culture nonetheless relied on the same constellation of ideas, although they envisioned the use of force to destroy bearers of erroneous education and customs. Jonas Stockam, a minister in early Virginia, explained: "till their Priests and Ancients have their throats cut, there is no hope to bring them to conversion."[70] Whereas Jesuits believed Christianity could adapt to and survive in a variety of cultural situations, a position strengthened by the international scope of Roman Catholicism, English Protestants in Virginia associated Christianity with English culture, positing a hostile relationship between Christian and "heathen" ways. Religion, to them, did not shape culture as much as culture shaped religion, and English culture provided the setting in which real Christianity might take root. One author even linked the transformative power of divine grace, perhaps its very existence, to English culture: "concerning the baptisme of Infidelle children...after the manner of primitive guerre, such as mak servants or bondmen to Christians, and more xpetially[sic] to remane among them might be baptized."[71]

Colonial authorities recognized the power of the natives' culture because they had seen how it transformed settlers whose work as translators for the colony forced them to spend long periods of time among the natives. Living as they did on the margins of English and native society, these men were often described as men "that had in [them] more of the Savage then of the Christian" or had "in a manner turned heathen." Only

---

Virginia, 1619-1658/1659 (Richmond: Virginia State Library, 1915) 23; Morgan, *American Slavery, American Freedom*, 47, 98.

[70] John Smith, *Generall History of Virginia*, Barbour, *Works of Captain John Smith*, 2:286.

[71] Richard Ferrar to [George Thorpe], December 13, 1618, Ferrar Papers, Magdalene College, Cambridge University f. 93.

language betrayed the cultural origins of one Englishman who had spent several years among the natives and in every other aspect had been transformed. He had become, in the words of Ralph Hamor, "both in complexion and habit like a salvage"[72] Living outside colonial society, cut off from their traditional cultural institutions, the natures of English people could change; they could cross the divide and become "savage" themselves. "We have sent boies amongst them [natives]," the Reverend Jonas Stockham worried, "but they returne worse than they went."[73] Another English minister, John Brinsley, pushed a similar analysis, arguing further that the very existence of natives and their culture made North America an ominous place, applying to English colonists the same logic settlers used to argue the merits of converting native children. Native culture presented "manifold perils...especially of falling away from God to Sathan, and that themselves, or their [English] posterity should become utterly savage, as they are [natives]."[74] Actions could speak across linguistic divides. Native culture might entice Englishmen to forsake their customary ways just as easily as English society might "allure" natives to Christianity. Nor were the natives ignorant of this cultural competition. "In their own villages," as Bernhard Sheehan has demonstrated, natives were in fact "ardent proselytizers" of captured Europeans.[75] Thus,

---

[72] McIlwaine, *Journals of the House of Burgesses of Virginia, 1619-1658/1659*, 15; Morton, *Colonial Virginia*, 1:78-80; Ralph Hamor quoted in Nicholas Canny, "The Permissive Frontier: Social Control in English Settlements in Ireland and Virginia, 1550-1650," in K. R. Andrews, N. P. Canny, and P. E. H. Hair, eds., *The Westward Enterprise: English Activities in Ireland, the Atlantic, and America, 1480-1650* (Detroit: Wayne State University Press, 1979): 32. The best account of Indian interpreters is J. Frederick Fausz, "Middlemen in Peace and War: Virginia's Earliest Indian Interpreters, 1608-1632," *Virginia Magazine of History and Biography* 95 (1987): 41-64.

[73] John Smith, *Generall History of Virginia*, Barbour, *Works of Captain John Smith*, 2:286.

[74] John Brinsley, *The Consolation of Our Grammar Schools...* (London, 1622) A2-A3.

[75] Sheehan, *Savigism and Civility*, 110-113, quotation on 113.

neither in theory nor in practice did colonists hold a monopoly in the subtle contest of "cultural evangelism." Settlers in Virginia, at least if you were one of the leaders, were engaged in cultural warfare to defend their understanding of English identity.

Constructing a polity in Virginia meant accounting for English theories of human nature and pedagogy as well as for the threat posed by a rival culture, a threat created partly as a result of those theories. It also meant accounting for the settlers who came to Virginia, the matter on which the form of government would operate. Many of the colonists who came to Virginia only exacerbated the threat to identity since they had adopted traits in England that men in authority found more akin to savage than civil, Christian society. Virginia's early settlers were a rough lot who swore often, got drunk frequently, and worked little—not the sort of people who might voluntarily behave in ways that would create a settlement pleasing either to God or man. Authors of colonization literature sometimes seemed to compete with one another to see who could describe these men in the basest of terms. "The *superfluitie*, or if you will, the very *excrements*" of England, wrote one;[76] people "no more sensible then beasts," claimed another;[77] "persons God hateth even from his very soule," accused a third.[78] The vantage point of time has not softened descriptions of the first settlers. Modern historians have agreed with the literature of the era. "Worthless and unruly," they have termed these men, the "scum of England."[79] Vagrants, convicted felons, debtors, and the unemployed of London all found their way to Virginia, their emigration sometimes inspired by Company policies. At the company's insistence, for example, the mayor of London in 1609 cleaned up his city by sending to the colony its "swarme of unnecessary

---

[76] Crashaw, *Sermon Preached in London,* E-3.

[77] Hamor, *True Discourse of the Present [E]state of Virginia*, 2.

[78] Whitaker, *Good Newes,* 11.

[79] Morton, *Colonial Virginia,* 1:31; Miller, "Religion and Society in the Early Literature of Virginia," 131.

inmates."[80] More interested in escaping English society's traditional restraints than in replicating them abroad, these men worried little about maintaining the settlement's relationship with God.[81] They were, in the common assessment of contemporaries and historians alike, lazy, idle, and irreligious. Labor, religion, and moral behavior to such men were not necessarily respected facets of England's cultural inheritance.

Early resident leaders complained bitterly about their fellow colonists, not that the men under their charge were stupid, incompetent, or unable to perform simple tasks; they were lazy and idle. Unless compelled, they refused to work. Even then they refused to perform the minimal amount of work necessary to plant and harvest corn enough to feed themselves. When Sir Thomas Dale arrived to govern the colony in May 1611, prime planting season, he found but a few private gardens sown with seeds and the people at "their daily and usuall workes, bowling in the streetes."[82] Men who "would rather starue in idlenesse...then [sic] feast in labour" wrote one observer of the colonists.[83] John Smith believed that had he not forced them to prepare food for themselves they would have turned to cannibalism.[84] For authors who believed the colonists were a slothful rabble, Proverbs 6:10-11 became a favorite Bible verse: "Yet a little sleep, a little slumber, and a little folding of the hands to sleep: so thy poverty cometh, as one that travaileth by the way, and thy necessity like an armed man."[85]

Colonists had not developed these bad habits in North America, however, so the New World's natural bounty was not to

---

[80] Morgan, *American Slavery, American Freedom*, 86; A Letter from the Councill and Company of the honourable Plantation in Virginia to the Lord Mayor, Alderman and Companies of London, Brown, *Genesis of the United States*, 1:252-53.

[81] Canny, "The Permissive Frontier," 27; Whitaker, *Good Newes*, 11.

[82] Morgan, *American Slavery, American Freedom*, 73; Hamor, *True Discourse of the Present [E]state of Virginia*, 26.

[83] Hamor, *True Discourse of the Present [E]state of Virginia*, 2.

[84] Morgan, *American Slavery, American Freedom*, 78.

[85] Strachey, *Voyage to Virginia*, 66-67.

blame. Late-Elizabethan and early-Jacobean England was overpopulated with little work to go around—a condition made worse by early modern English economic views that envisioned a world with both a fixed amount of wealth and a fixed amount of labor. Unable to create more wealth or more work and faced with the prospect of rising numbers of unemployed and hungry men, Parliament passed laws advocating a policy Edmund Morgan termed the "conservation of labor." To remedy the mounting crisis caused by too many people and not enough work to go around, lawmakers passed statutes compelling employers to spread around, as much as possible, what work there was. Begun with the best of intentions, these laws nonetheless encouraged idleness, and thus idleness became the habitual custom of most English laborers.[86] The result was to establish a contradiction in English identity, for English economic practices came into conflict with English religious ideas about the value of labor.

With the members of this chronically underemployed English laboring class comprising a significant portion of Virginia's early settlers they threatened English identity overseas as well. When colonial authorities and supporters of colonization described the majority of these colonists as base, disordered, beastly, and idle, they were also saying that these men had come to North America possessing characteristics similar to those of England's Native American cultural rivals. Sir Thomas Dale lamented that few settlers "give testimonie beside their names that they are Christians,"[87] thus implying that most colonists likely needed Christianizing nearly as much as the natives and offering support for Christopher Hill's controversial thesis that many English people in the seventeenth century were still enthralled with idolatry. Such men made better proselytes than missionaries of cultural evangelism, and instead of drawing

---

[86] Morgan, *American Slavery, American Freedom*, 62-68, quotation on 65; Johnson, *Nova Britannia*, 18.

[87] Thomas Dale to Lord Salisbury, 17 August 1611, Brown, *Genesis of the United States*, 1:506-507.

natives to English society, some of them fled English Virginia for native Virginia, thereby threatening the colony's existence. For a settlement with a death rate approaching 85 percent,[88] any colonist, no matter how base, was a treasure to be maintained, for the colony's survival rested upon keeping Virginia populated and putting men to work at tasks that would make the venture pay so that investors would risk more capital on empire. Yet complaints of this nature do not appear in the literature. Instead of grousing about how runaways might drain the colony of vital population, the literature of colonization objected to Englishmen who chose to live like "savages." Unlike their fearful descriptions of translators who had been transformed by native culture, accounts of those who turned native are angry attacks on men who willingly rejected English ways. Leaders' self-righteous depictions portray defectors as selfish men who fled the colony in order to "live Idle among the Salvages" or to embrace "prophane course[s] of life," descriptions that closely mirror similar accounts of the faults endemic to native culture.[89] Running away to the natives was to commit an act of apostasy. Voluntarily forsaking Christianity for savagery was both an abomination and a threat to English identity. Challenged by powerful cultural rivals possessed of a way of life the common sort found attractive, colonial leaders demonized the natives. By doing so, they told colonists what they were not; the polity that attempted to maintain the colony's relationship with God would teach these men just what they were, or, at the very least, what they ought to become.

The settlers who peopled Virginia and the realities of North American cultural adversaries combined to influence Virginia's political society. Together with the constellation of ideas about education and human nature, these factors created an intel-

---

[88] Woolverton, *Colonial Anglicanism in North America* 246n.16.

[89] Morgan, *American Slavery, American Freedom*, 78; Kupperman, *Settling With the Indians*, 157; Canny, "The Permissive Frontier," 32-33; Smith, *Generall History of Virginia*, Barbour, *Works of Captain John Smith*, 2:215.

lectual context for colonial polity far different from Europe's obsession with creating state-church systems united by religious party theology. Virginia was not Europe, and in the colony the traditional religious dichotomies employed by historians and some contemporaries did not work. English recusants, Puritans, and Anglicans may well have been suspicious of neighbors who held different opinions about theology and religious ceremonies, but in Virginia two variants replaced historians' traditional Roman Catholic/Protestant and Puritan/Anglican rifts. Settlers found themselves divided between Christian Englishmen and "savage" natives as well as between English rabble and those "truer" Englishmen who professed Christianity. Company and resident leaders confronted in the New World not the religious passions of Europe, but the religious indifference of nominally Christian settlers whose behavior threatened both the colony's relationship with God and the validity of Christian morality as part of English identity. While people in England struggled to define the Church of England as an institution central to their lives, resident authorities in Virginia struggled even to maintain religion as a part of their cultural identity.

Threatened not only by a powerful cultural enemy but also by English settlers who seemed to have more in common with the natives than with English culture, Virginians shaped their relationship with God through behavior rather than belief. Written especially "for the Colony in Virginea Britannia," the *Lawes Diuine, Morall and Martiall* envisioned an English identity based on labor, worship, and Christian morality. Those who crafted Virginia's polity based their infant commonwealth on God's will as revealed in the prescriptions of the Deuteronomic code and threatened punishment of "all breaches of the sacred Tables, divine, and morrall, to GOD and man."[90] With a few modifications suitable to the seventeenth century, the divine portion of the *Lawes* followed the Ten Commandments in precise order. Section one encompassed both the first and second commandments, stating that the settlers owed their "highest and

---

[90] *Lawes Diuine, Morall and Martiall*, 41.

supreme duty" to him "from whom all power and authoritie is deriued, and flowes," followed by two statutes upholding the Decalogue's decree not to take God's name in vain. A fourth divine law modified the command to honor father and mother, replacing it with an admonition to speak no "traiterous words" against the King or royal authority, an expansion typical of the age. Although Virginia's code neglected the decree against coveting, the remaining statutes in this section reflect both in content and order the demands established by God in the second table of the Mosaic law.[91] A rigorous liturgical regimen prescribed by the *Lawes* strengthened this foundation, demanding that colonists attend church twice each workday and once on Sundays and allowing them their daily allotments of food only after divine service ended.[92] The persuasive rhetoric of sermons presumably complemented the statutes by encouraging settlers to keep the deity's decrees. A supporter back in London rejoiced over the *Lawes*: "Good are these beginnings, wherein God is thus before."[93]

To ensure that settlers followed the commandments, the *Lawes* set them to work. Idle hands were the devil's playthings and a sure cause of greater sins. "Where idleness is once received," the Church of England's *Book of Homilies* admonished, "there the Devil is ready to set in his foot."[94] In their battle to prevent Satan from tempting men already too inclined by custom to avoid labor, the company's statutes attacked idleness, just as John Smith had done a few years earlier. The code organized them into work gangs, appointed them tasks to be completed, and regular hours in which to perform their duties. Labor expected from the settlers was minimal both by modern standards and contemporary practice: between three to six hours a day in winter and five to eight hours in summer. Nonetheless,

---

[91] Ibid., 9-12. Compare the *Lawes* with the Ten Commandments in Deuteronomy 5 and Exodus 20. The divine laws are summarized a second time in *Lawes*, 32.

[92] Ibid., 10-11.

[93] Johnson, *New Life of Virginia*, 8.

[94] *Book of Homilies*, 438-39.

it was labor and that on a regular basis. Forced labor and compulsory church attendance structured colonists' time around a daily cycle of labor, prayer, rest and refreshment, labor, prayer, and retirement for the evening. This framework was hardly oppressive and left plenty of time for recreation.[95] Forcing colonists to work and compelling them to attend divine services (if not actually to worship the deity) removed from them traits they had shared with the natives of Virginia. Christians labored; Christians worshipped God.

The *Lawes* not only distinguished Englishmen from natives culturally through labor and worship but also by separating the two groups physically. As Edmund Morgan has demonstrated, Virginia's polity by 1611 "did not even contemplate that the Indians would become a part of the English settlement."[96] Resident authorities limited contact between natives and colonists as much as possible. Ordinary settlers could neither trade nor speak with natives without the permission of the colony's leaders. Running "away from the Colonie, to Powhathan, or any sauage Weroance else whatsoeuer" meant death. A prayer appended to the *Lawes* and repeated twice daily suggests that both groups presented a clear threat to the colony and formally cursed both Native Americans and those settlers whose actions might harm the settlement.[97]

The *Lawes Diuine, Morall and Martiall* created physical and cultural spaces that defined English identity overseas. Within

---

[95] Morgan, *American Slavery, American Freedom*, 60, 78-80, 88-89; John Smith, *Proceedings of the English Colonie in Virginia*, Barbour, *Works of Captain John Smith*, 1:259; Edmund S. Morgan, "The Labor Problem at Jamestown, 1607-1618," *American Historical Review* 76 (1971): 603-606; *Lawes Diuine, Morall and Martiall*, 45. In some ways, the pattern in early Virginia replaced the ritual of the Roman Catholic mass with a ritual based on labor and prayer.

[96] Morgan, *American Slavery, American Freedom*, 80.

[97] *Lawes Diuine, Morall and Martiall*, 13, 16; Morgan, *American Slavery, American Freedom*, 80-81. For more on curses in early Virginia, see Edward L. Bond, "Source of Knowledge, Source of Power: The Supernatural World of English Virginia, 1607-1624," *Virginia Magazine of History and Biography*, 108 (2000): 105-38.

English Virginia, colonial leaders applied to the rabble of England the same epistemological and pedagogical concepts that guided their few efforts to convert the natives, confident that an English cultural environment could make Englishmen pleasing to God, even of the most dissolute riffraff. In their distinct ways, church, court, and scaffold taught the behaviors expected of God's friends. Ministers preached, catechized, and celebrated the sacraments. The *Lawes* themselves were written down and posted so that all could see these statutes and their sanctions, a fact which impressed contemporary chroniclers. To make sure that even those who could not read got the point, colonial ministers read the divine and moral portions of the code aloud once a week as part of their regular catachetical instruction, thus infusing positive law with divine sanction. Habitual repetition of the statutes served to make the fleeting nature of the spoken word more memorable. Reflecting Jacobean social assumptions as well as traditional pedagogical notions, religious and civil leaders were enjoined to turn their lives into visible sermons: make "profession, and practise of all vertue and goodness for examples vnto[sic] others to imitate, it being true that examples at all times preuaile farre aboue precepts, men being readier to bee led by their eies, then their eare."[98]

Virginia's judicial system provided more vivid examples for wayward settlers to contemplate. For a vast number of offenses ranging from blasphemy to bearing "false witnesse" to stealing vegetables while weeding a garden, the *Lawes* prescribed death.[99] Historians agree that Marshall Thomas Dale enforced even the most "stringent provisions of these statutes to the letter,"[100] inflicting punishments with "arbitrary rigor."[101] Men who had

---

[98] Hamor, *True Discourse of the Present [E]state of Virginia*, 27; *Lawes Diuine, Morall and Martiall*, 19, quotation on 30; Morton, *Colonial Virginia*, 1:32. See also Gray, *Good Speed to Virginia*, D2-D3.

[99] *Lawes Diuine, Morall and Martiall*, 10-13; Morgan, *American Slavery, American Freedom*, 80.

[100] Billings, Selby, and Tate, *Colonial Virginia*, 39; Morton, *Colonial Virginia*, 1:32.

[101] Morgan, *American Slavery, American Freedom*, 80.

robbed the store of supplies Dale had "bownd faste unto Trees and so sterved them to deathe." For stealing a few pints of oatmeal another colonist "had a bodkinge thrust through his tongue and was tyed wth a chaine to a tree untill he starved." Those who "turned native" met similar fates. In 1612 Dale recaptured several colonists who had fled the settlement to live among the natives: "Some he apointed to be hanged Some burned Some to be broken upon wheles, others to be staked and some shott to death."[102]

Historians have justly pointed out the violence of these punishments, and certainly at least a bit of anger and vengeance lay behind Dale's brutal treatment of men who had "turned native." Yet men are not beasts; they resort to violence for a reason. Unlike brute animals whose use of force is innocent, men enter it rationally and with a design.[103] Executions in early Virginia were harsh, visceral, and public, visual experiences designed to impress social realities upon observers. As public spectacle they formed part of the colony's pedagogy. George Percy wrote of those executed by Thomas Dale for running away to the natives: "All theis extreme and crewell tortures he used and inflicted upon them To terrefy the rest."[104] When he arrived in the colony, Lord De la Warr announced to the settlers that he meant to continue these practices, and if they persisted in their idle and dissolute ways he would not hesitate to "draw the sword of justice to cutt off such delinquents" from the polity.[105]

---

[102] George Percy, "A Trewe Relaycon of the Proccdeinges and Occurrentes of Momente which have hapned in Virginia from the Tyme Sir Thomas Gates was shippwrackte uppon the Bermudas anno 1609 until my departure outt of the Country which was anno Domini 1612," *Tylers' Quarterly Historical and Genealogical Magazine* 3 (1922): 280; "The Tragical Relation of the Virginia Assembly, 1624," Tyler, *Narratives of Early Virginia*, 423.

[103] de Grazia, *Machiavelli in Hell*, 109. See also J. A. Sharpe, *Crime in Early Modern England, 1550-1750* (New York: Longman, 1984) 13.

[104] Percy, "True Relaycon," 280; Morton, *Colonial Virginia*, 32.

[105] Strachey, *Voyage to Virginia*, 85.

Afraid of God's wrath, possessed of an unsettled identity, and threatened by the fragility of their own culture and the strength of nearby cultural enemies, colonial leaders established laws for a nominally Christian population that would both maintain God's friendship and define English identity overseas. The issues were linked: the identity problem was the problem of sustaining God's friendship. Steps necessary to maintain the colony's relationship with God would also establish a cultural environment for English people to inhabit. The cultural context constructed by the *Lawes Diuine, Morall and Martiall* said little about particular Christian beliefs, and when literate Virginians mentioned what they thought separated them from God they invariably referred not to European fears of religious mixture but to particular actions: theft, swearing oaths, idleness, avarice, not attending divine worship, political faction, and drunkenness. Spreading the religion which bore their savior's name may have been one of the Virginia Company's goals, but colonists referred little to Christ, his teachings, or to such peculiarly Christian concepts as individual salvation. Virginia's polity instead represented the logical application of the Renaissance idea equating the good Christian with the good citizen.[106] The emphasis was on the salvation of the state, which meant empire for England and confirmation of colonizers' imperial hopes. Virginia's early polity showed more concern for its corporate relationship with God than with the personal relationships individuals might have shared with the deity. A corporate relationship was the way to gain empire. In the process, leaders in Virginia constructed their own definition of English nationhood, one predicated on the broad cultural unity of behavior rather than belief and reflecting a Mosaic definition of the relationship between the colony and God.

Virginia's Mosaic polity began with Old Testament morality and ended with force. Dale's laws established the relationship with God and prescribed the boundaries of identity. But laws without force are impotent guides. Colonial authorities realized

---

[106] J. A. Sharpe, *Crime in Early Modern England*, 26.

that human beings might act out of choice as well as necessity. The prayer appended to the *Lawes Diuine, Morall and Martial* indicated as much, asserting that those who failed to follow the commandments did so "willfully" by "chusing those things which thou hast most justly & severely forbidden us."[107] But since neither law, nor preaching, nor the examples of virtuous leaders could compel individuals to embrace the faith and behave in ways pleasing to God out of choice, by introducing harsh necessity and eliminating choice as much as possible, punishments might still force settlers to conform to the outward principles of the Decalogue that defined the colony's relationship with God. State violence in early Virginia was a compelling teacher that demarcated the boundaries of acceptable English behavior. Ralph Hamor described the people put to death by colonial leaders as "dangerous, incurable members, for no use as fit as to make examples to others."[108] Executions not only served as lessons in virtue but also as ritual purifications of the community. For those who desired empire, destroying men who harmed the settlement's relationship with God were acts of imperial mercy. "Evil persons that be so great offenders to God and the commonweal," proclaimed the *Book of Homilies*, "charity requireth to be cut off from the body of the commonweal, lest they corrupt good and honest persons."[109] Killing English people who transgressed the commandments or fled the colony to live with the natives thus became at once acts of patriotism as well as devotion. Enforcing God's laws furthered the creation of a national empire and a colonial identity. The polity the colonists established offered nothing less than a Mosaic answer to the question of English identity overseas, marked by an implied covenant and designed to maintain God's

---

[107] *Lawes Diuine, Morall and Martiall*, 63.

[108] See, for instance, Hamor, *A True Discourse of the Present [E]state of Virginia*, 27; Instructions to Sir Thomas Gates, Governor of Virginia, 1 May 1609/10, Kingsbury, *Records of the Virginia Company of London*, 3:14; and Instructions to Sir Thomas West Knight Lo: La Warr, 1609/10, *Records of the Virginia Company of London*, 3:27.

[109] *Book of Homilies*, 55.

favor by choice if possible and violence if necessary. Virginia's polity under the *Lawes* taught virtue and threatened harsh punishments not primarily to save individuals from the clutches of Hell, but in order to save the colony from the judgments of God.

The *Lawes Diuine, Morall and Martiall* institutionalized the nation's soteriology of empire, mixing with it a defense of English culture based upon civility and labor, and backing both intentions with violent necessity. At the same time as the *Lawes* attempted to maintain Virginia's relationship with God, they also tried to establish and defend a cultural environment in which a sincere Christian faith might develop over time. Although brutal and more closely associated with the old than the new covenant, these statutes were perhaps the first and only organized religious mission to the many nominal Christians in Virginia. Just as civilizing always preceded the process of Christianizing the natives, it did the same for the many nominally Christian colonists who peopled Virginia.[110] In Virginia's wilderness, behavior took on a nearly sacramental character, an outward and visible sign of Englishness that distinguished civilization from savagery. The colony's leaders found a veiled religious unity in an English culture that contained the outward behavioral signs of Christianity. Frightened by the strength and appeal of native culture, they separated the two societies through law, taught the lower orders to hate Indians,[111] and forced English people to behave in ways that might please God—ways they also believed were identified with English culture—hoping they would someday decide to act this way out of choice rather than force.

And although they may not have realized it, they wounded the very religion they had come to spread and hoped to teach to the nominal Christians. The abiding concern with preventing and disciplining actions that offended God resulted in an

---

[110] David Bertelson, *The Lazy South* (New York: Oxford University Press, 1967) 21-26; Gray, *Good Speed to Virginia*, C-2.

[111] Morgan, *American Slavery, American Freedom*, 80.

emphasis on the behavior itself rather than on the motivation that accompanied the action. Force may have compelled settlers to behave, but violence could not ensure that those actions would be committed with the proper religious grounding necessary to lead a person to salvation. Whether Arminians or Calvinists, Christians in early seventeenth-century England believed faith was necessary to salvation, and Virginia's leaders were no different. John Smith wrote: "Our good deeds or bad, by faith in Christs merits, is all wee have to carry our soules to heaven or hell."[112] The most stringently enforced laws, however, could not ensure that deeds acceptable to God would be done in faith. Laws could constrain, coerce, and create a cultural environment; they could perhaps compel the commission of good actions; they might even create good pagans. They could not on their own lead men and women to salvation. A system of public morality and private faith emerged, a pattern influenced by the short supply of ministers sent from England to fill the colony's pulpits. Virginia's leaders settled for the outward marks of civility, the superficial signs of Christian society that distinguished English people from "savages."

To be sure, Dale, Gates, and other colonial leaders hoped the settlers would become good Christians. The *Lawes*, in fact, required every colonist upon arriving in Virginia to give an account of his faith to a minister. Those whose faith or knowledge about Christianity was found wanting were ordered to receive additional catechetical instruction. Other portions of the code instructed settlers to prepare in private for public worship. Yet, given the descriptions of the rabble that populated early Virginia, much of this may have been wishful thinking. Given the context and the nature of the many nominal Christians who populated Virginia, a compelled moral behavior associated with English civility was the only form of devotion leaders could hope for, a sort of Old Testament Christianity. Although the Old

---

[112] John Smith, *Advertisements for the Unexperienced Planters of New England*, Barbour, *Works of Captain John Smith*, 3:277; see also Whitaker, *Good Newes from Virginia*, 7, 36.

Testament polity began to fade after 1618, it remained part of the legacy of early Virginia, and the emphasis on behavior rather than belief continued to shape Virginia's public life and identity throughout the seventeenth century. Writing in 1670 to a friend in England who had sent a dissolute youth to the colony, Governor William Berkeley attributed to Virginia's cultural environment the same vague sort of undertones that might encourage individuals to behave while at the same time setting a context that could make it possible for them at a later date to embrace the faith: "This is an exelent school to make...disorderly wild youths to repent of those wild and extravagant courses that brought them hither."[113] Virginia's society could tame, order, and make unruly persons tractable. If the colony's religious leaders, of whom there were few until the end of the seventeenth century, could not make good Christians of the colonists, they attempted to maintain the social context in which a sincere faith might take root by upholding the standards of English civility. Eternal salvation became a private matter between the individual and God, often outside the formal institutions of the established church.[114] This was part of the religious legacy of Virginia's early years.

---

[113] Sir William Berkeley to Sir Richard Browne, 2 April 1670, British Museum, Additional Manuscripts 15857, f. 40.

[114] Edward L. Bond, "Anglican Theology and Devotion in James Blair's Virginia, 1685-1743: Private Piety in the Public Church," *Virginia Magazine of History and Biography* 104 (1996): 313-340.

CHAPTER THREE

CREATING AN IDENTITY: GEOGRAPHY, PROFIT, AND THE INVISIBLE HAND OF JAMES I

As people of faith, colonists in Virginia were not all that different from men and women back in England. Although colonial leaders during the colony's earliest years often complained about the large numbers of lower-class rabble whose idleness and other sins were a constant threat to the polity's survival, there were also in Virginia men of prayer who knew that as human beings they were more than missionaries of empire. To English men and women of the early modern period both groups were Christian, one by culture or by virtue of birth in a Christian nation, the other by faith or by virtue of choosing to become Christians. Virginia's *Lawes Diuine, Morall and Martiall* recognized both groups, and despite the statutes' emphasis on the collective identity of an expanding nation and on moral behavior rather than on personal relationships with a living God, some colonists nevertheless worshiped God out of choice rather than coercion, out of faith rather than fear of brutal punishments. They desired the sacraments of the Church, they quoted scripture in their letters, prayed to God, asked his blessing upon their labor, and searched the natural world for signs of his intervention. The divine infused their universe with meaning. The age-old rhythms of religion shaped the colonists' understanding of time as well, just as it had for centuries of English people, and settlers often marked time with reference to the traditional dates in the Church of England's liturgical calendar. William Strachey revealed just how deeply ingrained were notions of religious time to some of the colony's earliest settlers when he noted that a great tempest struck the fleet in which he traveled to Virginia "on St. James his day." Likewise, George Archer could date precisely when a group of settlers began to explore the new land, for they left Jamestown on "Sonday, Whitsonday."[1] Other settlers left evidence of their religious devotion in the ground rather than in words. We can only imagine that settlers to guide their prayers and devotions used the crucifixes, rosary beads, and religious medallions unearthed by archaeologists at Jamestown.[2]

Men and women of faith who were apparently devout Christians appear with some regularity in the spotty extant records of early Virginia. Nevertheless, these documents afford us tantalizing scenes of faith rather than doctrinal controversy between competing groups of Christians or detailed information about theology and religious practices. They are more timeless than particular, revealing questions about the nature of man's relationship to God common to all people of faith at all times. In this regard, the religious-minded among Virginia's early settlers were not so much Englishmen as they were men in quest of the divine.

In mid-June of 1610, during the spring following the starving time, Jamestown was in ruins—the palisade had collapsed, numerous houses either lay in rubble or had been used for firewood,

---

[1] William Strachey, *A Voyage to Virginia in 1609*, ed. Louis B. Wright (Charlottesville: University Press of Virginia, 1967) 4; George Archer, "A Relayton of the Discovery of our River, 21 May-22 June 1607," in Edward Arber and A. G. Bradley, eds., *Travels and Works of John Smith, President of Virginia, and Admiral of New England, 1580-1631* 2 vols. (Edinburgh, 1910) xlv. Archer also noted St. James Day, xcv.

[2] For evidence of the various religious items uncovered by the Association for the Preservation of Virginia Antiquities, see Nicholas Luccketti and Beverly Straube, *Interim Report on the APVA Excavations at Jamestown, Virginia* (Richmond: Association for the Preservation of Virginia Antiquities, 1998) 22-23.

the gates to the fort had fallen from their hinges. It was a desolate sight, "a verie noysome and unholsome place" in the words of one settler. But Sir Thomas West, the third Lord De la Warr, had arrived, and he intended to make a go of the colony, perhaps strengthened in his purpose by William Crashaw's sermon citing God's defense of the colonial venture. The new governor's men formed an honor guard and la Warr came ashore, fell to his knees on Virginia's soil, and offered a silent prayer to God, thanking him for the mercy of a completed voyage and asking for divine blessings upon his efforts to lead the colony.[3] He then proceeded to the chapel where he heard a sermon preached. The church was in ruins like the rest of the settlement, and this symbol of institutional religion la Warr ordered reconstructed. An impressive sixty-by-twenty-four-foot building with a "chancel of cedar and a communion table of black walnut, and all the pews of cedar with...a pulpit of the same" took the old chapel's place. Services were held in it daily at 10 A.M. and 4 P.M., the traditional times for morning and evening prayer in the Church of England. West introduced pomp and ceremony into Sunday worship as well, arriving each Sabbath with brightly clad officers and veterans. He sat in the choir in a green velvet chair, a velvet cushion before him to use when the colony's Governor and Captain-General kneeled in prayer. Perhaps la Warr was one of those men who later tended toward Laudian ceremonials and the "diverse flowers" with which he had the building "trimmed up" an example of the beauty of holiness.[4]

---

[3] Richard L. Morton, *Colonial Virginia*, 2 vols. (Chapel Hill: University of North Carolina Press, 1960) 1:21; Strachey, *Voyage to Virginia*, 44-45, 69-71; Lord De la Warr to Earl of Salisbury, July 1610, in Alexander Brown, *Genesis of the United States*, 2 vols. (New York: Russell & Russell, Inc., 1964) 1:415.

[4] Strachey, *Voyage to Virginia*, 80-81; Alexander Whitaker to M. G., 18 June 1614, in Ralph Hamor, *A True Discourse of the [E]state of Virginia* (Richmond: Virginia State Library, 1957) viii; Horton Davies, *Worship and Theology in England*, 5 vols. (Princeton: Princeton University Press, 1961-

A few years later in 1614 John Rolfe fell in love.[5] The problem he wrestled with was an age old one—religion had come into conflict with romantic passions, for the woman Rolfe had fallen in love with was an Indian maiden, "an unbeleeving creature" he called her, Pocahontas. Clergymen in both Virginia and England had warned in general against Englishmen marrying native women. The English, some ministers claimed, were contemporary Israelites and could not soil themselves by mixing with these contemporary Canaanites. God, they suggested, found such impurities damnable. Other authors offered more practical reasons for preventing such "abominable mixtures" by arguing that native women lacked the proper cultural background and thus could not be expected to raise Christian children in a proper English cultural environment.[6] Rolfe did not know what to do. He poured out his feelings in a letter to a man he may well have considered a spiritual superior, Sir Thomas Dale. It was the letter of a soul in torment. He had prayed daily about his dilemma, yet could find no solace. Did the devil tempt him to

---

1975) 2:103; William Meade, *Old Churches, Ministers and Families of Virginia*, 2 vols. (Philadelphia: J.B. Lippincott & Co., 1878) 1:71.

[5] Copies of Rolfe's letter may be found in "Letter From John Rolfe to Sir Thomas Dale," *Virginia Magazine of History and Biography* 22 (1914): 150-57; Lyon Gardiner Tyler, ed., *Narratives of Early Virginia, 1606-1625* (New York: Barnes & Noble, 1952) 239-44; Hamor, *True Discourse*, 61-68; Meade, *Old Churches, Ministers and Families of Virginia*, 1:126-29. Perry Miller, "Religion and Society in the Early Literature of Virginia," in *Errand Into the Wilderness* (Cambridge: Harvard University Press, 1956) 107-108. For very different views of Rolfe's letter, see Kathleen Brown, *Good Wives, Nasty Wenches, and Anxious Patriarchs: Gender, Race, and Power in Colonial Virginia* (Chapel Hill: University of North Carolina Press, 1996) 63-64; and Paul Brown, "'This Thing of Darkness I Acknowledge Mine': The Tempest and the Discourse of Colonialism," in Harold Bloom, ed., *William Shakespeare's The Tempest* (New York: Chelsea House Publishers, 1988) 131-34.

[6] David B. Smits, "'Abominable Mixture': Toward the Repudiation of Anglo-Indian Intermarriage in Seventeenth-Century Virginia," *Virginia Magazine of History and Biography* 95 (1987): 177, 180.

sin, or did God call him to "labour in the Lords vineyard" and make a Christian of this rudely educated woman, or was his longing merely evidence of the "frailty of mankinde, his prones to evil" and carnal desires? Portions of the letter bear some resemblance to the confession of sin in the *Book of Common Prayer*. In outlining the reasons for his decision did Rolfe ask in a strange way for absolution? The letter was a statement as well as a question. He would marry Pocahontas. Let the vulgar sort and overly rigid clergymen think what they would of his decision. After much time in prayer and contemplation he believed that taking her as his bride was in keeping with God's will both for him and for her. If he had erred and God judged him for this, "I will heartily accept of it as a godly taxe appointed me." John Rolfe was a man whose piety and devotion had led him to stand against the common religious assumptions of his age. He found courage in his faith.

Robert Evelyn, a producer of gunpowder and saltpetre, showed less confidence about his place before God. He was preparing in 1611 to travel to the colony, a voyage he knew would be "long and dangerous." But he was in debt and hoped to make enough money in Virginia to pay off his creditors. The possibility of death frightened him, since it would leave his wife and children in "very poor and mean" conditions. He found little consolation in his belief that his sins "deserved these punishments and far greater at God's hands." Contemplating the uncertainties of an Atlantic crossing, he pleaded for God's mercy: "but we must all be contented with the pleasure of Almighty God...it is His pleasure to dispose of us."[7]

During the colony's earliest years, such expressions of religious devotion were confined largely to colonial leaders, men like John Rolfe, John Smith, and Sir Thomas West, or so the extant records suggest. Over time, however, the extant records suggests that scenes of a religious nature increased in number and began to take place throughout larger segments of Virginia's

---

[7] Robert Evelyn to his mother, November 1611, Brown, *Genesis of the United States*, 1:440-42, 2:887.

population, a shift that accompanied the rising number of immigrants to Virginia from the middle and yeoman classes during the years from 1610 through 1621. References to the immemorial patterns of sacred time from the church's calendar that men and women had used for years to order the days and months appear with greater frequency in the years after 1620. Observe the settlers of Berkeley Hundred in 1624, the last year of the Virginia Company of London. An unpleasant dispute had developed between a minister, Robert Pooley, and a member of his congregation, Richard Pawlet, a physician who had charged the parson with simony, bribery, and "speakinge false latten." Not to be outdone, Pooley in turn had accused Pawlet of failing to pay his tithes and of singing bawdy songs. At heart, this is a petty dispute over whether or not the minister had fulfilled the terms of his contract between two men who apparently had a history of mistrust. Ministers were in short supply, and Pooley had agreed to hold services at Berkeley Hundred once every four weeks. It had been six weeks, however, since he last read prayers for the residents there and Pawlett saw the minister's failure as an opportunity to attack an old foe. Similar disputes between clergy and parishioners would fill the colony's courts for over a century.[8] The case is striking in one way: the precision with which court witnesses noted the date of this eruption, St. Stephen's Day. Celebrated on 26 December, this holy day commemorates the church's first martyr. Settlers at Berkeley Hundred met on the morning of Monday, 26 December 1624, to say and hear divine service on what the Church of England recognized as a feast day. This tells us something about the colonists' liturgical regimen, as does the fact that deponents referred to the feast day

---

[8] On the difficulties ministers often encountered in receiving their tithes, see Clara Ann Bowler, "The Litigious Career of William Cotton, Minister," *Virginia Magazine of History and Biography* 86 (1978): 281-94; Jon Butler, *Awash in a Sea of Faith: Christianizing the American People* (Cambridge: Harvard University Press, 1990) 43; James Horn, *Adapting to a New World: English Society in the Seventeenth-Century Chesapeake* (Chapel Hill: University of North Carolina Press, 1994) 388-89.

itself rather than to the day after Christmas, implying a certain familiarity with the feast and fast days in the Church's liturgical calendar.[9] Similar markings of time were common. Contracts in early Virginia often ran from Christmas to Christmas;[10] ships were expected to arrive "before the feast of St. Thomas ye Apostle next comeing"; a steer would be ready for sale "two days before Whitsontide." In March 1625, Roger Reades, an indentured servant, wagered a portion of his indenture with his master on the month in which Easter fell that year, and he won.[11]

By 1620 or so, growing numbers of colonists also showed evidence of their personal relationships with God. In the face of a protracted native war and a recent plague, George Harrison, a planter in Charles City County and a participant in one of Virginia's first duels, could still refer to the deity in the most intimate of terms: "our friend god."[12] Governor George

---

[9] H. R. McIlwaine, ed., *Minutes of the Council and the General Court of Colonial Virginia*, 2nd ed. (Richmond: Virginia State Library, 1979) 88; Brown, *Genesis of the United States,* 2:962.

[10] York County Deeds, Orders, and Wills, 1645-1649, Book 2, f. 178; York County Deeds, Orders, and Wills, 1657-1662, Book 3, ff. 57, 123; Susie M. Ames, ed., *County Court Records of Accomack-Northampton Virginia, 1632-1640* (Washington, DC: American Historical Association, 1954) 40, 63; Susie M. Ames, ed., *County Court Records of Accomack-Northampton, Virginia, 1640-1645* (Charlottesville: University Press of Virginia, 1973) 124, 348; Norfolk County Records, Minute Book, 1637-1646, f. 126; Charles City County, Deeds, Orders, Depositions, vol. 1, 1655-1658, f. 6; McIlwaine, *Minutes of the Council and the General Court of Colonial Virginia*, 10, 20, 89, 163, 173; Northumberland County Court Order Book 2, 1652-1665, f. 33.

[11] McIlwaine, *Minutes of the Council and the General Court of Colonial Virginia*, 97. Religious dates also appear in the colony's laws. See William Waller Hening, *The Statutes at Large: Being a Collection of all the Laws of Virginia...* 13 vols. (Richmond, 1809-1823) 1:125-26, 170, 268.

[12] George Harrison to John Harrison, 24 January 1624/1625, Public Records Office, Colonial Office 1/2 ff. 113-14; Brown, *Genesis of the United States*, 2:913.

Yeardley, on the other hand, offered a somewhat more fatalistic view of the relationship between God and man. "But what am I," he wrote, "that I should be able to doe any thing against wch the Lord of Lords hath otherwise disposed, or what are wee all, that we should gaynesay the Allmyghty...yf the Lord will lay his hand upon us and crosse us with sickness and mortality...what then shall he say unto these things but that it is the Lord lett him doe what he please."[13]

Other settlers were apparently fluent enough with the Bible to quote or allude to scripture seemingly from memory. Thomasin Woodshawe, a condemned felon, petitioned Governor Francis Wyatt for clemency in a letter that referred not only to the parable of the fig tree but also to the Church of England's Ash Wednesday liturgy.[14] Richard Freethorne, an indentured servant, did not think highly of Virginia, tobacco cultivation having dispelled any illusions he may have held about the opportunities Virginia offered men like himself. His master exploited him in planting tobacco, and he received little in return for his toil. For Freethorne, Virginia was no longer the promised land of Canaan. He closed a letter to his parents by comparing Virginia to the Biblical land of slavery: "I end prayeing to God to send me good success that I may be redeemed out of Egipt."[15] In 1621 William Powell wrote to Sir Edwin Sandys about a dispute he was then

---

[13] Sir George Yeardley to Sir Edwin Sandys, 1619, Susan Myra Kingsbury, ed., *Records of the Virginia Company of London*, 4 vols. (Washington, DC: United States Government Printing Office, 1905-1936) 3:127; John Rolfe to Sir Edwin Sandys, January 1619/20, Kingsbury, *Records of the Virginia Company of London,* 3:242; Virginia Company to the Governor and Council in Virginia, 6 August 1623, Kingsbury, *Records of the Virginia Company of London* 4:263.

[14] Thomasin Woodshawe, Petition to the Governor of Virginia, between October 1622 and (January 1622/23), Kingsbury, *Records of the Virginia Company of London*, 3:681. The biblical reference may be found in Matthew 3:10 and Luke 3:9. See also, Ezekiel 33:11.

[15] Richard Freethorne to his father and mother, 20 March, 2-3 April 1623, Kingsbury, *Records of the Virginia Company of London*, 4:58-62, quotation on 61.

engaged in with the colony's present governor, Sir George
Yeardley. Powell justified his letter to the company treasurer by
alluding to "the lawfulnes of a complainte" in St. Paul's warnings
against Alexander the coppersmith. Much of the letter, in fact, is
a series of allusions to various biblical and religious texts that
support his position. "We are all by nature the sonnes of wrath:
servinge the prince of the aire," he wrote of human beings, a
description straight from Paul's letter to the Ephesians.[16]

Some men alluded as well to a practical theology, which
many colonists must have adhered to: "repent, amend, pro-
ceed."[17] If you sinned, admit it, ask for forgiveness, resolve to
live a better life with God's help, and move on. This is solid
advice—even if it lacks the theological subtlety of controversial-
ists—and would have been difficult for members of any English
religious group to quibble over. Despite colonial laws establishing the Church of England, it is hard to give these expressions of
devotion any designation more particular than Christian.

These sentiments are not in the least extraordinary. The
questions which colonists puzzled over and the uses to which
they put scripture were typical of centuries of faithful Christians.
Some people found courage in their religion; others, aware of
their grievous sins, showed a resignation to God's will which
became confidence that ultimately God ruled the world for the
best; still other people found support for various arguments in
the books of the Bible. What differs for the colonists is not the
sentiments but the setting. And again it is the land—there is no
escaping the importance of the North American continent to
religion in early Virginia. As the English went about the process
of fulfilling God's promise to Abraham by possessing their

---

[16] William Powell to Sir Edwin Sandys, 12 April 1621, Kingsbury,
Records of the Virginia Company of London, 3:436-437. The biblical
references are to I Timothy 1:20, 2 Timothy 4:14, and Ephesians 2:2-3. An
additional portion of Powell's letter may allude to a verse from the
"Magnificat."

[17] George Yeardley to Edwin Sandys, 1619, Kingsbury, *Records of the
Virginia Company of London*, 3:127.

"good" land, the continent in turn possessed them back. The people may have made the land English as a matter of national identity, but the land also changed the people who settled it and their institutions in ways they may not have completely realized.

Significant interaction with the land began within a few years of settlement. The first wave of colonists had established Jamestown about thirty-five miles from the mouth of the James River on Virginia's lower peninsula. With a deep channel, a convenient source of fresh water, and easily defended terrain, it had seemed like a good spot to establish a settlement. The first settlers had been wrong. The site's natural advantages were equal to if not outweighed by the disadvantages. The land was marshy, making it a perfect breeding ground for disease-carrying mosquitoes; the water was brackish and made the settlers ill. Jamestown's dismal reputation improved little throughout the course of the century, and as late as 1667 Governor William Berkeley described it as a site best avoided: "all the Summer time [it is] so infested with Mosqetos & other troublesome flyes, that it will be impossible for men to live there."[18] In addition to unfavorable environmental factors, Jamestown's close proximity to native enemies kept the settlement under the constant threat of sudden destruction. If all of this was not trouble enough, none of the first colonists really knew how to hunt or grow food. Virginia in the early seventeenth century was hardly a glittering jewel of English overseas empire. Death dominated the memories of many early settlers. George Percy wrote: "Our men were destroyed with cruell diseases as Swellings, Flixes, Burning Fevers, and by warres, and some departed suddenly, but for the most part they died of meere famine."[19]

---

[18] Governor William Berkeley and the Council in Virginia to Charles II, ca. 1667, Public Records Office, Colonial Office 1/21, f. 112.

[19] Warren M. Billings, ed., *The Old Dominion in the Seventeenth Century: A Documentary History of Virginia, 1606-1689* (Chapel Hill: University of North Carolina Press, 1975) 25; Morton, *Colonial Virginia*, 1:29; Warren M. Billings, John E. Selby, and Thad W. Tate, *Colonial Virginia: A History* (White Plains NY: KTO Press, 1986) 30-32.

Important people back in England found this situation entirely unsatisfactory. The Virginia Company wanted profit; England wanted empire; and whether death came from native raids or the flux it brought neither money nor imperial stature. To alleviate the problems of the Jamestown site and to secure better their own and the nation's goals, Company officials instructed resident leaders to find a more suitable place for establishing settlements. Authorities in the colony followed these orders, and between 1610 and 1616 they oversaw the expansion of English Virginia up and down the river from the original site, founding the equivalent of the many small villages and towns of their homeland. Settled about forty miles west of Jamestown and fifteen miles south of the James' falls, the settlement of Henrico was typical. Begun by Sir Thomas Dale in 1611 (and named after his friend Prince Henry), Henrico occupied a seven-acre site on a peninsula located on the river's north bank. By early the next year a new town had been constructed, with a watchtower, a church, storehouses, and dwellings built from bricks made in the settlement. On the lands nearby, Dale fenced off a hog range and several acres on which to grow corn. To fortify the small settlement, he had a stockade built across the peninsula's neck, thus physically separating English from native Virginia in ways common to English notions of possession.[20] In a strange land, the settlement nonetheless reflected ancient patterns of living and the traditional face-to-face English communities, in which people lived close to one another, drew water from the same wells, prayed together in the local church, and shared similar daily experiences.

By 1616 the colony consisted of four other settlements in addition to Jamestown and Henrico. Kecoughtan lay near the easternmost point of the lower peninsula and guarded the mouth of the James River. A few colonists occupied a small island, Dale's Gift, off the Atlantic side of the Eastern Shore and there processed salt and caught fish. Two settlements lay about fifteen miles by water south of Henrico, just north of where the

---

[20] Morton, *Colonial Virginia*, 1:29-30.

Appomattox River empties into the James. Shirley Hundred occupied the north bank and Bermuda Hundred the south.[21]

Finding healthier spots to plant settlements was not the only reason for the colony's growth. Peace came to English and native Virginians in 1614 and peace helped the colony expand by making it safer for settlers to move further into the continent and, if they chose, away from the protection of their infant towns. Peace opened up the continent; potential profit made taking the territory worth the risk of moving further away from the colony's center at Jamestown and possibly angering the land's native inhabitants. Various moneymaking schemes had been advanced in the years before 1614, but for one reason or another they had all failed to turn a profit. Silk failed, wine making failed, and the colonists had shipped home so much sassafras that they succeeded only in destroying the market. There was no gold or silver to refine, and the high cost of transporting lumber made it a risky investment. Colonists had also tried tobacco, since the tobacco imported to England from the Spanish West Indies was selling in London for the impressive price of 18 shillings a pound. But tobacco grown in Virginia lacked the island variety's quality. It was described as "but poore and weake, and of a byting taste" and attracted few buyers. Undeterred by the poor quality of native tobacco and enticed by the profits successful cultivation of a palatable weed might bring, John Rolfe had begun experimenting in 1612 with the Orinoco and sweet-scented tobacco plants of Venezuela and the West Indies. His experiment succeeded. Two years later Rolfe shipped four hogsheads of tobacco to England; within four years the colonists were shipping nearly 50,000 pounds a year back to markets on the other side of the Atlantic.[22]

---

[21] Morton, *Colonial Virginia*, 1:43.

[22] Edmund S. Morgan, *American Slavery, American Freedom: The Ordeal of Colonial Virginia* (New York: W. W. Norton, 1975) 87-91; Morton, *Colonial Virginia* 1:39-40; Billings, Selby, and Tate, *Colonial Virginia*, 43; J. Frederick Fausz, "An 'Abundance of Blood Shed on Both

Colonial tobacco met a rising English demand for the weed. Europeans had first started smoking tobacco for medicinal reasons since they believed it possessed curative powers able to relieve numerous ailments. They soon learned, however, that smoking this yellow weed was just plain enjoyable, and consequently its price rose. Despite Company admonitions to find some other profitable product, be it silk (a favorite of James I), glassware, wine, salt, or lumber, colonists in Virginia believed their land's promise lay in producing a noxious weed smoked in brothels and taverns, and they set about planting it with a vengeance.[23]

As disturbing as some Virginia Company leaders found the prospect of raising a crop vaguely associated with immoral activities, tobacco fit well within the religious context established by the *Lawes Diuine, Morall and Martiall.* Raising tobacco was a labor intensive activity which required nearly constant attention from the time seedlings were planted in the spring to the time the cured leaves were shipped in the fall. Not only did a man have to sow the seeds and then transplant the young tobacco, but he also had to take care to keep weeds and worms away from the developing plants. Towards fall the leaves were harvested and cured for shipping to English markets. The numerous tasks demanded by tobacco helped keep men inclined to idleness—like many of those who peopled the colony—at work. Some men worked at growing the weed because they wanted to get rich. Less fortunate settlers toiled at tobacco cultivation because men greater than they wanted to get richer.[24] Whether they owned their own labor or were indentured servants betting their futures

Sides': England's First Indian War, 1609-1614," *Virginia Magazine of History and Biography* 98 (1990): 3-54, esp. 47-48.

[23] Morton, *Colonial Virginia*, 1:40-41, 93; Morgan, *American Slavery, American Freedom*, 90-91.

[24] Billings, Selby, and Tate, *Colonial Virginia*, 66-68; Morgan, *American Slavery, American Freedom*, 177; T. H. Breen, *Tobacco Culture: The Mentality of the Great Tidewater Planters on the Eve of Revolution* (Princeton: Princeton University Press, 1985) passim, especially 82.

on another's current profit, tobacco left little place for idleness. For a people who equated idleness with "savagery" and Christianity with labor, tobacco must have seemed a near perfect crop. If labor did indeed take on a sacramental quality in early Virginia, then the toil required of tobacco demonstrated an individual's place in a Christian society, even if the work was forced and even if the laborers rejected the tenets of the faith. And who could tell if labor might not lead the English rabble to civility and then to a professed Christianity? At the very least, the labor required of tobacco cultivation mixed well with a religious orientation that emphasized moral behavior and labor as the distinctive features of a Christian people. Although he did not explicitly mention the role of tobacco, Governor Francis Wyatt noted the ideal relationship between religion and labor in the frontispiece of his commonplace book: "Each House, a Church, each Church, an Hive should be, And every Hive, should have his Christaine Bees."[25]

The colonists' discovery of a cash crop also dovetailed nicely with the Virginia Company of London's attempt to make the colony a success by giving those who lived there greater financial incentives. Company leaders believed, correctly as it turned out, that if men worked their own lands rather than those belonging to the company they might put forth more effort, thereby keeping the colony afloat and increasing the odds that investors might make some money themselves. To implement this plan, Virginia Company leaders introduced the headright system, a method of encouraging people to go to Virginia by giving them lands in the colony. Old planters, those settlers in Virginia before spring 1616, received one hundred acres of land at the end of their indentures or immediately if they had paid their own way to Virginia. Those people who settled in the colony after 1616 received fifty acres apiece. For the future, a person who paid his own way would get fifty acres of land when he arrived in Virginia—with an additional fifty acres for everyone else whose

---

[25] Sir Francis Wyatt Commonplace Book, 1625-1629, frontispiece, Virginia Historical Society.

transportation costs he paid. The company did not intend that the settlers who took advantage of this land bonanza would plant tobacco. They envisioned instead the production of a variety of more reputable goods, from silk and lumber to wine and fish and even put restrictions on the amount of tobacco people in Virginia could legally plant.[26]

Colonists in Virginia, however, already had an independent streak, and they ignored the company's orders and planted tobacco anyhow. It became an obsession. Samuel Argall, a mariner and sometime pirate who served as Virginia's governor in 1617, found tobacco everywhere when he arrived at this outpost of English empire. "The Colonie," he reported, was "dispersed all about, planting Tobacco." Settlers cleared land and planted it in fields; they planted it in the streets and in the marketplace; they planted it anywhere it would grow and sometimes where it would not.[27] Raising the weed was a profitable pursuit, but to make money a man needed fields of his own on which to grow this new staple. And men being men and thus subject to the passions of human nature, most wanted to make as much money as possible, which meant more fields on which to plant more weeds. Virginia was in the process of becoming a "boom country" by this time, and tobacco reigned. Demand for the weed grew so strong that through the mid-1620s industrious planters could reasonably expect profits of two hundred to three hundred percent on their investments.[28] Men could get rich by planting tobacco, yet getting rich in Virginia

---

[26] Morgan, *American Slavery, American Freedom*, 93-96; "A Briefe Declaration of the present state of things in Virginia," Brown, *Genesis of the United States*, 2:774-80.

[27] John Smith, *The Generall History of Virginia, New-England, and the Somer Isles* (London, 1624) in Philip L. Barbour, ed., *The Complete Works of Captain John Smith*, 3 vols. (Chapel Hill: University of North Carolina Press, 1986) 2:262.

[28] Jon Kukla, "Order and Chaos in Early America: Political and Social Stability in Pre-Restoration Virginia," *American Historical Review* 90 (1985): 284; Morgan, *American Slavery, American Freedom*, 108-30.

meant spreading out across the land in ways that threatened English ideas about community and the public practice of religion. With readily available land and a profitable commodity to exploit, settlers ventured ever further into the rich lands of the James River Valley, in the process leaving behind traditional English patterns of settlement. Colonists soon stopped planting themselves in towns like inhabitants of England or the nation's other colonies, and like they had done during the settlement's first few years; instead they scattered out across the countryside to grow tobacco. Leaders new to Virginia seemed shocked by the colony's settlement patterns and complained that colonists had stopped living like English people: "[the settlements were] so dispersed & [the] people so straglingly seated, that we were not only bereft of the frendly comerce and mutuall societie one of another in religious duties, the first fruites of Civility; but were also disabled any way to prouide for the comon safety either against forraine or domesticke invasion, the carefullest charge of Christian charity."[29] Such remarks about the impact of the colony's environment on traditional religious practices foreshadowed those of immigrant English ministers later in the century who found that the institutional facets of Virginia's church were as foreign to them as the land.[30]

The colonists' accommodation to the land and the tobacco culture that the land fostered weakened the influence of Virginia's institutional church; filling the land with English settlers shaped the development of Virginia's ecclesiastical polity. The colony's ecclesiastical polity began with the Church of England, which was formally established in 1619 at the General Assembly's first meeting. (Earlier charters and the *Lawes Diuine, Morall and Martiall*, however, had assumed that colonists in Virginia would follow the English Church "in all fundamentall

---

[29] Sir Francis Wyatt, Commission to Sir George Yeardley, 20 June 1622, Kingsbury, *Records of the Virginia Company of London*, 3:656.

[30] The impact of Virginia's tobacco culture on the colony's religious institutions and personal piety will be taken up in much greater detail in chapter five.

pointes".)[31] The Church of England, Virginia's established church, formed one of the more peculiar branches of the Reformation. It adhered to an episcopal form of church government, and it combined Calvinist theology with the yearly Christological cycle of the Roman Catholic liturgical calendar purged of some of its Marian festivals offensive to all Protestants. With the exception of St. Paul, they limited celebrations of saints days to those Biblical saints who had witnessed Christ's resurrection. Advent, Christmas, Epiphany, Lent, Easter, and Ascension Day came each year with unceasing regularity, although strict Protestants found no scriptural justification either for the seasons of the Church's calendar or for the approximately two-dozen holy days celebrated throughout the year. In addition to the liturgical feasts and fasts, the Church also observed two holy days to commemorate occasions when God had shown his mercy to the English nation. Beginning in 1606, English people annually celebrated Gunpowder Treason Day on 5 November as a day of prayer and thanksgiving. Following the Restoration, Anglicans marked 30 January as a day of humiliation and fasting in remembrance of Charles I, king and martyr. Containing set forms for prayer services and the celebration of the sacraments, the *Book of Common Prayer* served both as the Church of England's service book and as a symbol of its unity.[32]

Established church or not, the Virginia Company of London wanted to fill the colony with settlers, and they, as well as

[31] Richard Beale Davis, *Intellectual Life in the Colonial South, 1585-1763*, 3 vols. (Knoxville: University of Tennessee Press, 1978) 2:633; Samuel M. Bemiss, ed., *The Three Charters of the Virginia Company of London, with Seven Related Documents; 1606-1621* (Williamsburg: Virginia 350th Anniversary Celebration Corporation, 1957) 57, see also 15; *For the Colony in Virginea Britania. Lawes Diuine, Morall and Martiall, &c.* in Peter Force, ed., *Tracts and Other Papers Relating Principally to the Origin, Settlement, and Progress of the Colonies in North America*, 4 vols. (Gloucester MA: Peter Smith, 1963) 3:2:10-11.

[32] David Cressy, *Bonfires and Bells: National Memory and the Protestant Calendar in Elizabethan and Stuart England* (Los Angeles: University of California Press, 1989) 2-6, 13-33; Davies, *Worship and Theology* 2:224-28.

resident leaders, often gave "in all fundamentall pointes" a
liberal interpretation. Instructions issued to Governor Yeardley
in 1618, for instance, did not even define a particular
institutional religious expression, although they demanded that
the colonists set aside glebe lands for the maintenance of
ministers.[33] Notwithstanding the established church, behavior
rather than belief continued to shape the colony's religious
polity. The Assembly set penalties, milder than those of the
Lawes but maintaining the same pattern, for drunkenness,
swearing, "ungodly disorders," and Sabbath breaking. In a clause
which allowed authorities to separate from the polity notorious
sinners who might draw down God's wrath, clergymen were
directed to meet with the governor four times a year to discuss
excommunicating men and women who persisted in "enormous
sins."[34] For the colonists to worship God and follow his moral
laws remained more important to both Company and resident
authorities than any particular form of worship or theology. The
Lawes Diuine, Morall and Martiall, with their emphasis on
behavior, had established a political framework in which an
infant religious toleration could develop. Virginia's growth and
its particular form of economic mandate only encouraged this
pattern.

The burden of peopling the colony fell largely on Sir Edwin
Sandys, an "assistant" or director of the Virginia Company by
1616 and later its treasurer. Sandys was not picky about religion,
so long as it was Christian, and he put empire above religious
purity. His own religious views demonstrated a certain eclecticism. The son of an archbishop, he once claimed the church
government of Geneva was the best in the world, and not only
consulted with his former teacher Richard Hooker on the latter's

---

[33] Instructions to Governor Yeardley, 18 November 1618, Kingsbury,
Records of the Virginia Company of London, 3:102.

[34] John Pory, "A Reporte of the Manner of proceeding in the General
Assembly convented at James City," 30-31 July, 2-4 August 1619,
Kingsbury, *Records of the Virginia Company of London*, 3:172-73. See also
Hening, *Statutes at Large*, 1:123.

Laws, but also gave financial support to ensure publication of this work that attacked John Calvin and the other Genevan reformers. In Sandys' own book, *A Relation of the State of Religion, and With What Hopes and Policies it Hath Been Framed, and is Maintained, in the Several States of These Western Parts of the World,* published in 1605, he argued that any hope for Christian unity was illusory. Yet he did not find this a cause for mourning. He found instead something positive in his negative assessment of the possibility of creating a reunited Christendom and advocated, according to his most recent biographer, "what today we would call peaceful coexistence," the first person following the Reformation to do so.[35] Ideas about "peaceful coexistence" among religious groups shaped Sandys' policies toward Virginia, and he may well have viewed the colony as an experiment in applied political theology. In any case, his policy of establishing particular plantations gave the company a way of peopling the colony that also avoided religious conflict and allowed the colony to experiment with religious diversity. The practice led to the creation of something similar to a confederal system in which different particular plantations followed their own local customs in worship and theology under the broader colony wide relationship with God based on Christian morality, a halfway step to the full coexistence outlined in Sandys' *Relation.* Yet Virginia's system created a mixture within the polity as a whole that many people in England would soon find disturbing.

Under Sandys' guidance, a wide variety of English religious groups received permission to settle in Virginia. William Throckmorton and Richard Berkeley, who in 1619 received a

---

[35]Kingsbury, *Records of the Virginia Company of London*, 4:194-95; George MacLaren Brydon, *Virginia's Mother Church and the Political Conditions Under Which it Grew*, 2 vols. (Richmond: Virginia Historical Society, 1947-1952) 1:72; Richard Hooker, *Of the Laws of Ecclesiastical Polity*, ed. Arthur Stephen McGrade (Cambridge: Cambridge University Press, 1989) xiii; Theodore K. Rabb, *Jacobean Gentleman: Sir Edwin Sandys, 1561-1629* (Princeton: Princeton University Press, 1998) 36-38, 330.

patent to found Berkeley Hundred, wanted their new settlement to adhere to the rites of the Church of England, and they gave explicit instructions to those who settled their lands to make sure that "the lorde day be kept in holy and religious order and that all bodily labour and vaine sporte and scandalous recreations be refrained, and that morning and evening prayer (according to the englishe booke of common prayer) be Dayly read and attended unto...And that all other such festivalls and holidayes be observed and keept wch are authorised and appoynted by the lawes and statutes of this realme of England."[36] That same year, with Sandys leading the discussions, the company also gave the Pilgrim fathers who later settled Plymouth colony leave to establish a settlement in Virginia, planning to settle them somewhere in the James River Valley. It did not matter that they came ashore several hundred miles to the north rather than along the Chesapeake, for Company authorities had intended to locate these Separatist Puritans in Virginia. On this point, Perry Miller's observation about religion in early Virginia seems on the mark: "history is often more instructive as it considers what men conceived they were doing rather than what, in brute fact, they did."[37]

Although the Pilgrims happened to settle elsewhere, other Puritan groups did establish settlements in Virginia, and they lived free of any obvious harassment through the 1630s. Several former members of the English Separatist congregation in Amsterdam known as the Ancient Church established particular plantations in Virginia. Edward Bennett, a onetime elder of the church, received a patent from the Virginia Company of London in 1621. Two years later Puritans Christopher Lawne and Nathaniel Basse established settlements on the Southside of the James near Bennett's. Lawne, a button maker, had also been an

---

[36] William Throckmorton, Richard Berkeley, et. al., *Ordinances Direccons and Instructions to Captaine Jon Woodlefe,* 4 September 1619, Kingsbury, *Records of the Virginia Company of London,* 3:208.

[37] Morton, *Colonial Virginia,* 1:63-68; Rabb, *Jacobean Gentleman,* 330; Miller, "Religion and Society in the Early Literature of Virginia," 101.

elder of the Ancient Church until a falling out with the group's minister over the question of separatism led to his expulsion. He returned to England and was close enough to the established church to author an anti-Brownist tract, *The Prophane Schisme of the Brownists or Separatists*. All three men found a place in Virginia and even served in the House of Burgesses.[38] Henry Jacob, who had established one of England's first Independent Congregational Churches, died on his way to the colony to found a particular plantation to be named "Jacobopolis."[39] Several other Brownists had arrived in Virginia a decade earlier, their journey interrupted when the *Sea Venture* crashed on Bermuda during a storm at sea.[40] Men persuaded by Roman Catholics also lived in the colony unpersecuted for their religious opinions. John Pory wrote to Edwin Sandys in 1620 to tell him of a Roman Catholic then residing in the settlement: "that Mr. Chanterton smells to much of Roome...as he attempts to work myracles with his Crucyfixe." The resident governor, however, had decided to "take no notice" of the man unless he later perceived that Chanterton presented a threat to the colony.[41]

---

[38] Davis, *Intellectual Life in the Colonial South*, 2:643-44; John Bennett Boddie, "Edward Bennett of London and Virginia," *William and Mary Quarterly* 2nd ser. 13 (1933): 117-30; Babette M. Levy, "Early Puritanism in the Southern and Island Colonies," *Proceedings of the American Antiquarian Society* 70 (1960) 93-94, 105-107.

[39] Butler, *Awash in a Sea of Faith*, 38; Davis, *Intellectual Life in the Colonial South*, 2:643-44.

[40] Strachey, *Voyage to Virginia*, 42-43.

[41] John Pory to Sir Edwin Sandys, 12 June 1620, Kingsbury, *Records of the Virginia Company of London*, 3:304. For more on Pory, see William S. Powell, *John Pory/1572-1636: The Life and Letters of a Man of Many Parts* (Chapel Hill: University of North Carolina Press, 1977) 74-131.

In their efforts to people the colony and thus maintain dominion over this portion of English territory overseas, Sandys and his colleagues did not use religious views to establish some form of seventeenth-century litmus test. Even the ardent anti-papist, anti-nonconformist William Crashaw was, by the late 1610s, forwarding to Company leaders get-rich-quick-schemes absent a religious motivation.[42] Colonial laws establishing the Church of England in Virginia likely did more to appease any English authorities in London worried about nonconformity than they did to define Virginians' ecclesiastical polity. Although a departure from early modern European political theories of state organization, the situation in Virginia closely approximated contemporary English practices. English law did not tolerate the mischief of nonconformity, but nonetheless a wide range of religious beliefs and practices flourished in Jacobean England, only the most radical of which were attacked with any consistent vigor. An extraordinarily shrewd politician, King James I managed to craft unity within his Church of England by playing both ends of the religious spectrum (Puritans on the left and Roman Catholics on the right) off against Anglicans in the middle. James held his own religious sympathies, but as long as the wrangling among England's many religious parties did not upset politics he was content to allow people their own private religious opinions.[43] A similar practice emerged in Virginia.

The story of Virginia's early experiment in "peaceful coexistence" can hide some very real problems. In truth, religion's institutional presence failed to keep pace with the colony's growth, and during the same period colonists were beginning to show a sharp increase in religious sentiments. The institutional church lagged so far behind by 1620 that over half the boroughs in Virginia went without the services of a minister.

---

[42] Kingsbury, *Records of the Virginia Company of London*, 1:370.

[43] Kenneth Fincham and Peter Lake, "The Ecclesiastical Policies of James I and Charles I," in Kenneth Fincham, ed., *The Early Stuart Church, 1603-1642*, ed. Kenneth Fincham (Stanford: Stanford University Press, 1993) 23-50.

Despite the thousands of people Edwin Sandys had encouraged to go to the colony, in 1620 only three ministers and perhaps two deacons resided there.[44] The shortage was not new. It had grown so acute a few years earlier in 1617 that Samuel Argall took the extraordinary step of asking company leaders to solicit English bishops in hopes that one would be willing to ordain in absentia Mr. William Wickham, who had assisted the Reverend Alexander Whitaker at Henrico before the latter's death earlier that year.[45] Soon the colonial assembly began petitioning English leaders for aid in words that would become a familiar refrain for nearly a century: "the Informatione given you of the wante of wourthie Ministers heere is very trew...soe it is our earnest request, that you woulde bee pleased to send us over many more learned and sincere Ministers."[46] Yet Virginia Company leaders did not seem concerned with this deviation from traditional English ways of life and did not respond adequately to the colonists' requests. Despite instructing settlers to support the Church of England, neither the company, the Crown, nor the English Church organized an official mission to Virginia's settlers in the seventeenth century. English authorities consistently showed more interest in converting natives to Christianity than in meeting the religious needs of English colonists, as obsessed with this fancy as Virginians themselves were with planting tobacco. But few colonists shared the company's missionary zeal, and by 1620, whatever mission to the

---

[44] Philip Alexander Bruce, *Institutional History of Virginia in the Seventeenth Century: An Inquiry into the Religious, Moral, Educational, Legal, Military, and Political Condition of the People Based on Original and Contemporary Records*, 2 vols. (New York: The Knickerbocker Press, 1910) 1:118; Edward Lewis Goodwin, *The Colonial Church in Virginia* (Wilwaukee: Morehouse, 1927) 55.

[45] Governor Argall to Council for Virginia, 9 June 1617, Kingsbury, *Records of the Virginia Company of London*, 3:74; Brydon, Virginia's Mother Church, 1:26-28.

[46] Council in Virginia to the Virginia Company of London, January 1621/22; Kingsbury, *Records of the Virginia Company of London*, 3:583.

native Virginians had ever existed had been disrupted by the
colonists' pursuit of wealth. This neglect worried some devout
settlers, but they were a distinct minority. Using words that
echoed the confession of sin in the *Book of Common Prayer*,
George Thorpe and John Pory worried that God's judgment
would soon be visited upon the colony for "wee doe not as wee
ought to doe, take his service a longe wth us by o[u]r serious
endevours of convertinge the Heathen."[47] Virginians even
diverted funds donated by pious Englishmen to support the
College of Henrico's efforts to convert natives to uses they
deemed more practical: they used the funds to finance an iron
works on Falling Creek.[48] George Thorpe captured the colonists'
attitude precisely in 1621: "There is scarce any man amongest us
that doth soe much as afforde [the natives] a good thought in
his hart and most men with their mouthes give them nothinge
but maledictions and bitter execrations."[49] Colonists did not
want native children in their midst learning civility and
Christianity—too much prejudice, too much bother, yet another
task to keep them from growing tobacco. Virginians did not wish
to be agents of cultural evangelism, and the natives wanted
neither the gift of Christianity nor having English Christians in
North America.

Nor did Virginia's native people share the resurgent
enthusiasm for the Virginia venture that came as a result of
Sandys' successful efforts to people the colony. Larger numbers
of English settlers meant that larger segments of North America
would be carved out by Europeans and the natives did not
believe the land was the company's to distribute. By early March

---

[47] George Thorpe and John Pory to Edwin Sandys, 15-16 May 1621,
Kingsbury, *Records of the Virginia Company of London*, 3:446.

[48] Charles E. Hatch, Jr. and Thurlow Gates Gregory, "The First
American Blast Furnace, 1619-1622: The Birth of a Mighty Industry on
Falling Creek in Virginia," *Virginia Magazine of History and Biography* 70
(1962): 257-68.

[49] George Thorpe and John Pory to Edwin Sandys, 15-16 May 1621,
Kingsbury, *Records of the Virginia Company of London*, 3:446.

1622, Opechancanough, Powhatan's successor, had had enough of the English and their encroachment upon his peoples' lands. He conceived, planned, and executed an attack upon the eighty or so English settlements in Virginia that nearly succeeded in destroying this portion of England's overseas empire. The natives struck on 22 March 1622. Their surprise attack, coordinated among the thirty "kingdoms" in the area, killed almost 350 settlers, including several councilors and George Thorpe, one of the few colonists who thought well of the natives and one of the only settlers in Virginia who ever seriously entertained hopes of converting Indians to Christianity. After hearing of the attack, a minister in England, the Reverend Joseph Mead, compared the massacre to European forms of religious violence: "It seems this God of theirs is something of kind to that manages the massacres now in France, & other parts of Christendome."[50]

Opechancanough's uprising of 1622 reinforced the boundaries established by the *Lawes Diuine, Morall and Martiall* that had been forgotten during the early years of economic success. Natives were "savages," and English people were Christians. Called into convocation by the Council, Virginia's remaining clergy met and approved a plan to destroy the natives by conducting a "holy war" against this people who had shed the "inocent blood of so many Christians."[51] Native Virginians had killed English Christians; now they would be made to feel God's wrath through the military might of those whose land Virginia truly was. The English hoped to obliterate the natives' presence from their promised land. Company leaders directed the

---

[50] Morton, *Colonial Virginia*, 1:74-75; Robert C. Johnson, ed. "The Indian Massacre of 1622: Some Correspondence of the Reverend Joseph Mead," *Virginia Magazine of History and Biography* 71 (1963): 408. Easter Day fell on 21 April 1622, so the massacre did not occur on Good Friday.

[51] Treasurer and Council for Virginia to Governor and Council in Virginia, 1 August 1622, Kingsbury, *Records of the Virginia Company of London*, 3:671-72; Governor and Council in Virginia to [?], September 1624, Ferrar Papers, f. 556, Magdalene College, Cambridge University.

colonists "to roote out [the natives] from being any longer a people."[52] One definition of religion changed in Virginia once the colonists began trying to annihilate the native Virginians. Instead of being a gift the English offered to men enslaved by Satan, Christianity became a justification for ethnic prejudice and the use of violence against an infidel foe. No matter how nominally Christian some of the colonists may have been, the colonists' view of Christianity became more clearly what it had been all along, the possession of English men and women. At the time of the uprising, Virginia was an expanding colony comprised of Anglicans, Puritans, Roman Catholics, Brownists, and people who could not have cared less about religion—a volatile combination of contrary theological beliefs that in England was already beginning to come apart. Yet the assault baptized the settlers with a common Christianity even as it demonized the natives. As part of their own identity in Virginia's wilderness, the colonists had demonized the natives, seeing in them what one historian has called a "threatening Other."[53] Although Virginia's leaders recognized the natives as men like themselves, they were nonetheless "other" in a way that rival Europeans were not. Company policies had encouraged a broad understanding of Christian unity as had the behavioral emphasis of the *Lawes Diuine, Morall and Martiall*; the massacre only confirmed preexisting sentiments. It confirmed both the practicality and the wisdom of the *Lawes'* vision of colonial identity. If Virginia's religious mixture held the potential for religious conflict like that of Europe, the colony's cultural enemies helped contain it by vividly demonstrating that Christian Virginians had enemies more alien than other Englishmen who held peculiar opinions about theology and religious ceremony. Virginia would face religious conflicts in the

---

[52] Treasurer and Council for Virginia to Governor and Council in Virginia, 1 August 1622, Kingsbury, *Records of the Virginia Company of London*, 3:671-72.

[53] Stephen Greenblatt, *Renaissance Self-Fashioning: From More to Shakespeare* (Chicago: University of Chicago Press, 1980) 9.

coming years, but they would be unlike those in England. Puritans would not battle Anglicans; in Virginia, the traditional practice of religion would contend with the tobacco economy.

The imperatives which flowed from the colonists' decision to make tobacco their staple crop had a tremendous impact on the institutional facets of the Church of England that they had transplanted to Virginia. Settlers wanted both religion and tobacco, yet it proved more and more difficult to satisfy the demands of both and by mid-decade there was obvious conflict. At its 1623/24 session, and again in 1626, the colony's General Assembly passed a law modifying the rhythms of religious time, implicitly testifying to the Anglican slant of Virginia's church establishment. "By reason of our necessities," the Burgesses reasoned that when two holy days fell together "betwixt the feast of the annuntiation of the blessed virgin and St. Michael the archangell, then only the first to be observed."[54] Largely unnoticed in the modern world, holy days represented sacralized time, significant days set aside from ordinary time, days when "lawful bodily labour could be set aside."[55] The feasts and fasts regulated by colonial law fell between 25 March and 29 September, a period when most colonists would have been tending to the stages of tobacco production. (A roughly contemporaneous law set the beginning of the planting season no later than 25 March, then New Year's Day.)[56] The law suggests several potential interpretations. Perhaps too many people took feast days off to attend religious observances, just as the people at Berkeley Hundred had gathered to commemorate St. Stephen's Day. Or perhaps like their countrymen on the other side of the Atlantic, the colonists joined great merriment to their holy days by putting on revels and church ales following religious observances, thus unfitting themselves for serious labor the next day. London poet John Taylor described contemporary English Shrove Tuesday festivities as days of "boiling and

---

[54] Hening, *Statutes at Large*, 1:123.
[55] Cressy, *Bonfires and Bells*, 7, 35.
[56] Hening, *Statutes at Large*, 1:161.

broiling...roasting and toasting...stewing and brewing." After so much drinking and feasting, men in their cups frequently brawled with other revelers, and riots broke out on no less than twenty-four Shrove Tuesdays between 1603 and 1642. Ascension Day, Pentecost, St. Bartholomew's Day, and the Eve of the Feast of St. John the Baptist included goodly measures of merrymaking as well.[57] Perhaps people who took the day off in Virginia followed English custom and celebrated too much, thus turning the observances into mob revels. Whatever the reason, the abundance of religious festivals in the spring, summer, and early fall threatened tobacco cultivation and made an accommodation necessary.

By modifying but not abandoning the Church of England's traditional religious calendar, the General Assembly's law of 1623/24 attempted to maintain in Virginia two values competing for the colonists' time: religion, which brought familiar traditions, structures, and a sense of stability to a strange land, and tobacco, which offered settlers the opportunity to acquire temporal wealth from that novel environment. Too many festivals and the drinking that often accompanied them did not incline a man to labor vigorously the next day. In a context where labor differentiated Christians from savages, potential idleness was a great threat not only to economic success but also to English identity. Shaped by what men believed was the necessity of planting tobacco, Virginia's church developed as best it could, maintaining as much as possible of the traditional institution while nevertheless making allowances for colonial "occasions." "Occasions," in the words of theologian Paul Avis, provide the "political, social, and cultural context...for a church and contribute to the shaping of its outward form." They "cannot provide a definition of a church or its *raison d'etre*." In other words, "occasions" influence the development of a church's institutional arrangements but not that church's

---

[57] Peter Burke, "Popular Culture in Seventeenth-Century London," in Barry Reay, ed., *Popular Culture in Seventeenth-Century England* (New York: St. Martin's Press, 1985) 35-38.

theology. For Virginians, "occasions" included not only the social, political, and cultural institutions peculiar to English society in Virginia, but also the geographical setting and the natives against whom colonial leaders defined themselves.

Modifying the celebration of traditional English holy days accommodated Virginians to their tobacco culture—to one of their most significant "occasions"—and in the process gave tobacco cultivation and the search for wealth primacy over traditional religious practices. The land had made the accommodation with tobacco desirable; its native inhabitants also shaped the traditional church calendar to the exigencies of a novel environment. An additional portion of the statute adapted traditional religious time to the colony's peculiar cultural context by setting aside 22 March as a holy day to be observed in commemoration of Virginia's deliverance from Opechancanough's warriors. Although people at the time did not necessarily understand things this way, a distinct colonial religious identity was not only in the process of emerging, but also, through the actions of colonial leaders, it was already being institutionalized.[58]

All of these laws about the church seem out of place. Virginia had become a "boom country" by this time, and it is an odd boom country that pays so much attention to religion. Yet we can doubt neither the mad scramble for wealth taking place in the colony nor the exploitation of servants that accompanied it. Some indentured servants believed their conditions so harsh that they no longer thought of Virginia as a promised land. Noting the ill treatment of servants like himself, Richard Freethorne maintained the Old Testament analogies popular in the literature of colonization but compared his experiences in Virginia to that of the Israelites during their captivity in Egypt. Nonetheless, combined with the search for wealth and the brutal usage of servants was the growing sense of religion's place in the

---

[58] Paul Avis, "What is 'Anglicanism?'" in Stephen Sykes and John Booty, eds. *The Study of Anglicanism* (Philadelphia and London: S.P.C.K., 1988): 406.

colony. Certainly tobacco cultivation challenged community development in early Virginia; yet following traditional English religious practices also helped early settlers maintain some semblance of order despite this threat. Whether observed by attending divine services, by participating in revels, or both, saints' day celebrations testify to some degree of social cohesion and an attempt to preserve what order existed. Divine service required people willing to travel to a church or a house which served as a church, in order to meet and hear prayers. Secular celebrations, if they took place in Virginia, required even greater organization. Hogs or calves had to be slaughtered or other food prepared, a convenient location for the revelers to meet would have been necessary, and if the colonists followed English practice, someone would have had to prepare a bonfire or two.

To English people, worship and the punishment of moral offenses were two of the props holding the community together, and other aspects of colonial religion belied its role in maintaining order and community for Virginia's early settlers. Consider, for instance, how men described the Church of England's communion service. Whatever spiritual solace the Eucharist may have brought individual colonists, it nonetheless served the polity as a ritual and traditional form of spiritual weaponry that could foster concord within the settlement. Even stripped of the mysteries associated with the Roman Catholic Mass, the Protestant Eucharist nonetheless brought God immediately into the world in a very tangible way that could be both intimidating and terrifying. Anglican Eucharistic doctrine steered a middle path between Catholic transubstantiation and Zwinglian memorialism, a position illuminated well by Nathaniel Eaton, a minister who served an Eastern Shore parish in the 1630s:

> That when the holy Elements are blest
> By the Priest's powerful lips, though nothing there
> To outward sense but bread and wine appear,
> Yet doth there under these dark forms reside

The Body of the Son of Man that died.[59]

This acceptance of Christ's real presence in the sacrament meant that the words of institution, "This is my Body.... This is my Blood," conveyed the reality of God breaking into the world at a particular time among a particular people under the guise of bread and wine. To ingest the elements was to ingest God, a terrifying God English people knew both as judge and prescriber of penalties. This understanding made easy the ritual and traditional use by the Tudor-Stuart Church of communion as a form of a poison ordeal. Individuals accused of crimes could offer testimony of their innocence and then receive the sacrament to ratify their honesty on the assumption that a lie would invite God's judgment. Similar notions governed people who made agreements with each other, such as when newly married persons received communion in order to confirm the vows they had just made in the marriage service. More generally, communion as a poison ordeal carried an implied threat that anyone who violated the peace and quiet of the community after sharing Christ's body and blood with their neighbors opened themselves to God's wrath. Communion, as the name implies, referred to the community who prayed and ate together—be it individuals or families who had resolved a dispute, wedded couples, the local parish, or even a colonial settlement. Persons who received the sacrament essentially swore by Christ's body and blood that they would honor their agreements. To do otherwise turned the elements of the sacrament from foretaste of the heavenly banquet to notice of divine sanction—to Italians, the "vendetta of God."[60]

---

[59] Davies, *Worship and Theology in England*, 2:294.

[60] Keith Thomas, *Religion and the Decline of Magic: Studies in Popular Beliefs in Sixteenth and Seventeenth Century England* (London: Weidenfeld and Nicolson, 1971) 44-45; Edward Muir, *Ritual in Early Modern Europe* (New York: Cambridge University Press, 1997) 162-63. For a more detailed discussion of supernatural weapons in early Virginia, see Edward L. Bond,

This understanding of the Eucharist as a poison ordeal continued in Virginia among Company members and colonists alike who from time to time marked the resolution of disputes by receiving the sacrament. In 1621, Governor George Yeardley and Captain William Powell, a burgess from James City, engaged in a protracted disagreement, each man sending charges and countercharges to Company superiors in London. Before Virginia Company officials decided how best to resolve the dispute, Powell and Yeardley privately reconciled. John Pory, secretary of the colony and a former member of Parliament, described the religious element of their reconciliation when he reported that both men had "receyved ye Sacrament" in pledge of their reconciliation and were "unwillinge, that ye matter should be any way revyved; but rather desirous yt might be forevr buryed." So common was this understanding of the Eucharist in Virginia that even when facts dictated a different interpretation some settlers thought of communion as an "outward and visible pledge of reconciliation." John Smith related the standard series of events—conflict, resolution, and communion—in the tale of his admission to the resident council in 1607. Yes, Smith admitted, he had not gotten along well with all of the other leading planters, yet the Reverend Mr. Hunt had resolved the dispute, and Smith had taken his place on the Council. "The next day," he continued, "all receaved the Communion." Smith erred on the communion's date. It was celebrated eleven days, not one, after he had joined the Council, and may have been in observance of the Feast of St. John the Baptist. Smith, however, viewed the rite as part of the resolution of a conflict. Perhaps this explains why Virginians celebrated the sacrament monthly rather than quarterly as in most English parishes and, in part, why the shortage of ministers proved so disturbing.[61]

"Source of Knowledge, Source of Power: The Supernatural World of English Virginia, 1607-1624," 108 (2000): 105-38.

[61] George Thorpe and John Pory to Sir Edwin Sandys, 9 May 1621, Kingsbury, *Records of the Virginia Company of London*, 3:445; Brown, *Genesis of the United States*, 2:969-71; Morton, *Colonial Virginia*, 1:58-60;

Maintaining a sense of community in Virginia's novel environment could be difficult, and in the years immediately following the Powhatan uprising of 1622, the few religious scenes in the records suggest the importance of religion in maintaining social cohesion and order throughout the growing colony. Most prominent in the colony's court records, these scenes reflect the colonists' abiding fear that actions offensive to God might draw down his wrath. Sabbath breaking appears often. Burgesses noted it particularly in 1631/32 as a sin that "almighty God may justlie punish his people for neglectinge." Typical penalties combined civil and religious sanctions: a fine to help keep the church in good repair and public acknowledgement of error before the congregation, a ritual apology to other members of the community who may have suffered had God chosen to smite the settlement for the offender's sin. William Capps, an "old planter" who occasionally found himself at odds with the colony's leaders, ran afoul of the law mandating church attendance in 1629 for routinely failing to attend divine services at Elizabeth City Parish. The court fined him and put a lien on his next crop for the value of the fine.[62]

Mixed with Sabbath breaking in the court records are other faults not only "hateful" to God, but also threatening to the peace and quiet of the community, behaviors such as gossip, slander, and fornication. When it came to social control, Virginia's courts were particularly interested in punishing offenses that threatened social harmony. Found guilty of fornication in 1626, John Ewing received forty lashes at James City and another forty stripes the next week at Shirley Hundred where he had committed the offense. Jane Hill received a less physically brutal but still humiliating sentence. She was ordered to stand up in James City Parish during divine service wearing the

---

John Smith, *The Proceedings of the English Colonie in Virginia* (London, 1612), Barbour, *Works of Captain John Smith*, 1:207.

[62] Hening, *Statutes at Large*, 1:155; McIlwaine, *Minutes of the Council and the General Court of Colonial Virginia*, 194.

traditional white sheet of sexual offenders and to do the same the next week at Shirley Hundred's church.[63]

A year later, settlers at Archers Hope complained about the "abominable contentions" disrupting their lives. "Scoldings railings & fallings out" had erupted between Amy Hall and several other people, all to the increasing weariness of Mrs. Hall's neighbors and perhaps more importantly to the "dishonor of God." The case soon found its way on to the General Court's docket. The justices ordered six colonists to pay bond for their good behavior, while Mrs. Hall, the apparent source of much of the strife, was to be "toughed [towed] round aboard the Margaret & John & ducked three times."[64] Another woman, Eleanor Sprague, created a stir after agreeing to marry two different men. She was required during divine service to ask forgiveness of the congregation and of Almighty God.[65]

Duckings, asking forgiveness of a sin on the Sabbath in front of the congregation gathered for prayer, and similar punishments were all forms of penance, proceedings designed not so much for retribution as "for the soul's health," to reform offenders and put them back in proper relationship with God and their neighbors.[66] Throughout the first half of the century, Virginia's county court system enforced the traditional English penitential rituals, acting in the capacity of an English ecclesiastical court and frequently addressing social conflicts detrimental to the peace and quiet of the community. Gossip,

---

[63] McIlwaine, *Minutes of the Council and the General Court of Colonial Virginia*, 142; Martin Ingram, *Church Courts, Sex, and Marriage in England, 1570-1640* (Cambridge: Cambridge University Press) 53; Clara Ann Bowler, "Carted Whores and White Shrouded Apologies: Slander in the County Courts of Seventeenth-Century Virginia," *Virginia Magazine of History and Biography* 85 (1977): 411-26.

[64] McIlwaine, *Minutes of the Council and the General Court of Colonial Virginia*, 119.

[65] McIlwaine, *Minutes of the Council and the General Court of Colonial Virginia*, 15.

[66] Ingram, *Church Courts, Sex, and Marriage*, 3.

slander, and tale-telling could prove particularly disruptive to society, setting neighbors at odds with each other, perhaps leading them to take sides in disputes, thus tearing at the colony's tender social fabric. Whereas English moralists may have worried about fornication provoking God's wrath and the religious minded may have shown concern about the sin's effect upon the sinner's soul, many people had more practical worries such as the impact fornication might have upon their finances since the local community had to support the bastard children and sometimes their mothers as well.[67] Human beings are rarely happy to pay the costs for the sins of another, and this enforced charity was not taken lightly.

Among Virginia's scattered court records of the 1620s recounting the numerous instances when colonists disrupted the community there is a peculiar absence. Cases for heresy do not appear. It was the 1620s, and for English people not to be hurling epithets at religious opponents was peculiar indeed. Back in England, religious animosity had begun more and more to mark public life. During the latter half of the decade William Laud, then bishop of London and as anti-Puritan as ever, began to harry Puritans out of the land in an effort to rid England of what he considered an objectionable religious impurity. Aware of the rising tensions between Puritan and Anglican wings within the Church of England and hoping to limit them, James I had several years earlier limited the right to preach on controversial theological issues such as predestination to conforming ministers.[68]

Virginia, however, had developed differently, shaped by the colony's own peculiar circumstances. As a result, during the

---

[67] Ingram, *Church Courts, Sex, and Marriage*, 286.

[68] Leo F. Solt, *Church and State in Early Modern England, 1509-1649* (New York: Oxford University Press, 1990) 164-73.

same years that theological controversies were heating up in England, Virginians were struggling to keep religion as a part of their public life at all. Following the uprising of 1622 and the dissolution of the Virginia Company of London in 1624 by James I, who had grown tired by then of the members' squabbling and the corporation's general lack of profit, the formal ecclesiastical presence of religion in the colony deteriorated. Although the company's efforts were often weak and its leaders more interested in converting natives than in offering spiritual sustenance to Christian Englishmen, the Virginia Company of London had nonetheless attempted to maintain a clerical presence in the colony. Between 1607 and 1624 the company sent no less than twenty-two ministers to Virginia, although most of them soon died or returned to England. In the wake of the company's collapse, the shortage of ministers in Virginia became acute, as neither Crown nor Church stepped in to fill the void and the colonists suffered as a result. As the years advanced toward 1630, settlers' religious needs were met with less and less regularity. In 1629, Governor John Harvey, noting the colony's "want of sufficient and able" clergy, implored Charles I's Privy Councilors to supply Virginia with six or seven "grave and conformable ministers." To attract clergy to preach the Word and celebrate the sacraments in Virginia, he recommended that the Privy Council grant each minister willing to come to the colony a travel allowance to help defray the costs of an Atlantic crossing. England returned a blunt answer to its missionaries of empire in the New World. They refused Harvey's request for funds, asserting that Virginia had become a voluntary missionary field: "Such voluntary ministers may go over as will transport themselves at their own charge."[69]

Only two decades had passed since Englishmen had first landed on the shores of the James River, bringing with them a

---

[69] "Governor John Harvey's Propositions Touching Virginia, [1629]," and "Certaine Answeares to Capt. Harvey's Proposicons Touching Virginia," *Virginia Magazine of History and Biography* 7 (1900): 369-71; Bruce, *Institutional History,* 1:118-19.

soteriology of empire that required them to please God if England was to gain its desired imperial status, but by 1630 English leaders seemed little concerned with Virginia's religious life—either with converting the natives or with continuing the Church's traditional pastoral mission to the English people. A disillusioned John Smith, bitter over English authorities' lack of attention to religion, had come to believe that the whole venture had been a farce from the beginning. In 1631 he charged English leaders with making "religion their colour, when all their aime was nothing but present profit."[70] A few years later some settlers, desperate for Christian guidance and solace, embraced the Roman Catholicism offered by missionaries from nearby Maryland, a colony that had been founded in 1634 as a haven for this persecuted minority. Some people in Virginia complained about the apostasy, certain that a plot had been conceived by Marylanders who were in their words "withdrawing our people from our Religion." Such criticism, however, came from newcomers who did not yet understand that although Englishmen may have peopled Virginia it was very different from their homeland. Whereas people in England had begun to view religion in partisan terms, Virginians were happy for any religious presence at all.[71]

In 1632 Governor Harvey once again asked the Crown to send suitable ministers to England's outpost of empire on the James River. The problem was not only that there were too few clergy in Virginia, but also that many of those then resident in the colony were more inclined to card playing, drinking, and tossing dice than to prayer and quiet meditation on the Scriptures. One author described the colony's clergy as men who

---

[70] Cited in Karen Ordahl Kupperman, *Settling With the Indians: The Meeting of English and Indian Cultures in America, 1580-1640;* (Totowa NJ: Rowman & Littlefield, 1980) 165.

[71] Charges by the Virginia Company of London Against Governor John Harvey, 1635, Bankes Manuscript 8, f. 3; Bodleian Library, Oxford University, "Governor Harvey to Secretary Windebanke," *Virginia Magazine of History and Biography* 8 (1900): 161.

could "roare in a Tavern" and "babble in a Pulpet."[72] They were poor role models, and people had begun to complain. Members of the General Assembly, either unwilling to wait for a response to Harvey's request or weary of English indifference, took matters into their own hands at their next meeting, making the colony's religious establishment their first order of business. The resulting statutes marked the development of what have been called "native institutions."[73] Colonial leaders defined Virginia's Church as they had in the past, declaring that "theire bee a uniformitie throughout this colony both in substance and circumstance to the cannons and constitution of England as neere as may bee."[74] The acts of 1631 and 1632 went beyond mere establishment and also defined the religious duties of both ministers and lay people. Clergy were directed to preach at least one sermon each week, to celebrate the Eucharist at least three times a year, to spend their time reading scriptures, and to busy themselves with labor on a daily basis. Satan could tempt the idle hands of ministers as readily as those of lower class settlers. In addition, the acts enjoined ministers to catechize youth and ignorant persons in their parishes on Sunday afternoons prior to evening prayer, the Church of England's traditional time for religious instruction (and a time Puritans preferred to set aside for a second Sunday sermon).[75] Lay people wanted religious

---

[72] Hening, *Statutes at Large*, 1:158; John Hammond, *Leah and Rachel, or, The Two Fruitfull Sisters Virginia and Maryland: Their Present Condition Impartially Stated and Related* (London, 1656), in *Force, Tracts and Other Papers*, 3:14:9.

[73] Brydon, *Virginia's Mother Church*, 1:90-95.

[74] Hening, *Statutes at Large*, 1:155. The General Assembly had passed a law more strictly defining conformity in 1629, although there is no evidence that it changed Virginia's religious polity in any way. Passed as it was early in the reign of Charles I, who held more rigid ideas about orthodoxy than his father had, this law likely appeased English authorities more than it changed the colony's ecclesiastical arrangements.

[75] The Church of England's Canons of 1604 refer directly to the clergy's duty of instructing ignorant and young persons. See Reay, "Popular Religion," 97-98.

instruction, but apparently were neither attending church regularly themselves nor sending their children for catechetical lessons, situations likely aggravated by the distances people had to travel to get to their local parish and by card playing, heavy-drinking clergy whose lives showed little evidence that they were men of piety and prayer. Burgesses also instructed the laity to attend church each Sunday and holy day as well as to ensure that their children attended the minister's catechism hour each Sunday afternoon.

To enforce ecclesiastical justice, and to maintain both "quiet and peace as befitteth Christians" and an identifiably Christian cultural context, the burgesses in 1631 and 1632 charged each parish to choose two church wardens to present to the monthly court all ecclesiastical offenders: fornicators, slanderers, and Sabbath breakers. Within two years, the administration of ecclesiastical justice became the purview of the newly organized county court system. In 1634, the growing number of settlers and their increasing disbursement throughout English Virginia led the General Assembly to formalize the colony's political and legal structure by dividing Virginia into eight shires or counties and placing judicial authority in the hands of local county courts. The new county courts then took on the function of English church courts and began punishing people who refused to behave as colonial leaders expected Christians to behave. The devotional side of religion was as important to the burgesses as the judicial, and they accommodated the colony's growth in this regard by allowing ministers to appoint deacons to read services in remote areas. As Virginia expanded further, the Burgesses created additional parishes, counties, and courts to oversee the civil and religious aspects of day-to-day existence.[76]

Throughout the period from 1634 to the end of the 1650s, county courts punished ecclesiastical offenses with regularity,

---

[76] Hening, *Statutes at Large*, 1:155-56, 208; Warren M. Billings, "The Growth of Political Institutions in Virginia, 1634-1676," *William and Mary Quarterly* 3rd ser. 31 (1974): 225-30; Morton, *American Slavery, American Freedom*, 412. Morton, *Colonial Virginia*, 1:125-29.

often prescribing a specific act of public penance in addition to any civil penalties. In 1648, for instance, the Reverend Charles Grymes and the wardens of New Poquoson Parish in York County presented Oliver Segar, a laborer, for "profaneing the sabath Day by going a fishing," a lapse made worse because Grymes had celebrated the sacrament of Holy Communion that Sunday. Since Segar had abandoned the community at one of its important ritual moments, the gentlemen of the court believed he deserved a punishment greater than the usual fine for Sabbath breaking of 150 pounds of tobacco. They ordered a community-minded penance that helped other members of the community get to church more easily. The justices directed him to build a "sufficient bridge" over a local swamp, it "being ye Church way."[77] Cases such as Segar's were typical in Virginia's courts.

Segar's act of Sabbath breaking was one of the offenses most likely to result in prosecution and public penance prior to the 1660s. As the colony grew and settlers took more and more land from their cultural rivals, ministers, justices, and churchwardens singled out for prosecution those sins which they believed distinguished English Virginians from native Virginians: fornication, Sabbath breaking, and bastard bearing were all reminiscent to English minds of native ways. "Savages" did not attend church, and English people questioned native sexual morality. Kathleen Brown has claimed, in fact, that English sexual notions based on Biblical morality served as a "litmus test for barbarism that enabled the English to distinguish themselves from native peoples."[78] Prosecuting these offenses thus helped English people maintain their Christian identity in a novel environment.

---

[77] York County Deeds, Orders, and Wills, 1645-1649, Book 2, f. 386; Caroline Julia Richter, "A Community and its Neighborhoods: Charles Parish, York County, Virginia, 1630-1740" (Ph.D. diss., College of William and Mary, 1992) 211.

[78] Kathleen M. Brown, "Gender and the Genesis of a Race and Class System in Virginia, 1630-1750" (Ph.D. diss., University of Wisconsin-Madison, 1990) 73-74; Morgan, *American Slavery, American Freedom*, 412.

Beneath this colony-wide prosecution of sinful behaviors, an ecclesiastical localism was developing. The tendency had been inherent in Edwin Sandys' policy of allowing particular plantations wide latitude in conforming to the Church of England and its continued growth built upon this preexisting pattern. Different Virginia counties held different religious preferences that they revealed through their ceremonies and approaches to ecclesiastical justice. The Reverend Charles Grymes, for instance, had fled England as a Royalist exile during the English Civil War and his New Poquoson Parish in York County adhered to the Church of England.[79] About forty miles away in Nansemond County, a Puritan settlement thrived, and like other Virginians, they were often in search of a minister. There is evidence as well of Roman Catholics on the Eastern Shore, where there was some trade in crucifixes, a Roman Catholic devotional object. In 1640, Stephen Charlton, a local merchant and trader as well as a vestryman of Hungar's Parish, complained to the Accomack County Court that he had yet to receive compensation for a "silver Crucifix" he had purchased from a local doctor.[80] And Nicholas Harwood, another Accomack resident, alluded to the Roman Catholic practice of offering prayers for the dead when he stipulated in his will that the parish minister "may make a sermon for me and soe I leave this worlde desiringe all good people to pray for my soules helth."[81] Puritans, Anglicans, and Roman Catholics inhabited English Virginia and managed to get

---

[79] J. Randolph Grymes, Jr., "A Short Biographical Sketch of the Reverend Charles Grymes, Immigrant," Virginia Historical Society, 1.

[80] Ames, *Accomack-Northampton, 1632-1640*, 144-45; Susan Stitt "The Will of Stephen Charlton and Hungar's Parish Glebe," *Virginia Magazine of History and Biography* 77 (1969): 259-60. For evidence of Roman Catholics on the Eastern Shore later in the century, see Ralph T. Whitelaw, *Virginia's Eastern Shore: A History of Northampton and Accomack Counties*, 2 vols. (Richmond: Virginia Historical Society, 1951) 2:1403.

[81] Ames, *Accomack-Northampton, 1632-1640*, 54; Whitelaw, *Virginia's Eastern Shore*, 1:425. For another will containing hints of Roman Catholicism, see will of Abraham Persey, PRO CO 1/8, f. 15.

along, perhaps because the colony wide government had established a confederal system over several widely dispersed and divergent local groups, leaving plenty of room in the colony for both the beauty of holiness and the plain style of the Puritans.

This emerging localism extended to patterns of ecclesiastical justice as well as to theology and devotional practices. In York County prior to 1661, only one person was whipped for a religious offense, and he had slandered a minister, declined religious instruction, and refused to receive the sacrament of Holy Communion. He may well have been suspected of atheism. Justices in Puritan Nansemond County, however, took a harder line, and offenders there commonly received lashes in addition to penance in the public church.[82] Northampton justices testified to that county's Anglicanism when in 1646 they ordered Richard Buckland, who had written a scandalous poem about a local woman, at the "next sermon that is preached at Nussawattocks, stand at the Church door from the beginning of the 1st lesson untill the 2nd be ended with a paper upon his hat, & on it shall be written in capital letters Ininrius Libellos desireing forgiveness of God & also in particular the aforesaid defamed."[83] Reading more than one scripture lesson at divine worship was an Anglican trait; Puritans read only one because ministers' sermons contained numerous quotations from holy writ. This localism in moral reformation extended in some cases to extra-legal levels of the colony's judicial system as well. Hungar's Parish, for instance, took care of some offenses without recourse to the

---

[82] My argument comes from my survey of York County, Deeds, Orders,and Wills, Books, 1-3. The case cited is on Book 3,f. 386. See also 2, ff. 350, 387;3, ff. 1-2; Ingram, *Church Courts, Sex, and Marriage*, 52-53; Warren M. Billings, "English Legal Literature as a Source of Law and Legal Practice for Seventeenth-Century Virginia," *Virginia Magazine of History and Biography*, 87 (1979): 415; Billings, "Growth of Political Institutions in Virginia," 229. For a slightly different view, see Brown, *Good Wives, Nasty Wenches, and Anxious Patriarchs*, 96-97.

[83]"Northhampton County Records in [the] 17th Century", *Virginia Magazine of History and Biography*, 4 (1897): 407.

county courts. At least the parish vestry did so with Betsy Tucker and several other women during the summer of 1634. Tucker was a notorious gossip and scold "who, by ye violence of her tongue had made...ye neighborhood uncomfortable." William Cotton, the parish minister, had intervened and tried to bring peace to the community. Following what may have been local custom and what was certainly common English practice, he had warned Tucker three times to stop her scolding and backbiting. Despite Cotton's efforts at private persuasion, Tucker persisted in her disruptive behavior, thus forcing the parish to take the next step and formally involve the civil magistrates. After hearing the case informally, they ordered her to be ducked until she swore never to "sin in like manner again." On the appointed day at the appointed hour the Accomack sheriff led Tucker to a suitable pond where a ducking machine awaited. Public penance was a community ritual and a large crowd had gathered, some simply out of curiosity, others out of a sense of justice since they were among those injured by Tucker's scandal-mongering, and still others who wanted to see a sinner reconciled to God and the community. A witness described both machine and punishment:

> It is a platform with 4 small rollers or wheels, and two upright posts between which works a Lever by a Rope fastened to its shorter or heavier end. At ye end of ye longer arm is fixed a stool upon which sd Betsey was fastened by cords, her gown tied fast around her feete. The Machine was then moved up to the edge of ye pond, ye Rope was slackened by ye officer, and ye women was allowed to go down under ye water for the space of half a minute.

Only after being ducked five times did Tucker submit and cry out, "Let mee go! let mee go! by God's help I'll sin so no more." The public ritual complete, the sheriff released her from the machine and allowed this "hopefully penitent woman" to return home.[84] Like penance in the public church and whippings, these were visceral public punishments that appealed to the sense of sight and not only shamed sinners but also warned others of the humiliation and pain they could expect if they too chose to violate God's laws and the community's peace. No account either of Tucker's case or the three other duckings at Hungar's Parish in the summer of 1634 exists in the Accomack County Court records, suggesting the existence of informal parish or community proceedings beyond the gaze of historians, perhaps knowingly sanctioned by the county court system and the colony's General Assembly. The existence of such parish-level punishments may help account for the low number of ecclesiastical presentments in seventeenth-century Virginia.[85]

Despite a few additional scenes of this nature, what strikes the student of Virginia's religious history during the 1630s and early 1640s most is the relative peace and quiet of the colony's religious life, a quiet that did not extend to other elements of Virginia's existence. The tobacco boom had gone bust by the 1630s, its price falling from a high of three shillings per pound in the 1620s to but three pence a pound by 1639.[86] As a result, debt cases filled court dockets throughout the colony, accounting for 80 percent of all court cases in Accomack County between 1632 and 1638.[87] Persistent factionalism marked Virginia's civil polity as competing groups of wealthy men attempted to use their offices to enrich themselves at the

---

[84] "The Ducking Stool," *American Historical Record*, 1 (1872): 204-206; David Underdown, *Revel, Riot, and Rebellion: Popular Politics and Culture in England, 1603-1660* (New York: Oxford University Press, 1985) 17. Even when cases ended up in Accomack's courts, ministers often served as "arbitrators in various law suits." See Levy, "Puritanism in the Southern Colonies," 142.

[85] Horn, *Adapting to a New World*, 404-405.

[86] Morgan, *American Slavery, American Freedom*, 134-35; Russell R. Menard, "A Note on Chesapeake Tobacco Prices, 1618-1660," *Virginia Magazine of History and Biography* 84 (1975): 401-410.

[87] Kukla, "Order and Chaos," 287.

expense of rival factions. Although they competed with each other for political and economic power, Virginia's great men cooperated in zealous defense of what they believed was their collective right to manage the colony's affairs, occasionally treating royal governors as meddlesome outsiders. In 1635 they tired of Governor John Harvey, whose policies they believed ran contrary to the colony's interests, and in what has been called the "thrusting out" of the governor, seized him and shipped him back to London with a letter explaining that they hoped their actions would "be acceptable to God, not displeasing to His Majesty, and an assured happiness unto this Colony."[88] Harvey soon returned to Virginia, and the bickering between the governor and his enemies continued on both sides of the Atlantic as both groups tried to revenge themselves on the other by appealing to King Charles, mistreating their opponent's friends, and spreading tales in the taverns of London.[89] Virginia's wealthy planter leaders got along no better with inhabitants of the newly established colony of Maryland than they had with Harvey. Disturbed by the Marylanders' encroachment upon Virginia's territory and the accompanying competition to their tobacco trade, Virginians began to see residents of this new colony as enemies, not in religion but in economics.[90] Harvey wrote of the attitude of many Virginians toward the new colonists when he explained to Secretary Windebanke that many residents of the first colony "would rather knock their cattell on the heads then sell them to Maryland."[91] Strife soon arose between Marylanders and Captain William Claiborne over Kent Island in the upper reaches of the Chesapeake Bay. Claiborne

---

[88] Cited in Morton, *Colonial Virginia*, 1:137.

[89] Morton, *Colonial Virginia*, 1:136-37; Morgan, *American Slavery, American Freedom*, 145; J. Mills Thornton, "The Thrusting Out of Governor Harvey," *Virginia Magazine of History and Biography* 76 (1968): 11-26.

[90] Kukla, "Order and Chaos," 286.

[91] "Governor John Harvey to Secretary Windebanke," *Virginia Magazine of History and Biography* 8 (1900): 161.

had long roots in the colony, having served as a surveyor for the Virginia Company of London, "Indian" fighter, successful fur trader, as well as the colony's secretary, a position to which Charles I had appointed him. His fur trade centered on Kent Island, where he and a few other Virginians had established an outpost long before Lord Baltimore gained patent to the territory as a place to settle English Roman Catholics.[92]

Such contentiousness was confined neither to Virginia nor to political affairs. Settled several hundred miles to the north of Virginia, Massachusetts Bay experienced religious factionalism during these years as well, and led by a woman at that. Anne Hutchinson challenged the colony's Puritan religious establishment between 1636 and 1638 and was banished to Providence, a town founded in 1636 by Roger Williams, who too had contested the orthodoxy of Massachusetts Bay's religious practices and had likewise received a sentence of banishment.[93] In England, religious divisions began taking shape in politics as Puritan supporters of Parliament and Anglican friends of the Crown moved towards open warfare. Men there used terms of abuse such as "Puritan" and "Arminian" as cudgels with which to discredit or destroy opponents.[94] By the 1630s, James I's Church of England had broken apart. Non-separatist Puritans had already begun fleeing to Massachusetts Bay; Roman Catholics, now feeling greater persecution, had established a haven in Maryland; Puritans and Anglicans remaining in England were rapidly moving further apart. If James' church polity continued to exist at all, it did so in the first North American colony established during his reign, Virginia.

---

[92] Morton, *Colonial Virginia*, 1:134-36, 143.

[93] Edmund S. Morgan, *Roger Williams: The Church and the State* (New York: Harcourt, Brace & World, 1967).

[94] Andrew Foster, "Church Policies of the 1630s," in Richard Cust and Ann Hughes, eds., *Conflict in Early Stuart England: Studies in Religion and Politics, 1603-1642* (New York: Longman, 1989) 193-224, especially 195.

With the exception of Virginia, much of the trans-Atlantic English world between 1630 and 1660 bubbled in a cauldron of religious hostility. And unlike other facets of the colony's life, the religious element there remained fairly quiet. A few cases of Sabbath-breaking, fornication, and gossip surfaced in the county records, but the religious violence and abusive language common to England or its other North Atlantic colonies did not exist. Of course, with so few ministers in the colony, men found it difficult to find theological differences to complain about. Yet, even as Governor Harvey and the councilors squared off, neither side accused the other of irreligion or wrong belief. Three thousand miles away back in England such slurs were common. Granted, there were men in the colony who—perhaps for reasons little related to faith—made an issue of Lord Baltimore's Roman Catholicism. Even so, Virginia's statute of 1641 regarding Catholic recusants is muted. It banished priests, weather permitting, and it disabled lay Catholics from holding political office, yet it nevertheless allowed Roman Catholic lay people to remain in the colony.[95] Suspicion of Baltimore and the Marylanders reflected not so much Virginians' wariness of religious rivals as their mistrust of outsiders, especially outsiders who threatened their tobacco profits.

The contrast with contemporary England is striking. Calvinist, Laudian, Arminian, and so forth—these terms describing English religious parties rarely appeared in Virginia. More often than not Virginians described themselves simply as Christians, or, more precisely, as English Christians. The absence in the colony of the religious hostility common to early modern Europe suggests either that residents there did not care one way or the other about religious adherence or that Virginians had found a way to diffuse the religious passions of Europe. It would have been extraordinarily peculiar for religion not to matter, and there is no reason to suspect that religious faith evaporated when Englishmen and women touched American soil. Surviving the uncertainties of an Atlantic crossing, in fact, would more likely

---

[95] Hening, *Statutes at Large*, 1:268-69.

have increased an individual's devotion. The sentiments of royalist exile Henry Norwood who reached Virginia in 1650 were common: "As soon as I had set my foot on land, [I] rendred thanks to almighty God for opening this door of deliverance to us, after so many rescues even from the jaws of death at sea."[96] Nor should a quiet and unpretentious religious life necessarily show evidence of a lukewarm faith, and acceptance by historians of this position suggests their capitulation to the tyranny of Geneva. The "self-validating godly" should be allowed to set a religious standard for themselves alone.[97] For Virginians to have shown little interest in religion would have made them utterly remarkable English people. And the view fails to square with what we know of the growing importance of religion to Virginians and of their continuing desire for ministers. In the importance of the divine to their lives, Virginians were much like other English people.

Yet the colony still seems out of place. While the rest of the English trans-Atlantic world seethed with religious discontent and theological disputes, Virginia remained quiet and distinctly atypical. The colony seems out of place, however, only if one accepts the English pattern as normative, that there was but one legitimate expression of English Christianity and that all people who disagreed with that opinion were traitors, scoundrels, and heretics. For the Church of England the big question remained one of identity, of determining legitimate ecclesiology, theology, and devotional practices. And by the 1640s English people were no closer to defining their national church than they had been at the time of Virginia's founding. The institution's peculiarities only made the task more difficult for English men and women. Of all the reformed churches in the seventeenth century, the Church of England held only the vaguest notion of orthodox doctrine. No written confession outlined Anglican faith and

---

[96] Colonel [Henry] Norwood, "A Voyage to Virginia," in Force, *Tracts and Other Papers,* 3:10:20.

[97] Judith Maltby, "'By This Book,': Parishioners, the Prayer Book, and the Established Church," in *The Early Stuart Church, 1603-1642,* 116.

dogma as a guide to what constituted right belief, certainly not the Thirty-nine Articles which "allowed plenty of room for personal theological emphases and idiosyncrasies." When pressed, most authorities found truth in antiquity and simply referred to the decisions of the first four ecumenical councils held at Nicaea, Constantinople, Ephesus, and Chalcedon as the basis of Church doctrine. However, that still left plenty of room for disagreement, especially in the religiously charged atmosphere of Caroline England. Although by the 1660s the lack of theological cohesion in the Church of England became a standard joke,[98] it also ran counter to European "state-church systems" and helps account for much of the doctrinal squirming and writhing within England's later-Stuart religious polity.

What the English Reformation lacked in theological and doctrinal certitude, however, it more than made up for in its chief document, the *Book of Common Prayer*. Not a creed, a confession, or a lengthy series of anathemas, but a book of worship, it implied in its title the importance of shared devotion to God rather than common belief. "We are Englishmen and we are Christians," it seems to say, "let us pray together as Christians for the sake of our souls and for the health of the nation for that is what God demands. Whatever we may believe of grace, predestination, and other theological subtleties, these divine mysteries transcend human understanding, and perhaps it is best to leave such matters to God." Whether this arrangement was brilliant, cynical, common sensical, or splitting the middle about as sharply as it could be split, England's peculiar contribution to the Reformation (still largely intact) promised no theological unity. Rather, it asked men and women to participate in a relationship with God, to act, and to pray. Given European understandings of what constituted unity, it is not

---

[98] John Spurr, *The Restoration Church of England, 1646-1689* (New Haven: Yale University Press, 1991) 185; Paul Elmer More and Frank Leslie Cross, eds., *Anglicanism: The Thought and Practice of the Church of England, Illustrated From the Religious Literature of the Seventeenth Century* (London: S.P.C.K., 1962) 162-63.

surprising that this religious arrangement festered until Civil War erupted.

Despite what we know of the religious turmoil in Stuart England, the Church of England and the *Book of Common Prayer* embraced in theory what has been called a "rich ecumenical potential." One man who grasped the Church of England's ecumenical possibilities had ruled England from 1603 until his death in 1625: King James I. James believed Christian unity rested upon a "very limited number of crucial Catholic doctrines," and outside of these few points, various opinions on secondary issues such as predestination and the theology of grace could be tolerated as long as those holding them did not disrupt the polity.[99] Pervading England for nearly the first two decades of Virginia's existence, this atmosphere helps explain the colony's religious calm. James' broad approach to religious uniformity found a ready home in Virginia. In fact, the king's desire for "a formal acceptance of conformity, often mitigated by a good deal of tolerance of practical non-conformity or laxity,"[100] closely approximates what can be learned of Virginia's religious polity through the mid-1640s. In the colony's "novel environment" far from their English homeland, threatened by "savage" cultural rivals, and their traditional religious presence hindered by a shortage of clergy, Virginians showed little interest in the theological controversies that gripped their countrymen. Many of the few religious scenes in early seventeenth-century Virginia share an emphasis on church services and the punishment of men and women who had violated Christian morality, two elements which clearly separated civil English Christians from uncivilized, heathen natives. Shaped by a cultural environment foreign to England, short of clergy, and burdened by a weak institutional church, Virginians developed in practice an

---

[99] Davies, *Worship and Theology*, 2:224; Fincham and Lake, "The Ecclesiastical Policies of James I and Charles I," in *The Early Stuart Church*, 31.

[100] Peter Lake, "The Laudian Style: Order, Uniformity, and the Pursuit of the Beauty of Holiness in the 1630s," in *The Early Stuart Church*, 182.

ecclesiastical polity that the English Reformation had suggested in theory.

In the absence of contrary evidence, we might assume that most Virginians accepted the central tenets of the Christian faith on which all believers might agree. The preamble to Nicholas Dale's 1648 will contains no controversial elements and is typical of others: "not knoweing how soon it may please him [God] to take me out of this transitory life I commend my soule into the hands of Almighty God and Creator whoe gave it and my body to the earth from whence it came to be buried in Christian buriall...trusting and believing through the merritts of Iesus Christ my only sauiour and Redeemer to rise again to life euerlasting."[101] Beyond these verities, we might also assume that Virginians believed the Bible was true and that good Christians should worship God and follow the commandments. In all likelihood, most Virginia parishes also used the *Book of Common Prayer* or closely followed its order. The extant evidence, though fragmentary, suggests that even Puritan-minded settlers used this service book. In 1643, Basil Haynes and Julia Underwood of Lower Norfolk, a Puritan stronghold on the south side of the James River, were found guilty of adultery and ordered to atone for their sin by making "a public acknowledgement of their fault" and by asking God's forgiveness "in time of divine service, between the first and second lessons in the forenoon," a

---

[101] York County, DOW (2), f. 366. See also James Blair, *Our Saviour's Divine Sermon on the Mount, Contain'd in the Vth, VIth, and VIIth chapters of St. Matthew's Gospel, Explained; and the Practice of it Recommended in divers Sermons and Discourses*, 5 vols. (London:) 5:177-78, 203, where he defines faith: "Christian Faith, implies not only a Belief in God, but a Belief and Trust in the Mediation and Intercession of Jesus Christ...Faith implies not only a general Belief in God, and that he is to be addressed through the Mediation of Jesus Christ; but likewise a Belief of this particular Promise, that God for Christ's sake will hear and grant our Prayers...Faith, is a fundamental Duty we owe to God; now as this is necessarily presupposed as the Foundation of all our Prayers...so it is chiefly conversant about his Goodness; one Instance of which, namely, his sending Christ into the World to bring us to Heaven, is the Foundation of all our Faith."

description reflecting Anglican peculiarities and the *Book of Common Prayer's* morning prayer service. Puritans traditionally punished sinners in the afternoon rather than at the morning service. They also tended to read but one passage of scripture at each meeting—unlike the several lessons in the *Book of Common Prayer*—because Puritan ministers included numerous Biblical quotations in their sermons.[102] Along with moral behavior, the *Book of Common Prayer* may have given Virginia's diverse religious elements some additional measure of unity. It appears in numerous estate inventories, and phrases from its burial service occasionally appear in the preambles of Virginians' wills. On the more troubling issues of predestination and the nature of the sacraments, however, Virginians were silent, leaving those matters to individual settlers and God. As a political society, behavior, including the fact of worship rather than its practice, united the colonists, not theology.

Virginia's religious polity had emerged out of numerous sources, from England's soteriology of empire to the Virginia Company's desire to fill the colony with settlers, from the rough and rude men who populated Virginia during the colony's earliest years to the native cultural rivals who peopled the land, and it gradually became the colony's customary arrangement (although it may have taken shape in a less conscious way than we might care to believe). England's soteriology of empire had stressed the importance of behaviors pleasing to God rather than the strict doctrinal purity of a religious faction. Colonial authorities too had emphasized behavior, not only because they believed that labor and morality pleased God but also because these behaviors provided clear evidence of English differences from native Virginians, a people who colonists believed possessed

---

[102] Norfolk County Record Book, 1637-1646, ff. 225-26; "Lower Norfolk County Records, 1636-1646," *Virginia Magazine of History and Biography* 40 (1932): 41-43: Charles E. Hambrick-Stowe, *The Practice of Piety: Puritan Devotional Disciplines in Seventeenth-Century New England* (Chapel Hill: University of North Carolina Press, 1982) 110, 130; Davies, *Worship and Theology in England*, 1:266.

neither Christianity, Biblical morality, nor industrious work habits.

The development of the colony's religious system was also part of the colonial leaders' intellectual milieu. Prior to 1641, the men who ruled Virginia had come to maturity in the England of Elizabeth and James I and had thereby imbibed the political craftsmanship of the Elizabethan Settlement and its Jacobean consolidation. They had seen the wisdom of political unity coupled with religious ambiguity. The image of martyrs, Protestant and Roman Catholic alike, burning for a faith they did not share in an England that only embraced these opinions by turn gave way before a polity that found a place for both. Company and resident leaders lived in an England shaped by a king who had allowed men of differing religious views a great luxury: to love both their God and their England. He allowed men the opportunity to be arrogant for England rather than partisan for religious party theology.[103] Men of this age founded Virginia and shaped its polity for over a decade after James' death in 1625. And Virginia's religious polity continued to reflect Jacobean ideals long after the strife-ridden church of Charles I began to come apart. Here was a "city upon a hill" had anyone cared to pay attention to the colony for something greater than the profits it might bring in smoke.

England changed, not Virginia. The colony remained stuck in a religious world out of place in the 1640s, and despite the colony's growing religious sentiments, denies them completely because its difference from the rest of the English world makes it seem as though religion did not matter. It is this quiet which is so extraordinary and bids us to listen to the achievement. It is the Puritan hegemony of Massachusetts Bay and the strife-ridden Church of Charles I which do not fit the Jacobean model. James had crafted a more conciliatory and expansive Church than his son or his son's archbishop of Canterbury, William Laud, could

---

[103] Fincham and Lake, "The Ecclesiastical Policies of James I and Charles I," 23-49, especially 23-24.

abide.[104] James' hopes, were of a more modern time, and there are clear hints in early Virginia of a Lockean religious world. It was yet neither John Locke's toleration nor Thomas Jefferson's "wall of separation," but the pattern had been set. Several disruptions would arise to challenge the silence and calm of Virginia's customary practice, but the custom returned. Ultimately, it would gain the force of law.

One disruption to Virginia's Jacobean religious polity occurred in the early 1640s, and the incident was directly related to the colony's new governor, Sir William Berkeley. A staunch royalist and firm advocate of the Church of England, Berkeley represented something of a shift in Virginia's governmental structure. Foremost, the new governor was of a different generation than Virginia's earlier leaders. Born in 1605, the thirty-seven-year-old Berkeley had come of age in Caroline England. After an education at Oxford and the Middle Temple, followed by the requisite European tour, Berkeley spent a decade at the court of Charles I. And Charles' religious views were not those of his father James. Where James had found unity in his ambiguous ecclesiastical policies, Charles saw merely illusions and inconsistency. He believed the lack of doctrinal and ceremonial uniformity tolerated by his father had allowed the Puritan menace to emerge as a threat to the concept of monarchy. His fear of Puritans led him to transform the Oath of Allegiance—originally designed to check Roman Catholics—into a device for attacking Protestant nonconformists. Taken as a whole, Charles replaced James' flexibility and accommodation to all but the most extreme nonconformists and recusants with new policies emphasizing order, deference, and authority. During his ten years at court, Berkeley had either picked up similar ideas

---

[104] James, in fact, refused to elevate Laud to Canterbury. In 1621, James had made Laud bishop of St. David's, perhaps as a result of pressure from Charles.

about the threat of Puritans to the polity or had his own ideas confirmed by men in high places.[105]

From Charles' court, Berkeley arrived in Virginia to fill his new post in February 1642 with instructions identical to those of the colony's preceding governors. Identical instructions or not, this Caroline courtier and devout Anglican took a more partisan position than earlier leaders had on the admonition that Almighty God be "served according to the form of religion established in the Church of England both by yourself and all the people under your charge." The colony's entire religious organization may well have surprised the recent immigrant, running contrary as it did to contemporary English attitudes. Virginia's General Assembly unwittingly made a potentially uncomfortable situation more difficult by making preparations at its 1642 session to divide Lower Norfolk County into three parishes. Puritans populated this Southside region and had lived there for years unpersecuted on account of their religious opinions. "Godly" immigrants had begun settling the area in 1621, first at Edward Bennett's particular plantation, then at neighboring settlements established by Christopher Lawne and Nathaniel Basse. Despite suffering tremendous casualties during the Powhatan uprising of 1622 and the ensuing Anglo-Indian War, their numbers had recovered and by 1642 a sizable community of Puritan Virginians made their homes in the counties of Lower Norfolk, Nansemond, and Isle of Wight. They "lived together in their place," as a conforming minister later put it, working, raising families, planting tobacco, and scattering across the land in order to plant more of the weed much like other Virginians with whom they seemed to be on good terms. With the exception of an Anglican minister or two, few of the other settlers had complained about their presence. The

---

[105] Biographical Sketch, Warren M. Billings, ed., *The Papers of Sir William Berkeley, 1605-1677* (forthcoming); Stephen D. Crow, "'Your Majesty's Good Subjects': A Reconsideration of Royalism in Virginia, 1642-1652," *Virginia Magazine of History and Biography* 87 (1979): 158-73; Fincham and Lake, "Ecclesiastical Policies of James I and Charles I," 49.

Southside Puritans were active and accepted participants as well in the colonywide life of Virginia's polity. They sent representatives to the General Assembly, and at least one Lower Norfolk nonconformist, the wealthy Richard Bennett, served on the governor's Council. And like other settlers, they also endured a shortage of clergy. Lacking "godly" ministers to lead them, some of the Puritan settlers had begun "backsliding" and falling away either to irreligion or to the Anglican wing of the Church of England. They lived, wrote one of the Puritans, William Durand, "scattered in the cloudy and darke day of temptation, beeing fallen from their first love, and are even as the wife of youth forsaken and desolate." In the summer of 1642, the Southside Puritans attempted to remedy the situation by asking their brethren in New England to send three "godly" ministers to serve the county's three parishes.[106]

If Berkeley had indeed found Virginia's religious arrangement surprising, he was no doubt shocked in January 1643 when three Puritan divines from Boston showed up in Jamestown carrying letters of introduction from Governor John Winthrop of Massachusetts Bay who described the ministers as "seed sown, which would bring us in a plentiful harvest." William Thompson, John Knowles, and Thomas James had come in response to the Puritans' plea the previous summer for clergy and planned to settle in Lower Norfolk and minister to the people who lived there. Their plan had been widely known throughout the colony among both conforming and nonconforming Virginians. Aware of the religious deficiencies under which they all suffered, most settlers either approved of the Southside Puritans' proposal or

---

[106] Biographical Sketch, Billings, ed. Berkeley Papers; Charles I, Instructions to Sir William Berkeley, 10 August 1641, PRO CO 5/1354; Hening, *Statutes at Large*, 1:250-51, 287; Bruce, *Institutional History*, I:253; Edward Johnson to John Ferrar, 25 March 1650, Ferrar Papers, f. 1160, Magdalene College, Cambridge University; Jon Butler, ed., "Two 1642 Letters from Virginia Puritans," *Massachusetts Historical Society Proceedings* 84 (1972): 99-109, quotation on 108; Butler, *Awash in a Sea of Faith*, 47; Horn, *Adapting to a New World*, 389-90.

kept their complaints private. Members of the colony's General Assembly, in fact, planned to make a provision in law for people on the Southside by dividing the area into three parishes, one for each of the three immigrant Puritan ministers.[107]

Berkeley, however, considered the arrival of Puritan religious leaders a threat to the colony's political and ecclesiastical order. Knowing the English Civil War between Puritan supporters of Parliament and royalist defenders of Charles I had broken out a few months earlier only intensified the governor's fears, thus making the situation in Virginia more tense. Berkeley banished the three ministers, two of who soon returned to New England. Thompson, however, found the colony pleasing to him both in body and spirit, and despite the governor's threats, remained in Virginia and continued his work, making, in the words of Cotton Matther, a "constellation of great converts there."[108]

Likely at Berkeley's prodding, the General Assembly passed at its next session an act for the "preservation of the puritie of doctrine & unitie of the church" which required all ministers in the colony to be "conformable to the order and constitution of the church of England...and not otherwise to be admitted to teach or preach publickly or privately." The law further demanded that upon due notice of their offense, "all nonconformists" be compelled to leave the colony.[109] It not only represented a striking breach with the colony's customary practices but also differed radically from a similar statute dealing with Roman Catholics passed at the same session. The act regulating colonial recusants merely repeated the provisions of

---

[107] Morton, *Colonial Virginia*, 1:151-52; James Kendall Hosmer, ed. *Winthrop's Journal: "History of New England," 1630-1649*, 2 vols. (New York: Charles Scribner's Sons, 1908) 2:73-74; Butler, "Two 1642 Letters from Virginia Puritans," 104, 109.

[108] Morton, *Colonial Virginia*, 1:151-52; Butler, "Two 1642 Letters from Virginia Puritans," 99; Cotton Mather, *Magnalia Christi Americana; or, The Ecclesiastical History of New England...* (1792; rpt. Hartford CT: 1855) 1:440.

[109] Hening, *Statutes at Large*, 1:277.

an act passed two years earlier, and therefore introduced no new ideas into Virginia's religious establishment. Like the Burgesses' previous law, it disabled all people who refused to take the oaths of allegiance and supremacy from holding public offices and banished from the colony any Roman Catholic priests. Catholic lay people, however, could remain.[110] Taken together these two statutes represented an attempt to modify Virginia's ecclesiastical polity and bring it more in line with Charles I's Church of England. Uneven treatment of nonconformists and recusants was typical of Charles for he did not equate these religious minorities as threats. Puritanism loomed far larger to him as a disruptive force in need of control, and Virginia's own departure under Governor Berkeley reflected the position of the king to whom he was devoted.

In his efforts to ensure the loyalty of Virginia's Puritans during a time of civil war, Berkeley also borrowed tactics used earlier by Charles I. He ordered all colonists to swear an oath of allegiance to Charles or face sanctions for their refusal. One Puritan Virginian suggested in 1644 that Berkeley's innovations may have brought the colonists close to war over religion themselves when he complained that "divers of the most religious and honest inhabitants, were mark't out to be plundered and imprisoned for the refusall of an Oath that was imposed upon the people, in reference to the king of England." By forcing a special oath upon Virginians, Berkeley once again adopted the tactics of his monarch who had transformed the original anti-Roman Catholic intent of the Jacobean Oath of Allegiance into an instrument with which to attack English Puritans soft on monarchy. Berkeley blundered less in his dealings with Virginia's religious minorities than Charles did with England's Puritans, but he nevertheless threw a people otherwise content in their religious ambiguity into a "great mischiefe." As a result, Virginians grew more contentious in their

---

[110] Hening, *Statutes at Large,* 1:268-69.

dealings with those who did not share their religious opinions and came close to open warfare themselves.[111]

Other hostilities, however, reminded Virginians that Englishmen though they were, Virginia was not England and radically different circumstances shaped the colony's religious polity. In April 1644, Opechancanough, now old, feeble, and nearly blind, rallied what remained of the old Powhatan Confederacy in one last attempt to drive the English from his ancestral homeland. A brief skirmish on the James River between a London ship supporting Parliament and a ship from Bristol supporting the king led the natives to believe English colonists were at war with each other and thus might enjoy a good chance of success. Although the attack came as a surprise, at least a few colonists suspected that the natives were up to something. Virginians, like most people in the early-modern world, believed in signs and portents. Strange or unexplained phenomena might be premonitions sent by God to warn of difficult events in the near future.[112]

In the spring of 1644, an anonymous colonist saw what he believed were disturbing indications of impending judgments. While washing a bucket of clothes on the first of April, his wife had noticed globs of blood in the wash pail. Alarmed, she called her husband, who stirred the gore, only to discover that the blood stained neither his hands nor the dirty linens. Taking this as a sign from God portending "some designe of the Indians," he made preparations to defend his dwelling. Seventeen days later,

---

[111] Kukla, "Order and Chaos," 291; Joseph Frank, ed., "News From Virginny, 1644" *Virginia Magazine of History and Biography* 65 (1957): 85; Fincham and Lake, "Ecclesiastical Policies of James I and Charles I," 49.

[112] Morton, *Colonial Virginia*, 1:153-54; Hosmer, *Winthrop's Journal*, 2:168. "The Beginning, Progress, and Conclusion of Bacon's Rebellion, 1675-1676," in Charles M. Andrews, ed., *Narratives of the Insurrections, 1675-1690* (Bowie MD: Heritage Books, 1992) 15-16. Additional references to portents may be found in Original Letters, John Catlett to Thomas Catlett, 1 April 1664, John D. Rockefeller, Jr. Library, Colonial Williamsburg Foundation; Ashmolean MS 242, f. 126, Bodleian Library, Oxford; and Nicholas Perry to King Charles II, PRO CO 1/21, ff. 126-27.

on Maundy Thursday, Opechancanough attacked. It succeeded; nearly five hundred settlers fell to native warriors that day.[113] The assault revealed to Virginians on the verge of war with each other that given their North American context, perhaps Puritan Virginians and Anglican Virginians had more in common with each other than their nascent religious factionalism might have suggested. The massacre pulled the remaining colonists together to fight against a common enemy, thus containing any potential violence based on disagreements about theology or devotional practices. The Anglo-Indian War of 1644-1646 was a "hinge-point" in Virginia's history, a moment when the colony's history could have swung dramatically in another direction.

A few months after hostilities broke out, Berkeley returned to England on a mission to acquire weapons with which to fight Opechancanough. Once there, and aware of Charles' difficulties, he stayed for nearly a year and helped to fight the Roundhead champions of Parliament. He returned to Virginia in June 1645 and found war with the natives still smoldering. Sir William quickly gained control of the situation, took the fight to the old chief, and captured him. Within a year the natives sued for peace.[114] In the aftermath of the Anglo-Indian War and his brief but turbulent sojourn in England, Berkeley abandoned his former practice of compelling religious uniformity through force, and, with the exception of the most extreme elements, stopped his harassment of lay Puritans.[115]

Berkeley's new approach posed a brilliant solution to the problem of a religious minority largely confined to a few parishes in one geographic area. Rather than banishing nonconformists or forcing oaths of allegiance upon them, the General Assembly passed an act in 1647 allowing parishioners the freedom to withhold tithes from ministers who refused to read services from

---

[113] Frank, "News From Virginny, 1644," 87; Morton, *Colonial Virginia*, 1:153.

[114] Biographical Sketch, Billings, ed., *Berkeley Papers*; Morton, *Colonial Virginia*, 1:154.

[115] Kukla, "Order and Chaos," 291.

the *Book of Common Prayer*.[116] Although formally upholding the Church of England as the colony's established church, the statute still allowed a great deal of local flexibility and may have been designed as well to spare any conforming congregations who somehow found themselves saddled with a Puritan divine from the indignity of supporting a minister whose orthodoxy they questioned. Since vestries by an act of 1643 chose ministers for their parishes,[117] such controversies must have been rare. If the vestry and parishioners of a particular parish, however, chose to hire a dissenting minister, the law allowed them to pay him just as conforming parishes supported conforming ministers. As a practical matter, the issue of whether or not to pay a nonconformist clergyman was largely moot. The question remained not one of what ministers believed, but if there would ever be enough of them to fill the colony's growing number of parishes.

Yet one incident did occur, and it may have been the motivation behind the Assembly's 1647 law. Controversy broke out in the mid-1640s concerning the governor's former chaplain, the Reverend Thomas Harrison, who had been converted to the godly way, possibly by the tarrying Mr. Thompson. Harrison served the church at Elizabeth River, a parish in Lower Norfolk County divided against itself. Church wardens Matthew Phillips and Thomas Ivey, who had the power to present ecclesiastical offenders, were Anglicans who preferred the *Book of Common Prayer* and its rites. Most of Elizabeth River's parishioners, however, favored Harrison and his brand of Puritanism. In 1645 the wardens haled their minister before the county court for "not reading the booke of Common Prayer and for not adminstring the Sacrament of Baptisme according to the Cannons and order pscribed and for not Catechising on

---

[116] Hening, *Statutes at Large*, 1:341-42.

[117] Brydon, *Virginia's Mother Church*, 1:91-92; Hening, *Statutes at Large*, 1:302; John Frederick Woolverton, *Colonial Anglicanism in North America* (Detroit: Wayne State University Press, 1984) 77-78.

Sunnedayes in the afternoone according to Act of Assembly."[118] The gentlemen of the court avoided a decision and referred the matter to Berkeley and his Council. After meeting with Harrison they decided that he could remain at his post. Historians have speculated about what went on at this meeting—whether Harrison promised to conform, whether the governor showed unusual leniency to a close acquaintance, or whether Berkeley and the Council gave the minister a set period in which to conform to the cannons of the Church of England.[119] Given the circumstances of Harrison's case, Virginia's Jacobean religious polity suggests another answer. "Under Charles I, nonconformist clergy escaped prosecution by promising to conform; under James I, it was sufficient to promise to confer about conforming,"[120] which is exactly what Harrison had done. He continued his ministry to the people of the Southside until early in 1648, when he left Virginia, bound first for Boston (where he married one of Governor Winthrop's cousins) and then Ireland.[121] Harrison may have been banished by Berkeley in 1648, certainly the Puritan Parliament believed this to be the case, and they censured the governor for allegedly depriving Harrison of his living.[122] But he may just as likely have left Virginia for love or to spread the Parliamentary cause in Ireland where he served as chaplain to Henry Cromwell. A debt action filed against him in the Lower Norfolk courts might also help explain his sudden disappearance from the colony.[123]

---

[118] "The Church in Lower Norfolk County," *The Lower Norfolk County Virginia Antiquary* 2 (1897-1899): 12.

[119] Morton, *Colonial Virginia*, 1:152; Babette Levy, "Early Puritanism in the Southern and Island Colonies," 127; Butler, *Awash in a Sea of Faith*, 47; Horn, *Adapting to a New World*, 391.

[120] Kenneth Fincham, *Prelate as Pastor: The Episcopate of James I* (New York: Oxford University Press, 1990) 228-29.

[121] Morton, *Colonial Virginia*, 1:152.

[122] Public Records Office, State Papers, Domestic 25/84, f. 482.

[123] "The Church in Lower Norfolk County," *Lower Norfolk County Virginia Antiquary* 2 (1897-1899): 13. Harrison's saga is treated in Bruce, *Institutional History*, 255-57; Davis, *Intellectual Life in the Colonial South*,

With Lower Norfolk once again destitute of clergy, a layman named William Durand took it upon himself to begin preaching the Gospel to his brethren, relying upon notes from Puritan sermons that he had heard in England. This was highly irregular activity, both for conformists and nonconformists alike. To make matters worse, Durand began to develop a following that some people viewed as a "faction."[124] Certainly beyond the bounds of acceptable religious behavior, Durand was ordered to leave Virginia. He and many of his followers left the colony for Maryland by late in 1649, a departure that delighted the Reverend Edward Johnson, a friend of the Ferrar family. From his parish on Mulberry Island, Johnson wrote John Ferrar that he was "glad we are soe quitt of them." Other correspondents of the Ferrar's in Virginia held more moderate views. Mitch Upchurch saw little problem with the colony's Puritans, since no "New England men" had come down to meddle in Virginia's affairs. "They are at peace with al men," he wrote to John Ferrar's daughter, Virginia, a sentiment echoed by John Stirrup as well.[125]

With this source of contention gone, the parish's life once again settled down to dull order. Parishioners elected a vestry, half of whom had been presented to the county court by the other half a few months earlier as "seditious sectaries" who refused to hear prayers from the *Book of Common Prayer*, and together this group hired a new minister and returned the parish

---

2:644; Levy, "Puritanism in the Southern and Island Colonies," 126-30; Butler, *Awash in a Sea of Faith*, 46-47; Brydon, *Virginia's Mother Church*, 1:120-21; Winthrop's Journal, *William and Mary Quarterly* 1st ser. 13 (1905-1905): 54-56; Francis Burton Harrison, "The Reverend Thomas Harrison, Berkeley's 'Chaplain,'" *Virginia Magazine of History and Biography* 53 (1945) 302-311.

[124] "The Church in Lower Norfolk County," *Lower Norfolk County Virginia Antiquary* 2 (1897-1899): 15.

[125] Edward Johnson to John Ferrar, 25 March 1650, f. 1160; Mitch Upchurch to Virginia Ferrar, 27 March 1651, f. 1204; John Stirrup to John Ferrar, 26 January 1649/50, f. 1151; all in the Ferrar Papers, Magdalene College, Cambridge University.

to its peaceable and quiet existence.[126] The congregation at Elizabeth River left no record of its internal divisions over theology and worship. Yet it seems likely that the entire Durand matter came about as moderate and radical Puritans contended for control of the parish once their previous minister left, using the *Book of Common Prayer* as a means of getting colony-wide authorities involved. Durand probably led a faction more radical than the other, and he in fact turned to Quakerism in Maryland, perhaps suggesting a disturbing proclivity to adopt the violent and confrontational tactics of the early Friends.[127]

---

[126] "The Church in Lower Norfolk County," *Lower Norfolk County Virginia Antiquary* 2 (1897-1899): 14-17; Horn, *Adapting to a New World*, 391-93.

[127] Tension simmered into the next decade, and it revealed a peculiar aspect of Virginia's ecclesiastical localism. Sampson Calvert, the first minister the parish had hired after the departure of Durand, the lay preacher, had been convicted six months after his arrival of committing adultery with a parishioner's wife. After enduring the humiliation of reading his confession to the congregation of Elizabeth River Parish on two successive Sundays, Calvert left the colony. A subsequent clergyman died a year or so into his term, leaving the county once again without a minister. In 1654, a "General Inquest" presented the entire county for breach of the Sabbath since no ministers were then resident despite continued efforts by the people to attract a clergyman. The problem was not merely that there was no minister in the county, but that none cared to preach God's word to the settlers of Lower Norfolk. County representatives had contacted several prospects, but none wanted to harvest the godly in this troubled field. Confronted by this series of disappointments, the people of Lower Norfolk started to do what members of many other early-modern communities did in times of crisis, they began accusing their neighbors of witchcraft. Like Essex County in England, although on a much smaller scale, witchcraft accusations were far more prevalent in Lower Norfolk than in any other Virginia County. Residents of that region had endured a series of religious difficulties, and by 1655 tensions were once again running high. These were serious allegations for which an individual could be banished or executed. Virginians, like other people of that era, believed in the existence of witches and their ability to harm both individuals and property by using supernatural powers. From time to time, settlers in the colony had accused suspected witches of

With Durand's departure overt religious conflict in Lower Norfolk County came to an end, and Virginians spent much of the remainder of the Interregnum in relative peace as the colony's religious polity of the 1650s continued practices developed years earlier in the 1620s. Decades of custom backed that arrangement by mid-century. In the context of the larger English world, Virginia's few pseudo-theological controversies are almost laughable and seem more like petty bickering than serious disputes, a farce in which custom wins out over innovation, even when that custom to the minds of many English authorities was the innovation. Some men of different persuasions, to be sure, held private animosities against those who did not share their beliefs, but they did not allow their private opinions to upset the public polity. Anthony Langston, a royalist planter who had fought for the monarchy during the

---

prophesying deaths, causing the deaths of animals, making people ill, and, in one case, of hindering a man's ability to shoot and kill game. Although allegations of witchcraft were extraordinarily rare in Virginia, the problem had become so great in Lower Norfolk by 1655 that the county's justices went beyond existing colonial statutes and ordered anyone making a false accusation of witchcraft to pay a fine of 1,000 pounds tobacco, a sizable sum. Residents of Lower Norfolk were far more likely than other Virginians to suspect their neighbors of using occult powers, and witchcraft accusations plagued the county's justices throughout the second half of the seventeenth century, a peculiar facet of the county's localism, and likely evidence of the county's continuing social tension. Bruce, *Institutional History of Virginia in the Seventeenth Century*, 1:210; Lower Norfolk County Records, 1646-1651, f. 129; Horn, *Adapting to a New World*, 393. On witchcraft in seventeenth-century Virginia, see Richard Beale Davis, "The Devil in Virginia in the Seventeenth Century," *Virginia Magazine of History and Biography* 65 (1957): 131-49; Butler, *Awash in a Sea of Faith*, 68-70, 83, 85-86; Horn, *Adapting to a New World*, 411-18; McIlwaine, *Minutes of the Council and the General Court of Colonial Virginia*, 111-12, 114; Bruce, *Institutional History of Virginia in the Seventeenth Century*, 1:278-88. The abundance of witchcraft cases in one location is hardly unique in the early-modern world. In England, a great many cases appear in Essex County while other counties record none.

English Civil War, enthusiastically described the colony's polity in the 1650s when he portrayed Virginia as a place where men could "take up Land (untaken before) and there seat, build, clear, and plant without any manner of restraint from the Government in relation to their Religion, and gods Service."[128]

Virginia's surrender to Oliver Cromwell's Commonwealth forces changed the colony little. Three of the four commissioners had spent long periods in Virginia and had ready experience with the colony's ways.[129] When the Commonwealth representatives and their forces arrived, Governor Berkeley called out the militia and made a great show of force before he and the House of Burgesses formally agreed to surrender. The terms were liberal. Those regarding religion allowed colonists use of the *Book of Common Prayer* for one year if the majority in a parish wanted it—although this service book had been outlawed in England—a condition which recognized Virginia's ecclesiastical localism. Even the customary Anglican practices of shooting guns and drinking healths at weddings and funerals, the latter a practice Puritans despised, were allowed to continue. Rooted in Virginia's peculiar circumstances themselves, the commissioners were more liberal than their instructions, and Anglican Virginians went unmolested in their use of the prayer book long after the year-long deadline had expired.[130]

After surrendering Virginia to the Commonwealth, Sir William retired to his Green Spring estate about three miles from the capital at Jamestown and reflected upon his efforts to

---

[128] Horn, *Adapting to a New World*, 140; "Anthony Langston on Towns and Corporations; and on the Manufacture of Iron," *William and Mary Quarterly* 2nd ser. 1 (1921): 100-106; *Virginia Magazine of History and Biography* 1 (1893-1894): 453; *Virginia Magazine of History and Biography* 28 (1920): 139-40.

[129] Morton, *Colonial Virginia*, 1:171-73.

[130] Morton, *Colonial Virginia*, 1:173, 180; Hening, *Statutes at Large*, 1:401-402; William H. Seiler, "The Church of England as the Established Church in Seventeenth-Century Virginia," *Journal of Southern History* 15 (1949): 488; Brydon, *Virginia's Mother Church*, 1:123.

diversify the economy of his adopted "country."[131] The
Burgesses interrupted his retirement in 1660, asking Berkeley to
become Virginia's governor once again. He accepted and served
as the colony's last governor under Cromwell's Protectorate and
as the first royal governor under Charles II's restored monarchy.
Back in power, however, Berkeley did not disrupt Virginia's
religious polity again. Although he still nursed a private hatred
of Puritans and would later interpret King Philip's War in New
England as God's judgment upon men who sought Charles I's
death,[132] he left Virginia's Puritans alone. Moderate Puritans
Daniel Richardson (fl. 1660-1676) of Hungars' Parish and
Francis Doughty (fl. 1648-1668), who was the minister in turn at
Hungars', Farnham, and Sittenbourne parishes, served Virginia
parishes unharrassed for their nonconformity during the
remainder of Berkeley's tenure as Virginia's governor.[133]

Why did William Berkeley change his course? Any answer is
speculative, for the governor left no explanation. Perhaps the
fighting that Berkeley had observed during his sojourn to
England in 1645 frightened him or led him to realize that this
was no way to administer either a country or a colony. Maybe
the shift had something to do with Berkeley's personality. Hot
tempered to begin with, Sir William's tenure in Virginia was
marked by periodic episodes of anger followed closely by
accommodation. Often directed at religious minorities with
whom he disagreed, his blustering and threatening ultimately
gave way to more conciliatory responses. He reacted this way

---

[131] Warren M. Billings, "Sir William Berkeley and the Diversification of
the Virginia Economy," *Virginia Magazine of History and Biography* 104
(1996): 444.

[132] Sir William Berkeley to Secretary Coventry, 2 February 1676/77,
Coventry Papers of the Marquess of Bath, Longleat House, vol. 77, ff. 356-
59, Biographical Sketch, Billings, ed. Berkeley Papers.

[133] Butler, *Awash in a Sea of Faith*, 47; Brydon, *Virginia's Mother
Church*, 1:131; *Virginia Magazine of History and Biography* 5 (1897-1898):
288. For a very different view of Berkeley and the Puritans, see Brydon,
1:117-23.

with Puritans in 1643, representatives of the Commonwealth in 1652, and followed the same course with Quaker missionaries in the early 1660s. In each case, a surprising amiability followed the initial rage. Or perhaps the governor simply came to see the wisdom of Virginia's pre-existing, Jacobean religious polity. Such a course may have come naturally over time to a man like Berkeley who identified so closely with the people he ruled and whose interests he consistently advanced over a thirty-four-year career in the colony.[134] And part of being a Virginian by mid-century meant providing a comfortable degree of religious accommodation. Governor Berkeley, in the light of power and at the center of events, may have undergone publicly a transition to Virginia's ecclesiastical arrangement that other immigrants accomplished privately. Perhaps becoming a Virginian meant returning to the England of James I or leaping ahead to the theoretical one John Locke constructed in his *Letter on Toleration*. Virginians by 1650 were stumbling towards a Lockean religious world long before Locke ever wrote. At the very least, they had come to embrace the idea that religious opponents could peacefully coexist within the same polity.

Yet Virginia's leaders rarely accepted religious minorities immediately, and an additional disruption to the colony's religious polity took place towards the end of the 1650s. Members of perhaps the most radical religious sect to emerge out of the English Civil War, Quaker missionaries arrived in Virginia for the first time in the late 1650s. As a religious movement, Quakerism offered both an antidote to Puritanism and an alternative to the formal liturgical style of the Church of England. Friends preached the message of general redemption, by which they meant all men could be saved, not just those God had predestined to heaven, a doctrine not completely at odds with the Church of England's soteriology.[135] In England as well

---

[134] Kukla, "Order and Chaos," 291-92; Biographical Sketch, Billings, ed., *Berkeley Papers.*

[135] Rufus Matthew Jones, *The Quakers in the American Colonies* (London: McMillan and Company, 1911) 265-69; Howard Beeth, "Outside

as Virginia, Quakers drew converts among anxious Puritans to whom the Friends' broad offer of salvation to all men offered greater solace than John Calvin's ironclad predestinarianism. George Fox, the movement's founder, was one of those who took the path from Puritanism to a more radical religious expression. Calvin's doctrine brought the Puritan Fox no comfort, and he spent many of his pre-Quaker days sitting in a hollow tree contemplating his despair. Counsel from conformist and nonconformist ministers alike failed to heal his brokenness of spirit. Tobacco, acquaintances suggested, or perhaps a good bloodletting might cure his malaise. Yet Fox found no comfort. Peace finally came to him through a direct revelation from God: "The Lord hath opened to me by his invisible power how that every man was enlightened by the divine light of Christ." Consequently he and the Quakers saw no need for ministers to act as spiritual intermediaries or superiors for the laity or for formal liturgical spaces or rituals. Quakerism as a devotional movement emphasized a quiet, meditative faith based on the existence in each individual of what they called the "Inner Light." If men and women only opened their hearts in faith, God would respond by feeding their souls with divine grace, helping them to lead holy and moral lives. Men and women could open their hearts to the divine anywhere, in a barn, on a ship, or outdoors in the forest, as easily as in a church.[136]

Virginia's deficiencies made the colony a near perfect setting in which Quakerism could take root and flourish. To Quakers,

---

Agitators in Southern History: The Society of Friends, 1656-1800" (Ph.D. dissertation: University of Houston, 1984) 292; J. F. McGregor, "The Baptists: Font of All Heresy," in J. F. McGregor and B. Reay, eds., *Radical Religion in the English Revolution* (New York: Oxford University Press, 1984) 61. See chapter 5 for a discussion of Anglican soteriology and theology.

[136] Michael R. Watts, *The Dissenters: From the Reformation to the French Revolution* (New York: Oxford University Press, 1978) 186-88, 200-203; B. Reay, "Quakerism and Society," in *Radical Religion*, 141-43; Horn, *Adapting to a New World*, 398-99.

the shortage of ministers and the scattered population, which so
hampered the worship of both Puritan and Anglican Virginians,
were but minor inconveniences since the faithful needed neither
clergy nor formal places for worship. To people unchurched by
circumstances more than by choice, Quakerism offered a viable
pastoral alternative to both Puritanism and the Church of
England.[137]

Many Virginians welcomed the Friends. Their simple faith
and direct appeal to God won converts among slaves, elites,
servants, and middle class farmers alike. Elizabeth Harris, the
first Quaker missionary to the colony, arrived in 1656, and she
received opposition from neither church nor state. Some people
may have found a local Quaker meeting more convenient than
the long trek through wind, rain, and heat to the parish church
or chapel of ease, while servants and slaves likely found the
Friends' teachings about the spiritual equality of all persons a
reaffirmation of their worth as human beings in a setting where
they were valued only for their labor. Chesapeake Friends
"provided a religious environment in which marriages could be
solemnized, God worshipped with apostolic purity, and children
raised in a vibrant Protestant atmosphere,"[138] all without the
difficulties that the shortage of clergy and Virginians'
accommodation to tobacco culture caused the Church of
England. Quakers did all the things an ordained clergy
did—upheld the moral universe, offered guidance about faith

---

[137] Horn, *Adapting to a New World*, 398-99.

[138] Beeth, "Outside Agitators in Southern History," 292; Kenneth L.
Carroll, "Elizabeth Harris, the Founder of American Quakerism," *Quaker
History* 17 (1968): 96-111; Michael Graham, "Meetinghouse and Chapel,"
in Lois Green Carr, Philip D. Morgan, and Jean B. Russo, eds., *Colonial
Chesapeake Society* (Chapel Hill: University of North Carolina Press, 1988)
260. See also, Levy, "Puritanism in the Southern Colonies," 122-23, 133,
156-57; Warren M. Billings, ed., "A Quaker in Seventeenth-Century
Virginia: Four Remonstrances by George Wilson," *William and Mary
Quarterly* 3rd ser. 33 (1976): 127-30; Bruce, *Institutional History*, 1:222-
51.

and the individual's journey to heaven, and provided support at life's crucial moments—only Friends placed these burdens on the priesthood of the laity rather than on a professional clergy.[139] Quakerism seemingly fit the colony's religious customs, and a number of people throughout Virginia filled their need for religious community by embracing the Gospel as preached by the Society of Friends. In 1659 Quaker missionary William Robinson wrote of the numerous "convincements": "There are many people convinced, and some in several parts are brought into the sense and feeling of truth."[140]

Yet the colony's leaders, both Commonwealth governors and Sir William Berkeley once he returned to his former position, saw Quakers less as a religious movement than as a political threat to order and showed little enthusiasm for the children of light. Their fears were justified, for Quakerism was not only a devotional movement, but also an extreme movement of radical religious, social, and political protest. It carried with it dangerous social ideas and a well-deserved reputation for turbulence and violence. Their initial support in England came from disaffected groups: agrarian radicals, participants in anti-tithe riots, and men and women who had earlier been in conflict with their landlords over manorial duties and rents. Their radical commitment to the Protestant notion of the priesthood of all believers implied a social leveling which threatened traditional ideas about proper social order. And the prominence of women in the movement, not only as workers but also as leaders, threatened Virginia's patriarchal society.[141]

Nor were Quakers the gentle people linked in the American imagination with tolerant Friends schools and pacifism. In

---

[139] Horn, *Adapting to a New World*, 399.

[140] Jones, *Quakers in the American Colonies*, 273.

[141] Jones, *Quakers in the American Colonies*, 270; Wesley Frank Craven, *Red, White, and Black: The Seventeenth-Century Virginian*, (Charlottesville: University Press of Virginia, 1971) 44; Reay, "Quakerism and Society," 141-45; Kathleen Brown, *Good Wives, Nasty Wenches, and Anxious Patriarchs*, 143-44; Horn, *Adapting to a New World*, 398.

England, members of the sect had plotted rebellion, disturbed the peace, disrupted worship services, and, in general, were obnoxious to those with whom they disagreed. Their religious protests could be spectacular. James Nayler differed from other Quakers only in the outrageousness of his actions. In 1656, he claimed he was Christ and rode into Bristol on an ass to signify the fact, all the while his female followers threw palms in his path. When local magistrates asked his identity, he replied: "I am the son of God." One of the women even claimed Nayler had resurrected her from the dead—an outrageous claim to be sure, but typical of Quaker rhetoric. Several Friends claimed the power to work miracles; George Fox kept a record of his, which included curing smallpox, scabs, ague, and a broken neck. Arrogant and self-righteous, Quakers engaged in verbal violence that was not only vulgar and crude but also made compromise and debate difficult. Using words from the Bible that were offensive, George Fox, once told a religious opponent: "Thou must eat thy own dung, and drink thy own piss that comes from thee, for all that in thy book is but dung."[142]

Their reputation for turbulence and dissension preceded Quakers across the Atlantic, and it shaped colonial perceptions of what members of the sect might do. Colonial authorities expected the worst. Burgesses described them in a manner which still echoes of fear and panic: an "unreasonable and turbulent sort of people...teaching and publishing, lies, miracles, false visions, prophecies, and doctrines which have influence upon the communities of men both ecclesiasticall and civil endeavouring and attempting thereby to destroy religion, lawes, communities and all bonds of civil societie, leaveing it arbitrarie to everie vaine and vitious person whether men shall be safe."[143] It was not quite the specter of barbarians at the gates, but in reputation if not in local actions, the Friends' arrival nonetheless raised anxieties. "There are Quakers in our midst," the General

---

[142] Reay, "Quakerism and Society," 148-49, 158-59; Watts, *The Dissenters*, 194, 210-11. The biblical reference is to II Kings 18:27.

[143] Hening, *Statutes at Large*, 1:532.

Assembly seemed to say, "God only knows what mischief and chaos they might sow." In modern parlance they were loose cannons on the ship of state. The seventeenth century would have used the analogy of disease in the body politic as Governor Berkeley did when he called them a "pestilent" sect. Quakers were akin to an infection not strong enough to be fatal, but popularly believed capable of killing, a source of disorder feared for its potential ability to destroy the state. Although there is little evidence that Virginia Quakers wanted to do much more than hold their meetings in peace—no showing up naked at services of the established church, no plotting rebellion—the abusive and confrontational encounters of a few Friendly malcontents, some who refused traditional hat honor to social superiors, merely confirmed authorities' preconceptions. Thomas Bushrod, a York County Quaker, was particularly troublesome. He followed the Reverend Justinian Aylmer and a councilor, Augustine Warner, aboard a merchant vessel at anchor in the York River, then accosted the men and verbally assaulted them. He called the minister "a lying knave[,] an ugly Rogue & blind Rogue" and the councilor "a dogg and a rogue." Not content with these insults, he taunted Aylmer for his inability to prevent some York County residents from choosing Quakerism over the Church of England, decried Anglican clergy as "Antichrists... preceded from the pope," and finished his tirade by daring Aylmer or the Council to break up Quaker meetings. When colonial leaders termed the Friends "dangerous, turbulent, seditious," they did so with good reason.[144]

Virginia's broad religious polity did not include Quakers. The result more of their reputation for disruptive behavior rather than any organized activities, Quakers in Virginia were perse-

---

[144] Charles City Court Orders, 1661-1664, ff. 424, 437; York County, Deeds, Orders, and Wills (3) ff. 66, 131; Brown, *Good Wives, Nasty Wenches, and Anxious Patriarchs*, 142-44; Horn, *Adapting to a New World*, 397. For another treatment of the Quakers, see Jay Worrall, Jr., *The Friendly Virginians: America's First Quakers* (Athens GA; Iberian Publishing Company, 1992).

cuted for several years during the late 1650s and early 1660s.
Meetings held in conspicuously private places—the woods or
individual residences—raised suspicions about Quaker intentions. Only people with something to hide gathered in such
clandestine ways. They were whipped and fined, if not for their
religious beliefs then for their suspected revolutionary activities.
Some county authorities attacked Quakers in creative ways.
Charles City County relied upon old anti-vagrancy statutes to
persecute Quakers who had crossed the county line to attend
meetings. Justices had the violators rounded up, and then
removed them from the county with a warning never to return.
English Friends in the colony as missionaries, such as Thomas
Thurston and Josiah Cole of Gloucestershire, were arrested and
given sentences of banishment. In his mid-twenties, Cole was a
particularly able preacher, described by a contemporary Quaker
historian as "a son of thunder" and by William Penn as a man
whose words fell "like an axe, a hammer, or a sword." So
frightened were Virginia's authorities of the social discord
Thurston and Cole might sow, that during their time in custody
they were allowed no "pen, ink, or paper or correspondence"
with any of the colony's citizens lest they communicate the
plague to others and spread the pestilence further. A revision of
the colony's laws completed at the General Assembly's spring
1658 session placed the Quakers well beyond Virginia's religious
pale. The statutes institutionalized what had by then become
Virginia's customary ecclesiastical localism. Referring to no
particular theology or style of worship, the new laws left these
matters as well as decisions about church government in the
hands of each parish, yet explicitly exempted Quakers from the
implied toleration. In the same year, the General Court ordered
that the colony undertake a "general persecution" of the sect.[145]

---

[145] Charles City County, Court Orders, 1661-1664, f. 444; McIlwaine,
Minutes of the Council and the General Court of Colonial Virginia, 506;
Beeth, "Outside Agitators in Southern History," 292-93; Hening, *Statutes
at Large*, 1:433; Morton, *Colonial Virginia,* 1:180-81.

Unlike differences earlier in the century between Anglicans and Puritans that had set lay people against lay people as well as authorities against nonconformists, persecution of the Quakers was apparently a governmental endeavor. Most Virginians seemed not to care about the Friends' presence and may, in fact, have been pleased that someone was working to maintain a Christian presence in the colony. By the early 1660s conflict had emerged between colonial authorities and colonists over the validity of the Quaker threat to order. When William Berkeley, who was no more a friend to the sect than previous executives had been, returned to the governor's office in 1660, he chastised the long-suffering sheriff of Lower Norfolk County, Richard Conquest, for "not stopping the frequent meetings of this most pestilent sect of the Quakers" and ordered him not to "suffer any more of theire meetings or Conventicles." Citizens of Lower Norfolk, however, held broader ideas about what constituted acceptable religious expressions than the colony's leaders. Just as they had once welcomed Puritans they had done the same for Quakers. So ingrained was this attitude in Lower Norfolk, colonial Virginia's moderate equivalent of a "burned-over district," that when a local justice attempted to "suppresse the quakers" at Isabel Spring's house, she accused him of being a "traitor."[146]

Quaker difficulties were doubtless exacerbated by greater than normal tensions in the colony's life during the early years of the Friends' presence. In 1656, the year Quaker missionaries had first arrived in Virginia, the colony's traditional conflicts with the natives had flared up once again. This time, natives had begun encroaching upon English territory near the falls of the James River. With memories of Opechacanough's uprising twelve years earlier still vivid, Virginians acted to remove the threat. Unfortunately, the man sent to resolve the conflict, Colonel

---

[146] Lower Norfolk County, Wills and Deed, D (1656-1666), ff. 6, 237, 264, 302, 305-307, 312-13, 328.

Edmund Hill, proved so inept a leader that the colonists suffered a spectacular defeat and were forced to sue for peace.[147]

In addition to their problems in foreign affairs, Virginians also confronted a series of internal problems during the late 1650s. Burgesses jealous of their powers squabbled with Governor Samuel Mathews, who tended to overstep the bounds that had traditionally limited executive power. Three years later colonists began to have trouble with their servants, those "angry young men" in one historian's words. Many were English convicts or prisoners of war—former members of Cromwell's Model Army, a hotbed of religious radicalism, who had ended up on the losing side—none too pleased with their bondage. A servants' rebellion broke out in York County in 1661 and another was narrowly averted two years later in nearby Gloucester County. Colonel John Catlett of Rappahanock County captured the country's fear in a letter to a cousin in England: "there was a combination of severall servants, who had complotted first to arme themselves with their Masters armes and then 2ly [sic] to make their own termes which was their freedom and in case of denial to kill all that should oppose them." Unrest comprised but a portion of the problems created by laborers. A small but troubling number of servant suicides caused, in the words of the York County Court, by the "instigation of the devill at York," brought colonial Virginians as close as they ever came to claiming that Satan was rampaging through their midst. When they were not threatening the colony's order and their master's lives and investments by plotting rebellion or killing themselves, they became a menace to the colony by doing their masters' bidding. Frustrated by the low prices that came from a saturated tobacco market, at least one planter ordered his servants to destroy other men's crops so that his would rise in value. Put plainly, it was an inauspicious

---

[147] Morton, *Colonial Virginia*, 1:178-79.

moment for a people with a reputation for agrarian radicalism and general troublemaking to show up in Virginia.[148]

Persecutions reached their height in 1662, several months after the servant uprising of the previous year. With Berkeley in England, and likely with his blessing, the burgesses asserted their idea of colonial religious identity by defining conformity more strictly than in the past. Once again they passed statutes making church attendance mandatory and levying a £20 sterling fine on those who refused to comply. Frequenting Quaker meetings carried an additional fine of 200 pounds of tobacco. Quaker persecution took off after passage of this statute. Numerous people were arrested and imprisoned to await trial, including George Wilson, a Quaker missionary from Cumberland, England.[149]

Wilson had arrived in Virginia in 1661, having been banished from Massachusetts Bay earlier in the year for his proselytizing efforts there, and began preaching the Gospel of Light to Virginia's largely unchurched population. By spring the next year he had a run in with colonial authorities and lay languishing in James City jail. Despite his imprisonment, Wilson persisted in the confrontational tactics typical of many Quakers. Somehow he acquired pen and paper and wrote a series of remonstrances in which he railed against deputy governor Francis Moryson and called divine wrath down upon him and the colony for Virginia's continued attempts to suppress the Friendly heresy. Wilson likewise warned the burgesses against sponsoring further harassment of his coreligionists lest they too become explicit subjects of God's displeasure. Wilson's threats changed no one's mind, and he remained in jail, at one point "chained to an Indian,

---

[148] Morton, *Colonial Virginia*, 1:180-82; Morgan, *American Slavery, American Freedom*, 246, 286-87; John Catlett to Thomas Catlett, 1 April 1664; York County, Deeds, Orders, and Wills (3) 1657-1662, ff. 74, 88, 122.

[149] Billings, "A Quaker in Seventeenth-Century Virginia," 128; Hening, *Statutes at Large*, 2:49.

which is in prison for murder; we had our Legs on one boolt made fast to a post with an ox chaine."[150]

We do not know why Wilson's jailers treated him in this manner. Possibly they chained the two men together for their own amusement. Yet the image hints at something deeper, and maybe there is a strange symbolism here. Virginia's leaders cared neither for Native Virginians or Quakers. Missionary efforts to the people of the land had long been forgotten. Governor Berkeley, in fact, showed greater interest in converting Turkish slaves than in bringing Christianity to Virginia's native peoples. Even the few efforts undertaken to convert natives were often criticized. In 1654, the king of the Roanoke Indians approached Colonel Francis Yeardley of Accomack County about having his son baptized and taught to read and write English. Yeardley liked the idea and invited the king's son into his family where he could be instructed in English religion and civility. Many people complained, however, and when the Roanoke king attended church one Sunday with Yeardley's wife, "some [of] our Justices of this place...after sermon, threatned to whipp him and send him awaye." Natives remained to Virginians a frightening and perverse culture beyond the margins of civilization. Somewhat less human than English Christians, they were best enslaved, and best of all, enslaved by people who would take them far away from Virginia. In any case, relations with the natives took a turn for the worse in 1661. Rumors trickled back to James City of scalps being taken by "strange" natives on the frontiers who threatened both colonists' lives and their trade with friendly tributary Native Virginians. The situation grew so grave that within a few years the formal spatial division of Virginia in English and Native territories was once again formalized. Laws allowing Englishmen to sell arms to natives were repealed, and settlers were once again ordered to take weapons along to church, court, or any other public gathering.[151] It is possible

---

[150] Billings, "A Quaker in Seventeenth-Century Virginia," 130.

[151] John Clayton, *The Defence of a Sermon, Preach'd upon the Receiving into the Communion of the Church of England, the Honorable Sir Terence*

given Virginia's setting and some colonists' delight in the ironic linking of opposites that the image of the native murderer and the Quaker missionary represented the two great threats to the colony's polity—disorder without and disorder within.

Fear of Quaker disorder, however, began fading by the end of 1663, and persecution of the sect fell dramatically. Years would pass before Virginians completely accepted the Friends, yet there were already indications of a new attitude, and, as in England, persecution varied from place to place over time. Thomas Bushrod, who had slandered the Anglican clergy as "episcopal knaves" in 1661 was back in the court's favor less than a year later, acting as a representative of the court to divide an estate. As long as Quakers paid their parish levies, a symbol of their support for morality and the state's role in upholding it, they were generally left alone. A few obstinate confrontationalists, however, courted persecution and often ended up before county justices. Edward Thomas trespassed on the Reverend Anthony Sclater's property and chopped down the parson's trees. On a different occasion he made a great show of working on Christmas Day in order to affront members of the established church. Another Quaker malcontent, Richard Brown, threw blocks of wood at a minister's wife. Such disturbances were rare, and colonial authorities, grudgingly perhaps, allowed most Quakers to practice their religion. By the early 1670s, Governor William Berkeley—old, deaf, and more irascible than ever—found it possible to show members of the sect some kindness, although he still despised nonconformists. He hosted the Quaker missionary William Edmundson at his Green Spring estate outside Jamestown, a remarkable show of tolerance for a man

---

Mac-Mahon Baronet, and Christopher Dunn. Converts From the Church of Rom ...(Dublin, 1701), preface, no pagination; Francis Yeardley to John Ferrar, 8 May 1654, Rawlinson Manuscript A-14, ff. 84-87, Oxford University; Virginia Ferrar to Mrs. Yeardley, October 1654, Ferrar Papers, f. 691, Magdalene College, Cambridge University; Morgan, *American Slavery, American Freedom*, 233-34; Morton, *Colonial Virginia*, 1:228-29.

who a decade earlier had established a commission to see that
"the abominate seede of ye Quakers spread not."[152]

Different times bring different attitudes. Although the social
tensions which troubled Virginians had changed little between
the mid-1650s when Quaker missionaries had first arrived in the
colony and in 1663 and 1664 when persecution of the sect
declined, authorities' perceptions of the Friends' relationship to
the polity were different. Commonwealth leaders as well as
Governor Berkeley had good reason to worry about the Quaker
menace. Their penchant for disruption was well known. Virginia's
leaders no doubt knew as well that English peoples' hatred of
Quakers was so great that Cromwell's indulgence of the sect had
helped bring down his regime. The root of colonial laws against
Quakers was a well-founded fear: fear of disorder, fear of
innovation, and fear perhaps of losing support for the
government if leaders did not act against these radicals. Yet by
the end of 1663 and the beginning of 1664, colonial authorities
had come to different understandings both of Quakerism and of
what constituted the real threat to the colony.[153]

Following the English Civil War, Quakers renounced
violence, thus giving authorities less reason to fear their
meetings as potential threats to social and political order. More
important was the realization that Quakers meant what they said
and intended to forsake this disruptive aspect of their history, a
fact born out in Virginia by experience. The colony's Quakers
had supported neither rebellion nor social leveling, and, in fact,
adhered to the Quaker "peace testimony" sooner than their

---

[152] Billings, "Quaker in Seventeenth-Century Virginia," 128; York
County Deeds, Orders, and Wills (3), f. 145; Horn, *Adapting to a New
World*, 395-97; *William and Mary Quarterly* 1st ser. 11 (1902): 31; William
Edmundson, *A Journal of the Life, Travels, Sufferings and Labour of Love in
the Work of the Ministry, of that Worthy Elder and faithful servant of Jesus
Christ, William Edmundson* (2nd ed., London, 1774), 70, Virginia Historical
Society.

[153] Levy, "Puritanism in the Southern Colonies," 154.

brethren across the Atlantic.[154] Virginia's Quakerism remained what it had always been, a religious movement well suited to both the colony's environment and the deficiencies of its institutional church. At the very least, Quakerism taught Biblical morality and, in fact, defined "true Christianity as moral conduct," a belief compatible with Virginia's religious pattern. There is no evidence in the colony of the radical agrarianism or the organized efforts to overthrow authority associated with English Quakerism. While the colony's circumstances were ideal for Quakerism as a religious movement, they were not conducive to the sect's radical political and social elements.

As in so many things, Virginia was not England, and the Quakers of Virginia were not the Quakers of England, either in their degree of social disruption or in their demographic makeup. English Quakers drew "substantial numbers" from the lower classes, people dissatisfied with their conditions and willing to challenge the political and social order. In Virginia, however, a significant number of Quakers came from the colony's ruling class, including county justices, sheriffs, and at least one former burgess. Quakers or not, these leading men challenged neither patriarchy nor rule by those possessing land and wealth. Their interest, from all indications, lay in piety not revolution.[155] Most Virginians, in fact, seemed unfazed by the sect's presence, quite willing to tolerate them and their religious peculiarities. Many English people, however, despised members of the sect, and one man, speaking for himself in words that others supported, pronounced: "I would not leave a Quaker alive in England...I would make no more...to set my Pistol to their Ears, and shoot them through the Head, than I would to kill a dog." Unlike in England, where large numbers of citizens harbored an ill-concealed hatred of the group and often showed their feelings by destroying Quaker meeting houses and businesses, Virginians

---

[154] Reay, *Quakers and the English Revolution*, 107-109.

[155] Reay, "Quakerism and Society," 144; Brown, *Good Wives, Nasty Wenches, and Anxious Patriarchs*, 417n.11; Levy, "Puritanism in the Southern Colonies," 155-56.

displayed none of this popular animosity.[156] Colonial leaders had worried about Quakers, and when their own attitudes toward the sect changed, the government could turn a blind eye to their activities without risking a public outcry. The colony was in the enviable position in which it neither had to defend itself against Quakers nor protect the Friends from their neighbors.

The real threats to Virginia's polity came not from Quakers but from unhappy servants and a Stuart imperial policy predicated on economic authority rather than colonial autonomy. Given this situation and the continuing lack of pastoral care by the Church of England, a few Quakers spreading Gospel lessons about morality did not seem so seditious after all. Largely mythic in reality to begin with, Virginians' fear of Quakers had always been more vivid in imagination than in reality, and easily gave way to the more tangible concern of servants plotting to kill their masters and Virginia's abiding need for a religious presence. If upper class Quakers wanted to hold a meeting at their houses or in the woods and invite their servants and slaves, they just might be able to help stay the colony's unrest. Colonial realities had transformed a potential source of disorder into one of the props maintaining colonial society.

Is not Berkeley's and other Virginians' gradual approval of Puritans and Quakers not the story of religious minorities in America—a pattern of animosity and confrontation, followed by begrudging accommodation, and then indifferent acceptance? It is in Virginia's relative quiet at mid-century that the colony had achieved something extraordinary. Virginia was different from England, and whether longtime residents realized it or not, they had begun to construct a religious identity separate from that of the mother country. They had created their own fast days, 22 March and 18 April—the anniversaries of Native uprisings in 1622 and 1644, to commemorate moments when God had delivered their "country" from their native enemies. They had

---

[156] Barry Reay, *The Quakers and the English Revolution* (London: Temple Smith, Ltd., 1985) 62-78, 105-106, quotation on 106; Reay, "Quakerism and Society," 144, 156.

also established lay vestries with powers far greater than those in England. Over time those powers would grow, and those powers would need to be defended not against Native Americans, but against English encroachments. As a result of the English Civil War and English neglect of the colony, Virginia by the 1650s had been developing its own customary methods of dealing with government and religion for nearly fifty years.

On the shores of the James River, these seventeenth-century Virginians, long viewed as a people who cared little about man's religious nature, established in the New World an ecclesiastical polity which recognized that strife between religious parties would have to be minimized for the sake of the polity's existence. It was yet neither religious toleration nor religious freedom, but it was a step in that direction. They had solved the problem of unity and identity by creating a system that left faith a private matter.

Emphasizing the peaceful coexistence of religious groups within the polity allowed Virginians to see other threats more clearly, particularly economic ones. The strength of financial incentives after 1615 and the enduring weakness of the colonial church had encouraged Virginians to find another source of unity. Consumed by tobacco cultivation, colonists in Virginia worried more about economic threats to the colony than religious ones and often united in defense of the colony's common economic interests. Thus when Roman Catholics began settling Maryland in the 1630s, few colonists groused about their religious proclivities. What disturbed Virginians was the economic competition for their lands and the profits settlers, in the first colony, might reap from tobacco and furs. Lord Baltimore and many of the new settlers may have been papists, but social deference nonetheless reigned. Thomas Tindall found himself in the pillory for two hours after "Giving my Lord Baltimore the Lye and threatening to knock him down."[157] In the 1650s colonists once again showed their mutual devotion to

---

[157] "Extracts from Virginia Records, 1630-31," *Virginia Magazine of History and Biography* 17 (1909): 7.

the colony's economic self-interest, this time against the mother country. Puritan Virginians and Anglican Virginians combined to resist efforts of both Charles I and supporters of Parliament to wage war against their Roundhead and Cavalier enemies by preventing Virginia's trade with their opponents. They likewise balked at the Commonwealth government's attempt to restrict their trade with the Dutch.[158] Virginians were happy to avoid divisive religious questions and trade their tobacco with anyone willing to offer payment. Domestic tranquility made good business sense. Getting along with men of different religious persuasions enhanced economic success. Virginians' commitment to their economic self-interest encouraged them to remove religious struggles from domestic politics. Colonists would soon learn that the greatest threat to their polity, political as well as religious, no longer came from nonconformists in religion or from native cultural enemies, but from Englishmen who harbored their own ideas about how Virginia should function.

---

[158] Crow, "'Your Majesty's Good Subjects': A Reconsideration of Royalism in Virginia, 1642-1652," 166-70.

CHAPTER FOUR

AMBIGUOUS ENGLISHMEN

Early in 1665 Charles II belatedly declared what had been apparent for several months: England and the Dutch were at war. The reasons had to do not with territory or politics but with commerce, particularly trade with England's overseas' colonies. With the restoration of Charles II to the throne in 1660, a half century of Crown inattention to England's North American colonies came to an end as the Stuart monarchy attempted to bring order to England's growing number of colonial possessions, in part by enforcing the oft-neglected mercantile laws governing colonial trade and manufacturing. England's colonial policy of vigorous indifference had come to an end. For their part, Dutchmen cared little for England's new policy and saw her revived interest in colonial commerce in a very different light. Dutch merchants after all had sailed Virginia's waters for decades, and despite Commonwealth statutes outlawing the practice, their tobacco trade during the English Civil War had spared the colony from poverty. Virginians now believed they had the right to trade with whomever they chose. English leaders thought otherwise. If merchants from Holland or Spain or France or any place else could trade at will with England's North American colonies, then how did these possessions benefit the mother country? England had planted, nurtured, and defended her colonies, and the nation would go to war in order to defend the exclusive right to the marvelous bounty and the equally fine profits produced by those North American territories.

No one, however, seemed terribly concerned about what Virginians thought of all this. Writing in 1666 of England's war with the Dutch in words that revealed the ambiguity of being English yet living in a land far from England, Governor William Berkeley mused: "We live here after the simplicity of the past age...and unlesse this danger of our country gave our feares toungs and language we should shortly forget all sounds that did not concerne the businesse and necessities of our farmers."[1] Largely removed from the hostilities, it still made sense for Berkeley and other Virginians to worry about foreign depredations of their homeland for they considered themselves English. Most colonists had immigrated to Virginia from England and at the very least still possessed ties to the mother country of kinship, language, religion, the common law, and that ambiguous abstraction called the "rights of Englishmen." Colonial elites aped the latest English fashions and tried to recreate on their Virginia estates something of the appearance of English aristocratic ways. As Englishmen, Virginians were prepared to defend the colony against rival powers. In 1667 when the Dutch navy showed up in colonial waters and burned the English tobacco fleet at anchor in Chesapeake Bay, the colonists took to arms and prevented the invaders from landing. Their military sympathies were clear. Alluding to Psalm 72, Sir William wrote: "as we are farther out of Danger so we approach nearer to heaven with our prayers that his sacred Matis Ennimies may either drinke the sea or licke the Dust."[2]

Yet an ocean away from England with lives shaped by the exigencies of another continent, it also made sense for Virginians to put foreign matters aside and concentrate on their own interests, for whether the mother country was in peace or at war "the businesse and necessities" of colonial farmers remained abiding concerns. Their chief business was tobacco, and it shaped colonial life by influencing the contours of civil and

---

[1] Sir William Berkeley to [?],1 May 1666, Public Records Office Colonial Office 1/20 f. 117.

[2] Sir William Berkeley to [?],1 May 1666, PRO CO 1/20, f. 117. See also, Thomas Ludwell to Lord Arlington, 1 May 1666, PRO CO 1/20, f. 118.

ecclesiastical arrangements. Colonists lived, worked, worshiped, and governed themselves in Virginia where local circumstances rather than Stuart policies often determined the routines of everyday life, dictating how Virginians prayed to God, earned a living, controlled laborers, and got along with their neighbors. Heirs of two cultures not wholly compatible—one rooted in English precedents, the other based both on colonial self interest and colonial adaptations of English precedents—Virginians by the 1660s were a people of divided loyalties. They were proud to be English and wanted to be part of the empire, but they preferred to do so on their own terms. In matters of truly national interest, which for Virginians meant threats from foreign enemies, Virginians were English. But when it came to economic policies and civil or religious government, Virginians were a local people, devoted to themselves, their own interests, and their own "prescriptions." Loosely defined as custom or tradition, "prescription" encompassed a people's cultural patterns and the expectations those patterns created. As an organic metaphor it described the evolution of societies as an inheritance rooted in a people's particular cultural circumstances, gradually changing over time, firmly rooted in both the customs and practices of the past as well as the necessities of the present. People did not adopt "prescriptions" by reading of them in books or through the conscious use of reason so much as they picked them up accidentally by experience as part of living in a particular society. "Prescription" elevated to supremacy the wisdom of experience over mere reason. "It is," in the words of Edmund Burke, "made by the peculiar circumstances, occasions, tempers, dispositions, and moral, civil, and social habitudes of the people, which disclose themselves only in a long space of time." Explaining the concept further, he wrote: "Circumstances are infinite, are infinitely combined, are variable and transient: he who does not take them into consideration is not erroneous, but stark mad."[3]

---

[3] Edmund Burke, "Speech on Reform of Representation of the Commons in Parliament" (1782), in *The Writings & Speeches of Edmund*

By 1660, Virginians had established a religious polity suitable to their circumstances. By accentuating the colonists' common Christian inheritance rather than the religious factionalism typical of Europe, Virginia's "prescription" fostered concord within the polity by removing a traditionally divisive issue from political importance. Experience suggested that Virginia's Jacobean polity worked well. With its elevation of public behavior over private belief as a unifying factor and Virginia's accommodating ecclesiastical localism, the colonys "prescription" had spared Charles II's "old dominion" from much of the religious conflict that had swept portions of the English trans-Atlantic world in the 1640s and 1650s. While England endured several years of civil war and the execution of Charles I, and just across the Potomac River to Virginia's north, Maryland had nearly returned to the political state of nature in 1645 as a result of Ingles' Rebellion—a clash emerging directly out of local religious animosities and their relation to civil war in the mother country—Virginians enjoyed relative calm. So chaotic did English people find conditions during the Civil War that it gave them an enduring example of how not to effect revolution. Maryland's rebellion demonstrated just how easily European-style religious faction could be manipulated for both public and private gain. Some Puritan Marylanders saw the disruption back in England as an opportunity to wrest control of the colony away from the Roman Catholic Calverts and thereby put the colony on a proper footing. Robert Ingles, for whom the incident is named, and a few other Maryland Puritans held less ideological views, yet nonetheless saw a good opportunity when it came along. They intended not only to attack the colony's papist proprietors but also to plunder wealthy Marylanders of any creed who disagreed with them. Frightened Marylanders found refuge

---

Burke in Twelve Volumes (Boston: Little, Brown, and Company, 1901): vol. 7, 94-95; Second quotation, from Speech on the Petition of the Unitarians. While a member of Parliament in the 1770s, Burke supported colonial independence. See also, Edmund Burke, "The First Letter on a Regicide Peace" in Paul Langford, ed., *The Writings and Speeches of Edmund Burke*, 9 vols. (New York: Oxford University Press, 1991) 9:242.

in Virginia, and only with assistance from Governor Berkeley was the colony restored to order.[4] Virginia's Jacobean religious polity, however, helped colonists there avoid denominational strife, just as it helped them avoid religion becoming a divisive issue in late seventeenth-century colonial politics. Although colonists in Virginia suffered their share of conflict in the second half of the century—two aborted servants' rebellions in addition to Bacon's Rebellion in 1676, and a plant-cutting riot to drive up the price of tobacco in 1682—religion played at most a negligible role in each.

Yet there was more to Virginia's religious tradition than relations between Christian persuasions. Although the Crown and the Church of England's lack of pastoral concern for the North American colonies contributed to the development of a more modern polity in Virginia which placed economics above traditional notions regarding religious unity, that same neglect had not had an altogether salutary effect on the colonists' spiritual lives. Years before the Puritans of New England had, in Perry Miller's phrase, been "left alone with America,"[5] the Church of England had abandoned colonists to the south in Virginia. Four ministers served the colony's 350 people in 1616.[6] By 1661 nearly 26,000 people lived in Virginia; twelve were ministers.[7] The statistics are meaningless. Whether one

---

[4] James Horn, *Adapting to a New World: English Society in the Seventeenth-Century Chesapeake* (Chapel Hill: University of North Carolina Press, 1994) 370-72.

[5] Perry Miller, "Errand Into the Wilderness," in *Errand into the Wilderness* (Cambridge: Harvard University Press, 1956) 15.

[6] Jon Butler, *Awash in a Sea of Faith: Christianizing the American People* (Cambridge: Harvard University Press, 1990) 38.

[7] R[oger] G[reene], *Virginia's Cure: or an Advisive Narrative Concerning Virginia...*, in Peter Force, ed. *Tracts and Other Papers, Relating Principally to the Origin, Settlement, and Progress of the Colonies in North America*, 4 vols. (Gloucester MA: Peter Smith, 1963) 3:15:4-5; Patricia U. Bonomi, *Under the Cope of Heaven: Religion, Society, and Politics in Colonial America* (New York: Oxford University Press, 1986) 16; Edmund S. Morgan, *American Slavery, American Freedom: The Ordeal of Colonial Virginia* (New York: Norton, 1975) 404.

clergyman presumably served as pastor to ninety persons or to over two thousand, the enduring reality was that there was an absence of any organized or unorganized missionary effort by English authorities. A crisis in pastoral care accompanied Virginia's factional peace.

Whether Puritan or Anglican, Virginians needed educated clergy to bring spiritual comfort in times of crisis and to provide religious instruction on a regular basis. Members of both persuasions felt the absence of ministers, albeit in different ways. To word-centered Puritans, the word of God expounded by learned and "godly" preachers took the central role in their religious meetings. Ordained ministers were just as important to Anglican Virginians; they not only preached (usually for about twenty minutes) but also celebrated the sacraments of baptism and Holy Communion, the most important of the Church's rites. Puritans without preaching and Anglicans without sacraments were something less than full religious beings, people slightly uprooted from their religious moorings. Richard Bennett, then governor of the colony, captured the sadness and despair of many devout Virginians: "the greatest want that Virginia hath is in the power purity & spirituality of its Ministery of ye word, for want whereof we know not God, we Live as without God in the world."[8] Without a minister, to whom did one turn for solace when ill or for guidance if one's faith began to wane? To whom did one turn to in the time of death, that constant companion of Chesapeake settlers? Where did the faithful Puritans turn for assurance that the life they had lived showed evidence of their election and that they need not fear the terrors of judgment? Who reminded Anglican Virginians of the "sure and certain hope of the resurrection"?

---

[8] Richard Bennett to John Ferrar, 12 February 1652/53, Ferrar Papers, f. 1217Magdalene College, Cambridge University. For additional background material on Bennett, see the entry for Richard Bennett in John T. Kneebone, J. Jefferson Looney, Brent Tarter, and Sandra Gioia Treadway, eds., *The Dictionary of Virginia Biography:* Aaroe-Blanchfield (Richmond: The Library of Virginia, 1998) 1:445-47.

Without traditional clerical leadership, Virginians attempted throughout the first half of the century to address these deficiencies in fairly traditional ways. The General Assembly ordered deacons to lead prayer services so that areas without ministers could nonetheless enjoy public worship.[9] Although imperfect, the solution was successful enough that sheriffs had to be told not to serve warrants during church services since this practice needlessly discouraged church attendance.[10] On other occasions, colonists made use of books as replacements for the pastoral counsel of ministers. They treated the libraries of deceased ministers as public property, saving them for use by the next clergyman who showed up, perhaps circulating volumes among literate settlers in ways that have been lost to researchers. Seventeenth-century Virginians took special delight in religious volumes, aids to private piety as well as symbols of a spiritual world that transcended the colony's religious difficulties.[11] At mid-century, Edward Johnson, the Anglican minister at Mulberry Island, showed palpable gratitude after receiving a package of devotional books from Virginia Ferrar: "I went into the church and fell on my knees to pray for you and your religious family."[12]

---

[9] George MacLaren Brydon, *Virginia's Mother Church and the Political Conditions Under Which It Grew*, 2 vols. (Richmond: Virginia Historical Society, 1947-1952) 1:435; William Waller Hening, *The Statutes at Large: Being a Collection of All the Laws of Virginia...*, 13 vols. (Richmond: 1809-1823) 1:208.

[10] Hening, *Statutes at Large*, 1:457.

[11] Richard Beale Davis, *Intellectual Life in the Colonial South, 1585-1763*, 3 vols. (Knoxville: University of Tennessee Press, 1978) 2:503.

[12] Edward Johnson to Virginia Ferrar, 11 March 1650/51, Ferrar Papers, f. 727. Books of any kind were of great importance to literate colonists. The previous year, Johnson had written to Virginia Ferrar: "For the meane time, I could wish that as Virginia gave you its name, you could give Virginia your bookes, this the onely plank, that is wanting in that countrye." Edward Johnson to Virginia Ferrar, 25 March 1650, Ferrar Papers, f. 1159. See also John Stirrup to Virginia Ferrar, 26 January 1649/50, Ferrar Papers, f. 1152. Quakers were also glad to recieve books from their brethren in England; Howard Beeth, "Outside Agitators in

Among some settlers, guides to the spiritual life were possessions so highly sought after that contention resulted. A dispute in 1658 over ownership of two volumes of St. Augustine's writings had to be resolved in the York County court.[13] The result of these efforts was a haphazard ministry of second-hand sources that even in maintaining a religious presence in the colony told Virginians that they were second-class citizens of the empire. Books traditionally assisted public worship just as deacons traditionally assisted ministers—in Virginia, both claimed greater primacy.

By the second half of the seventeenth century, Virginians had begun to rely less upon the charity of Church and Crown to meet their religious needs and more on their own initiative. Burgesses turned to financial incentives that often bordered on bribery to entice clergy to come to Virginia. In 1656 the General Assembly granted ministers willing to serve colonial parishes tax breaks in the form of exemptions from "publique levies" for themselves and up to six servants.[14] Clergymen, however, were not the only ones to profit from the colonists' growing sense of urgency, and the burgesses offered economic inducements to the laity as well, in the process recognizing the validity of the colony's ecclesiastical localism. A law passed at the same session as the one granting tax inducements to clergy willing to emigrate to Virginia stated that anyone who successfully recruited a minister for the colony received not only reimbursement for transporting the man from England to Virginia, but also a reward of £20, an act that merely confirmed contemporary practice by making the effort more financially attractive. [15] Virginians already wrote to friends in England for help finding clergy, often placing the counsel of a devout man over partisan theological opinions in the manner of Puritan Richard Bennett's

---

Southern History: The Society of Friends, 1656-1800" (Ph.D. diss., University of Houston, 1984) 292.

[13] York County, Deeds, Orders, and Wills (3), f. 33.

[14] Hening, *Statutes at Large*, 1:424.

[15] Hening, *Statutes at Large,* 1:418.

appeal to John Ferrar, an Anglican: "the greatest good and most Reall & Beneficiall servis that you or any can possibly doe is to be helpfull to us in this great pticular [locating ministers to serve Virginia]."[16] County justices likewise used the power of their offices to request that Virginians planning to travel abroad solicit likely candidates for colonial pulpits. In 1655 when the Lower Norfolk County Court learned that Captain Thomas Willoughby planned to travel to England, they seized the opportunity and asked him to help "pvide a Minister of God's word for us."[17] With demand high and supply low, a savvy minister could fix quite a deal for himself. The Reverend Alexander Cooke certainly did. He agreed in 1652 to serve a parish in Lancaster County, demanding not only "double tythes confirmed to me for ye first year," but also that the parish "send at your own charges boate & hands" to assist him in moving to the Northern Neck.[18]

Despite these economic enticements, between the dissolution of the Virginia Company of London in 1624 and the late 1670s, ministers simply did not want to come to Virginia. Even the numerous Anglican clergy turned out of their livings after Parliament's triumph in the Civil War often preferred unemployment or harassment at home to a colonial cure. Conse-quently, both Puritan and Anglican parishes in Virginia languished for

---

[16] Richard Bennett to John Ferrar, 12 February 1652/53, Ferrar Papers, f. 1217. Three years earlier, Edward Johnson of Mulberry Island Parish had written a similar letter to Ferrar: "But Sr what in truth is most wanting and best for us shalbe my last and Earnest request to you: That you would recommend to Virginia Tow [sic] or three more Orthodox Minister[s]: whoe must needes be paynefull and pious"; Edward Johnson to John Ferrar, 25 March 1650, Ferrar Papers, f. 1160.

[17] Horn, *Adapting to a New World*, 393; "The Church in Lower Norfolk County," *Lower Norfolk County Virginia Antiquary*, 3 (1899-1901): 31-32.

[18] Lancaster County, Deeds, Wills, Settlements of Estates, Book 1, 1652-1657, 26 September 1652, Alexander Cooke to [?], f. 41. This document may also be found in "Some Extracts from the Records of Lancaster County," *William and Mary Quarterly* 1st ser. 20 (1911): 136-37.

want of clergy. In truth, the colony's reputation did not offer many inducements to clergymen who may have wished to make the long and dangerous journey across the Atlantic. Letters and pamphlets written by colonial clergy provided a catalog of discontents reviling both Virginia and Virginians. Often disturbed by an environment to which they had not yet grown accustomed and the colonists' manner of accommodating to its demands, ministers complained bitterly to their superiors in England. Nicholas Moreau of St. Peter's Parish in New Kent County griped to the archbishop of Canterbury, Thomas Tenison, and others of the church hierarchy: "I have got in the very worst parish of Virginia and...am reduced to that great necessity to drink water constantly." So dreadful did he find Virginia that even Ireland seemed preferable: "when I doe reflect upon Ireland, [I] should find myself very happy if I could but live upon the most dark place of that Kingdom." The colony's climate was intolerable, his fellow clergymen ignorant, the people base—and, to make matters worse—his wife had not accompanied him to America.[19] The Reverend John Clayton's complaints were muted when compared to Moreau's but nonetheless damning, resurrecting earlier charges that the colonists had stopped living like English people: "The Country is thinly inhabited; the Living solitary & unsociable; Trading confused, & dispersed; besides other Inconveniences." Other clergy quit Virginia, then published memoirs of their trials in England. Since it made pastoral visits impossible without detriment to other clerical duties, the colonists' damnably inconvenient settlement pattern became easy fodder. "If they [ministers] should spend time in visiting their remote and far distant habitations," railed Roger Greene, "they would have little

---

[19] Nicholas Moreau to Archbishop Tenison, 12 April 1697, Fulham Palace Papers, vol. 11, ff. 22-23, Lambeth Palace Library; Nicholas Moreau to Bishop of Lichfield, 12 April 1697, Fulham Palace Papers, vol. 11, ff. 24-25; William Stevens Perry, *Historical Collections Relating to the American Colonial Church,* 5 vols. (New York: AMS Press, 1969) 1:31.

or none left for their necessary Studies and to provide necessary spiritual food for the rest of their Flocks."[20]

Salaries were another problem. Although clergy were paid largely in Virginia's common currency, tobacco, its quality varied throughout the colony. Sweet-scented tobacco fetched a good price in London, but it needed the good soil north of the James River in order to flourish. Ministers serving parishes on the Southside where lands were of poorer quality received the same amount of tobacco but it was of lesser quality and so brought in less hard cash at market. Taking a parish in "a part of ye countrey where ye tobacco is not quite so good" could mean economic hardship for the minister.[21] Getting paid at all in the seventeenth century could also become a problem. More than one colonial minister found that like the Reverend John Almoner of Wickomico Parish in Lancaster County the only way to receive payment for services rendered was by filing suit against his parishioners.[22] Nor did ministers necessarily believe that Virginians possessed much desire for God. Lionel Gatford, a Puritan minister, labeled the colonists "wicked and ungodly wretches."[23] His Anglican counterpart and contemporary, Edward Johnson, agreed: "[Virginia] it selfe it is a most Gallant Country: The People for the most parte beinge the worst thinge that growes

---

[20] "A Letter from Mr. John Clayton to the Royal Society," in Force, *Tracts and Other Papers*, 3:12:12, 21; G[reene], *Virginia's Cure*, 6.

[21] Lawrence de Butts to Mr. Berriman, 1 July 1722, Fulham Palace Papers, vol. 11, ff. 294-95; William H. Seiler, "The Anglican Parish in Virginia," in James Morton Smith, ed., *Seventeenth-Century America: Essays in Colonial History* (Chapel Hill: University of North Carolina Press, 1959) 121.

[22] Lancaster County Order Book I, 9 December 1653; Jon Butler, *Awash in a Sea of Faith*, 43. See also entries for James Boulware, William Cainhoe, John Carnegie, John Davis, William Towers in the Protestant Episcopal Church Papers, Virginia Historical Society.

[23] Quoted in Edward D. Neill, *Virginia's Carolorum: The Colony Under the Rule of Charles the First and Second, A.D. 1625-A.D. 1685...*, (Albany, 1886) 244.

there: I meane not the Natives."[24] On top of these discouragements, English ministers found Virginia's ecclesiastical localism
confusing since it was at odds with European ideas about church
order. Virginia's church polity caught Gatford off guard.
Annoyed by the colony's ambiguous religious polity, Gatford
longed for the mythic structure of European state church
systems. Using the language of someone who has found a
situation more complex than he had imagined, Gatford urged
that in Virginia a "publick profession of Religion, both for
Doctrine and worship, be established, and such a sense of
discipline set about it, as that both those, who would remove
from hence thither, may before hand know what Religion they
may there enjoy, and when they come thither, be assured to
enjoy it."[25]

Whether bitter over their economic fortunes, homesick for
England, or simply unnerved by the demands the tobacco
culture imposed upon the church, ministers often found the
situation in Virginia unpleasant and consequently sketched
unappealing portraits of a colonial clergyman's life. Ministers
lived unhappy lives, often separated from their families who had
not risked the journey. They were overworked and underpaid;
they toiled among a vulgar people who resented their presence.
True or not, letters and rumors recounting such tales of clerical
hardships found their way back to England, then circulated
through the ecclesiastical community, making it even more
difficult for colonial parishes to attract ministers. Letters that
stopped returning home brought additional concerns. Nearly
two-thirds of Virginia's clergy before 1660 either died within five

---

[24] Edward Johnson to John Ferrar, 25 March 1650, Ferrar Papers, f.
1160. See also Johnson's remark in Edward Johnson to Virginia Ferrar, 11
March 1650/1651, Ferrar Papers, f. 727: "you must expect as little of other
comodities [tobacco] as there is worship of god amonst them."

[25] Lionel Gatford, *Publick good without private Interest. Or, A
compendious remonstrance of the present sad state and condition of the English
colonie in Virginea* (London, 1675), epistle dedicatory (no pagination), John
D. Rockefeller, Jr. Library, Colonial Williamsburg Foundation.

years of reaching the colony or soon returned to England.[26] Problems in Lower Norfolk and Lancaster counties were typical. When Willoughby's attempts to find a minister for the Southside Puritans failed, the people of Lower Norfolk decided to invite a Manhattan clergyman to come live among them and preach God's word. He refused. A similar pattern developed in Lancaster County in Virginia's Northern Neck. After taking charge of the parish there, the Reverend Cooke soon died or departed. A successor died in 1656. Yet a third minister arrived in 1657, but died two years later.[27]

The colony's sordid reputation did not help the development of its religious life either. John Hammond summed up the attitude of many Englishmen: "But *Virginia* savouring not handsomely in *England,* very few of good conversation would adventure thither, (as thinking it a place wherein surely the fear of God was not)."[28] Other chroniclers condemned the ministers sent from England to serve the settlers rather than the people of Virginia, suggesting that many colonists had more fear of God than their ministers. A resident of the Eastern Shore who believed the clergy were nothing more than religious scoundrels referred to them collectively as "Black Cotted Raskolls." Hammond's characterization of Virginia's clergy as drunken thieves who could at best babble their way through a sermon said much the same thing, only he published his opinion in England.[29] Lionel Gatford found it a toss-up. He believed that both clergy

---

[26] John Fredrick Woolverton, *Colonial Anglicanism in North America* (Detroit: Wayne State University Press, 1984) 38.

[27] Horn, Adapting to a New World, 393; "Church in Lower Norfolk," *Lower Norfolk Virginia County Antiquary,* 3 (1899-1901): 33-34.

[28] John Hammond, *Leah and Rachel, or the Two Fruitfull Sisters Virginia, and Maryland: Their Present Condition, Impartially stated and related...*, in Force, *Tracts and Other Papers,* 3:14:2.

[29] James P. Walsh, "'Black Cotted Rascals:' Anti-Anglican Criticism in Colonial Virginia," *Virginia Magazine of History and Biography* 88 (1980) 21-36; Hammond, *Leah and Rachel,* 2.

and colonists were "wicked," and he condemned most ministers as ecclesiastical charlatans afraid to remain in England.[30]

With such aspersions in the air, even the most dedicated servants of God must have thought long about risking their lives and careers in Virginia. What of a man's reputation if he chose to return to England? Would an English parish afford him an opportunity after being tainted by service in the colony? Given what many people thought of Virginia and its religious life, the shortage of ministers is easily understood, and the problem continued with little relief well into the eighteenth century. "There are many vacant parishes in the Colony," the Reverend Walter Jones informed the bishop of London in 1733, "I have writt to several clergy-men of my acquaintances in Wales advising 'em and inviting 'em to these parts, but all to no purpose."[31]

By the 1660s, Virginia's burgesses had learned the lessons of experience: "By reason of our great distance from our native country...able & faithfull ministers cannot in probability be allwaies supplied from thence." They had a proposal, however, to take care of the problem themselves, a shrewd one at that and potentially seditious: establish in the colony a college to educate native men who wished to enter the ministry.[32] Their plan would have addressed two of Virginia's most pressing religious problems—the shortage of clergy and ministers' discontent with the demands of the colony's tobacco culture—by filling colonial pulpits with Virginians already accustomed to the colony's circumstances. Englishmen who wanted to pursue their vocations in Virginia could also be trained at the college, thus

---

[30] Gatford, *Publick good without private Interest*, 14-15.

[31] Walter Jones to Bishop Edmund Gibson, 27 March 1733, Fulham Palace Papers, vol. 12, ff. 199-200.

[32] Hening, *Statutes at Large*, 2:25, 56. For a broad overview of many of the laws governing Virginia's seventeenth-century Church of England, see William H. Seiler, "The Church of England as the Established Church in Seventeenth-Century Virginia," *Journal of Southern History* 15 (1949): 478-508.

easing their transition to Virginia by immersing them in the colony's cultural setting long before they took a parish there.

The burgesses, however, envisioned more than a colonial college to educate Virginia men for Virginia parishes. They sought English sanction not only for ecclesiastical autonomy but also for their traditional economic freedom. By the 1660s, when Virginia "farmers" took their crops to market they confronted a lengthening series of English laws telling them with whom they could trade (England or another English colony), how they could trade (in English or colonial bottoms with crews no less than three-quarters English), and how much tax they would have to pay as a duty when the cured tobacco reached England (two pence for each pound, or about fifty percent of its market value).[33] Virginians mostly ignored the statutes, just as they ignored most everything they thought damaging to their economic interest. Burgesses spoke for other colonists in 1660 when they condemned the English laws and passed a statute reaffirming their own commitment to free trade. With the recently restored Charles II on the throne, they hoped he could be persuaded by his father's old friend, William Berkeley, to exempt Virginia from these onerous Navigation Acts that attacked the "libertye of the Collonie."[34] Hopeful of gaining royal support for schemes that would have placed Virginia at the center of a system originating in James City rather than on the periphery of one based in London, the General Assembly drew up petitions and sent Governor Berkeley to England to plead the colony's case at Whitehall. They also sent two respected ministers, Philip Mallory and Roger Greene, to work ecclesiastical channels and recruit ministers for the immediate future.[35]

---

[33] Morgan, *American Slavery, American Freedom*, 197.

[34] Morgan, *American Slavery, American Freedom*, 146; H. R. McIlwaine, ed., *Journals of the House of Burgesses, 1619-1658/59* (Richmond: Virginia State Library, 1915): 74.

[35] Hening, *Statutes at Large*, 2:37; Brydon, *Virginia's Mother Church*, 1:180.

When Berkeley, Mallory, and Greene set off for London in the spring of 1662, there was at least some reason for optimism. Virginians, had, for the most part, their way with the Commonwealth commissioners sent by Cromwell to demand the colony's surrender in 1652, gaining terms so liberal that little if anything changed in the way Virginians ran their polity. Berkeley still possessed influential contacts at court potentially able to sway Charles' opinion.[36] Hopeful colonists could hold out expectations that Berkeley's friendship with Charles I and their own loyalty to the Crown might bear fruit in special preferments. Who could complain about the college for ministers? Crown and Church had abandoned the colony's religious establishment thirty years earlier. If they were willing, why not let Virginians take on this responsibility themselves?

Charles II, however, had different aspirations for England's overseas colonies, ones predicated on control rather than freedom. He thought well of Cromwell's attempts to reign in the empire, especially the Navigation Acts, which brought lucrative tax revenues to the Crown. Unfortunately for Virginians and their desire for less imperial oversight, the greatest revenue came from yellow weeds planted in the Chesapeake colonies, and Virginia's tobacco contributed more to the royal accounts than sugar, furs, or any other product harvested in England's colonial empire. A good mercantilist, Charles accepted the theory that the world contained only a fixed amount of wealth and that the best way for a prince to make his own nation powerful was to control as much of that fixed amount as possible. It only made sense to the Stuarts and their advisers that the mother country, rather than foreign interlopers, should profit from the nation's investment in empire. Stuart imperial policy therefore placed strict controls on colonial trade, excluding foreign traders and merchants from English ports and planters' wharves up and

---

[36] Richard L. Morton, *Colonial Virginia*, 2 vols. (Chapel Hill: University of North Carolina Press, 1960) 1:172-73; Warren M. Billings, "Sir William Berkeley and the Diversification of the Virginia Economy," *Virginia Magazine of History and Biography* 104 (1996): 447.

down the North Atlantic coast.[37] Berkeley nevertheless lobbied, argued, and urged the colony's case for months, eventually overstaying his welcome. His efforts resulted in few tangible successes. Charles dashed the burgesses' attempts to legitimate a rival version of English society. Although he offered lukewarm support for an economic diversification scheme put forward by Sir William, the king refused to lift the Navigation Acts, ordering the governor to make sure that "care may be taken for the severe prosecution & punishment of those who shall Transgress the said Act of Navigation."[38]

Attempts to solve Virginia's pastoral difficulties met with little better success. Philip Mallory died shortly after arriving in London, leaving the colony's lobbying efforts in the hands of Roger Greene, who had by then come to believe, like the Stuart regime, that what Virginia needed most was a good dose of authority. Now on the side of the Stuarts, he recommended sending a bishop to the colony as soon as possible to help establish traditional English ecclesiastical authority. The center-piece of the burgesses' plan to reform religion in Virginia—the college proposal—also failed, likely the victim of its own ambiguity. A seminary college in Virginia cut two ways. Depending upon who ultimately controlled the institution, it could result in either greater autonomy for the colonists or greater control for the Stuarts, perhaps a first step towards introducing a bishop and further English interference in colonial affairs.[39] For his part, King Charles showed neither support for

---

[37] Morgan, *American Freedom, American Slavery*, 196-98.

[38] Billings, "Sir William Berkeley and the Diversification of the Virginia Economy," 449, 451-52.

[39] Brydon, *Virginia's Mother Church*, 1:180; G[reene], *Virginia's Cure*. In addition to the college's ambiguous place in Stuart imperial policy, the proposed institution had faced numerous difficulties from the start. Establishing a college meant constructing buildings and hiring a faculty, both of which cost great sums, and most colonists seemed less willing to support it with their treasure than Virginia's great men. A college was also a grand means of introducing unnecessary controversy—who would control it? Where would it be located? What particular Church of England party

the proposed institution nor much interest in the colony's religious life. To him and other Stuart imperialists, colonies were warehouses of English agricultural treasure that the Crown could exploit to fill the royal accounts. Speaking over thirty years later of another college proposal, Sir Edward Seymour captured the attitude of English civil leaders set no later than the early 1660s: "*Souls!* damn your Souls. Make Tobacco."[40]

Dashed hopes turned to bitterness. Burgesses had asked their king to acknowledge Virginia's special circumstances and the variant form of English identity it engendered, but Stuart imperial policy told them they had no identity separate from the mother country, that they were but laborers and warehouse managers of agricultural bounty. Virginians resented this treatment. Governor Berkeley denounced England's economic exploitation of the colony which also happened to hamper his and other Virginians' dreams of greater riches: "The vicious ruinous plant of Tobacco I would not name, but that it brings more money to the Crown than all the Islands in *America* besides."[41] What had been to that point vague feelings of frustration about the colony's religious deficiencies, expressed mostly in frequent pleas for more clergy, found focus as well. The Crown, the Church of England, private citizens, universities, ministers in England and other colonies—had all been solicited for assistance, and all the efforts had come to nothing. Virginians did not blame themselves (they rarely did), yet someone had to be at fault for this deplorable situation: Charles Stuart. In an act that both revealed Virginians' pique at having been snubbed as a

---

theology would it support? The plan's inherent centralizing tendencies may have been unwelcome to some, threatening as it did the colony's easy-going ecclesiastical localism.

[40] Brydon, *Virginia's Mother Church*, 1:177; Parke Rouse Jr., *James Blair of Virginia* (Chapel Hill: University of North Carolina Press, 1971) 70-71; Thad W. Tate, "The Colonial College, 1693-1782," in *The College of William & Mary: A History*, 2 vols. (Williamsburg: King and Queen Press, 1993)1:11.

[41] William Berkeley, *A Discourse and View of Virginia* (London, 1663; reprint, Norwalk CT: W.H. Smith, Jr., 1914) 2.

people and foretold future events, the General Assembly in 1663 chided King Charles for his selfish neglect of the colonial church, implicitly accusing him of impiety. Frustrated and disappointed over the failure of the college scheme and colonists' continuing inability to attract clergy, burgesses claimed the situation in Virginia was now out of the hands of men; it would only improve if God intervened to "turn his majesties pious thoughts towards us and provide a better supply of ministers."[42] It was hardly hyperbole when a few years later Lionel Gatford summed up both the colonists' perceptions and over a half century of reality in Virginia's religious life in a short phrase: "poor neglected despised *Virginea*."[43]

Despised and neglected as Virginia was, a smattering of ministers still came to the colony. Their expectations and the colony's realities combined to frame perhaps the most ambiguous facet of Virginia's relationship with England, the relationship with the English Church. It was Virginia's established church as it was England's and most colonists' religious persuasion of choice. With English Anglicans, Virginians shared the *Book of Common Prayer* and the exhortations in the Elizabethan *Book of Homilies*, symbols of a common faith occasionally sent as gifts to Virginia's parishes by the reigning monarch.[44] Church canons for "celebrating divine service and administration of the sacraments" set the liturgical standard for the colony's church. Like their counterparts in England, Virginians used words implying sainthood to refer to the "blessed and glorious" Charles I and commemorated January 30th as a day of fasting and prayer.[45] But the liturgy did not exhaust all there was of the Church, and in Virginia's first half century, the colony's Church

---

[42] Hening, *Statutes at Large*, 2:43.

[43] Gatford, *Publick good without private Interest*, epistle directory.

[44] Warren M. Billings, *Virginia's Viceroy: Their Majesties' Governor General: Francis Howard, Lord Howard of Effingham* (Fairfax VA: George Mason University Press, 1991) 79; Brydon, *Virginia's Mother Church*, 1:191.

[45] Hening, *Statutes at Large*, 2:47, 49.

of England, through necessity and adaptation, had developed its own ecclesiastical "prescription": a hybrid creation, English in theology, colonial in structure, Virginian in fact.

Immigrant ministers understood the differences more readily than most people, and by the mid-1660s their complaints began to reflect not only problems unfamiliar to earlier generations of clergy but also the existence in Virginia of an ecclesiastical polity incompatible with the practices of the English Church. Virginia's novel environment and its demands lost prominence in their descriptions of the colony's religious failings. They no longer complained as much about the environment as they did the people, and not the ones Lionel Gatford called the "scum and off-scouring" of England either.[46] Those folks ranted, cursed, got drunk, had sex outside of marriage, and said God damn too much. But like the poor, people who ranted, cursed, got drunk, had sex outside of marriage, and said God damn too much would be around until the end of the age. The problems came from the good God-fearing Church of England elites and those who aspired to reach elite status. Many of them did the same things as the poorer sort; only since they were more respectable one might assume that they realized they had erred in doing so. More immediately troubling was the fact that they had adopted a form of ecclesiastical government at odds with English notions of proper church order and that they resisted ministers' efforts to Christianize slaves.

Ministers found Virginians' treatment of the natives and slaves particularly disturbing. Whether a product of the age, a special area of instructional emphasis in seminary, or simply an attribute of men willing to journey three thousand miles to serve God, spreading the Gospel to natives and slaves gripped many immigrant ministers as though the ghost of old Edwin Sandys had returned to pursue the lost dream of a biracial Christian society. The colonists' lack of missionary zeal reflected poorly in ministers' minds on the English nation and was contrary to the gentle nature they were certain typified English Christians. Some

---

[46] Gatford, *Publick good without private Interest*, 4.

ministers became so incensed at this neglect that they resorted to hyperbole: "and (which is a grand shame both to our Nation and to our Religion) instead of converting or civilizing any one of the Natives...they give them all too just occasion to be scandalized at the very name of Christianity."[47] Other clergymen persisted in the wishful thinking of "allurement," either too stubborn or too ignorant to accept that Virginians did not care about native souls. Such wishful thinking sometimes forced adherents of the allurement doctrine to revise history so that it more accurately supported their own contemporary goals. If only Virginians would settle in towns, these men argued, their religious lives would improve, natives would see the example of peaceful Christian communities, and pious ministers could reap the harvest of souls, thus making good the colony's original purpose.[48] Improving the quality of Virginia's religious life meant radically reforming the colony's existing social arrangements, but the colonists were unwilling to forego the pursuit of wealth from tobacco that clergy recommendations would have required. Tobacco, not religion, determined their settlement pattern. In addition to Virginians' stubborn adherence to tobacco cultivation (which Crown polices encouraged), experience had taught colonists that natives did not want the gift of the Gospel, and most English people in the colony had long ago put away any thoughts of cultural evangelism. At any rate, worsening native relations in the years after 1661 did nothing to encourage English proselytizing efforts. Rumors of scalps being taken on the frontiers made men place safety and the threat of dying, "suddenly and unprepared," over charity.[49]

With the shift to a formalized race-based slavery early in the 1660s, ministers increasingly directed their missionary ardor toward Christianizing African and African-American slaves. The

---

[47] Gatford, *Publick good without private Interest*, 2.

[48] G[reene], *Virginia's Cure*; Brydon, *Virginia's Mother Church*, 1:514-15.

[49] *Book of Common Prayer*, Great Litany; Morton, *Colonial Virginia*, 1:228-30.

roles of heaven would swell overnight if they could only bring the Gospel to Virginia's growing number of slaves. Some ministers buttressed their efforts to proselytize Virginia's significant population of black bondsmen by applying company-period models to slaves instead of Native Americans. Histories of the ancient world retained primacy for ministers who thought this way and fancied themselves modern partners with the Roman Empire in spreading the Gospel's light to the remaining spiritually dark populations of the globe. Filled with evangelical ardor and inspired by Bede's *Ecclesiastical History of the English Nation* and its saga of how the Romans had brought Christianity to the motley tribe of ancient Britons, Morgan Godwyn, a young Oxford graduate, arrived in Virginia in 1665 ready to act upon the Great Commission and spread the Gospel to all nations. He concerned himself particularly with converting Africans, whom he reasoned made better potential converts than some Europeans; at least they were not Irish, a people he thought truly barbaric. Colonists, however, balked at attempts to Christianize slaves and thus make their chattels more like themselves—at the very least, masters of their own economic freedom. Slaves after all did the work of beasts—better to treat them as beasts. One woman illuminated the commonly held view of white Virginians when she told Godwyn that if he insisted on baptizing slaves he might as well sprinkle water on "her black Bitch" for all the good it would do.[50] To baptize was to acknowledge humanity; cattle could not be Christians, neither could horses or mules. Since Africans did the work of beasts, intellectual convenience demanded that Virginians treat them in this regard as beasts.

To baptize was also to acknowledge the potential freedom of the individual, something Virginians did not wish to admit about their slaves, although English law and colonial custom both argued the incompatibility of slavery and Christianity. As a willfully chosen faith identity Christianity transcended race and cultural identity, the invisible and indelible marks of grace obliterating temporal appearances, with freedom one of its

---

[50] Woolverton, *Colonial Anglicanism in North America*, 71-72.

earthly benefits. The equation of Christianity with liberty and economic opportunity was so commonplace in the 1660s that Governor William Berkeley bribed three Turkish slaves with offers of manumission and plantations if they would reject their inherited heathenism and become Christians.[51] Colonial legal precedents confirmed this truth by commonly freeing slaves judged to be Christians. Elizabeth Key, for instance, received her freedom after proving her Christianity, the justices declaring "That shee hath bin long since Christian...and that by report shee is able to give a very good account of her fayth."[52] A case brought before the colony's General Court in 1665 revealed the same verity, that Christianity bestowed freedom. A black slave who sued for his freedom and was judged to be a Christian was nonetheless returned to his master, but as an indentured servant. As one historian has pointed out, "All of the identifiable free blacks had Christian names." Other blacks bound as slaves were less fortunate and declared frauds masquerading as Christians in vain attempts to steal their freedom.[53]

Black people had lived in Virginia since at least 1619 and despite the effects of traditional English racial animus had occupied an anomalous position in the colony. Some Africans were enslaved, while others enjoyed rights and responsibilities

---

[51] John Clayton, *The Defence of a Sermon, Preach'd upon the Receiving into the Communion of the Church of England*...(Dublin, 1701), preface; Philip S. Foner, *History of Black Americans: From Africa to the Emergence of the Cotton Kingdom* (Westport CT: Greenwood Press, 1975) 192; Winthrop D. Jordan, *White Over Black: American Attitudes Toward the Negro, 1550-1812* (Chapel Hill: University of North Carolina Press, 1968) 180-81.

[52] Warren M. Billings, ed., *The Old Dominion in the Seventeenth Century: A Documentary History of Virginia, 1606-1689* (Chapel Hill: University of North Carolina Press, 1975) 167; Warren M. Billings, "The Cases of Fernando and Elizabeth Key: A Note on the Status of Blacks in Seventeenth-Century Virginia," *William and Mary Quarterly* 3rd ser. 30 (1973): 467-74.

[53] Billings, *Virginia in the Seventeenth Century*, 149, 164-71; H. R. McIlwaine, ed., *Journals of the House of Burgesses of Virginia, 1659/60-1693* (Richmond: Virginia State Library, 1915) 230, 243; Woolverton, *Colonial Anglicanism in North America*, 70.

similar to white people. Black people in the latter group owned property and servants, bought and sold cattle, and did penance in the public church in traditional English fashion like other malefactors. The colonial leaders had not always attempted to keep the Gospel's message from black people. Earlier in the century colonial laws had dictated that when ministers were available, both white and black servants were expected to attend catechetical instruction (although the purpose may have been to give both groups of servants a strong dose of teachings about behavior).[54] This clearly would not do by the 1660s. Slavery was still a fragile institution and granting black Christians freedom threatened the long-term labor force of white Virginians as well as white economic supremacy. To secure these ends, Virginians denied to Africans and African Americans what they had offered in the past by expanding the cultural definition of "savagery" to include Africans and applying it with a consistency they had neglected in the past. Morgan Godwyn described the arrangement: "These two words, Negro and Slave, being by custom grown Homogeneous and Convertible; even as *Negro* and *Christian*, *Englishman* and *Heathen*, are by the like corrupt Custom and Partiality made *Opposites*; thereby as it were implying that the one could not be *Christians*, nor the other *Infidels*."[55] White Virginians wanted to justify their control. Linking cultural identity with religious faith prescribed the world they wanted to exist, thus making it easier to legitimize their superior place in society.

---

[54] Morgan, *American Slavery, American Freedom*, 154-56; Michael L. Levine, *African Americans and Civil Rights, From 1619 to the Present* (Phoenix: Oryx Press, 1996) 16-18; T. H. Breen and Stephen Innes, *"Myne Owne Ground": Race and Freedom on Virginia's Eastern Shore, 1640-1676* (New York: Oxford University Press, 1980). For a discussion of Africans in Virginia before 1619, see William Thorndale, "The Virginia Census of 1619," *Magazine of Virginia Genealogy*, 33 (1995): 155-70.

[55] Woolverton, *Colonial Anglicanism in North America*, 72; Morgan Godwyn, *The Negro's and Indian's Advocate suing for their Admission into the Church* (London, 1680) 36.

Although many clergy, like Godwyn, found the easy division between Englishness and heathenism ontologically irrational, the prescription had deep roots in colonial custom. An earlier critic, had he wished, could have said much the same thing as Godwyn no later than 1622 when the Powhatan uprising had crystallized the differences between English Christians and "savage" natives. Christianity in that year had become the possession of English Virginians, even those who lived lives so base that in James Blair's later phrase they were "Christians by birth" rather than choice.[56] In Virginia, Christianity served not only as a faith but also, and perhaps more importantly, as a cultural identity. As Blair's phrase implied, individuals inherited this identity at birth, and as a purveyor of meaning the cultural inheritance meant more than the faith.

Virginians put religion as an identity to different uses to bring order to their dealings with Native Americans and African slaves. As a cultural possession received at birth by English Virginians, Christianity defined the boundaries between natives and colonists, thus justifying the separation of the two cultures. Separation, however, was not a feasible approach to take with African and African-American slaves. They lived within English Virginia, and colonists who coveted their labor encouraged greater importation. Whereas Christianity as an inherited cultural identity peculiar to white people justified the exclusion of natives from English Virginia, by the 1660s it legitimated not exclusion of Africans but English control of slaves who, of necessity, would remain in English territory. Furthermore, when colonial leaders described natives as "savage" or "heathen," they did so to legitimize excluding from their society a dangerous culture. Africans did not present the same cultural threat, since white Virginians believed that Africans were by nature

---

[56] Jordan, *White Over Black*, 210; James Blair, *Our Saviour's Divine Sermon on the Mount, Contain'd in the Vth, VIth, and VIIth chapters of St. Matthew's Gospel, Explained; and the Practice of it Recommended in divers Sermons and Discourses*, 5 vols. (London, 1722) 3:282, John D. Rockefeller, Jr. Library, Colonial Williamsburg Foundation.

submissive. Therefore African culture did not constitute the danger that Native American culture did. English Virginians might defile their baptisms in debauchery or reject every tenet of the faith, but as Christians by birth they still controlled their own labor and economic potential or as indentured servants could aspire to do so in a few years time. To be identified as Christian by the mid-1660s was to be on the side of control. Intellectual consistency meant excluding Africans from Christianity.

This solution proved untenable, in part because ministers like Godwyn saw through the illusion and forced Virginians to confront their spiritual dissembling. Virginians responded by dissembling in other ways. In 1667, perhaps as a result of Godwyn's complaints, the General Assembly replaced the liberty of the Gospel with the Pauline injunction to remain in the condition one enjoyed at the time of conversion. In other words, baptism no longer conferred freedom. Allegedly passed to "endeavour the propagation of Christianity"[57] the statute changed little about Virginians' efforts to convert their slaves to true religion. By leaving conversion efforts in the hands of masters, the new law created a peculiar variant of ecclesiastical localism.

This statute decreased the importance of faith as a facet of identity and at the same time it elevated, as a defining feature, the culture that had first possessed the faith. English Virginians maintained Christian cultural supremacy by pre-empting the significance of baptismal identity as new creatures in Christ through positive law enactments making cultural inheritance the determining factor in Christian identity. The law created no less than four separate identities: Christians by birth, Christians by birth and choice, heathens by birth, and heathens by birth who later became Christians by choice. Despite the new pronouncement, the last hybrid creature remained a trouble-some beast. Custom was stronger than law, and Virginians continued to equate freedom with Christianity, resisting the conversion of

---

[57] Hening, *Statutes at Large*, 2:260.

their slaves for fear that they would become "immediately free." Ministers throughout the century offered variants on the complaint that slaves "had been there lamentably Neglected," and, consequently, the law may have been passed again in the mid-1680s.[58] Once again, in the conflict between religion and tobacco, tobacco cultivation took primacy in the public sphere.

Although they did not link their cause with the slaves, emigrant ministers after 1665 believed Virginians mistreated the clergy as well, reducing them to a form of ecclesiastical servitude.[59] All the ministers who served Virginia parishes in the seventeenth century were trained in Europe, usually at schools in England or Scotland. Ministers trained in England and familiar with English ecclesiastical customs that gave the clergy independence from the laity found a different situation in Virginia. Familiarity with English practices did not prepare a man for the colony's aberrant form of church government. Ministers had braved dangers at sea and the mysteries of an unknown continent to bring a traditional religious presence to a people long neglected, and they quite likely expected gratitude and respect in return. But clergymen there were treated like servants, or so they complained, who toiled at the pleasure of "Plebian Junto's, the Vestries; to whom the Hiring (that is the usual word there), and admission of Ministers is solely left."[60] Although Virginia's vestries had evolved out of English precedents and both groups shared many of the same bureaucratic responsibilities—caring for the poor, providing for bastard and orphaned children, presenting moral offenders (in Virginia to county rather than ecclesiastical authorities),

---

[58] John Clayton, *Defence of a Sermon*, preface.

[59] But see the *Virginia Gazette*, 3 April 1752, for an eighteenth-century charge that: "There are too a very small Number, who are not so over nice, as to distinguish between a black Gown and a black Skin, but look on the one, to be as great a Mark of Disgrace, and as certain a Badge of Servitude, as the other." Copies of the *Virginia Gazette* may be consulted at the John D. Rockefeller, Jr. Library, Colonial Williamsburg Foundation.

[60] Brydon, *Virginia's Mother Church*, 1:512; Woolverton, *Colonial Anglicanism in North America*, 73-74.

maintaining the church building and grounds—circumstances had allowed Virginians to assume powers unknown to their English and colonial counterparts.[61] In the mid-1630s as a result of the colony's own ecclesiastical localism and the burgesses' attempt to establish order for a colonial church abandoned by English authorities, vestries had gained the right to "elect and make choyce of their ministers," a practice confirmed by statute in 1643.[62] English custom recognized no such vestry authority over clergy. In England, the parish patron nominated a minister to be rector, then the diocesan bishop inducted the nominee into office. Once inducted, a minister enjoyed the equivalent of tenure, the vestry in effect agreeing to support him as long as he wished to remain, with only serious moral offenses justifying the minister's removal from his cure. Virginia's vestries, however, not only had power to choose their ministers but also were reluctant to present clergy for induction, preferring in the words of a Hungars' Parish contract, to "hire from yeare to yeare," allowing ministers salary and use of the glebe and any accompanying lands for a set term. This was part and parcel of what one scholar has termed the "laicization" of the colony's church.[63]

Lay control over Virginia's church was not a completely unjustified innovation, and, all in all, vestries were one source of continuity in the colony's religious life. Ministers came and went, often in rapid succession, and many a vestryman must have attended the funerals of more than a few parish clergy. Nor were all ministers of the best quality, and vestry authority helped Virginians control the reprobate clergy they were certain

---

[61] Borden W. Painter, Jr., "The Anglican Vestry in Colonial America" (Ph.D. diss., Yale University, 1965) 56, 86.

[62] Hening, *Statutes at Large*, 1:302; Woolverton, *Colonial Anglicanism in North America*, 77-78.

[63] Clive Raymond Hallman, Jr., "The Vestry as a Unit of Local Government in Colonial Virginia" (Ph.D. diss., University of Georgia, 1987) ch. 1, 12-13, 37; Woolverton, *Colonial Anglicanism in North America*, 74-78; Northampton Order Book, X, 1674-1679, f. 137. For the functions of a Church of England parish in colonial Virginia, see Seiler, "The Anglican Parish in Virginia," 119-42.

England dumped on the colony. Taking the colonists' view that English authorities often treated Virginians shabbily, Governor William Berkeley in 1670 quipped that most clergy who served Virginia were, like other English exports to James City, "as in all things the worst."[64] The natural tendency of human beings to maintain the authority they have along with Virginia's peculiar circumstances led the colony's vestries to guard their powers jealously.

By the mid 1660s, vestries no longer went begging for clergy the way Lancaster County Parish had in 1652 when the vestry there had consented to pay Alexander Cooke "double tythes" for a year. These avaricious bands of imperious men now called the shots. In some cases fiscally shrewd vestrymen who knew they could pay lay readers less than ordained ministers and thus allow residents of a parish to keep more of their tobacco for market often hired these "leaden lay-Priests of the vestries ordination" to read prayers from the liturgy and sermons from the *Book of Homilies*. Governor Berkeley introduced an even more irregular practice when he took the unprecedented step of using his civil authority to ordain men to the deaconate, not to save money but to put men with some sort of orders into the colony's parishes. Vestries defended their powers and the colony's ecclesiastical arrangements in other ways as well, and, as a consequence, ministers who pressed English tradition too enthusiastically sometimes lost their jobs. After serving Christ Church Parish in Middlesex County without complaint for over two years, for example, the Reverend Richard Morris asked the vestry to present him to the governor, who by colonial law filled the bishop's role of inducting clergy, for lifetime tenure in his cure. The vestry offered to continue as before. When Morris refused their offer, the vestrymen dismissed him and hired a lay reader to lead prayer services. Occasionally, vestries showed their displeasure with ministers who balked at signing another yearly contract in more public displays. John Munro of King and Queen Parish was not the only minister who, after a dispute with

---

[64] Billings, *Virginia's Viceroy*, 79-81; Hening, *Statutes at Large*, 1:517.

vestrymen over a contract, showed up on Sunday to preach and read divine service to find the doors of the church shut against him and a confused congregation milling around outside. The vestrymen of King and Queen were, however, more creative in explaining away the shut doors. They said they had presumed the parish vacant and did not want cows wandering in to defile the chapel.[65]

Colonial custom irritated English ministers used to the freedom and security of induction. The high-handed practices of Virginia vestrymen left both ministers and the English church hierarchy angry and bewildered. Clergy in Virginia abused by the vestries thought themselves treated as hirelings—no better than common laborers at an Elizabethan work fair searching for another year's contract. The situation perplexed Archbishop of Canterbury, Thomas Tenison: "This seems to me a very strange way they have there that their Ministers are not inducted, but may be removed like domestic Servants by a Vote of the Vestry. Who would be a Minister in that Country?"[66] Writing from his Fulham Palace residence in 1677, Henry Compton, bishop of London, under whose jurisdiction the church in the foreign plantations fell, summed up the nature of the clergy's complaints, erring only in assuming that a power not found in theory was necessarily imaginary: "the vestries there pretend an Authority to be intrusted with the sole management of Church

---

[65] Brydon, *Virginia's Mother Church*, 1:513; Lord Howard of Effingham to Nathaniel Crew [?], in Warren M. Billings, ed., *The Papers of Francis Howard Baron Howard of Effingham, 1643-1695* (Richmond: Virginia State Library and Archives, 1989) 458; C. G. Chamberlayne, ed., *The Vestry Book of Christ Church Parish, Middlesex County, Virginia, 1663-1767* (Richmond: Old Dominion Press, 1927) 6, 9, 12; H. R. McIlwaine, *Executive Journals of the Council of Colonial Virginia* (Richmond: Virginia State Library, 1979) 1:328; George MacLaren Brydon, "Parson Sclater and His Vestry," *Virginia Magazine of History and Biography* 53 (1945): 288-301.

[66] "A True Account of a Conference at Lambeth, 27 December 1697," in Perry, *Historical Collections Relating to the American Colonial Church*, 1:47, 49.

Affaires, & to exercise an arbitrary power over the Ministers themselves."[67]

Virginians did not see their authority as pretended, whether in law or not. They were a people for whom custom was more important than law, or better still, of customs in the process of becoming law. If Bishop Compton revealed the conflict of traditions in theory, then Morgan Godwyn outlined the practical consequences by turning an ironic question into a declaration: "this is the recompense of leaving their hopes in England... together with their Friends and Relations, and their Native Soil, to venture their lives into those parts amongst strangers and enemies to their Profession."[68] Godwyn, like William Berkeley, a royalist and strong supporter of the Church of England (his father was a canon, one grandfather a bishop), arrived in the colony in 1666. Arrogant, self-righteous, and a devotee of proper ecclesiastical government, Godwyn found Virginia's customs troubling. To surmise from his record in the colony (three parishes in four years), colonial vestries found him equally vexing. He was one of the first to encounter the colony's powerful vestries and the most eloquent spokesman of immigrant ministers in the second half of the century. "Plebeian Junto's," "leaden lay-Priests," "hungry Patrons"—the terms are his.[69] In words calculated to enflame, Godwyn compared the vestries' treatment of ministers unfavorably to the Church of England's sufferings under Oliver Cromwell's illegal government: "our Discouragements there [Virginia] are much greater, than ever they were here in England, under the Usurpers."[70] His repeated attempts to impose English ecclesiastical ideas on his provincial parishioners did not sit well with colonists who believed their

---

[67] Henry Compton, A Memorial of what abuses are crept into the Churches of the Plantations, PRO CO 1/41, ff. 48-49; Arthur Lyon Cross, The Anglican Episcopate and the American Colonies (New York: Longmans, Green, and Company, 1902) 27.

[68] Brydon, Virginia's Mother Church, 1:512.

[69] Brydon, Virginia's Mother Church, 1:512-14; Woolverton, Colonial Anglicanism in North America, 71-72.

[70] Brydon, Virginia's Mother Church, 1:512.

own experience had taught them what was necessary—London, Canterbury, or Oxford be damned.

Godwyn encountered a Virginia far different from what it had been a few years earlier. Race-based slavery formalized in law, angry over Stuart threats to economic freedom, and feeling abandoned once again by the Church of England, Virginia possessed a society that in terms of religion had come to terms with its novel environment and had found ways of getting by. Roger Greene, the most ardent spokesman for the clergy prior to Godwyn, had railed about the colony's accommodation to tobacco culture and how Virginians' failure to live in towns, their damnably inconvenient settlement pattern, and the long distances that a man or woman had to travel to get to church, hindered the public practice of religion. Tobacco, in fact, is the great villain of Greene's *Virginia's Cure* for it led to the troublesome ways of life.[71] Godwyn, however, identified a new villain for a new era in the colony's development, the vestries. Previous ministers, still fascinated by the prospect of converting natives through "allurement," had urged gathering colonists into towns where ministers could more easily spread religion among the English, and pious settlers could then more easily attract natives to Christianity. To be sure, Godwyn wanted to convert natives as much as any Virginia Company minister had, yet his concerns reflected something different—not the culture of a weed, but colonial elites jealous of their right to rule Virginia as they saw fit. Whereas ministers prior to 1665 had complained primarily about colonial "occasions," ministers after 1665 shifted the focus of their complaints to the institutions the "occasions" had fostered. The first offered a critique; the second sounded a warning.

Ministers who did not like Virginia's customs essentially reduced their complaints to the issue of ecclesiastical authority. Salaries, induction, missionary efforts to slaves and Native Americans, proper church order and practice—all could be set right, they believed, if only the Church of England sent a bishop

---

[71] G[reene], *Virginia's Cure.*

to North America. It was Roger Greene's solution; it was Morgan Godwyn's solution; and sixty years later it was Hugh Jones' solution as well.[72] They hoped for a strong bishop as well, not some political appointment to whom the king owed debts, preferably one willing to take on the vestries, break their power, and, in general, show these provincials in Virginia just how the Church of England ought to be run. Writing from his parish in New Kent County in 1697, Nicholas Moreau claimed the church would flourish in Virginia if only your "Lordship would send here a good Bishop, with a severe observation of the Canons of the Church, eager for the Salvation of Souls."[73] For dissatisfied colonial clergy, a colonial episcopate became something of a panacea, their hopes conjuring up images of a resident bishop waving a magic crosier over Virginia's peculiar arrangements and setting everything right. A faulty logic grounded their assumptions—the supposition that authority implied the force requisite to effect the necessary changes in Virginia's church and the assumption that confronted by authority Virginians would obey. They had a long history of doing just the opposite.

Different understandings of the problems with Virginia's church belied conflict between two different "prescriptions" in religion. When emigrant ministers urged the Church hierarchy to appoint a bishop, they framed Virginia's religious problems in such a way that ecclesiastical government became the focus, thus making departures from English practice the source of friction. Virginians framed the question another way. They had neither asked for a bishop nor shown any interest in having one resident in the colony. For them the issue was not church government but pastoral care, and the problems originated not with the colonists but with the Church and the Crown. Grievances drawn

---

[72] G[reene], *Virginia's Cure*, 18; Brydon, *Virginia's Mother Church*, 1:513; Hugh Jones, *The Present State of Virginia, From Whence is Inferred a Short View of Maryland and North Carolina*, ed. Richard L. Morton (Chapel Hill: University of North Carolina Press, 1956) 119-22.

[73] Nicholas Moreaux to the bishop of Lichfield, 12 April 1697, Fulham Palace Papers, Vol. XI, ff. 24-25.

up by Rappahanock County after Bacon's Rebellion in 1676 not
only attested to the colony's enduring problem, but were also
phrased in such a way as to make England rather than Virginia
responsible for God's judgment on the colony: "The first thing
that wee complaine of...is the great want of honest able sober
pious orthodox Ministers the want whereof & of ye due
administration of divine ordinances have bin the originall cause
of the severe Judgments that have fallen upon this Land,
wherefore it is desired that yor honor would be pleased to ask his
Matie to send us an annuall supply thereof."[74] Virginians wanted
ministers to fill Virginia's empty pulpits, and a bishop after all
was but one man. He could ordain men to the priesthood, to be
sure, but that took years of study for each candidate, all the
while, for want of clergy, children died unbaptized,[75] their souls
damned by English indifference. To the colonists, all that
English officials could speak of was authority—economic, political, now ecclesiastical.

When pressed on the issue of their ecclesiastical difficulties,
Virginians dissembled, shifted the terms of the debate, and
charged the English Church with hypocrisy. As Thomas Ludwell
coyly explained to Lord Arlington in 1667, Virginia was "yett
unfitt for a Bishop to reside here by reason of the fewness of our
Numbers & other Inconveniences." But, if the bishop of
London, Humphrey Henchman, and other superior clergy took
the colony "a little more into their care" and sent additional
ministers, colonial parishes would happily accept them and
present these men to the governor for induction into their

---

[74] Grievances of Rappahanock County, 13 March 1676/77, PRO CO
1/39, f. 197; David John Robinson, "Roots of Anti-Clericalism in Colonial
Virginia Down to 1750 with Particular Reference to the Career of James
Blair" (Ph.D. diss., University of Southampton, 1980) 200.

[75] Lord Howard of Effingham to the bishops of Durham, Peterborough,
and Rochester, February 1687, *Papers of Lord Francis Howard Baron
Howard of Effingham*, 282.

livings.[76] Asked to provide an accurate description of the colony's government, Ludwell told English officials what Virginians wanted them to hear—that the colony's religious life was in sufficient order and, rumors to the contrary, not in need of closer supervision. To their minds, the colony's ecclesiastical government worked well. All Virginia needed was a better supply of clergy, preferably men willing to adapt to the colony's ways. A bishop was neither necessary nor suitable in Virginia, especially since episcopacy meant additional English control. Already chafing at Stuart imperial policies that limited their economic freedom, Virginians thought of a colonial bishop as yet another unwelcome interference in the colony's affairs. It set a bad precedent as well, for Virginia's elite were men new enough both to power and slavery to realize just how easily power could be taken away.

Church government was a moot point for most Virginians. They did not bring up the question because they had settled the issue, or more accurately, circumstances and "occasions" had helped settle the issue for them. When colonists and ministers clashed over issues such as induction and the role of vestries, they did not argue about the Church's spiritual purpose but about its outward form. Both followed an Anglican custom which argued that church government was adiaphora, or a thing indifferent, until it was settled, then for the sake of order the form established should remain. By the 1660s when conflicts over colonial church government first appeared, the Church of England on both sides of the Atlantic had established due forms of church order. For people in England, the Church of England meant episcopacy and the powers associated with the bishop's office, not only to ordain men to the priesthood but also to impose ecclesiastical order. Virginians did not disagree with all of that. They wanted ordained clergymen, preferably English rather than Scottish ones, and they were content to allow the bishop of London to determine a man's suitability for the

---

[76] Thomas Ludwell to Lord Arlington, 17 September 1666, PRO CO 1/20, f. 220.

priesthood. Throughout the colonial period, Virginians submit-
ted to this aspect of episcopal authority by sending postulates to
England for ordination despite the inconvenience.[77]

Yet Virginians did not necessarily consent to a bishop's
authority in church government. To make a priest was one thing;
to govern the clergy and laity was another thing altogether. The
analogy may be pushed too far, but Virginians were leaving
behind in religion the Aristotelian world that claimed that the
one was better than the few or the many and were beginning to
mix the forms of government. While Virginians clearly conceded
the spiritual power of the one, the bishop, to ordain priests, they
preferred their own more democratic (actually aristocratic) form
of church government. Now, vestries were hardly democratic
institutions, as many people during Bacon's Rebellion pointed
out; they had a disturbing tendency in the seventeenth century
to become closed, self-perpetuating bodies run by local elites.[78]
In relations with England, however, they were democratic to the
extent that vestrymen had been elected and represented the
interests of the people of a parish, the many, against the power
of the one, be it bishop or Crown. The struggle was not simply
one between Virginians and the Church of England over
authority, but the creation of a new institutional structure with a
new understanding of authority. In England, the advowson, or
right to appoint ministers, was a form of property that could be
inherited or sold as its owner saw fit, essentially making it a

---

[77] Peter Lake, *Anglicans and Puritans? Presbyterian and English
Conformist Thought from Whitgift to Hooker* (London: Allen & Unwin,
1988) 221-22; John Spurr, *The Restoration Church of England, 1646-1689*
(New Haven: Yale University Press, 1991) 135-36; Joan R. Gundersen,
"The Search for Good Men: Recruiting Ministers in Colonial Virginia,"
Historical Magazine of the Protestant Episcopal Church 48 (1979): 453-64.

[78] Billings, *Virginia's Viceroy*, 81. After 1720, however, this was not
necessarily true. See Joan R. Gundersen, "The Myth of the Independent
Virginia Vestry," *Historical Magazine of the Protestant Episcopal Church* 44
(1975) 133-41.

private right beyond the control of a majority of the laity.[79]
Virginians made the power to appoint somewhat more
democratic in theory, thus giving the representatives of the
people power over the clergy in ways English tradition found
abominable. Virginia Anglicans by the 1660s were as devoted to
this structure as they were to the *Book of Common Prayer*.

The result was a new form of outward identity for the Church
of England in which vestries shared control of the church with
bishops. In spiritual matters such as making priests and defining
theology, Virginia churchmen conceded the traditional authority
of the church hierarchy, but in matters of church government,
Virginians believed local custom should come first and now
demanded the right to determine colonial church polity, a right
that had originally been thrust upon the colonists when the
English Church and Crown refused to take an interest in the
colonial church. There were other concerns as well. Virginians
saw themselves not only as defenders of the customs that had
emerged out of their "occasions," but also as protectors of the
colonial church from unfit clergy. Ministers, on the other hand,
found Virginia's church oppressive, an unorthodox innovation
harmful to the clergy's traditional independence and thus to
their prophetic role within society. Having settled the issue of
church government to their own satisfaction, Virginians wanted
above all else greater pastoral care. Ministers who spread the
Gospel in Virginia had no problems with providing the colonists
with pastoral guidance; they simply wanted to do their work in a
context governed by the customary English rules about
ecclesiastical order with which they were familiar.

The struggle between colonists and clergy for control of
Virginia's ecclesiastical polity was important, yet it was very
nearly a struggle about theory alone. Until English authorities
found either supplying Virginians with more ministers or
establishing ecclesiastical order an issue worth their trouble,
colonists were not going to get a larger supply of ministers or

---

[79] F. L. Cross and E. A. Livingstone, eds., *The Oxford Dictionary of the Christian Church*, 2nd ed. (New York: Oxford University Press, 1993) 20.

better pastoral care and ministers were not going to receive support for more ecclesiastical order.[80] The truth of the matter

---

[80] As a result either of caution, cowardice, or continued disinterest by the Church and Crown in Virginia's religious situation, little was done about a colonial bishop for several years. The first clear steps came in 1672, although who originated the plans and why they did so remains unclear. Nevertheless, a charter directed "that the place of James City and the church there be created, erected, founded and established as an Episcopal See and Cathedral Church." The site chosen was ridiculous and would have done little if anything to enhance the dignity of the Church of England. Ludwell had been on the mark: Virginia was not yet suitable for a bishop, especially at Jamestown. It made a pathetic metropolis and by whatever high-sounding name one wished to call it, James City was no see city. Three years later visitors and residents could still view the place with a glance—a church, a statehouse, "som 16 to 18 howses," most, but not all, of brick. Only a dozen families made their homes in town. Most residents earned a living running ordinaries at which they charged travelers and members of the General Assembly inflated prices for rooms and drink.

However implausible the place, Charles II's nominee for the post, Alexander Moray, was about as wise a choice as was possible. The whole scheme may have been repayment by the king for a decades' old debt of friendship. A royalist Scotsman, Moray had fought with Charles at the Battle of Worcester. He fled England after that debacle, ending up by 1665 at Ware Parish in Virginia's Gloucester County. He adapted easily to colonial society and was soon acting like a Virginian. Moray planted both tobacco and mulberry trees that he hoped would soon bring profit in silk, acquired servants (who may have been slaves) to tend his fields, and planned to purchase more laborers. If he could "procure two or three men servants more," Moray reasoned that he could quit preaching and take up full time as a planter, thus leaving him more time to pursue his beloved agricultural experiments. His piety based on the quiet of the desert fathers, Moray even found the colony's settlement pattern to his liking. If English authorities thought Virginia needed a bishop, then Moray was their man. Despite some anti-Scots prejudice, Moray fit in well in his adopted land.

But the plan failed. Trouble arose when word made it back to Virginia that Charles II intended to "settle Ecclesiasticall Government in Virginia by a Bishop." Men who either disliked Moray, the idea of a colonial bishop, or both, cast "false aspertions" and "black imputations" upon the minister. In a letter to Archbishop of Canterbury Gilbert Sheldon requesting an inquiry, Moray suggested that any animosity may as likely been directed at the office as at the man chosen to fill it. From that point on the plan collapsed. Mary Francis Goodwin, "The First Bishop-Designate of Virginia 1672-3," is that English authorities had long disregarded the colonists' religious life.

The fortunes of Virginia's church changed, however, in 1675 when Charles II translated Henry Compton from Oxford to the see of London. By tradition, expectation, or default, the bishop of London held jurisdiction over the Church of England overseas, although prior incumbents had mostly looked upon the colonial church as a nuisance to be avoided, leading one historian to claim the existence between 1630 and 1680 of an ecclesiastical "starving time."[81] Compton changed all of that. Whether justified legally or not, he considered himself the colonies' "diocesan"[82] and took responsibility for the spiritual welfare of men and women in the foreign plantations. In the process he formalized the bishop of London's control over the Church of England in the colonies in ways that would shape the colonial church until the American Revolution. Compton recognized both the pastoral difficulties Virginians faced as well as their penchant for syncretism in church government. The shortage of clergy was well known, but abuses were also rampant: men without orders exercised "ministerial function[s]," parishes sometimes remained vacant notwithstanding the availability of suitable ministers, and, most troublesome, the vestries maintained what he called a "pretended authority" to run the church.[83]

Historical Magazine of the Protestant Episcopal Church 12 (1943): 59-68; "Letters Written by Mr. Moray, a Minister to Sr. R. Moray, from Ware River in Mock-Jack Bay, Virginia, 1 February 1665," *William and Mary Quarterly* 2nd ser. 2 (1922): 157-61; Alexander Moray to Gilbert, Lord Archbishop of Canterbury, 1672/73, Harleian Mss. 3790, f. 1-4, British Museum; "Draft for the Creation of a Bishoprick in Virginia," *Virginia Magazine of History and Biography* 36 (1928): 45-53; Charles M. Andrews, ed., *Narratives of the Insurrections, 1675-1690* (Bowie MD: Heritage Books, 1992) 70, 135-36.

[81] Butler, *Awash in a Sea of Faith*, 42.

[82] Cross, *Anglican Episcopate in the American Colonies*, 25.

[83] Cross, *Anglican Episcopate in the American Colonies*, 27; Henry Compton, A Memorial of what abuses are crept into the Churches of the Plantations, PRO CO 1/41, ff. 48-49.

Bishop Compton believed that the colonists as well as English leaders had contributed to the difficulties in the colonial church and that both English and colonial errors warranted reform. Faced with a multitude of problems, Compton set out first to improve the quality and number of Virginia's clergy, hoping that success in this area might resolve the remaining difficulties. He was familiar with rumors about the colony's poor clergy and realized vestries had used this fact to justify their authority. Perhaps if deserving men filled colonial pulpits Virginians would be more inclined to follow church law and induct ministers into their livings as church law required. Compton therefore cracked down on dissolute clergy. In 1677 he instructed lieutenant governor Herbert Jeffreys to make "Inquiry" into the "lives, licence, abilities, and qualifications" of Virginia's clergy and to suspend or remove all "scandalous, unworthy Ministers."[84] Three years later he began ordering all colonial governors to allow no minister to serve a colonial parish "without a Certificate from the Lord Bp. of London" affirming the man's orthodoxy and good moral character.[85] He also took a personal interest in finding candidates for Virginia's many vacant pulpits. A botanist, whose Fulham Palace gardens were renowned for their exotic plants, Compton often chose for the colony men like himself who combined a religious vocation with an interest in science. The variety and curiosity of the colony's flora and fauna was well known by the late-seventeenth century, and Compton may have impressed upon potential missionaries the opportunities Virginia afforded both to serve God and to investigate firsthand hitherto unseen wonders of his creation. The bishop acted wisely when he emphasized the colony's natural wonders to potential missionaries. If the people proved stiff-necked in their refusal to abide by English church law, the

---

[84] Rouse, *James Blair of Virginia*, 61.

[85] Cross, *Anglican Episcopate in the American Colonies*, 26; Billings, *Virginia's Viceroy*, 79; Rouse, *James Blair of Virginia*, 61; Instructions to Governor Thomas Lord Culpepper, 6 September 1679, Fulham Palace Papers, Vol. XI, ff. 11-12.

country nonetheless helped ameliorate the unhappiness of many clergymen. Delight in their scientific endeavors helped soften the disappointment some clergymen-scientists experienced in their professional lives. At least that was the case with the Reverend Nicholas Moreau. Unhappy in his pastoral pursuits because he had difficulty adjusting to Virginia's ecclesiastical system, Moreau still enjoyed the opportunities Virginia offered for scientific explorations. John Bannister, John Clayton (the colony's first commissary), and the dedicated Hugh Jones were a few of the scientifically inclined ministers who came to Virginia at Compton's behest. The bishop encouraged men less interested in science to come to Virginia as well, such as Deuel Pead (later minister of St. James Clerkenwell in London and chaplain to John Holles, Earl of Clare), and James Blair (Virginia's second commissary).[86]

Sending clergy to Virginia not only filled many of the colony's vacant parishes but also served in an unobtrusive way to shape Virginia's religious ethos. As a result, the colony took on a more distinctly Anglican tenor in the years after 1675, an accomplishment reached not by official proclamation, which would have raised Virginians' suspicions about authority, but by the simple and gradual workings of parish clergy going about their work and from time to time encouraging stricter adherence to contemporary English liturgical practices. Virginia Anglicans, after all, were English in worship if not in church government. Although there was little that ministers could do to make church exteriors reflect English models—most colonial churches were wood-frame buildings that resembled tobacco warehouses—they could make the interiors look more like what they remembered of churches in England. After 1680 many parishes began to rail in their communion tables or introduce rood screens. These

---

[86] Edmund and Dorothy Berkeley, eds. *John Clayton: Parson with a Scientific Mind* (Chapel Hill: University of North Carolina Press, 1965) xxiii; Edward Lewis Goodwin, *The Colonial Church in Virginia* (Milwaukee: Morehouse, 1927) 248, 260, 298; Davis, *Intellectual Life in the Colonial South*, 2:717.

architectural elements served to set off the sanctuary from the rest of the building, thus indicating a more clearly defined Anglican understanding of the sacrament and the dignity of the sanctuary. Some parishes ordered new pulpit cloths in a variety of colors, perhaps to indicate the seasons of the church's liturgical year. Vestrymen made certain that the surplice was washed and kept in good repair for the clergy's use. Occasionally, ministers even emphasized the importance of liturgical posture. If Deuel Pead treated his parishioners at St. Peter's Parish in Henrico the way he did congregations he later served in England, he soon had them bowing at the name of Jesus as a sign of reverence, a high-church practice associated with Laudianism. Church construction picked up in the years after 1680 as well.[87]

The vestries were another matter altogether. Lord Thomas Culpepper, governor of the colony from 1677 to 1683, reported at the end of 1681 that these bodies remained obstinate on the matter of presentation of clergy for induction.[88] Local custom and local law both granted vestrymen authority to hire and fire clergy, and they had no intention of forfeiting rights they now counted among their property. A power used was a power assumed, and they refused to amend Virginia's system of ecclesiastical government. Nor were they convinced by

---

[87] Jon Butler, *Awash in a Sea of Faith: Christianizing the American People* (Cambridge: Harvard University Press, 1990) 99-101; Richard Beeman, *The Evolution of the Southern Backcountry: A Case Study of Lunenburg County, Virginia, 1746-1842* (Philadelphia: University of Pennsylvania Press, 1984) 54; Dell Upton, *Holy Things and Profane: Anglican Parish Churches in Colonial Virginia* (Cambridge: MIT Press, 1986) 73-76; C. G. Chamberlayne, ed., *The Vestry Book of Kingston Parish, Matthew's County, Virginia, 1674-1796* (Richmond: Old Dominion Press, 1929) 11-12; C. G. Chamberlayne, *The Vestry Book of St. Paul's Parish, Hanover County, Virginia, 1706-1786* (Richmond: The Library Board, 1940) 20, 26, 41, 43, 49, 56, 60, 85; Deuel Pead, *Jesus is God: or, The Deity of Jesus Christ Vindicated. Being an Abstract of some Sermons Preach'd in the Parish Church of St. James Clerkenwell* (London, 1694) 91.

[88] Governor Thomas Culpepper to Bishop of London, 12 December 1681, PRO CO 1/47, ff. 258-262.

Compton's imperialist logic that smacked to them of tyranny. The bishop of London argued that the king was the patron of all colonial parishes and therefore possessed the right to appoint ministers to the governor for induction into their livings.[89] Virginians found this line of argument dangerous. It put local control of a colonial institution under the authority of the king and his representative, the governor, thus concentrating power in the one and denying the few or the many any role at all. Colonists were willing to share authority over clerical appointments with the king and indicated this on those occasions when vestries presented ministers for induction, but they refused to concede to the Crown power to choose clergy for colonial parishes. Given the colony's ecclesiastical localism, to do so could have forced on Virginia a dangerous degree of uniformity.

The Stuarts eventually settled upon a two-pronged policy to bring order to Virginia's church. As part of a general attempt to consolidate power in the governor and his appointed council, Charles II sent instructions to Lord Howard of Effingham, the colony's governor, explicitly ordering him to break the power of Virginia's local government, the county courts and the vestries. A skillful governor could have achieved these ends by exploiting factionalism among the justices, burgesses, and vestrymen to his own advantage. But skillful governors were rare in the late seventeenth century, and the burgesses, already angry over royal vetoes of their General Assembly statutes, stymied Effingham's efforts. Stalemate marked much of his tenure as governor. Lord Howard scolded, cajoled, and reminded the burgesses of the king's desires; the burgesses delayed and objected, refusing to participate in the destruction of their liberties.[90]

The second prong of the Stuart assault granted greater authority to the bishop of London to supervise the colonial Church of England. Lack of ecclesiastical authority in the

---

[89] Cross, *Anglican Episcopate in the American Colonies*, 26-27.
[90] Morton, *Colonial Virginia*, 1:316-27; Morgan, *American Slavery, American Freedom*, 288-92. For a more detailed account of Effingham's administration, see Billings, *Virginia's Viceroy*.

colonies meant that clergy went unsupervised and liturgical irregularities such as Virginians' penchant for being buried in their orchards rather than the churchyard went unrebuked. Compton gained additional powers over the colonial church, including the right to appoint a commissary, or representative, to oversee church affairs in each colony, although certain bureaucratic functions such as induction, "granting licenses for Marriage[,] and probate of wills" were reserved to the governor.[91] Compton, most likely, had the plan in mind and had sent the scientist-clergyman John Clayton to Virginia in 1684, probably with informal instructions to take charge of the parish at James City, Virginia's capital, before beginning a colony-wide reformation of church government. Clayton's reputation as an outstanding minister and fine preacher preceded him to the colony. Expectations ran high when he was asked to address the General Assembly not long after reaching Virginia: "I am to preach so that something peculiar is expected." He did not disappoint and received £5 for his troubles. When formal word came from the Crown authorizing the establishment of commissariats overseas, Compton urged Effingham to confirm his choice for Virginia by nominating Clayton for the new position. The young man was highly esteemed by the governor and burgesses alike, and Effingham wisely obliged.

Whether or not he ever received his commission, Clayton nonetheless set precedents reflecting the colony's religious attitudes. He brought Anglican ritual to his parish at James City, later claiming that he had "Setled the Service of our Church very Regularly" and that he was the first there to wear a surplice, a white garment worn over the cassock by Anglicans during divine service and a point of special contention for nonconformists. Clayton also brought a quiet missionary zeal to his dealings with sectaries and nonconformists. To combat the significant number of dissenters in the colony, Clayton turned not to fire or proclamations of uniformity or rancorous argumentation, but to calm and reasoned persuasion, a practice in keeping with Charles

---

[91] Rouse, *James Blair of Virginia*, 61.

II's earlier order to Governor Berkeley that he not "suffer any man to be molested or disquieted in the exercise of his Religion, so he be content with a quiet and peaceable enjoying it, not giving therein offense or scandall to the Government."[92] Men dissented from the established church, Clayton believed, because they did not understand the excellence of the Church of England and its *Book of Common Prayer*. If ministers only took the time to explain the church's faith and the prayer book's understanding of the relationship between God and man, more nonconformists could be brought to true religion than through the use of economic sanctions or corporal punishment. To this end, Clayton held regular afternoon lectures on the Church and the liturgy, commending its logic and piety to dissenters and conformists alike. His method won numerous converts among sectaries, and no doubt kept countless Anglicans within the faith. Even some Anabaptists and Quakers after hearing Clayton's explanations requested baptism at his hands. By his own account, as well as governor Effingham's, Clayton did good work in Virginia and may have wished to push reform more strenuously, perhaps against Roman Catholics. With Compton sending more qualified men to Virginia and Clayton overseeing matters on-site, the colony's church gained a measure of stability.

Shortly thereafter the trouble came. Clayton left Virginia early in 1686, possibly before formally receiving his commission from Bishop Compton. European politics and the sickly winter of 1686 and 1687 brought worse trouble, nearly combining to wipe out Compton's accomplishments. Charles II died in 1685, and the man who inherited the throne—thus becoming king, defender of the faith, and temporal head of the Church of England—was his brother, James II, a Roman Catholic. The immediate consequences of this change of regime did not bode well for Virginia's religious life. Despite his latitudinarian beliefs and his indulgence of nonconformists, Compton held no great fondness for Catholics and soon fell from favor with the new monarch for refusing to silence an anti-papist preacher in his

---

[92] Neill, *Virginia's Carolorum*, 292.

diocese. Following a trial and conviction in 1686, James suspended his stubborn Lord of London and put the overseas plantations under the ecclesiastical jurisdiction of a committee headed by the bishop of Durham, Nathaniel Crew. Crew did not devote the attention to Virginia that Compton had, and coupled with the "fatall" winter of 1686 and 1687 when many ministers in the colony either died or fled for fear of disease, Virginia was once again thrown into ecclesiastical chaos. Disturbed by Crew's reversion to the traditional English inattention to the colony's religious welfare, Governor Effingham chided the bishop early in 1687, comparing his efforts unfavorably to Compton's: since "my Lord Byshop of Londons suspention...there hath not been such a supply of Ministers sent hither as usuall." Nor were all those who remained in the colony suitable. Many had no orders or lived lives so disordered that they disgraced the Gospel. Others had simply declared themselves ministers by an acclamation of one, an irregularity only slightly more bizarre than former Governor Berkeley's decision to ordain men to the deaconate. Virginians had long history of experience with the accommodations their "occasions" necessitated and when in doubt or forced by necessity, Virginians adapted. The colony's situation even made a Virginian of Lord Howard in this regard. He suspended the notorious livers and allowed the remaining clergy, even those who had acclaimed themselves ministers, to officiate in all capacities save celebrating the Eucharist and pronouncing absolution. His description of the revived ecclesiastical chaos reflected conditions that would continue until after the Glorious Revolution: "I am forced to permitt, that one Minister may officiate in three and some tymes in Four Parrishes, and in many places there is not one in neere an hundred Miles, that Children dye unavoidably unbaptised."[93] Virginia's crisis in pastoral care had returned once again.

---

[93] My account of John Clayton's commissariat comes from Billings, *Virginia's Viceroy*, 78-81; Clayton, *The Defence of a Sermon*, preface; "John Clayton of James City, Afterwards of Crofton, Yorkshire," *William and Mary Quarterly* 2nd ser. 1 (1921): 114-15; Edward Carpenter, *The*

Old attitudes and animosities shaped life both in England and Virginia as people in the two societies wrestled with conflicts traditional to their prescriptions. As was often the case, religion was at the forefront of the strife in England while in Virginia it remained but a cultural identity. Following his accession to the throne in 1685 James II ran afoul of England's customary anti-papist prejudices, and consequently his reign was not a happy one for the English people. It was bad enough that his brother had been a crypto-Catholic, albeit with the good taste to stay his formal conversion until his deathbed, but James was openly Catholic, and his subjects feared their monarch's challenge to their Protestant ways. Shared memories of a rumored Popish Plot in 1679 only made Britons more suspicious of James' intentions. The birth and baptism as a Roman Catholic of a male heir sent many English people into a panic.

James' religious opinions revived the traditional European religious animosities that never seemed far away in seventeenth and early eighteenth-century England. For many Englishmen, the Glorious Revolution—or, in Stephen Webb's words, "Lord Churchill's coup"—was about the defense of England's Protestant religion and Protestant political power. Residents of the nation's North Atlantic colonies often reacted in a similar manner as a "Protestant putsch" swept across the Atlantic seaboard in New England, New York, and Maryland.

Virginians endured some of the same animosity, mostly from designing men willing to take advantage of a chaotic political situation for their own ends. The minister Reverend John Waugh of

---

Protestant Bishop, Being the Life of Henry Compton, 1632-1713, Bishop of London (New York: Longmans, Greene, and Company, 1956), 78-104; Henry Compton to Lord Howard of Effingham, 14 September 1685; Henry Compton to Lord Howard of Effingham, 19 November 1686; Lord Howard of Effingham to the bishops of Durham, Peterborough, and Rochester, February 1687; Lord Howard of Effingham to Nathaniel Crew?, n.d., in Billings, *Papers of Francis Howard Baron Howard of Effingham*, 219, 274, 282, 458-59; Berkeley and Berkeley, *Parson With a Scientific Mind*, xxiv-xxxiv; McIlwaine, *Journals of the House of Burgesses of Colonial Virginia, 1619-1659/60*, 226.

Overwharton Parish in the colony's Northern Neck, was one such man. A rabble-rouser who actively courted public favor, and possessed of a penchant for disregarding colonial laws, Waugh and several supporters stirred up a tumult in Stafford and Rappahanock counties. He railed against Roman Catholics, claimed the existence of a plot between local natives and Roman Catholic Marylanders to kill all the Protestants, and, most disturbing, claimed that because of the revolution in England there was no government in Virginia, so the people should take up arms to protect themselves. The whole scheme was a pretense to plunder the property of well to do Virginians, and colonial authorities knew it. Nicholas Spencer informed the Privy Council that "unruly and unorderly spiritts laying hold of ye motion of affaires, and that under the pretext of Religion, soe as from those false glasses to pretend to betake themselves to Arms...from the groundless imaginacon that the few Papists in Maryland, comparatively to ye Protestants in Maryland and Virginia had Conspired to hyre the Seneca Indians, to ye Cutting off, and totall distroying of all ye Protestants."

Despite the very real disturbances in the Northern Neck, Virginia did not collapse into the religious political factions of other English colonies. Spencer's views were typical: that Roman Catholics were not to be feared, in part because there were simply too few of them. Other Virginians believed that European religious violence created colonial opportunities. Shortly after William of Orange was proclaimed the joint-sovereign of England in 1688/89, William Fitzhugh, expecting the subsequent persecution of English papists, suggested that portions of Virginia become "a Refuge & sanctuary for Roman Catholicks." He had no doubts that "our Governmt. will give it all the Indulgences that can be reasonably required." His proposal reflected the ideas of toleration and prudence that had been developing in the colony for years: "Neither do I believe that persuasion will be hindred from settling any where in this Country, especially [on the frontier], where being Christians they may secure us against the Heathen."[94]

---

[94] My account comes from Warren M. Billings, John E. Selby, and Thad W. Tate, *Colonial Virginia: A History* (White Plains NY: KTO Press, 1986) 119-21; Stephen Saunders Webb, *Lord Churchill's Coup: The Anglo-*

In 1689 the new monarchs, King William and Queen Mary, restored Henry Compton to his episcopal authority, and the "Protestant bishop" soon turned his attention once again to colonial affairs. He appointed a new commissary for Virginia, the Reverend James Blair. Blair was living in the colony at the time of his appointment, and for four years he had served as minister of Varina Parish in Henrico County. Nevertheless, his route to Virginia had not been an easy one. Two years into his ministry at a parish in Scotland, he had been deprived of his living for refusing to sign a test oath agreeing to accept the Roman Catholic James II as head of the Scottish Church when he ascended to the throne. Blair then fled to England, where his countryman Gilbert Burnet, then preacher of the Rolls Chapel in London, found the young cleric work as a law clerk. It was there that he also met Bishop Compton, who persuaded him in 1685 to become a missionary to Virginia. Blair had settled into colonial life since reaching Virginia, and was well acquainted with the colony and its ways. He had begun purchasing land, and his marriage to Sarah Harrison had introduced him to allies among Virginia families prominent for wealth as well as power. Sarah's father, Benjamin Harrison, was one of the most important men in the colony, and as his children grew to adulthood and married, a son into the Burwell family and a daughter to Philip Ludwell II, Blair gained even more potentially helpful contacts. Over time, family connections created political sympa-

---

American Empire and the Glorious Revolution Reconsidered (New York: Alfred A. Knopf, 1995) 171-218; Fairfax Harrison, "Parson Waugh's Tumult," *Virginia Magazine of History and Biography* 30 (1922): 31-37; Nicholas Spencer to [Privy Council], 27 April 1689, PRO CO 5/1305, ff. 28-29; Nicholas Spencer to Privy Council, 29 April 1689, PRO CO 5/1305, ff. 30-31; Bruce E. Steiner, "The Catholic Brents of Colonial Virginia: An Instance of Practical Toleration," *Virginia Magazine of History and Biography* 70 (1962): 387-409; William Fitzhugh to Nicholas Hayward, 1 April 1689, and William Fitzhugh to Nicholas Spencer, n.d., in Richard Beale Davis, ed., *William Fitzhugh and His Chesapeake World, 1676-1701* (Chapel Hill: University of North Carolina Press, 1963) 250, 253.

thies, and a Blair-Harrison-Ludwell faction later developed on the governor's council.[95]

Blair was an ambitious man, and his appointment to the commissariat proved fortuitous since the doors of opportunity in England and Scotland had been shut. A Scot, his native country was no place to seek riches, and anti-Scotch prejudice in England limited opportunities for preferment there. If Blair hoped to achieve wealth, position, or fame, Virginia offered the best shot. Yet like Virginia itself, Blair was a man of ambiguous loyalties. He was the quintessential Virginian—his chief interest, his own, how to achieve it, his objective. Blair would soon recognize the ambiguous nature of his new office, if he had not already, but as a clergyman and full with the excitement of new-found power, his sympathies (and the route to even greater power) lay with the Church of England and its hierarchy.

Blair wasted little time establishing his authority. At a convocation of the clergy he called in July 1690 (news of his appointment had arrived only a month earlier), he set forth a series of proposals designed to bring radical change to Virginia's Church of England. The plan was ambitious. It attempted to increase the authority of the Church and the dignity of the clergy at the same time as it attacked the colony's traditional lay control of church government. He began by announcing his intention of bringing some old-fashioned ecclesiastical justice to Virginia by establishing church courts to punish the moral failures of "both Clergy and Laity." His timing could not have been better, and the proposal revealed his political savvy. A passion for moral order swept England in the years following the accession of William and Mary as ecclesiastical and political leaders worried that the nation had been seduced by vice. One clergyman wrote: "the abuse of good wine and the use of bad women [is] strangely epidemical." Virginia was no better, where, according to one minister: "Drunkenness is a most common

---

[95] "James Blair," *Dictionary of Virginia Biography*, 1:539-43; Rouse, *James Blair of Virginia*, 16-21, 34-35; Morgan, *American Slavery, American Freedom*, 348; Carpenter, *Protestant Bishop*, 263.

sin....Rash swearing is too common....Great numbers, I think, are more ashamed of Chastity and modesty, than of impudicity and Ribaldry." Blair saw in Virginia what English leaders saw back home, an unabated reign of sin, often unpunished by county courts and not presented by church wardens. He also saw an opportunity for the church to reclaim its traditional role in punishing vice, which in Virginia had fallen to the laity through the county court system.[96]

Blair planned to divide Virginia into four districts or convocations, each with a "Substitute and surrogate" for himself presiding over ecclesiastical justice. Henceforth, "Cursers, Swearers & blasphemers...whoremongers, fornicators and Adulterers... drunkards ranters and profaners of the Lords day and...all other Scandalous Persons," likely most of Virginia in one way or another, would be subject to European-style church justice. Laws punishing the offenses Blair mentioned were already on the books, but with the exception of bastardy cases, which cost people money, or select dissenters who intentionally offended Anglican sensibilities, courts rarely enforced these statutes. Under clerical rather than civil jurisdiction, perhaps the colony would take moral reform more seriously.[97]

If his first proposal attempted to increase the clergy's authority and responsibilities, the second intended to use financial means to enhance the clergy's dignity and independence. Low salaries plagued the colony's religious establishment and contributed to the colony's pastoral crisis. As the price of tobacco plummeted in the 1680s and 1690s, payment in that currency left ministers in such "miserable poor condition....that

---

[96] Rouse, *James Blair of Virginia*, 37-42; Spurr, *The Restoration Church of England*, 237; John Spurr, "The Church, the Societies and the Moral Revolution of 1688," in John Walsh, Colin Haydon, and Stephen Taylor, eds., *The Church of England c.1689-c.1833: From Toleration to Tractarianism* (New York: Cambridge University Press, 1993) 128; Alexander Forbes to Bishop Edmund Gibson, 21 July 1724, Fulham Palace Papers, vol. 13, ff. 27-30; John Lang to Bishop Edmund Gibson, 7 February 1725/26, Fulham Palace Papers, vol. 12, ff. 97-98.

[97] Rouse, *James Blair of Virginia*, 39-40.

many of the better sort who can pay for their passage begin to
desert the Country, & Ministers of any worth, who know the
state of the Clergy there, refuse to go to it, by which means, one
half of their Parishes is now void."[98] Blair urged the burgesses to
remedy this problem by setting clergy salaries at an established
sterling rate rather than in tobacco that was subject to the
quality of the weed and to the shifting whims of the
marketplace.[99]

Despite the support of Virginia's Lieutenant Governor,
Francis Nicholson, a military man and strong supporter of the
Church of England, Blair's church courts failed to gain support
among the Burgesses or the people. The General Assembly
passed laws once again denouncing the various vices the
commissary had noted and promised once again to sanction
violators, but Virginia's elites proved unwilling to share their
powers, especially with a class of men linked more closely now to
authority in England. Nor did other colonists want ecclesiastical
justice, possessed as they were of "a great aversion to Spiritual
Courts."[100] Unwilling to authorize this innovation, the
burgesses allowed Blair's plan to die quietly in the General
Assembly. They squashed his attempt to improve salaries as
well.[101] Successful implementation of the commissary's proposals
would have given the clergy greater power at the expense of local
elites, increasing their dignity and role in colonial government.
His proposals were all the more dangerous for attempting to
create a class of men with authority who would have existed
economically outside the colony's tobacco economy. Ministers
would have been men in, but not of, Virginia.

---

[98] Memorial concerning the clergy of Virginia, 11 December 1691,
PRO CO 5/1306, f. 353.

[99] Report of the General Meeting of the Clergy, 23 July 1690, PRO CO
5/1305, ff. 94-95; Rouse, *James Blair of Virginia*, 39-43.

[100] James Blair to John Robinson, bishop of London, 18 November
1714, Fulham Palace Papers, vol. 11, ff. 221-22.

[101] Rouse, *James Blair of Virginia*, 42-43.

Blair's proposals revealed the tensions in the commissariat. As a representative of the Church he was an English bureaucrat in a foreign land; but he was also Virginian enough to advance the colony's interests. In his efforts to establish church courts and gain greater prestige and independence for the clergy, Blair was an outsider pushing on Virginia practices at odds with the colony's prescription. In other actions, however, he fit in with colonial goals, and the burgesses encouraged his actions, finding on those occasions his contacts in London an asset rather than a threat.

Such was the case with his proposals to establish a college in Virginia. He and the clergy envisioned an institution with three divisions: grammar school, undergraduate college, and divinity school. Unlike his plans to increase the pay and authority of ministers, it received an enthusiastic response from clergy, council, governor, and burgesses alike. At their next session, the burgesses formed a committee to petition the Crown for a charter and asked Blair to present the colony's case before King William and Queen Mary.[102] Once in England on the colony's business, he wrangled himself the college's presidency, writing to his friend, Virginia's Lieutenant Governor Francis Nicholson, that Bishop Compton and others in the church hierarchy believed it necessary to fill this office first. Blair played his familiarity with the colony to his advantage. A small college overseas, he suggested, would not satisfy the ambitions of English scholars otherwise deserving of the office; Virginia's tiring and troublesome "occasions" also dictated making a colonial president: "if we take a man from either of the Universitys who never saw any such Institution, but has been accustomed to a much more easy & idle way, that he will never bear it & will not at all be fitt for such a small College as ours will be."[103]

---

[102] Rouse, *James Blair of Virginia*, 43-44; Tate, "The Colonial College, 1693-1782" 4-11.

[103] James Blair to Francis Nicholson, 3 December 1691, "Papers Relating to Nicholson and the College," *Virginia Magazine of History and Biography* 7 (1899-1900): 162; Rouse, *James Blair of Virginia*, 76.

Nicholson and the General Assembly agreed and nominated the commissary for the post. Blair's efforts were successful, and in 1693 he returned to Virginia with the charter for the College of William and Mary. He had successfully furthered his own interests as well; the charter appointed him president for life. Governor Edmund Andros and the Council praised Blair's efforts, reimbursed him for expenses, and rewarded him with a generous honorarium as a token of their appreciation.[104]

As college president and commissary, Blair was already a major player in Virginia politics, a position solidified in 1694 when King William appointed him to the governor's council. He defended interests of the college, the clergy, and himself with great passion, three times travelling to England to plead—successfully as it turned out—for the recall of governors who did not fit his ideas of what was good for the colony or for himself. Failure to implement traditional English-style church government was one of his favorite charges. Blair pushed clergy issues throughout the 1690s, especially the right of induction and the need to improve salaries. He had some success on the pay issue, gaining ministers a raise in 1696 to 16,000 pounds of tobacco per year although this was far short of the sliding scale with an upper limit of 32,000 pounds paid in sterling that he wanted.[105]

Despite this moderate success, the burgesses refused to budge on induction. With salaries low and their livings still insecure, the clergy lived in what Blair called "precarious and uncertain" circumstances.[106] Yet the commissary blamed neither his inability to sway the burgesses nor the intransigence of the vestries and General Assembly for the ministers' plight. He instead attributed these inconveniences to Governor Andros for not forcing the legislators to make changes. The commissary and the

---

[104] Rouse, *James Blair of Virginia*, 76-77.

[105] Samuel Clyde McCulloch, ed., "James Blair's Plan of 1699 to Reform the Clergy of Virginia," *William and Mary Quarterly* 3rd ser. 4 (1947): 72-73.

[106] "Memorial Concerning Sir Edmund Andros," Perry, *Historical Collections Relating to the American Colonial Church*, 1:15.

governor did not like each other and had sparred over the college, the clergy, and Blair's right to sit on the Council. By 1697 Blair had had enough of Andros; he set out for London to argue for the governor's recall, using Andros' failure adequately to support Blair's college and his clergy as the centerpieces of his case. Andros had not raised clergy salaries enough. Andros did not support the induction of clergy into their livings, thus refusing to follow English practice. And, as Blair and his father-in-law, Benjamin Harrison, pointed out, the governor had quickly picked up on colonial ways and created majority factions on vestries in order to remove clergy he did not like. Archbishop Tenison was not pleased: "It must be a very pernicious thing. A minister will not know how to preach against any Vice, but some of the Great Men of his parish fancy the Sermon was made against him, and so make a faction to turn out the Minister, though perhaps the sermon was made seven years before."[107] Andros' "contrary" behavior, was, in Blair's opinion, directly responsible for the colony's current crisis in pastoral care— ministers served but twenty-two of Virginia's fifty parishes.[108] By portraying the unfortunate governor as an enemy of English custom in church government, Blair helped win Andros' recall.

Two years later in 1699, the commissary tried again to reform both the clergy and the colonists' treatment of them, still enthralled with what one historian has called the "pattern of English ecclesiastical organization."[109] Blair believed most problems with the colony's church could be divided into two areas: morals and economics. Although he had abandoned any attempt to impose ecclesiastical justice on the laity at the request of Bishop Compton, Blair still hoped to place his clergy

---

[107]"A True Account of a Conference at Lambeth," 27 December 1697, Perry, *Historical Collections Relating to the American Colonial Church*, 1:37-65, quotation on 48; Fulham Palace Papers, vol. 11, ff. 54-79.

[108]"Memorial Concerning Sir Edmund Andros," Perry, *Historical Collections Relating to the American Colonial Church*, 1:11; McCulloch, "James Blair's Plan of 1699," 73.

[109] McCulloch, "James Blair's Plan of 1699," 74.

under spiritual discipline.[110] The occasional sodomite or "habitual Drunkard" cast aspersions on the clergy as a whole, thereby reducing the Church's authority and dignity.[111] A morally exemplary clergy, however, could better preach against vice and compete with Quakers and nonconformists for colonists' souls. To that end, Blair proposed suspending scandalous ministers from their offices, actions that might help reform them, serve as examples to others, and demonstrate the commissary's intentions and authority. To combat vestry complaints of ignorant clergy, he suggested creating an examination committee consisting of the commissary and "some of the Learnedest Ministers of the Countrey" to pass judgment on any clergyman sent to a colonial cure. To help improve salaries, he proposed merging small parishes in order to create a larger economic pool from which to draw tithes. The solution may have increased ministers' remuneration, but it nonetheless showed a surprising ignorance of Virginia's circumstances and the potential difficulties of ministering to a larger parish. But Blair was fond of money himself and often saw the colony's pastoral crisis in economic terms. Better pay, he reasoned, would bring better clergy and make those in the colony more content. In addition to combining small or poor parishes, he once again urged the burgesses to raise clergy salaries, ensure that each glebe was large enough to be worked by at least four or five slaves, and force vestries to present ministers for induction. These attempts, like earlier ones to bring ministers greater independence, failed. Tobacco was a precarious source on which to base one's economic future, and burgesses believed vestries paid clergymen well enough already. Blair's plan, they griped, would have

---

[110] James Blair to Bishop Robinson, 18 November 1714. Fulham Palace Papers, vol. 14, ff. 221-22. The Privy Council had recognized the colony's different prescription in this regard by the mid-1720s, Action of the Privy Council to Bishop Gibson's Proposals, 26 April 1725, Fulham Palace Papers, vol. 36, ff. 63-66.

[111]"Conference at Lambeth," Perry, *Historical Collections Relating to the American Colonial Church*, 1:38.

afforded ministers more than "most of their own circumstances and of ye Country in Generall."[112]

Little came of the proposals other than to demonstrate their most consistent theme—James Blair's desire for clear authority over Virginia's church. Along with a proposed series of triennial parish visitations to see that all Virginia's church laws were in force—in other words, to make sure vestries did what they said they did—the commissary envisioned himself at the head of an ecclesiastical government with powers over not only the clergy but the vestries as well: advocate and judge of the clergy, disciplinarian of vestrymen. He would be Virginia's church.

By the turn of the century, Blair had begun to lose the support of his clergy, many of whom believed his authority and powers, rather than proper ecclesiastical government, were the commissary's goals. Commissary, college president, and councilor, Blair's duties dragged him further into colonial politics; and religious issues became a common device for attacking political enemies. Criticism of the commissary's "great worldly concerns" mounted.[113] Some clergy even accused him of removing ministers from parishes in disregard of church canons. Nor did they see him as a pastor of pastors; authority not counsel fascinated him: "[he] hath invested himselfe with many condemning powers without any protecting or relieving one." Others mocked him as a tyrant, complaining to Bishop Compton of the "Bigg words he trys to scare us with; as Schism, Canonical, obedience, the *Omnia* and *Omnimoda potestas Ecclesiastica* in ye Instrument for his commissary's place."[114]

When Blair fell out with his old friend Francis Nicholson after the latter's return to Virginia in 1698 as governor, the clergy joined the quarrel. Most supported the governor, a strong

---

[112] McCulloch, "James Blair's Plan of 1699," 76-86; Rouse, *James Blair of Virginia*, 148-49.

[113] Nicholas Moreau to the Bishop of Lichfield and Coventry, 12 April 1697, Fulham Palace Papers, vol. 11, ff. 24-25; Perry, *Historical Collections Relating to the American Colonial Church*, 1:29-32.

[114] Rouse, *James Blair of Virginia*, 149.

defender of the Church of England and its form of church government. Solomon Whatley, minister of Bruton Parish in Williamsburg, satirized the commissary's growing obsession with the governor: "Mr. Blair has got quite a trick of late, of crying out whenever he is put upon the fret, 'Govr Nicholson, Govr Nicholson,' that he will become a Common Swearer & with a new oath, upon every pet Cry out, 'By Govr Nicholson."[115] The real issue was Blair's desertion in 1703 "of the fight to secure permanent induction of ministers in their appointments and prevent vestries from keeping them on annual contracts," a right of the clergy that Nicholson fully embraced.[116] Blair chided his clergy in a sermon, proclaiming that Christ had left "Points of mere Order...under General Rules," and that it was best in these matters to "comply with such innocent Customs, as are established in the particular Church where we reside."[117] Although many traditions of the Church of England supported the commissary's position, most colonial ministers nonetheless believed that Blair's switch amounted to a form of apostasy. They resented him and his attacks on their patron. Several ministers got to the heart of the matter when they accused the commissary of "opposing her Majesty's Govr & Representative."[118] Yet for Blair, the route to power no longer ran through London and an alliance with royal authority, but

---

[115] "Papers Relating to a Clergy Conference Held in Williamsburg, 1705," Perry, *Historical Collections Relating to the American Colonial Church,* 1:166.

[116] Tate, "The Colonial College, 1693-1782," 44. That was the same year that Robert Quary wrote to the Board of Trade to complain that Virginia's burgesses had concluded that they were "entitled to all the Rights and Privileges of an English Parliament, and begin to search into the Records of that Honorable house for presedents to Govern themselves by," Robert Quary to the Board of Trade, 16 June 1703, Harleian Mss. 6273, f. 8, British Museum.

[117] Blair, *Our Saviour's Divine Sermon on the Mount,* 1:232-35.

[118] "Papers Relating to a Conference of the Clergy Held in Williamsburg, 1705," Perry, *Historical Collections Relating to the American Colonial Church,* 1:158.

with the "Virginia barons" who sat on the Council, in the Assembly, and on the vestries. Governors could be recalled easily enough but that these men were here to stay. So was Blair, and the only way to make it in Williamsburg was by becoming one of them, a Virginian.

In 1701 a pamphlet written by an anonymous Virginian entitled An Essay upon the Government of the English Plantations on the Continent of America *was published in London. Signed self-consciously "By an American," the tract contributed to a growing debate over the economic and political relationship of the colonies to the mother country within England's emerging colonial system. The author's primary interest was establishing in British North America what he called "a free Constitution of Government in the Plantations," and he mentioned religion only briefly. Yet his remarks on that subject reflected attitudes common among Virginians of the late seventeenth and early eighteenth centuries. Although a supporter of the established church, he believed it was neither convenient nor practical to expect all the colony's citizens to worship according to the rites of the Church of England, and he discussed religion just so far as it contributed to the "Maintenance and Support of the Civil Government." Appeals for both liberties of conscience and laws against profane and immoral behavior encompassed most of what the author had to say on this topic. The religious group an individual belonged to seemed to him a thing indifferent, for all Christian religions could help the state maintain order by teaching virtuous behavior. There the Essay placed its emphasis: "It is to be wish'd, that some Care be taken to instruct People well in Morality, that is, what all Perswasions either do, or pretend to desire."[119]*

---

[119] *An Essay Upon the Government of the English Plantations on the Continent of America*, ed. Louis B. Wright (San Marino: The Huntington Library, 1945) ix, 20, 38-39, 23. See also Carole Shammas, "Benjamin Harrison III and the Authorship of An Essay upon the Government of the English Plantations on the Continent of America," *Virginia Magazine of History and Biography* 84 (1975): 166-73.

"An American" also believed that religion helped order the world, but he did not think a single state church structured the polity's relationship with God. The Essay did not address prescriptive unity based on shared religious beliefs. The author, in fact, criticized for their arrogance religious groups that still held to the older view. In the colonies they controlled, Puritans, whom he called Independents, and Quakers, "abuse all Mankind that come among them, and are not for their Persuasion." And New York's various denominations oppressed each other in turn, depending upon which group held political influence at the moment. Against this background of contentious religious groups still attempting to establish in North America the mythic national religious purity common to Europe, "an American" implied that Virginia was different. Although nonconformists were few, the colony's Anglicans, Roman Catholics, Protestant dissenters, and "a greatly increasing" number of Quakers, got along in comparative harmony.[120]

Charity toward other denominations and support for biblical standards of morality formed the basis of the colony's religious life in James Blair's Virginia. If members of different denominations could agree on anything it was that biblical morality was a good thing. Anglican theology of the period, in fact, taught that a good life was evidence of a good faith. The anonymous Virginian who wrote the Essay avoided the question of unity that came from shared belief and encouraged religion because it taught people morality. His implication was not that good behavior pleased God, but that by teaching good behavior religion kept peace within the polity. This is what Virginians meant when they said "God be thanked [we] are in a peaceable state, and Intirely well quieted" or other words that expressed the same idea.[121] *Rather than dividing the world between those who professed true religion and those who adhered to false*

---

[120] *An Essay Upon the Government of the Plantations on the Continent of America*, 22; Butler, *Awash in a Sea of Faith*, 103. For a different view from that expressed here, see Butler, *Awash in a Sea of Faith*, 98-99.

[121] Nicholas Spencer to Lionel Jenkins, 16 July 1683, PRO CO 1/52, f. 54. See also Spencer to Jenkins PRO CO 1/61, f. 208: "I thank God....this...country enjoys peace and quiet, with fullness of liberty."

doctrine, Virginians by the end of the seventeenth century thought in terms of those who were Christians and those who were not. As long as they tolerated people professing other beliefs, good Christians made good citizens.

A fairly peaceful competition for souls took place between Christian groups in James Blair's Virginia. Full-scale pamphlet wars between Anglicans and Quakers took place in some parts of the colony, both sides doing a brisk business with London booksellers. In an effort to keep their colonial brethren up-to-date, English Quakers wrote to the Virginia Meeting, telling them "it may be proper for you to observe which sorts [of books] are most serviceable among your Neighbours, & to send to your Correspondts to buy and send you more of such sorts, had you mentioned what are ye Tytles of Adversaries Books that are disperced in your Province we could more Easily chosen answers suited to obviate their Calumnies."[122] *In other places, the rival parties held formal theological disputations, much to the delight of the large audiences of common folk and colonial officials who came to be both entertained and edified. These gatherings sometimes became quite raucous, spectators interrupting the disputants with questions of their own or discussing the points at issue while the debaters continued their arguments.*[123] *Commissary Blair welcomed debates between people of different persuasions, so long as these were "done in a friendly and peaceable Manner, and with a Design to find out the Truth." Preaching on the beatitude blessed are the peacemakers, which he thought contained the Savior's teachings on civil peace, Blair outlined the colony's emerging commitment to religious toleration: "if ever we Mind to cement into one Body, as our common Christianity obliges us...we must learn to*

---

[122] London Meeting to the Virginia Meeting, 1704, Epistles Sent, vol. 2 (1704-1738), f. 16, Library of the Society of Friends. See also Epistles Sent, vol. 2, f. 246; Epistles Received, vol. 1 (1683-1706), ff. 267, 383; vol. 2 (1705-1738), ff. 143-44; Miscellaneous Portfolio 16, f. 37; Meetings for Sufferings, vol. 2 (1680-1683), f. 176; vol. 15 (1701), f. 171; vol. 18 (1706-1707), f. 294, Library of the Society of Friends.

[123] Thomas Story, *The Journal of the Life of Thomas Story...*(Newcastle upon Tyne, 1747), dispute on pages 387-26, Earl Greg Swem Library, Special Collections, College of William and Mary.

be Friends of Truth and Virtue and Goodness, wherever we can find them, and to follow Peace with all good Men of whatsoever Denomination.[124]

The same prescription and the same "occasions" which had helped Virginians to create a polity with little open religious animosity had also shaped the colony's Church of England. Although the colony shared the Act of Toleration with England (Virginia's circumstances had militated in that direction for decades), the colony's established church had its own ways of church government contrary to English customs. The clergy's situation did not improve much in the coming decades. They were still treated like hirelings without the right of induction into their livings. Salaries throughout the colonial period remained at the 1696 rate of 16,000 pounds of tobacco. But all of that had been set by 1703 when James Blair switched sides on the induction issue. Virginia was so much like England, yet so different, that no one wanted to call the colony's treatment of ministers what it really was. In 1759 William Sherlock, the bishop of London, did. "In some times," he wrote, perhaps not aware that he had touched upon the more subtle point of the power of prescriptions and customs, to treat Anglican clergy the way Virginians had for so long "would have been called Treason, and I do not know any other name for it in our Law."[125]

---

[124] Blair, *Our Saviour's Divine Sermon on the Mount*, 4:212-14, 223.

[125] William Sherlock to the Lords Commissioners of Trade, 14 June 1759, Fulham Palace Papers, vol. 14, ff. 258-63

CHAPTER FIVE

THE RELIGION OF ANGLICANS IN JAMES BLAIR'S VIRGINIA

"When the wicked man turneth away from his wicked-
ness, that he hath committed, and doeth that which is
lawful and right, he shall save his soul."

Book of Common Prayer, 1662

Williiam Fitzhugh, an attorney and tobacco planter in
Stafford County, reflected briefly in January 1686/87
upon the difficulties of life in the Virginia colony.
Education for children was hard to come by; financial security
rested upon too many contingencies, forcing Fitzhugh to devote
more time to worldly affairs than he thought proper; and with
the exception of that found in books, "good & ingenious"
society was scarce. "But that which bears the greatest weight
with me," he wrote, "is the want of spirituall help & comforts, of
which this fertile Country in every thing else, is barren and
unfruitfull." It was a familiar complaint, common to laity as well
as clergy, and by the time Fitzhugh wrote, Virginians had been
complaining in this fashion for nearly seventy-five years.
Fitzhugh himself had twice asked friends in England to speak
with the bishop of London, Henry Compton, about the
problem, but despite these efforts and the bishop's own attempts
to find suitable ministers for the colony, Virginia's shortage of
clergy remained an abiding quandary.[1]

---

[1] William Fitzhugh to Nicholas Hayward, 30 January 1686/87, William
Fitzhugh to Captain Roger Jones, 18 May 1685, 168; William Fitzhugh to

Yet had ministers filled every vacant parish in the colony the church's work still would have suffered, only to a lesser degree, since a settled minister was no guarantee that colonists would attend divine service regularly. The Church of England's mission in Virginia was frustrated not only by a shortage of clergy, but also by the colony's "occasions."[2] As emigrant ministers never seemed to tire of pointing out, tobacco culture forced colonists to scatter about the countryside and hindered the public practice of religion. As if that were not a significant enough problem to be overcome, factors other than an insufficient supply of clergymen conspired to keep people away from church. "Extremes of Wind and Weather" thwarted some, "and divers of the more remote Families being discouraged, by the length or tediousness of the way, through extremities of heat in Summer, frost and Snow in Winter, and tempestuous weather in both, do very seldom repair thither." William Byrd II noted in his diary that rain and heat often kept him from divine services. Between 1709 and 1712 he attended church on less than forty-five percent of the Sundays covered by his diary, and the church was on his property, less than half a mile from his residence. The large size of Virginia's parishes also inhibited church attendance. An average parish covered about 270 square miles, and, in addition to the church building, most parishes contained one

---

John Cooper, 20 August 1690, 268, Richard Beale Davis, ed., *William Fitzhugh and His Chesapeake World, 1676-1701* (Chapel Hill: University of North Carolina Press, 1963) 203, 168, 268; Alexander Whitaker to William Crashaw, 9 August 1611, in Alexander Brown, ed., *The Genesis of the United States*, 2 vols. (New York, 1896) 1:499; Samuel Clyde McCulloch, ed., "James Blair's Plan of 1699 to Reform the Clergy of Virginia," *William and Mary Quarterly* 2nd ser. 4 (1947): 73, 76; Joan Rezner Gundersen, "The Anglican Ministry in Virginia, 1723-1776: A Study of a Social Class" (Ph.D. diss., University of Notre Dame, 1972) 32-34, 231; Joan R. Gundersen, "The Search for Good Men: Recruiting Ministers in Colonial Virginia," *Historical Magazine of the Protestant Episcopal Church* 47 (1979): 453-64.

[2] The notion of "occasions" is in Paul Avis, "What is 'Anglicanism?'" in Stephen Sykes and John Booty, eds., *The Study of Anglicanism* (London: S.P.C.K., 1988) 406.

and sometimes two or three chapels of ease. Colonial parsons served each on a rotating basis, officiating and preaching first at the "mother church" and then at the chapels of ease in their turn on succeeding Sabbaths. Although the parish clerk read the liturgy and a homily on Sundays when the minister served another part of his charge, colonists were reluctant to attend church when the minister was away. William Byrd, for instance, attended church only once between 1709 and 1712 when the minister was not officiating. Designed to encourage church attendance and the spread of religion, chapels of ease nonetheless resembled the European practice of clerical pluralism, the primary reason given by English ministers for non-attendance at divine services.[3] Consequently, Virginians did not abandon the

---

[3] Warren Billings, John E. Selby, and Thad W. Tate, *Colonial Virginia: A History* (White Plains NY: KTO Press, 1986) 65, 134-36; John C. Rainbolt, "The Absence of Towns in Seventeenth-Century Virginia," *Journal of Southern History* 35 (1969): 347, 343; T. H. Breen, *Tobacco Culture: The Mentality of the Great Tidewater Planters on the Eve of Revolution* (Princeton: Princeton University Press, 1985) 41; George MacClaren Brydon, *Virginia's Mother Church and the Political Conditions Under Which It Grew*, 2 vols. (Richmond: Virginia State Library, 1947), 1:372-73; R[oger] G[reene], *Virginia's Cure: or an Advisive Narrative Concerning Virginia* in Peter Force, ed., *Tracts and Other Papers, Relating Principally to the Origin, Settlement, and Progress of the Colonies in North America*, 4 vols. (Gloucester MA: Peter Smith, 1963), 3:15:4-5, 8-9; Louis B. Wright and Marion Tinling, eds., *The Secret Diary of William Byrd of Westover, 1709-1712* (Richmond: The Dietz Press, 1941) 24 July, 7 August 1709; 10 June, 26 November 1710; 21 January, 15 April 1711, and passim; Lord Howard to the bishops of Durham, Peterborough, and Rochester, 23 February 1687 in Warren M. Billings, ed., *The Papers of Francis Howard Baron Howard of Effingham, 1643-1695* (Richmond: Virginia State Library, 1989) 282; William Stevens Perry, ed., *Historical Collections Relating to the American Colonial Church*, 4 vols. (New York: AMS Press, 1969) 1:11; Patricia U. Bonomi and Peter R. Eisenstadt, "Church Attendance in the Eighteenth-Century British American Colonies," *William and Mary Quarterly* 3rd ser. 39 (1982): 254-55; Arthur Pierce Middleton, "The Colonial Virginia Parson," *William and Mary Quarterly* 3rd ser. 26 (1969): 425-40; Viviane Barrie-Curien, "The Clergy of the Diocese of London in

institutional church but their relationships with God often developed outside its formal structures.

Despite the lack of ministers and the weakness of the colony's established Church of England, religion remained an important part of many colonists' lives. In those parishes fortunate enough to have a pastor, ministers preached sermons, read the public liturgy, and celebrated the sacraments. Away from the sacred space of the church building individuals read devotional works and prayed in private, vindication of William Byrd II's belief that it was "natural for helpless man to adore his Maker in some form or other."[4] Many Virginians testified to the importance of religion in their wills, often mentioning the resurrection, forgiveness of sins, a sure and certain hope of salvation, or an explicit request for Christian burial. Over seventy percent of the wills in seventeenth-century York County include at least one of these sentiments. Among people explicitly listing a parish affiliation, the percentage mentioning these ideas rises to eighty-five. Other men and women showed their devotion by leaving donations of money, books, or property to their parish churches. Like many people who remembered the church in their wills, William Hawkins of York Parish had a specific request: he left 1,500 pounds of tobacco to be used to purchase a "Silver Flaggon" for use at communion. One of the more popular bequests among god-

---

the Eighteenth Century," in John Walsh, Colin Haydon, and Stephen Taylor, eds., *The Church of England c.1689-c.1833: From Toleration to Tractarianism* (New York: Cambridge University Press, 1993) 109. See also Henry Hartwell, James Blair, and Edward Chilton, *The Present State of Virginia and the College*, ed. Hunter Dickinson Farish (Williamsburg, 1940) 67; and "A Letter from Mr. John Clayton to the Royal Society," Force, *Tracts and Other Papers*, 3:12:12, 21.

[4] William Byrd, *History of the Dividing Line betwixt Virginia and North Carolina Run in the Year of Our Lord 1728, in* Louis B. Wright, ed., *The Prose Works of William Byrd of Westover* (Cambridge: Harvard University Press, 1966) 193.

parents combined religion and economic security by leaving a cow or calf to one's godchildren.[5]

Although hampered by the colony's "occasions," Anglicanism in James Blair's Virginia[6] was primarily a pastoral religion concerned with the spiritual care and guidance of individuals rather than with theological polemic, intellectual debate, or a "prying into adorable Mysteries" beyond comprehension by the human mind. Like Puritanism, Anglicanism addressed the

---

[5] The figures come from my survey of York County, Deeds, Orders, and Wills, bks. 1-10, Virginia State Library, Richmond Virginia, (microfilm) Colonial Williamsburg Foundation. Only 50 percent of the wills of those people not mentioning a parish affiliation contain additional religious sentiments of some kind. York County, Deeds, Orders, and Wills (3), f. 38A; will of John Yeates, Virginia State Library; Isle of Wight Records, 2, pt. 1, f. 53. There are numerous additional examples: York County, DOW (2), ff. 160, 180, 275, 295, 343, 372-373, 377, 394, 406; York County, DOW (3), ff. 24, 44, 49A, 54, 66, 98; York County, DOW (4), ff. 8, 186, 383; York County, DOW (5), ff. 3, 80; See also Warren M. Billings, review of *Holy Things and Profane*, by Dell Upton, in *Virginia Magazine of History and Biography* 95 (1987): 379-81; James Horn, *Adapting to a New World: English Society in the Seventeenth-Century Chesapeake* (Chapel Hill: University of North Carolina Press, 1994) 403.

[6] I have used the term "James Blair's Virginia" because the majority of extant sermons written by colonial Anglicans in Virginia —those of Blair (by far the largest single collection), Robert Paxton, John Clayton, Deuel Pead, Peter Fontaine, and even George Keith (who preached from time to time in Virginia) —are from the period covered by Blair's years in the colony. Thus, the major body of sources falls within the period 1685 to 1743. The Anglican theology discussed here did not come abruptly to an end in the mid-1740s, and I would content that similar views continued through the entire colonial period. Yet, although the few sermons of James Maury and other colonial ministers indicate the continuation of these religious views, there are limited primary sources on which to base such a hypothesis both before 1685 and after 1743. Therefore, to the extent that an Anglican theology can be recovered for colonial Virginia, that theology comes from the years of James Blair's commissariat. If the quotations tend to come from a small number of colonial Virginia's many ministers, it is because so few of the colony's ministers left sermons or other writings.

devotional life, which for members of the Church of England meant a life that began in faith, proceeded through repentance and amendment of life, and culminated with the "sure and certain hope" of a glorious resurrection at the last day. The Church's liturgy, ministers' sermons, the sacraments, devotional materials, and events in the natural world all helped create a general orientation pointing the faithful in the direction of God, while leaving the essential work of salvation in the hands of individuals who would work out their own salvation "with fear and trembling."[7]

Virginians often spoke of this process as a pilgrimage or a voyage to heaven. "Before I was ten years old," William Fitzhugh confessed to his mother, "I look'd upon life here as but going to

---

[7] James Blair, *Our Saviour's Divine Sermon on the Mount, Contain'd in the Vth, VIth, and VIIth Chapters of St. Mathew's Gospel, Explained; and the Practice of it Recommended in divers Sermons and Discourses*, 5 vols. (London, 1722) 5:374; The Burial Office in *The Book of Common Prayer and Administration of the Sacraments, and Other Rites and Ceremonies of the Church, According to the Use of the Church of England* (London, 1662) George Keith, *The Power of the Gospel, in the Conversion of Sinners* (Annapolis, 1703) 12; John Page, *A Deed of Gift to My Dear Son, Captain Matt. Page, One of His Majesty's Justices for New Kent County, in Virginia*, ed. William Meade (n.p., 1687; reprint, Philadelphia: Henry B. Ashmead, 1856) v, John D. Rockefeller, Jr. Library, Colonial Williamsburg Foundation. On the pastoral nature of Anglicanism, see also Blair, *Our Saviour's Divine Sermon on the Mount*, 2:173; Robert Paxton Manuscript Sermon Book, sermon no. 10, "Of Christs Resurrectn," 7, Houghton Library, Harvard University, (There is no pagination in Paxton's sermon book, but each sermon is precisely eight pages long. I have cited the appropriate page from one to eight for each individual sermon.); George Keith, *The Doctrine of the Holy Apostles and Prophets the Foundation of the Church of Christ* (Boston, 1702) 3; Deuel Pead, *Jesus is God: or, The Deity of Jesus Christ Vindicated. Being an Abstract of some Sermons Preach'd in the Parish Church of St. James Clerkenwell* (London, 1694) 43. Pead had served Christ Church Parish in Middlesex County, Virginia, from 1683 through 1691 before returning to England.

an Inn, no permanent being."[8] By the late seventeenth century, the pilgrimage motif was a well-known form of portraying the soul's journey to God, popular among Roman Catholics and Puritans as well as Anglicans. The classic of the genre was John Bunyan's celebrated *The Pilgrim's Progress*, but its roots lay in the works of medieval mystics such as Bernard of Clairvaux and Bonaventure, and in Walter Hilton's *The Scale of Perfection*. The Anglican notion of the journey, however, possessed its own distinct qualities, emphasizing neither the terrors of the wilderness stage typical of Puritan writers nor the mystical union with God common among Roman Catholic authors. Likewise, they wrote little of the rapturous joy of sinners admitted to redemption. Feelings of "Uneasiness," especially when thinking of one's sins, attended this voyage, but not dramatic events such as what the Puritans termed conversion. Theirs was a low-key piety, deeply felt and involving the "whole individual," but given to order rather than to passion or ecstasy. Anglicans worked out their salvation through a well-ordered journey to God. Extremes harmed the spiritual life. John Page, for example, warned his son against the emotional excesses of presumption and despair— those "two destructive rocks, upon either of which, if the ship of the soul dash, it is split in pieces"—as a missing of the religious life's golden mean. One deceived men and women into vain

---

[8] William Fitzhugh to Mrs. Mary Fitzhugh, 30 June 1698, in *William Fitzhugh and His Chesapeake World*, 358. See also Page, *Deed of Gift to My Dear Son*, 219; will of Edward Watts, York County Deeds, Orders, and Wills (5), f. 165; Blair, *Our Saviour's Divine Sermon on the Mount*, 4:80; Byrd, *History of the Dividing Line betwixt Virginia and North Carolina*, 193; *The Vain Prodigal Life, and Tragical Penitent Death of Thomas Hellier Born at Whitchurch near Lyme in Dorset-shire: Who for Murdering his Master, Mistress, and a Maid, was Executed according to Law at Westover in Charles City, in the Country of Virginia, near the Plantation called Hard Labour, where he perpetrated the said Murders* (London, 1680), 40, John D. Rockefeller, Jr. Library, Colonial Williamsburg Foundation; John Tillotson, *The Works of Dr. John Tillotson, Late Archbishop of Canterbury*, 10 vols. (London, 1820) 1:526; Donna Joanne Walter, "Imagery in the Sermons of James Blair" (M.A. thesis, University of Tennessee, 1967) 39-44.

hopes of mercy, the other tormented them with "hellish fears of justice." Together they threatened both halves of the spiritual life: "Presumption is an enemy to repentance, and despair to faith."[9]

As Page's allusion suggests, Virginians often described their spiritual journeys through the metaphor of a ship at sea returning to its home port, a particularly evocative image for anyone who had survived an Atlantic crossing. James Blair turned the metaphor into an analogy, comparing Christians to a well-disciplined ship's crew attending to its duties, "Such as stopping the Leaks, mending the Sails,...preparing the Guns to make a Defence against an Enemy; and especially the keeping of a good Reckoning, and looking out sharp to avoid Shelves, and Rocks, and Quicksands, and all other Dangers both attending the Voyage at Sea, and the Piloting right into Harbour." The image had become so commonplace that Blair did not bother to note for his listeners and readers that by the enemy he meant the devil and by rocks and shelves he meant temptations to sin.[10]

When Blair compared the spiritual journey to sailors going about their usual tasks of keeping the ship in order and sailing it to its intended destination, he captured the essence of the Anglican's movement to God. It was part of an individual's daily work, striking only in its ordinariness. People expected sailors to repair leaks, make preparations for enemy assaults, guide the

---

[9] Charles E. Hambrick-Stowe, *The Practice of Piety: Puritan Devotional Disciplines in Seventeenth-Century New England* (Chapel Hill: University of North Carolina Press, 1982) 54-55; John Spurr, *The Restoration Church of England, 1646-1689* (New Haven: Yale University Press, 1991) 373-74; Blair, *Our Saviour's Divine Sermon on the Mount*, 1:104; Page, *Deed of Gift to My Dear Son*, 94-95.

[10] Blair, *Our Saviour's Divine Sermon on the Mount*, 2:138, 198-99; 1:233. See also George Keith, *Power of the Gospel*, 17; Deuel Pead, "A Sermon Preached at James City in Virginia, the 23d of April 1686, Before the Loyal Society of Citizens born in and about London and inhabiting in Virginia," ed. Richard Beale Davis, *William and Mary Quarterly*, 3rd ser. 17 (1960): 376-77; Richard Beale Davis, *Intellectual Life in the Colonial South, 1585-1763*, 3 vols. (Knoxville: University of Tennessee Press, 1978) 2:376.

vessel to its intended port, and watch for shallow waters so as to prevent the ship from running aground. These were tasks common to the lives of seafaring men, and for sailors to neglect these chores would have been extraordinary; it would have made them poor seamen. This was perhaps the most distinctive quality of Anglican religion in colonial Virginia, it seemed unexceptional, a matter of doing the routine and habitual duties that naturally accompanied an individual's vocation. Religion was a practice rather than a set of propositions: "Christ's Doctrine is a practical Doctrine. Whosoever heareth these Sayings of mine, and doeth them."[11]

Virginians' emphasis on actions rather than on theological propositions reflected not only the colony's longstanding accentu-ation of morality over belief but also trends in the Restoration Church of England. Anglican divines of the Interregnum and Restoration periods believed the Puritan doctrine of "faith alone" had damaged the nation's moral life by inadvertently sanctioning antinomianism. They responded to this error by recovering the Church's "Catholic doctrine of salvation" and then establishing an ethical system suitable to the doctrine. The result was a practical theology stressing duty, one that the colonists accepted as readily as their brethren on the other side of the Atlantic. Ministers kept these ideas before the colony's faithful through their preaching; on their own, colonists read of it in the many Restoration religious tracts which they could not get enough of. Devotional materials written by Arminian divines such as Richard Allestree and Archbishop of Canterbury John Tillotson, the latter more influential in his lifetime than John Locke, were among the colonists' favorite books, and colonial parsons frequently "borrowed" heavily from these published editions when preparing their own sermons. Robert Paxton of Elizabeth City Parish often lifted whole passages from Tillotson's discourses, rephrasing them only slightly before delivering them from his pulpit. The Church of England's emphasis on duty and

---

[11] Blair, *Our Saviour's Divine Sermon on the Mount*, 5:374; 2:199, 204; Paxton, sermon no. 4, "Of the Tares in the Church."

practical theology found a ready setting in Virginia. As James Blair pointed out, despite aggressive Quaker proselytizing, there were few dissenters living in the colony to challenge the accepted orthodoxy, thus allowing ministers to focus on the "Practical Part of Religion[,] it being the Chief part of our Pastoral Care."[12]

Anglicans on both sides of the Atlantic thought mere belief in religious dogma denoted an insufficient faith. Properly understood, learning about theology was not an intellectual exercise but a spur to action. Typical was Commissary Blair's belief that people who assumed they could befriend God through their knowledge of theological tenets and arguments held erroneous ideas: "it is not the Authority of any Church, nor the Orthodoxy of any Opinions, that will entitle us to God's friendship, except these Orthodox Opinions work in us a real Change of Heart and Life, and make us good Men and Women."[13] Members of the laity held similar opinions. "Knowledge," one Virginian wrote, "is not an active quality, but only a means to direct a man in working. God reckons not so much our audience as our obedience."[14] Archbishop Tillotson, one of the colonists' favorite authors and the English divine from whose published sermons colonial ministers borrowed most frequently

---

[12] Spurr, *Restoration Church of England*, 305, 284; Davis, *Intellectual Life in the Colonial South*, 2:580-81; William Fitzhugh to Edward Hayward, 21 July 1698, *William Fitzhugh and His Chesapeake World*, 363; Blair, *Our Saviour's Divine Sermon on the Mount*, 1:ii. Prior to 1723 only two colonials made the trip to England for ordination. Every other minister who served a Virginia parish before then had been raised in Europe, most in England or Scotland, and thee vast majority had been educated at universities in the British Isles and were familiar with the Restoration Church's theology; Gundersen, "The Search for Good Men," 455. On Tillotson, see Norman Fiering, "The First American Enlightenment: Tillotson, Leverett, and Philosophical Anglicanism," *New England Quarterly* 54 (1981): 307-44; Louis G. Locke, *Tillotson: A Study in Seventeenth-Century Literature* (Copenhagen: Rosenkilde & Bagger, 1954).

[13] Blair, *Our Saviour's Divine Sermon on the Mount*, 3:240.

[14] Page, *Deed of Gift to My Dear Son*, 168.

when composing their own, also mocked the idea that "the Gospel is all promises, and our part is only to believe and embrace them."[15] The mark of a good Christian was neither right doctrine nor a command of theological subtleties, but a life adorned with good morals. An individual ought not to compartmentalize the sacred and the secular, for all of life was part of the sacred. John Page's words to his son were characteristic: "A good life is inseparable from a good faith—yea, a good faith is a good life."[16]

With the exception of a few fundamental articles, doctrine played little part in the religious life of late seventeenth- and early eighteenth-century Virginians. Jesus Christ, of course, was the Son of God, whose birth, life, death, and resurrection pointed the way to salvation. The prayer book proclaimed this doctrine, and ministers alluded to it in their sermons. Virginians seemed particularly convinced of the resurrection and referred to it often in their writings, frequently in their wills. Elizabeth Read of York Parish asserted in her testament: "being penitent and sorey from the bottome of my heart for my sines past...I give and Committt my soule unto Almighty God my Saviour and Redemer in whome and by the meritts of Jesus Crist I trust and believe assuredly to be saved."[17] Beyond this dogma, essentially a summary of the Apostles' Creed, Virginians meddled little with articles of faith. Some ministers even claimed that the Sermon on the Mount, with its teachings on behavior, contained

---

[15] Tillotson, *Works*, 1:496.

[16] Page, *Deed of Gift to My Dear Son*, 160, 210; George Keith, *Power of the Gospel*, 12; Gundersen, "Anglican Ministry in Virginia," 180-81. Portions of the liturgy reinforced the notion that faith without works was empty. The post-communion prayers included the phrase "to do all such good things has thou hast prepared for us to walk in," and the confession of sin referred to having "left undone those things which we ought to have done."

[17] Paxton, sermon no. 2, "Of the Resurrectn of Christ," 5-6; York County, Deeds, Orders, and Wills, (7), f. 257. There are numerous other examples in York County, Deeds, Orders, and Wills, books 1-10; *Secret Diary of William Byrd*, xxviii; Page, *Deed of Gift to My Dear Son*, 136-38.

everything necessary for salvation.[18] Nor did Virginians put much stock in ceremonial practices. In 1720, Robert Carter, one of the colony's great planters, affirmed that he was "of the Church of England way" and wanted his children raised as Anglicans, although he could not have cared less about liturgical styles: "Practical godliness is the substance—[ceremonies] are but the shell."[19] The lack of interest in doctrinal or ceremonial matters and the resulting emphasis on behavior underscored both the church's pastoral function and its understanding of soteriology. If salvation depended upon living a good life, then a minister's (or parent's) role was to teach that duty.

Anglicans in Virginia conceived of religion as a form of duty, and this idea guided the way in which they ordered their relationships with God. Sometimes, as when James Blair preached that "Good Morality is Good Christianity," they simply equated religion with virtue, often in simplistic terms that could be misleading to persons who did not share their understanding of religion. When Virginians referred to religion in this way, they meant more than the performance of moral duties or a rationalist incarnation of virtue. Duty was a necessary facet of the Anglican believer's journey to heaven, a response to God undertaken in faith. William Byrd II offered one of the clearest explanations: "Religion is the Duty which every Reasonable

---

[18] Blair, *Our Saviour's Divine Sermon on the Mount*, 5:364; Paxton, sermon no. 3, "Of Anger," 1; Tillotson, *Works*, 1:447; William Giberne, *The Duty of Living Peaceably with all Men* (Williamsburg, 1759), 11. See also Maude H. Woodfin, trans. and ed. Marion Tinling, *Another Secret Diary of William Byrd of Westover, 1739-1741* (Richmond: The Dietz Press, 1942) 280; Blair, *Our Saviour's Divine Sermon on the Mount*, 2:173; 3:240; 2:216: "Let us take Care to reserve our greatest Care and Industry for the Christian Morals, [for]...in the Great Day of Accounts, Holy Lives will be more enquired into, than Orthodox Opinions."

[19] Robert Carter to William Dawkins, 14 July 1720, in Louis B. Wright, ed., *Letters of Robert Carter, 1720-1727, The Commercial Interests of a Virginia Gentleman* (San Marino: The Huntington Library, 1940) 25.

Creature owes to God, the Creator and Supream Governor of the World."[20]

Byrd based his view of the duties owed to God on his belief "that there is a God, eternal in his Duration, and infinite in his Perfection." Had there been no God there would have been no reason to attempt to control one's passions, to confess one's sins, or to marvel at God's "wise and mercifull Providence." But God did exist. He was merciful and good; and he had sent "Christ into the World to bring us to Heaven." The proper and natural response to God's loving action was obedience, for Virginians believed obedience was "perfective of our Natures."[21] Mankind had been created in God's image, thus, men and women were to imitate God: "every man yt doth not imitate God but [acts] contrary to him, is so far unnatural because he acts contrary to his natural pattern & exemplar."[22] Duty, understood as a well-ordered life of prayer and obedience to God's laws, was the high mark of a person's earthly pilgrimage, the restoration of human nature as far as that was possible on earth.[23] To live such a life, like the sailor who did his duty in Blair's analogy, was natural and what God expected.

Since Adam's fall, however, men and women had been incapable of the obedience God demanded. Virginians realized they were sinners and that more often than not their wicked ways fell short of a holy life. Yet they could comfort themselves with the knowledge that despite their faults God was merciful and did

---

[20] Blair, *Our Saviour's Divine Sermon on the Mount*, 2:253. See also Page, *Deed of Gift to My Dear Son*, 183-95; William Byrd, "A History of the Jews Before the Birth of Jesus," 1, Virginia Historical Society; William Byrd Commonplace Book, 1722-1732, 51, Virginia Historical Society.

[21] Byrd, "History of the Jews," 1; Blair, *Our Saviour's Divine Sermon on the Mount*, 5:203; 4:148; Thomas Pender, *The Divinity of the Scriptures, From Reason & External Circumstances* (New York, 1728) 17.

[22] Paxton, sermon no. 6, "Of Imitating God," 2; see also Paxton, sermon no. 1, "Of the Son of God," 1; Pead, *Jesus is God*, 52.

[23] Blair, *Our Saviour's Divine Sermon on the Mount*, 5:157; 3:236; 2:186.

not want his creatures to suffer eternal damnation. For this reason he had sent his son, Jesus Christ, into the world as a propitiation for the sins of mankind.[24] Through the "Mediation of Christ, the old impossible Condition of Perfect Obedience to the Law [of Moses] in all Points, which brought Condemnation to All Men," had been supplanted by the New Testament's covenant of grace.[25] Christ's death had pacified God's wrath toward humanity, granting "a title to eternal life" to all who accepted the Gospel's terms.[26] God offered the promise of eternal life to the whole world, not just to a select few whom he had predestined for heaven. John Page, a royalist who had immigrated to the colony during the English Civil War, offered one of the most powerful illustrations of this belief. Christ, the mediator between God and man, was born not in a "private house, but [at] an inn, which is open for all passengers," and in the "commonest place," a stable. Likewise, the savior's crucifixion had not taken place within the city walls, "but without the gate, to intimate that it was not an Altar of the Temple, but the world."[27]

Although Anglican soteriology affirmed that Christ had died to redeem the whole world, universal redemption did not necessarily mean universal salvation. Salvation demanded human action and the obedience of which Blair, Byrd, and other colo-

---

[24] See, for instance, Blair, *Our Saviour's Divine Sermon on the Mount*, 2:189.

[25] Blair, *Our Saviour's Divine Sermon on the Mount*, 2:189.

[26] Paxton, sermon no. 2, "Of the Ressurectn of Christ," 6. See also Paxton, sermon no. 1, "Of the Son of God," 6; Page, *Deed of Gift to My Dear Son*, 126-29, 236-37.

[27] Page, *Deed of Gift to My Dear Son*, 141-42, 130. See also Paxton, sermon no. 1, "Of the Son of God"; sermon no. 11, "Of Salvation," 7; Blair, *Our Saviour's Divine Sermon on the Mount*, 4:87; 5:301; Ichabod Camp, *Men have Freedom of Will and Power, and their Conduct, whether good or evil, is of Choice* (New Haven, 1760) 4; Morgan Godwyn, *Trade Preferr'd before Religion, and Christ Made to Give Place to Mammon* preface (London, 1685) 11; text, 33. There are two separate paginations to Godwyn's sermon.

nists had written. Robert Paxton warned his congregation that the Gospel "does not bring Salvatn to all to whom it appears, not because it is insufficient, but because [men and women] do not accept of its offers...upon its terms by hearkening to its exhortatns & complying wt its commands."[28] "We are workers together with God," another minister proclaimed, "we must not be meerly passive...as so many Sticks and Stones...but following after him as he gently leads and draws us."[29] Men and women played a role in gaining their salvation; it was neither a free gift to the elect nor a presumptuous solifidianism. James Blair cautioned his parishioners about irresistible grace and "God's absolute and irrespective Election and Reprobation," doctrines he described as "dangerous Principles" since they discounted mankind's need to obey the Gospel precepts and thus enticed sinners to embrace antinomianism. These, to Blair, were irresponsible Calvinist dogmas. They tempted men and women to "lye easie till some wonderful Motion of God's Spirit" transformed them into new creations, rather than to cooperate with God in the painful work of "Prayers and vigorous

---

[28] Paxton, sermon no. 11, "Of Salvation," 3. See also, Thomas Warrington, *The Love of God, Benevolence, and Self-Love, considered together. A Sermon Preached at Norfolk, Before a Society of Free and Accepted Masons, December 27th, 1752* (Williamsburg: 1753) 7; Camp, *Men Have Freedom of Will and Power*, 13-14: "altho' God by his grace and Holy Spirit, assists us to a virtuous and holy life, yet he does not compel us; on the other hand, if we are wicked, we are so, not for want of sufficient help to be otherwise, but because of our wilful neglect of the assistance which is afforded us...whether we will co-operate with him, or resist him, depends wholly upon our own choice." John Clayton, minister of James City Parish for a few years in the 1680s, viewed his ministry as a form of cooperation between God and his own endeavors, in John Clayton, *The Defence of a Sermon, Preach'd upon the Receiving into the Communion of the Church of England, the Honourable Sir Terence Mac-Mahon Baronet and Christopher Dunn: Converts From the Church of Rome* (Dublin, 1701) 2nd page of preface (no pagination). Although Clayton's sermon does not specifically address Virginia, the two-page preface discusses his experiences in the colony.

[29] Keith, *Power of the Gospel*, 12.

Endeavours" which gave men and women hope for divine assistance in furthering their journeys to heaven.[30]

Virginians understood faith as a necessary but insufficient part of a Christian's pilgrimage to heaven. By faith men and women acknowledged God's omnipotence and Christ's saving death, but unless they responded to this knowledge with a sincere repentance their faith meant little. "If you welcome repentance, knocking at your door from God," John Page told his son, "it shall knock at God's door of mercy for you."[31] Every time an Anglican recited morning or evening prayer —at public worship, within the family, or privately in one's closet —God again called the world to repent. Through the words of the liturgy's invitation to worship taken from the prophet Ezekiel and cited in the epigraph, God called all people to lead lives of repentance, to forsake their transgressions, and to amend their lives. Repentance allowed men and women the opportunity to benefit from Christ's death and to apply the covenant of grace to themselves. Through the sacrifice of his son "God meets us half way, He is reconciled to us, It remains only yt we be reconciled to him yt we hearken to the message from him & be reconciled to God." Virginians knew that their sins, like those of the rest of the world, had crucified their saviour and left him dead in the tomb; only repentance could "reviveth him to us."[32]

When Anglicans spoke of religion as a duty, they used language as best they could to explain the temporal

---

[30] Blair, *Our Saviour's Divine Sermon on the Mount,* 300-302; 2:242. For the differences between Anglicans and Puritans on mankind's role in the process of salvation, see Hambrick-Stowe, *Practice of Piety,* 60, where he states that for the Puritans, God not only leads but takes men and women by the hand —a subtle but telling difference.

[31] Page, *Deed of Gift to My Dear Son,* 51. See also Paxton, sermon no. 8, "Of Repentance," 8; Pead, *Jesus is God,* 101.

[32] Paxton, sermon no. 11, "Of Salvation," 6; Paxton, sermon no. 2, "The Ressurectn of Christ," 8; Peter Fontaine, "A Fast Day Sermon Preached May 10, 1727," (typescript), John D. Rockefeller, Jr. Library, Colonial Williamsburg Foundation; Page, *Deed of Gift to My Dear Son,* v: "endeavor that Christ's death may become effectual to your soul."

manifestations of a life transformed through repentance. Thus a good life was a good faith, for faith was only good if it showed itself in works. Unlike conversion, which nonconformists often described in evocative terms—"Laying hold of Christ," "getting into Christ," and "rolling themselves upon Christ"—there was a certain poverty to the language of repentance.[33] Tears could express this disposition of the soul: "for Tears have an audible and significant Voice....God hears their secret, and special Voice, and in our weeping reads our Humility and Repentance."[34] But like moral behavior, tears too were externals, and such "outward testimonies" were poor reflections of a broken and contrite heart. How otherwise explain repentance than by pointing to its outward results? For without evidence of a good life, what people then called amendment of life, repentance remained incomplete.[35] Preaching a Fast Day sermon at Westover Parish, Peter Fontaine explained what most Virginians took for granted in words "borrowed" from one of Archbishop Tillotson's sermons: "We should prosecute our repentance & Good resolutions to the actual reformation of our lives, for in this repentance doth mainly consist."[36] Mere sorrow for past sins without amendment did not mark a penitential life: "they must not be reckoned true Penitents, who are for delaying and putting off their Repentance and Amendment as long as they can; and then amend as little as they can. True Repentance is no less than a sincere Endeavour to forsake all Sin, and to put in Practice all Duty."[37]

---

[33] Spurr, *Restoration Church of England*, 320.

[34] Deuel Pead, *A Practical Discourse Upon the Death of Our Late Gracious Queen* (London, 1695) 15. See also Wright and Tinling, *Secret Diary of William Byrd*, 175.

[35] Paxton, sermon no. 8, "Of Repentance," 3.

[36] Peter Fontaine, "A Fast Day Sermon Preached 10 May 1727," 6. The phrase is also in Tillotson, *Works*, 3:195. Most of Fontaine's sermon is a reworked version of a Fast Day discourse preached by Tillotson.

[37] Blair, *Our Saviour's Divine Sermon on the Mount*, 5:357; 2:167; Paxton, sermon no. 8, "Of Repentance," 6.

By placing such emphasis on repentance and human action, Virginians heightened the role of human endeavor in the economy of salvation. Yet to suggest that Virginians practiced moralism—placing unwarranted confidence in external duties rather than in faith and God's grace—is inaccurate.[38] Anglican theology muddled the traditional sequence of justification and sanctification, suggesting on its surface that good works could merit salvation. But Virginians were not Pelagians; they did not believe that men and women could take the initial steps toward salvation unassisted by divine grace. Reformed Protestantism had traditionally taught that God justified men as sinners without prior merit or effort on the part of individuals. By faith, the sinner "appropriated" God's promise of forgiveness demonstrated in Christ's atoning death. John Page could therefore write: "Justification by blood."[39] Sanctification, or "growth in grace through a life of obedience and good works" culminating in glory hereafter, had its basis in justification. Although related, sanctification followed justification and the two were distinct events.[40]

The soteriology espoused in Blair's Virginia conflated this chronology. God had justified sinners through the resurrection of Christ and had thereby invited all of humanity to partake of the covenant of grace. Through Christ's death and resurrection, God had communicated to all people a measure of grace sufficient to overcome the effects of original sin and to recognize

---

[38] For this interpretation of Anglicanism in Virginia and Restoration England, see C. FitzSimons Allison, *The Rise of Moralism: The Proclamation of the Gospel From Hooker to Baxter* (Wilton CT: Morehouse Barlow, 1966); Gundersen, "Anglican Ministry in Virginia," 180-81, 188; Jan Lewis, *The Pursuit of Happiness: Family and Values in Jefferson's Virginia* (New York: Cambridge University Press, 1983) 45-47, 212-14. For a good rebuttal to the moralist position, see Spurr, *Restoration Church of England*, 298.

[39] Page, *Deed of Gift to My Dear Son*, 40.

[40] Spurr, *Restoration Church of England*, 298-99; *Sermons or Homilies, Appointed to be Read in Churches in the Time of Queen Elizabeth, of Famous Memory* (New York: 1815) 19, (cited hereafter as *Book of Homilies*).

the truth of the Gospel. It remained, however, for men and women to take hold of the "title to eternal life" exhibited to them by responding with their own faith and repentance.[41] For without repentance there could be no justification. This sequence could suggest that sanctification occurred simultaneously with or preceded justification, thus making human action the means whereby God accepted persons as righteous. But to Virginians, God was always the original actor.[42] In technical language which Virginians rarely used but readily implied, God's preeminent or "preventing grace" called mankind to repent. His operative or "assisting grace" requested in prayer made men and women capable of repentance and the good works provided evidence of a life transformed by grace.[43] John Page best captured the paradox at the heart of Anglican theology in colonial Virginia: "You shall be saved for your faith, not for your works; but for such a faith as is without works you shall never be saved. Works are disjoined from the act of justifying, not from the person justified."[44]

In short, Virginians embraced the doctrine of the conditional covenant. God had satisfied his side of the covenant by offering mankind justification through the death of his son. By faith and repentance, demonstrated through a holy life of conformity to

---

[41] Paxton, sermon no. 2, "The Resurrectn of Christ," 6; Paxton, sermon no. 11, "Of Salvation," 2; Keith, *Power of the Gospel*, 2-7; Fontaine, "A Fast Day Sermon Preached in Williamsburg 10 May 1727"; John Frederick Woolverton, *Colonial Anglicanism in North America* (Detroit: Wayne State University Press, 1984) 184; Page, *Deed of Gift to My Dear Son*, 35. James Blair suggested that through the general propagation of the Gospel, and more particularly in the sacrament of baptism, God had given enough grace "even to the worst of Men, to make them inexcusable" if they did not accept His offer of salvation; Blair, *Our Saviour's Divine Sermon on the Mount*, 4:87.

[42] Blair, *Our Saviour's Divine Sermon on the Mount*, 4:148.

[43] Spurr, *Restoration Church of England*, 300; Page, *Deed of Gift to My Dear Son*, 25; Paxton, sermon no. 8, "Of Repentance," 7; sermon no. 2, "Of the Resurrectn of Christ," 5.

[44] Page, *Deed of Gift to My Dear Son*, 237.

God's laws, men and women met their part of the covenant's obligations. Through the gift of grace, freely given to those who asked this of him in prayer, God cooperated with man in the drama of salvation. Just as a good crop required both seasonable weather and the farmer's diligence, 'there must be a due Concurrence of these two, the Grace of God, and our own Endeavours, to produce a due Obedience" to the Gospel precepts. The liturgy's post-communion prayer also indicated the necessity of working with God to gain salvation: "assist us with thy grace, that we may continue in that holy fellowship, and do all such good works as thou hast prepared for us to walk in."[45] Charles Hambrick-Stowe, in attempting to illustrate the differences between Puritan and Roman Catholic spirituality, suggested that Puritans thought in terms of their having been elected by God, and Roman Catholics believed that they had elected God.[46] Anglicans in Virginia found a middle path, they cooperated with God in order to ensure their prior election by God. Robert Paxton could therefore preach: "Every one who perishes for want of mercy is his own murtherer & lost because he refused his own mercy."[47]

Virginians thus focused their attention on the pastoral task of preventing the faithful from committing spiritual suicide by failing to repent and amend. Ministers preached of this duty, devotional literature recommended it, parents introduced their children to this truth by teaching them the church catechism, and condemned criminals urged the crowds gathered to witness their executions to "repent now, and continue repenting so long as you have an hour to live." In 1678, one young indentured servant who had been sentenced to death for murdering his master and mistress admonished the crowds to make their "Election sure" by forsaking their wicked paths: "Leave off

---

[45] Blair, *Our Saviour's Divine Sermon on the Mount*, 5:315; *Book of Common Prayer*, Service for the Lord's Supper.

[46] Hambrick-Stowe, *Practice of Piety*, 45.

[47] Paxton, sermon no. 8, "Of Repentance," 8.

sinning, else God will leave you off."[48] God also took part in the pastoral work of calling Virginians to repent, periodically sending epidemics and plagues of insects upon the colony to remind the settlers that they were sinners who needed to amend their lives.

Repentance was central to the spiritual pilgrimage of Anglicans, as important a part of their journey to God as conversion was to nonconformists—a necessary part of the spiritual life without which all other religious exercises were of little value. Virginians occasionally equated repentance and conversion, thereby suggesting that repentance marked the onset of an active spiritual life in which the individual consciously began moving toward heaven. James Blair likened it to the "Pangs and Throws of the new Birth," and Robert Paxton called repentance the "change of life."[49] The intention to repent indicated a person's acceptance of God's offer of salvation, a decision to become a Christian by choice rather than by the accident of birth in a Christian nation.[50]

Yet Virginians did not view repentance as a mechanical round of sin, sorrow, and brief amendments repeated day after day, a cycle that reflected too closely what they equated with the Roman Catholic sacrament of penance; brief contrition followed by the mumbled words of a priest, and penitents were free to sin again without formally amending their lives.[51] Nor did they believe repentance should be left to the deathbed. Delaying so long left no opportunity for the necessary amendment of life, and a sickbed repentance often proceeded from the wrong

---

[48] *Vain Prodigal Life, and Tragical Penitent Death of Thomas Hellier*, 39-40.

[49] Blair, *Our Saviour's Divine Sermon on the Mount*, 1:104; Paxton, sermon no. 8, "Of Repentance," 7. See also Tillotson, *Works*, 1:479.

[50] Deciding to define oneself as a Christian through choice rather than through the possession of an English surname is a major theme in James Blair's sermons, *Our Saviour's Divine Sermon on the Mount*, 4:62; 2:14, 22, 31, 255; 3:186, 280; and 5:321.

[51] Blair, *Our Saviour's Divine Sermon on the Mount*, 2:167; 4:15.

motives, fear of judgment rather than love of God.[52] Nor was the repentance God demanded accomplished at one time; it was a process which continued throughout a lifetime: "an habitual Temper of the Mind and Course of Life."[53]

Repentance represented the essential reorientation of an individual's life. Despite the necessity of an amended life as evidence and the emphasis ministers placed on outward behavior, the process of repentance more accurately described an internal change within the believer's heart or mind (Virginians did not present a consistent anthropology) which then resulted in a life that increasingly conformed to God's laws. "The inner Man of the Heart, is the chief Thing that God aims to govern," for "like the main spring in a clock, the heart animates and directs all a person's thoughts and motions. As this main Spring of the Heart goes, the Man thinks, contrives, speaks and acts."[54] Virginians often used the pilgrimage motif to express this shift in direction. Preaching on Christ's admonition in Matthew's Gospel, "where your treasure is, there will your heart be also," James Blair suggested that the disposition of the heart determined the port toward which a person sailed.[55]

The heart's love also dictated the object that impressed itself upon the eyes. "Heavenly Treasures are fitted for our Heaven-born Souls," Virginia's commissary told his Bruton Parish congregation—thereby noting man's natural end—"the more good we do with an Eye to Heaven, the more heavenly minded shall we prove, and the more directly shall we steer our Course

---

[52] Blair, *Our Saviour's Divine Sermon on the Mount*, 2:31, 167; 4:31; 5:357-58; Paxton, sermon no. 8, "Of Repentance," 5; John Tillotson in Spurr, *Restoration Church of England*, 293. "It is a most desperate madness for Men to defer it till" they approached death warned *The Whole Duty of Man*, a devotional volume popular among Virginians, see [Richard Allestree], *The Whole Duty of Man* (1658; reprint, London: 1714) 121-22.

[53] Blair, *Our Saviour's Divine Sermon on the Mount*, 1:96.

[54] Blair, *Our Saviour's Divine Sermon on the Mount*, 2:332. See also Page, *Deed of Gift to My Dear Son*, 40-55; and Pead, *Jesus is God*, 35.

[55] Blair, *Our Saviour's Divine Sermon on the Mount*, 4:332.

to Heaven."[56] Men and women may have been formed form the dust, but they had been founded from heaven and were naturally inclined to return to God. Focusing one's eyes upon God was a metaphor indicating that the individual was properly oriented and moving towards the intended goal. In this, Virginians followed St. Augustine's belief that "the eye doth signify the intent...wherewith a man doth a thing."[57] What individuals saw or placed before their eyes was important to colonial Virginians, for they believed that sight conveyed knowledge more immediately than the elusive medium of sound. George Keith, a missionary for the Society of the Gospel in Foreign Parts who preached from time to time in Virginia, spoke for many in the colony when he observed that without frequent repetition spoken words were "as soon forgot as heard, for most part."[58] Blair went further, combining theories of sight and homiletics when he suggested that sermons received a better reception if the minister in the pulpit was higher than the congregation so "that his Voice may be the better heard, and his Person seen, which has no small Influence on the Authority and Freedom of Elocution, so necessary in all Orators, and so particularly noted by our Saviour in the End of the Sermon [on the Mount]."[59] To set God before one's eyes was both indicative of a well-ordered heart and to embark on the path leading to heaven. Felony indictments often illustrated this point in a negative way by noting the generally accepted explanation for the defendants' crimes: "not haveing the fear of God before thine eyes but being

---

[56] Blair, *Our Saviour's Divine Sermon on the Mount,* 4:225, 230; 3:344.

[57] *Book of Homilies,* 39; Blair, *Our Saviour's Divine Sermon on the Mount,* 3:5-6.

[58] George Keith, *The Notes of the True Church With the Application of them to the Church of England, And the Great Sin of Seperation [sic] from Her* (New York, 1704) 8. On the fleeting nature of the spoken word see also William Dawson to Dr. Bearcroft, 12 July 1744, Dawson Papers, vol. 1, f. 22, Library of Congress; Pead, "A Sermon Preached at James City," 378.

[59] Blair, *Our Saviour's Divine Sermon on the Mount,* 1:2; Pead, *Jesus is God,* 10, 12.

moved by the instigation of the devil." Lacking the proper orientation, men and women strayed from the precepts contained in the Gospels, threatening their own salvation and disrupting the polity through acts such as theft, murder, and suicide.[60] Robert Paxton urged his parishioners to follow a different course: "This yrfor is an essential part of our relign, to set God always befor our eyes as the great pattern of our lives & actns." So oriented, obedience to God's laws provided evidence of a person's faith.[61]

When viewed as a pastoral strategy within the context of the devotional life rather than as a rigorous systematic theology, Anglican soteriology falls into a logical and ordered sequence. That is how it should be understood, for Anglicans in the late seventeenth and early eighteenth centuries thought of religion more as a practice than as a belief. Virginians accepted the concept of universal redemption, and this fit well with an ecclesiology that defined the church broadly, including all members of the polity. The object for ministers, then, was neither to call the elect out of the world into a pure church nor to prepare individuals for their conversion by God, but to encourage all Christians to accept God's offer of salvation by living lives of repentance. By making use of the means of grace —"Reading and Hearing the Scriptures, Prayer, and Meditation, with the Use of the Sacraments"—all people could benefit from Christ's death.[62] Ministers and devotional manuals urged

---

[60] Warren M. Billings, "Pleading, Procedure, and Practice: The Meaning of Due Process of Law in Seventeenth-Century Virginia," *Journal of Southern History* 47 (1981): 580. See also York County, Deeds, Orders, and Wills, bks. 1-10, passim. For ministers encouraging criminals to confess their crimes, see Lord Howard to Philadelphia Pelham Howard, [1 May] 1684, *Papers of Francis Howard Baron Howard of Effingham*, 90.

[61] Paxton, sermon no. 6, "Of Imitating God," 3. See also Blair, *Our Saviour's Divine Sermon on the Mount*, 4:47: "If we set his Glory before our Eyes, as the ultimate Aim and Design of all our Actions, we shall be delivered from all base sinister Designs and Intentions."

[62] Blair, *Our Saviour's Divine Sermon on the Mount*, 2:171, 61, 64; 5:73 and passim.

Virginians to take up lives of prayer and devotion. It was a constant refrain from the colony's pulpits. Anglicans believed God was as unimpressed by works without faith as he was by faith without works. Without prayer, the best of duties was but "dull morality" and worthless in the eyes of God.[63] James Blair recommended "Prayer, Meditation, and Contemplation" both as a means of grace and as a form of "Vigilance against Temptations." On another occasion he said: "Let Prayer then begin, and let Prayer end all our own Endeavours; and let Prayer be ever intermixed in our religious Duties, to oil the Wheels of Action."[64] John Page highlighted the importance of acting from the proper motives when he warned his son to beware of doing a duty separate from faith: "External actions adorn our professions, where grace and goodness seasons them; but where the juice and vigor of religion is not settled in the soul, a man is but like a goodly heart-shaken oak, whose beauty will turn into rottenness, and his end will be the fire."[65]

An active, sincere, and regular devotional life was the key to what Virginians called "evangelical obedience." Prayer and spiritual discipline could turn nominal Christians—those who were "Christian" by virtue of their Englishness—into professing Christians, or people who had made a conscious decision to make their lives a pilgrimage to God. George Keith employed nautical imagery to explain the importance of the devotional life, comparing the Bible to a compass and Christ's life to a map that could guide the faithful on their voyages. Prayer entreated God to send the winds of divine influence to fill the sails of human

---

[63] Blair, *Our Saviour's Divine Sermon on the Mount,* 3:362.

[64] Blair, *Our Saviour's Divine Sermon on the Mount,* 1:101; 5:392; see also 3:346: "There is nothing like the constant Use of Prayer for keeping the Mind in a good Frame and Temper; nothng draws down the continually needful supplies of Grace like it; nothing does better oil the Wheels of Action."

[65] Page, *Deed of Gift to My Dear Son,* 246-47. See also John Clayton, *Christ Crucified; the Power of God, and the Wisdom of God;* (London, 1706) 3.

affections.[66] The devotional life offered the means of grace that helped individuals order their lives; it shaped the moral life and thus served as the link between faith, repentance, and salvation.[67]

In public as well as in private, the *Book of Common Prayer* was the greatest single influence shaping Virginians' devotional lives. Next to the Bible, it was the most common volume in colonists' libraries.[68] Its liturgy repeated weekly at public worship and read each day privately by many individuals, the prayer book provided a constant source of structure for the spiritual life. The Apostles' Creed and the Lord's Prayer were repeated at each office, and through the appointed lessons the Bible was read through every year. The liturgy echoed the Bible, many of its prayers crafted from the words of Holy Scripture. Day after day, week after week, it gave voice to the same themes in the same words, calling the faithful to repentance at every service and offering them the means of grace.[69]

By repeating the same words at each service and by using the same forms, the set liturgies of the *Book of Common Prayer* were intended to work a gradual transformation in the lives of individuals.[70] Thus, to describe Anglican worship (as some recent historians have) as "predictable and boring" misses the point, in effect defining the Anglican approach to religion from an evangelical perspective.[71] Yet the purpose of divine service was

---

[66] Keith, *Power of the Gospel,* 17.

[67] Blair, *Our Saviour's Divine Sermon on the Mount,* 3:346; Spurr, *Restoration Church of England,* 334, where the point is hinted at.

[68] Davis, *Intellectual Life in the Colonial South,* 2:580.

[69] Spurr, *Restoration Church of England,* 334.

[70] Spurr, *Restoration Church of England,* 334.

[71] Dell Upton, *Holy Things and Profane: Anglican Parish Churches in Colonial Virginia* (New York: MIT Press, 1986) 9. See also Rhys Isaac, *The Transformation of Virginia, 1740-1790* (Chapel Hill: University of North Carolina Press, 1982) 63-64. For a corrective to this view, see the insightful comments in Joan R. Gundersen, review of *Holy Things and Profane,* by Dell Upton, in *William and Mary Quarterly,* 3rd ser. 46 (1989): 380. The well-known complaint about Virginians altering parts of the liturgy, usually by shortening it, is not a significant deviation from practices in seventeenth-

neither entertainment nor excitement but edification and spiritual formation. In the "Tempestuous Sea" of life, tossed by passions and distractions, the prayer book remained exceptional in its constancy. Unlike evangelicals and nonconformists, Anglicans placed little emphasis on conversion, and their style of worship reflected this difference. Both as a devotional work and as a service book, the *Book of Common Prayer* aimed less at conversion than at helping the presumably converted maintain and deepen their faith. It served as the liturgy for a people who were assumed to be Christians because they were citizens of the English nation.[72] William Beveridge, a late seventeenth-century minister and sometime bishop of St. Asaph, explained in his discourse, *A Sermon Concerning the Excellency and Usefulness of the Common Prayer*, that prayer book worship was designed to form as well as to order the lives of English Christians. This process, however, occurred slowly, a gradual action instead of a sudden and dramatic change like that experienced by the Apostle Paul on the road to Damascus. Since the set prayers worked this transformation through sound rather than through the more immediate agency of sight, necessity demanded the frequent repetition of the same words and phrases.[73] Beveridge, in fact, based his argument on the elusive epistemology of the spoken word:

---

and eighteenth-century England and does not suggest that the colonists were less Anglican than their co-religionists in the mother country. Even in the most "conformable" of English parishes similar deviations occurred. See Spurr, *Restoration Church of England*, 187-88.

[72] Spurr, *Restoration Church of England*, 109. See also a "Draft Representation of the Society for Propagating the Gospel in Foreign Parts to King George I," 3 June 1715, Fulham Palace Papers, vol. 36, ff. 42-43, Lamberth Palace.

[73] William Beveridge, *A Sermon concerning the Excellency and Usefulness of the Common Prayer...*;(London, 1681). Horton Davies, *Worship and Theology in England*, 5 vols. (Princeton: Princeton University Press, 1961-1975) 2:196; See also Blair, *Our Saviour's Divine Sermon on the Mount*, 4:9.

> In order to our being *Edified*, so as to be made better and holier, whensoever we meet together upon a Religious account, it is necessary that the same good and holy Things be always inculcated and pressed upon us after one and the same manner. For we cannot but all find by our own Experience, how difficult it is to fasten any thing that is truly good, either upon our selves or others, and that it is rarely, if ever, effected without frequent Repetitions of it. Whatsoever good things we hear only once, or now and then, though perhaps upon the hearing of them, they may swim for a while in our *Brains*, yet they seldom sink down into our *Hearts*, so as to move and sway the Affections, as it is necessary they should do, in order to our being *Edified* by them. Whereas by a *Set Form of Publick Devotions rightly composed, as* we are continually put in mind of all things necessary for us to know and do, so that it is always done by the same Words and Expressions, which by their constant use will imprint themselves so firmly in our Minds, that...they will still occur upon all occasions; which cannot but be very much for our *Christian Edification.*[74]

Hence, divine worship following the rites of the prayer book was intended to grasp an individual's affections, thereby swaying the person toward living a holy life. Not that this occurred simply by hearing or reading the offices each day or each week. Individuals had to participate willingly in the service by opening their minds to the words they would hear, thus allowing the liturgy to bring their affections into the right frame and temper.[75] Repeatedly using the same set brief forms encouraged this process and allowed the faithful to "recollect" their prayers, or in Beveridge's words which alluded to things seen, "to look over our Prayers again, either in a Book, or in our Minds, where

---

[74] Beveridge, *Excellency and Usefulness of the Common Prayer*, 7-8. Also quoted in Isaac, *Transformation of Virginia*, 64; and Davies, *Worship and Theology in England*, 3:26-27.

[75] Beveridge, *Excellency and Usefulness of the Common Prayer*, 17, 21-23, 39.

they are imprinted."[76] Over time, spoken prayers thus gained the epistemological immediacy of sight.

In theory, the set liturgies in the *Book of Common Prayer* were to help form the souls of Anglican Virginians. The exhortation, which followed the opening sentence of scripture in the offices of Morning and Evening Prayer, explained the purpose of divine service. The congregation rendered God thanks for his blessings, praised him, heard his holy word, and asked of him "those things which are requisite and necessary, as well for the body as the soul."[77] Rightly understood, the liturgy of the prayer book represented a public and communal form of spiritual discipline for a people whose ethnic origin marked them as Christian. Upon the mere accident of their English births or upon their unconscious admission to the church as infants at baptism, the *Book of Common Prayer* attempted to mold nominally Christian people into active and professing Christians. Through the habitual performance of the same actions each week, the liturgy of the *Book of Common Prayer* evoked and strengthened the appropriate emotions within an individual.[78]

Unlike the colony's laws, which threatened transgressors with physical torments and economic sanctions, the set liturgies of the prayer book aimed at the affections. These rites attempted to transform people from within rather than to restrain them from without. Week after week, and in the same phrases, the *Book of Common Prayer* put those assembled for divine worship "in mind, both of what we ought, and what we ought not to do, that

---

[76] Beveridge, *Excellency and Usefulness of the Common Prayer*, 11. Some Anglican apologists argued that brief collects or "arrow-like prayers," required less time than the long prayers of the Puritans, and therefore ran less risk of losing the hearers' attention. James Blair believed short prayers addressed the infirmities of human nature more directly than longer ones. See Davies, *Worship and Theology in England*, 2:212; and Blair, *Our Saviour's Divine Sermon on the Mount*, 4:9.

[77] Beveridge, *Excellency and Usefulness of the Common Prayer*, 21. See also the offices in the *Book of Common Prayer*.

[78] Davies, *Worship and Theology in England*, 2:199, 528.

we may be saved."[79] Over time, active participation in the prayer life of the established church might lead people to practice self-discipline for the sake of salvation, thus providing evidence of the internal reorientation of the heart which had occurred as a result of repentance. Like the process of conversion, however, the means by which prayer transformed an individual was a mysterious one, and it transcended rational analysis. To the Reverend John Clayton, minister of Virginia's James City Parish during the 1680s, a clergyman could only do so much to effect this change. He could preach, read prayers, exhort people to practice holy living, and urge them to repent and amend their lives. Yet God and the individual ultimately had to cooperate in the process of Christian formation or as Clayton put it: "leaving it to God and their own Souls."[80] Anglican theology following the Restoration brought mankind to the center of the theological world, but it also placed greater responsibilities on the laity as they attempted to work out their salvation.

Like the Restoration Church of England, Virginia's Church encouraged the faithful to practice "holy living" for the sake of salvation. A term much abused by historians, "holy living" essentially denoted the existence of a lively faith and a godly life grounded on that faith, a life in which individuals worked towards resembling God as children do their parents.[81] Underlying this idea was the familiar concept that only like can know like, and as Anglicans progressed on their journeys to heaven and made use of the means of grace, they were expected ever more closely "to imitate [God] in all his imitable perfections."[82]

---

[79] Beveridge, *Excellency and Usefulness of the Common Prayer*, 17.

[80] Clayton, *Defence of a Sermon*, 2nd page of preface.

[81] Spurr, *Restoration Church of England*, 308; Paxton, sermon no. 6, "Of Imitating God," 1; Blair, *Our Saviour's Divine Sermon on the Mount*, 4:32.

[82] Blair, *Our Saviour's Divine Sermon on the Mount*, 4:32. See also Page, *Deed of Gift to My Dear Son*, 175.

The devotional life played an important part in shaping a holy life, and Virginians did not restrict their spiritual regimen to the public liturgy and the sacred space of the parish church. They never viewed public worship as an end in itself, and did not believe God could be approached only in the church building or through the set forms of the *Book of Common Prayer*. Nor did they believe public worship was necessarily the most important part of the spiritual journey. Unlike English divines who treated private devotions as a form of preparation for the Church's public worship, ministers in Virginia reversed this sequence, placing greater emphasis on private devotions than on public and communal prayer. Clergy, in fact, often looked upon public worship as preparation for private devotions. James Maury told his congregation that "Solitude is prerequisite to prayer" and recommended that persons interested in serious spiritual discipline follow Christ's example and retire from the presence of others when they attended to their prayers, suggesting that such devotions were "generally more serious and contemplative" because individuals were less likely to be disturbed in private than at public worship. William Byrd II certainly fit this model. Public worship provided numerous distractions that diverted him from the worship of God, especially the presence of attractive women in the congregation who were nearly certain to set the master of Westover meditating upon less holy desires than were proper at Sabbath services. Nor did the routine practices of the liturgy always point Byrd towards God. He treated preached sermons as an academic exercise in which he stood in judgment on the minister's effort, evaluating these public discourses as "good," "very good," or "poor." On at least one occasion, a minister alluded to contemporary events while preaching, thereby leading Byrd to think about his own place in colonial politics, thus disrupting his devotions. Byrd's attitude was different in private. Sermons he read at home touched his affections more directly than his intellect and he often noted in his diary having been edified or having repented as a result of this devotional reading.[83]

James Blair recognized that public worship could be problematic in other ways: "such is the Nature of Speech, that as it tires and flags the Spirit, so it dissipates a Spirit of Devotion, which as it is fed by Meditation, so it is spent by many Words and Talking."[84] The lack of attention paid to ecclesiastical laws in late seventeenth- and early eighteenth-century Virginia by the colony's civil leaders meant that the faithful needed to engage in private self-censure. Blair suggested that through the habitual practice of daily private prayer and self-examination "a Man becomes his own Reprover and Monitor, and from daily Experience, both of his own Good and Bad Actions, learns to improve himself for the future."[85] In a discourse on repentance Robert Paxton urged his parishioners to reprove themselves for their sins, a practice made more necessary since "the decay of publick & judiciall chastismt hath left us more in our own hands."[86]

The emphasis Virginia's ministers placed on private prayer likely reflected the necessity imposed on Anglicans by the colony's "occasions." If the public worship of the Church was to provide the focal point for the piety of the faithful, the Church had to provide regular opportunities for the devotion it encouraged. But relatively few ministers served Virginia's Church, the Lord's Supper was usually celebrated just three or

---

[83] John Spurr, "The Church, the Societies and the Moral Revolution of 1688," in *From Toleration to Tractarianism*, 138; Jeremy Gregory, "The Eighteenth-Century Reformation: The Pastoral Task of Anglican Clergy After 1689," in *From Toleration to Tractarianism*, 73; James Maury manuscript sermons, "2d sermon on Mat. vi. 6," 2-5, John D. Rockefeller, Jr. Library, Colonial Williamsburg Foundation. See also, Blair, *Our Saviour's Divine Sermon on the Mount*, 4:9. Wright and Tinling, *Secret Diary of William Byrd*, passim.

[84] Blair, *Our Saviour's Divine Sermon on the Mount*, 4:9; 5:385.

[85] Blair, *Our Saviour's Divine Sermon on the Mount*, 2:341-42.

[86] Paxton, sermon no. 8, "Of Repentance," 1.

four times each year, clerks appointed to read the liturgy in the minister's absence occasionally showed up at the wrong time, and divine service was held only on Sundays, a practice ministers new to the colony found disturbing and irregular. In comparison, by the mid-1680s nearly thirty churches in London offered the prayer book offices daily, and many churches had begun to celebrate the eucharist weekly or monthly. Deuel Pead of Christ Church Parish in Middlesex County celebrated the eucharist each month during the 1680s, and like some Anglican ministers in England, he preached a preparation sermon "on the Satterday in the afternoone afore the Giveing the Comunion." Despite his efforts, however, the practice remained uncommon in Virginia.[87] Clergy tried to accommodate themselves to these circumstances as best they could, often acting more like missionaries than settled ministers. Given their sporadic contact with the laity necessitated by the colony's large parishes, ministers encouraged the faithful to make use of the means of grace in private. Most sermons preached in colonial Virginia, in fact, were how-to discourses on repentance urging the duty of private prayer and explaining its necessity. Preaching thus served the faithful as a calm exhortation to action, to keep God before their eyes, and to deepen their spiritual lives away from the church building. Like many of the clergy, John Page believed that sermons at public worship served as preparation for private prayer. He warned his son not to "narrow up" God's service in "hearing," for sermons and public prayers did not exhaust his religious duty: "The word preached brings in knowledge, and knowledge rectifies devotion. So that preaching is to beget your

---

[87] John Lang to Bishop Edmund Gibson, 7 February 1725/26, Fulham Palace Papers, vol. 12, ff. 97-98. See also Francis Nicholson to Lucy Burwell, Francis Nicholson Papers, John D. Rockefeller, Jr. Library, Colonial Williamsburg Foundation; Spurr, "The Church, the Societies and the Moral Revolution of 1688," 138-39; Davis, *Intellectual Life in the Colonial South,* 2:717; C. G. Chamberlayne, ed., *The Vestry Book of Christ Church Parish, Middlesex County, Virginia, 1663-1767* (Richmond: Old Dominion Press, 1927) 44.

praying, to instruct you to praise and worship God."[88] Prayer and other devotional exercises were therefore duties to be undertaken within the family and in private, in addition to regular attendance at divine worship.

Not surprisingly, Anglicans in Virginia practiced much of their piety at home. Reading the Bible or other religious books, self-examination, and secret prayer were all forms of devotion individuals could make use of away from the sacred space of the institutional church. Clergy advocated these practices and often distributed religious volumes to their parishioners, thus making devotional manuals substitutes for ministers who could not adequately serve their parishes. (Their own spirituality forced to retreat during the Interregnum into the family or the private conscience, Royalist immigrants may have found these practices familiar already.) Such religious exercises were designed to help Virginians forge spiritual resolutions and then to act upon them, to order their lives in keeping with the divine pattern. Bible reading was widely encouraged. John Page urged his son to read the scriptures frequently and offered him the counsel of St. Ambrose: "Eat, and eat daily of this heavenly manna." The scriptures provided an "exact map of the heavenly Canaan, drawn by the pen of the Holy Ghost."[89] In the stories of Christ's earthly pilgrimage the Bible offered a model of the Christian life. Virginians viewed Christ as the divine teacher of virtue who had perfectly combined faith and works, thereby restoring human nature and demonstrating what men and women could become. They learned their duties through his model, and then tried to apply his teachings to their lives. "Examples are far better than Precepts," James Blair preached of Christ's life contained in the

---

[88] Page, *Deed of Gift to My Dear Son,* 169.

[89] Spurr, *Restoration Church of England,* 23; Page, *Deed of Gift to My Dear Son,* 12-14; Pead, *Jesus is God,* 48, 80-81. See also James Maury to James Maury, Jr., 17 February 1762, Fontaine-Maury Papers, John D. Rockefeller, Jr. Library, Colonial Williamsburg Foundation.

Gospels, "the perfect Pattern of all Virtue...gives a very great Light into our Duty."[90]

In addition to the Bible, Virginians turned to a variety of other religious works to guide their devotions. Philip Ludwell kept a "poor little old prayer book" worn from use in his closet to help order his private spiritual exercises. Another colonist believed that for family or private devotions one "cannot make a better choice than of the church prayers," by which he meant the *Book of Common Prayer*.[91] A number of English devotional writings also helped Virginians direct their journeys to heaven. *The Practice of Piety* by Puritan bishop Lewis Bayly, *The Whole Duty of Man*, likely written by Richard Allestree, a royalist minister, the *Book of Common Prayer*, *A Weeks Preparation Towards a Worthy Receiving of the Lords Supper*, and the Whiggish English minister John Lewis' *Church Catechism*, were all familiar titles in the colony. Lewis' little volume proved so popular that in 1738 William Parks, printer of the *Virginia Gazette*, published an edition out of his Williamsburg press, advertising it as "being very proper for a New Year's Gift to Children."[92]

In addition to devotional works, some colonists also owned books assumed to be less specifically Christian in nature, often

---

[90] Blair, *Our Saviour's Divine Sermon on the Mount*, 2:64, 116, 166; Pead, *Jesus is God*, 81-82. See also Robert Carter to Messrs. Micajah and Richard Perry, 22 July 1720, Wright, *Letters of Robert Carter, 1720-1727*, 34-35: "My son, I find, is on the stool of repentance....He begs of me to forget his past extravagances and desires I may not insist upon a particular account from him, and that he will give me no more occasion of future complaints. Upon these terms I am willing to shut up with him. Thus you see I am no stranger to the story of the Gospel." For Christ as an exemplar of unjust suffering for Christians to imitate, see William Berkeley to [King's Commissioners for Virginia], 23 April 1677, PRO CO 1/40, f. 62.

[91] Philip Ludwell to Philip Ludwell II, 20 December 1707, Lee Family Papers, section 5, Virginia Historical Society; Page, *Deed of Gift to My Dear Son*, 216. See also *Whole Duty of Man*, 109.

[92] *Virginia Gazette*, 15-22 December 1738; 9-16 February, 16-23 February, 23 February-2 March, 1738/39, John D. Rockefeller, Jr. Library, Colonial Williamsburg Foundation.

popular volumes written by "astrologer-physicians." Wealthy planters like Ralph Wormley, Edmund Berkeley, and Mathew Hubbard, as well as the Reverend Thomas Teackle of Accomac County all may have guided portions of their spiritual discipline with reference to books now classified as "occult." Volumes by the alchemist Albertus Magnus, Richard Mathew's work on "alchemical healing secrets," *The Unlearned Alchymist His Antidote*, and Jean Baptiste Porta's *Natural Magick* appealed to a small circle of well-to-do colonists. Like their contemporaries in England, these men may well have viewed alchemy as an "exacting spiritual discipline" aimed at the "spiritual transformation" of the individual practitioner, a means by which very religious people could gain spiritual insight not by study but by revelation.[93]

Although written by a range of authors representing nearly the entire theological spectrum, the religious volumes owned by colonial Virginians shared a common desire to encourage what one historian has called "the consecrated life of the laity." They advocated "holy living" and, like the Bible, urged Virginians to imitate Christ. Colonists were likely as practical in their purchase of books as in their theology. Books were bought in order to be used.[94] And apparently they were. In 1702 a group of Quakers in Chuckatuck complained that the Anglican practice of distributing devotional manuals hurt their efforts to attract con-

---

[93] Keith Thomas, *Religion and the Decline of Magic: Studies in Popular Beliefs in Sixteenth and Seventeenth Century England* (London: Weidenfeld and Nicolson, 1971) 269-71; Jon Butler, "Magic, Astrology, and the Early American Religious Heritage, 1600-1760," *American Historical Review* 84 (1979): 327-29.

[94] Davis, *Intellectual Life in the Colonial South*, 2:493, 580; Louis Wright, "Pious Reading in Colonial Virginia," *Journal of Southern History* 6 (1940): 385; Spurr, *Restoration Church of England*, 371. For specific ownership, see York County Deeds, Orders, and Wills, bks. 1-10, passim. For a specific recommendation from a minister to an ill parishioner, see James Maury to Mary Grymes, 16 January 1768, Sol Fienstone Collection of the American Revolution, section 924, letter 33, American Philosophical Society.

verts.[95] William Byrd II prepared for communion by reading in Jeremy Taylor's *The Worthy Communicant* to which he had added in his own hand a version of Psalm 51, a penitential psalm recommended by the *Book of Common Prayer* "if thou hast sinned, and art converted, and moved to do penance, desirous to have mercy."[96] Virginians of the gentry class were familiar not only with the Bible and devotional works but also with many of the classics written by the Church fathers and more recent theologians. John Page, Richard Lee, William Byrd II, and William Fitzhugh were among those who referred in their own writings either to canon law or the writings, among others, of Augustine, Ambrose, Hooker, Basil the Great, and John Chrysostom. They referred to them with the same ease with which earlier Virginians had alluded to the Bible. Widely read in theology, Lee used his knowledge of the Bible and the Church Fathers to dispute with a Puritan correspondent, arguing the importance of both tradition and scripture.[97] Fitzhugh utilized the scriptures in an equally practical way to help buttress some of his legal opinions.[98]

Family prayers too formed part of the Anglican spiritual regimen. Virginia's ministers promoted this exercise, as did the English clergy, especially for those people who were unable to attend public worship regularly.[99] John Page recommended the practice of family devotions to his son, not only as a means of grace but also as an example to his children. Since Virginians believed that praying for a person conferred grace upon that individual, habitual family prayer was also a way for husbands

---

[95] Epistles Received, vol. 1, f. 383, Library of the Society of Friends. See also Epistles Sent, vol. 2, f. 16, Library of the Society of Friends.

[96] William Byrd's copy of Jeremy Taylor, *The Worthy Communicant*, 3, Virginia Historical Society; *Book of Common Prayer* (no pagination).

[97] Richard Lee to [?], 21 October 1652, Morristown National Historical Park.

[98] William Fitzhugh to Robert Beverely, 1 January 1682/1683, *William Fitzhugh and His Chesapeake World*, 131.

[99] Gregory, "Eighteenth-Century Reformation," 74.

and wives mutually to support each other in their spiritual lives.[100] It also served to link family members spiritually across time and space. When Lord Howard of Effingham came to Virginia as the colony's governor in 1683 and 1684, his wife did not immediately accompany him, yet the couple nonetheless continued their practice of offering daily prayers for each other just as William Fitzhugh and his relations in England did. Prayer for the other on days when they would receive the sacrament was one of Lord Howard's special concerns: "pray remember me particularly on Easter day in your prayers, or any other holy time that our prayers may meet at the Throne of Grace for Each other."[101] In addition to praying for each other, family members often wrote to relatives and encouraged them to see the hand of God at work in the world, the laity thus taking on part of the pastoral role of spiritual counseling. William Fitzhugh often took this part in his family, especially when someone was ill or a child had died. Death was never far away in seventeenth-century Virginia, and the earthly pilgrimages of children were often brief. Fitzhugh believed that God "lent" children to parents as "Guest[s]," calling home these gifts at his pleasure. Yet death was not always an occasion for sadness. Fitzhugh, who had endured the deaths of three of his children, wrote to a cousin in 1687 and urged him to take heart at the sudden death of your two sweet Babes, which loss is easily & cheerfully born, if natural

---

[100] Page, *Deed of Gift to My Dear Son*, 189, 192-93.

[101] Lord Howard to Philadelphia Pelham Howard, 10 February 1684, *Papers of Francis Howard Baron Howard of Effingham*, 46, and passim. Holy Communion played an important role in the devotional lives of many Virginians fortunate enough to live in a parish that had a minister to celebrate the sacraments. Francis Nicholson offered a rare glimpse into the laity's view of communion in a letter to Lucy Burwell: "When I have been under any affliction[,] trouble[,] or when I have undertaken any business or employment I commonly received the most holy Communion, and I thank God that after I had done so I succeeded therein, either by obtaining what I desired or by being satisfied without it," Francis Nicholson to Lucy Burwell, Francis Nicholson Papers, John D. Rockefeller, Jr. Library, Colonial Williamsburg Foundation, f. 44.

affection be laid aside, & we truly consider as we ought, that they have changed a troublesome & uncertain terrestrial being for a certain & happy Celestial habitation, & you have this happiness continually to joy you, that you have of your Offspring in Heaven, continually singing Hallelujah's to the most highest, their Regeneration in Baptism washing off all Original Sin, & their fewness of years excusing them from all willful & obstinate sins.[102]

Besides public prayers within the family, Anglicans were expected to engage in the more serious work of private prayer, a duty "to be often performed, by none, seldomer than morning and evening."[103] William Byrd II followed this practice throughout his life, even on those days when he attended public worship at the local parish church.[104] Like family prayer and public worship, private prayer included praise, petition, confession, and thanksgiving. In their daily prayers Virginians thanked God for his temporal blessings or begged him to be merciful to their kin and the colony, at the same time acknowledging his omnipotence. "I comit you and yors to the divine tuition," and "the planter (if [God say Amen] designes) a great crop" were typical sentiments.[105]

---

[102] William Fitzhugh to William Fitzhugh, 30 January 1686/1687, *William Fitzhugh and His Chesapeake World*, 198. There are numerous other examples from Fitzhugh. See, among others, 171-74, 197, 200,

[103] Page, *Deed of Gift to My Dear Son*, 217. See also Lord Howard to Philadelphia Pelham Howard, 21-22 March 1684, Papers of Francis Howard Baron Howard of Effingham, 73; *Whole Duty of Man*, 110.

[104] On this point, see Byrd's diaries, passim.

[105] John Catlett to Thomas Catlett, 1 April 1664, misc. manuscripts, John D. Rockefeller, Jr. Library, Colonial Williamsburg Foundation; William Byrd I to [Perry & Lane], 29 March 1685, Marion Tinling, ed., *The Correspondence of the Three William Byrds of Westover, Virginia, 1684-1776*, 2 vols. (Charlottesville: University Press of Virginia, 1977) 1:30. The examples could easily be multiplied, but see *William Fitzhugh and His Chesapeake World*, passim; *Papers of Francis Howard Baron Howard of Effingham*, passim; Philip Ludwell to Philip Ludwell II, 9 February 1705/06, Lee Family Papers, Section 4, Virginia Historical Society; Francis

The more intense work of private devotion transcended both texts and forms. The colony's ministers advised Virginians to set aside words and to approach God in meditation or "mental prayer," for prayer was the "Language of the Heart to God."[106] By meditating upon God's goodness, his providences, or his mercy in sending Jesus Christ to redeem mankind, men and women focused their eyes upon the deity and thus oriented themselves for the journey to heaven.[107] These exercises brought the faithful "Face to Face" with God. So too did their daily observations of the natural world, which some colonists seemed to view as a type of spiritual exercise. Both in its design and its revelation of God's providences, creation pointed to an omnipotent and merciful deity. James Blair asked his Bruton Parish congregation to contemplate the natural world: "There are many wonderful things might be learned from the Works of Creation...for they bear the Marks and consequently the Proofs of God's Wisdom."[108] Nature fascinated Virginians, creating within them a feeling of wonder that both frightened them and attracted them to the creator. A great storm, the beauty of a flower, or the power of the sea which separated them from England all inspired this emotion, what one European philosopher called "a sudden surprise of the soul." Governor John Page said of the botanist John Clayton: "I have heard him say, whilst examining a flower, that he could not look into one, without seeing the display of infinite power and contrivance; and that he thought it impossible for a BOTANIST to be an

---

Nicholson to Lucy Burwell, 7 January 1702/1703, Francis Nicholson Papers; Joseph Tayloe to Mrs. Ruth Tayloe, 10 July 1705; "Letters of William Sherwood to Sir Joseph Williamson," *William and Mary Quarterly* 1st ser. 11 (1903) 112-13, 171-73.

[106] Blair, *Our Saviour's Divine Sermon on the Mount*, 4:9-10, 132; 3:359; 5:170.

[107] Blair, *Our Saviour's Divine Sermon on the Mount*, 1:203, 206; 5:170-71.

[108] Blair, *Our Saviour's Divine Sermon on the Mount*, 4:324-25, 50-51, 96, 100; 1:206; 3:258.

ATHEIST." The "most Dreadfull Hurry Cane" which struck Virginia in 1667 inspired a similar response. Councilor Thomas Ludwell believed "all the Ellements were at Strife," contending to see "wch of them should doe most towards the reduction of the creation into a Second Chaos, it was wonderfull to consider the contrary effects of that Storme." Rattlesnakes dazzled Thomas Glover who marveled that God could have created a beast this terrible yet placed a rattle at the end of its tail, "which seemeth to me a peculiar providence of God to warn people to avoid the danger." William Byrd II believed God had taken a pragmatic approach to creation by filling it with so many fascinating objects that men would want to apply their own God-given talents to learning more about the natural world.[109] Other colonists embraced illnesses, bad weather, and plagues of insects as calls to repentance. Sickness underscored God's omnipotence. After his sister died of a fever despite the best efforts of a good doctor, Philip Ludwell wrote to John Custis in words expressing his belief that God had ordered events: "but when God calls[,]

---

[109] Stephen Greenblatt, *Marvelous Possessions: The Wonder of the New World* (Chicago: University of Chicago Press, 1991) 20-23, 78-80; Edmund and Dorothy Berkeley, *John Clayton: Pioneer of American Botany* (Chapel Hill: University of North Carolina Press, 1963) 28; Thomas Ludwell to Lord Berkeley of Stretton, 7 November 1667, PRO CO 1/21, ff. 282-283; William Byrd II to Francis Otway, *Correspondence of the Three William Byrds*, 2:453; William Byrd II to [Sir Hans Sloane], 10 April 1741, *Correspondence of the Three William Byrds*, 2:585; Thomas Glover, *An Account of Virginia, its Scituation, Temperature, Productions, Inhabitants and their manner of planting and ordering Tobacco* (London: Royal Society, 1676) 20, Earl Gregg Swem Special Collections, College of William and Mary. See also Glover's manuscript edition in which he suggests that the great hurricane of 1667 "was a divine punishment laid on the Virginians because they had broken their promises not to plant tobacco," *Royal Society of London, Classified Papers, 1660-1740*, 7:1, a xerox copy is on file at the John D. Rockefeller, Jr. Library, Colonial Williamsburg Foundation, as part of the Virginia Colonial Records Project. See also Pead, *Jesus is God*, 10; the poetry of the Rev. Hartwell in *Virginia Gazette*, 25 January-1 February 1739/40, 4.

the best Phisitians still will not avail."[110] Understood properly, the entire world pointed toward God. Virginians' attitudes approximated those of Thomas Traherne, a contemporaneous English divine and mystical poet. He mused in a verse from one of his *Centuries*: "Would one think it possible for a man to delight in gauderies like the butterfly, and neglect the Heavens?"[111] The colonists' prose lacked the felicity of the poet's, but their sentiments were nevertheless the same: look closely enough at what seems most trivial, and you will find God.

Despite the emphasis Anglicans in Virginia placed on human effort in the economy of salvation, the focus of their devotional lives remained on God. Over and over he called them to repent, and his was the pattern they endeavored to imitate. They did not find humility in meticulous self-examination or in bemoaning the human condition, but in acknowledging God's goodness and striving to grow in grace and Christian perfection. Rather than meditating upon their sins, Virginians tended to focus their attentions on God. Although they practiced self-examination, no extant sermon delivered by an Anglican minister in the colony suggested that the faithful keep diaries of their religious pilgrimages or record their sins in detail. Virginians did not keep a diary of their spiritual lives in a book, but a book in their lives.

The devotional life shaped the moral life, providing the link between faith and repentance, between piety and living a holy life. Commissary Blair therefore recommended that Virginians

---

[110] Philip Ludwell to John Custis, 22 September 1708, Custis Papers, Virginia Historical Society. See also York County, DOW (4), f. 152.

[111] Thomas Traherne, *Centuries* (Wilton CT: Morehouse Publishing, 1985) 16. Compare Blair, *Our Saviour's Divine Sermon on the Mount*, 3:238: "Rare Miracles of Providence indeed we are apt to take notice of; but such daily Mercies, as the constant rising and setting of the Sun, the Seasonableness of the Weather, the sending of refreshing Showers, the regular Productions of Grass and Corn, and a thousand other daily Benefits we take no notice of at all, except we come to be pinched by the Want of them."

heed the Pauline injunction to pray without ceasing.[112] Throughout the day, as a means of spiritual maintenance and the "keeping out of Evil-Thoughts," he suggested the use of mental prayer and brief ejaculatory prayers—either with the heart or with the lips.[113] Ejaculatory prayer was similar to the Hindu OM and among Christians was a popular form of mystical prayer involving the frequent repetition of brief phrases. St. Augustine's "O Beauty of all things Beautiful," St. Francis' "My God, My God," and the Jesus Prayer, "Lord Jesus Christ, Son of God, have mercy upon me," are all examples from the Christian tradition. Blair believed this form of prayer should become as common in the spiritual life "as Breathing is in the Natural."[114] He also urged the faithful to pray the Psalms as an antidote to temptation, describing this portion of the Bible as a "Garrison at hand, to which we may retreat from a sudden Attaque of the enemy." Blair found Psalm 136 particularly useful, its refrain of "for his mercy endureth forever" a model of brief ejaculatory prayer.[115] By keeping mindful of God through habitual devotion, individuals drew down measures of grace to help them combat temptations and kept their eyes focused on God as they continued on the course to heaven.

---

[112] Blair, *Our Saviour's Divine Sermon on the Mount,* 5:166; 4:112. The Biblical reference is I Thessalonians 5.17.

[113] Blair, *Our Saviour's Divine Sermon on the Mount,* 2:344; 5:170-71; 4:10.

[114] Hambrick-Stowe, *Practice of Piety,* 184; F. L. Cross and E. A. Livingstone. eds., *The Oxford Dictionary of the Christian Church,* 2nd ed. (New York: Oxford University Press, 1974) 738; Blair, *Our Saviour's Divine Sermon on the Mount,* 2:344; 5:170-71. See also *Whole Duty of Man,* 110, 434-36. Compare Blair's views with those in James Walsh, ed., *The Cloud of Unknowing* (Ramsey NJ: Paulist Press, 1981). Blair, and many Virginians, may have continued the traditional practices of English contemplative prayer. This emphasis, rather than a lack of religious fervor, may help account for the small amount of material historians have uncovered about the practice of religion in colonial Virginia.

[115] Blair, *Our Saviour's Divine Sermon on the Mount,* 2:342; 3:239.

Like other Christian theologies, Anglicanism in late seventeenth- and early eighteenth-century Virginia tried to assist the faithful along the path to heaven. Although Anglican piety addressed the whole person by cultivating what James Blair called "the practice of the divine presence," Virginians demonstrated their piety most vividly through external behaviors. Such actions did not indicate the widespread acceptance of rationalism, moralism, or the ascendancy of works over faith. Doing one's duty was a statement of faith and the product of a sincere devotional life. Unlike many nonconformists, Anglicans did not seek in their earthly pilgrimages a mystical union with Christ, the "Bridegroom of the soul." Rather, they thought of Christ as a teacher of virtue, and with the assistance of God's grace they endeavored to imitate the divine pattern. William Byrd II could therefore define blasphemy as living a life of "Disorder." By so living, "instead of blessing his name, we are blaspheming it, & blotting out his Image in our Souls."[116]

Virginians viewed the spiritual life as a process in which the faithful, through God's assistance, tried to replace their sinful habits with the habits of Christian virtue. They were fond of citing the parable of the talents to indicate that sincere Christians were expected to grow in grace and come ever closer to Christian perfection throughout a lifetime. It was a process of becoming by doing. The habitual repetition of devotional behaviors strengthened an individual's relationship with God and led to the growth in grace necessary to continue the work of repentance and amendment. One could discern the state of a person's soul by observing his or her actions. A life marked less and less by sin was one oriented toward God, while a life that continually reflected "a long train of sins" was evidence that the work of repentance had not yet begun.[117]

The performance of devotional duties not only helped an individual grow in grace but also helped to establish a religious

---

[116] William Byrd Commonplace Book, 16.

[117] Tillotson, *Works*, 2:31. The parable of the talents is in Matthew 25:14-30 and Luke 19:12-27.

identity. This had always been true of those who took on the disciplines of family and secret prayer. But by the end of the century it was becoming true of regular church attendance as well. In 1699 the House of Burgesses reduced the legal requirement for church attendance to once every two months.[118] The decision to attend public worship regularly and to engage in private spiritual exercises, then, had largely become a matter of personal choice. A form of voluntarism was emerging within the structure of the institutional church, and colonial leaders were encouraging it. God had offered redemption to all men and women. To respond to his call, either by worshipping regularly at the parish church or by making use of the means of grace in private, was to begin the process of becoming a Christian by choice rather than by birth.

The colony's "occasions" had forced Virginians to adapt their devotional practices, not to abandon them. For those who wished to make use of them, the means of grace still existed. Virginia's ministers realized their church's problems, and pragmatic clergymen actively encouraged forms of prayer that might potentially threaten the centrality of the institutional church. Despite the church's difficulties, the faithful were able to practice their piety and to continue their pilgrimages to heaven. Although William Fitzhugh worried about the lack of "spirituall help & comforts" in Virginia, he also knew that a person could further her spiritual pilgrimage in the colony, even if the spiritual helps were not as readily available as some colonists may have wished. He wrote his mother in 1698, thanking her for the gift of her "choice Bible," urging her to face a present illness with Christian patience and to see God's hand in it, and reporting that his sister, who also lived in Virginia, had "died a true penitent of the Church of England."[119]

---

[118] William Waller Hening, ed., *The Statutes at Large: Being a Collection of All the Laws of Virginia...*, 13 vols. (Richmond, 1809-1823) 3:170-71.

[119] William Fitzhugh to Mrs. Mary Fitzhugh, 30 June 1698, *William Fitzhugh and His Chesapeake World*, 358.

Not only did the Anglicanism of James Blair's Virginia allow the faithful to continue their pilgrimages to heaven, it also created a mentality that helped to shape the colony's future. Although the private practice of piety that the colony's established church encouraged made it possible for Anglicans to adapt their devotional lives to a "novel environment," this emphasis carried with it a potential challenge to Virginia's institutional church. The origins of the Great Awakening in Virginia made that challenge a reality. "The first signs of the coming disturbance," in the words of Rhys Isaac, started "about 1743 when numbers of ordinary people...began reading religious tracts and absenting themselves from church."[120] Given the colony's "occasions" and the devotional life they had engendered, the Great Awakening's beginnings in the colony might be understood as the logical consequence of Virginia's approach to Anglican piety. Reading religious books beyond the sacred space of the parish church was hardly novel to Virginians. Ministers had encouraged the practice. For groups to eventually break away from the Church in this manner reflected less a disruption than an evolution of the colony's traditional approach to religion. Commissary Blair may have laid part of the intellectual groundwork when he publicly attacked what he called the "New Heresie" of Erastianism, a bold step for the representative of an established church. State control of the church destroyed its "Discipline and Government." Blair believed the church would be better off on its own so that it could concentrate fully on leading men and women to heaven, perhaps even introducing spiritual discipline for its voluntary members. Blair did not get his way, but if he had, piety would have become private in ways unimaginable to the late seventeenth and early eighteenth centuries.[121]

In addition to emphasizing a private piety that was potentially dangerous to the established church, the Anglican mentality in Virginia may have led people to view events within a

---

[120] Isaac, *Transformation of Virginia,* 148.

[121] Blair, *Our Saviour's Divine Sermon on the Mount,* 1:232; 2:27.

certain intellectual context as well. The religious notions preached from Virginia's pulpits encouraged the colonists to find patterns in events. Virginians, for instance, did not speak of individual sins in a teleological way, as a missing of the mark, but they viewed a series of actions in this way. Actions implied patterns, and "a long train of sins" was evidence of an unrepentant life, of a life that was moving toward an end other than heaven. Moreover, the pattern such a life demonstrated was the result of human choice. Although Anglicanism in James Blair's Virginia did not speak the classical republican language of power and conspiracy, and over two decades would pass after the commissary's death in 1743 before Virginians would discern a design against their liberty, the theology of the colony's Church of England still provided colonists with a teleological method of interpreting events.[122] Human actions were the result of human choice, they were evidence of the heart's intent, and they tended to point logically toward a particular end. At the very least, Virginia's Anglican Church offered the colonists an intellectual structure sympathetic to the logic of English opposition thought. It offered Virginians practices and structures that opened an unintended future.

---

[122] One should note, however, that Blair's sermons on government could easily have been cribbed from the writings of his friend, John Locke. Blair's sermons, in fact, may be one of the first means by which Locke's ideas were communicated to the colonial public. See Blair, *Our Saviour's Divine Sermon on the Mount*, 1: sermons 12 and 13

CHAPTER SIX

CONTINUITIES: THE RELIGIOUS JOURNEYS OF A COLONIAL VIRGINIAN

Devereux Jarratt discerned at an early age that he would not earn a living tilling the fields of his native Virginia. "Very irksome" labor, he called it. Unlike exercising racehorses or preparing gamecocks for matches, tasks he had enjoyed while working for one of his older brothers, Jarratt held no fondness for plowing and harrowing the soil. "I seemed out of my element," he later recalled, "while at the *plough*, or *ax*." Possessed of a ready intellect, a keen memory, Jarratt turned to teaching and for nearly a decade in the mid-eighteenth century earned a modest income as a schoolmaster. He first taught in Albemarle County and later in Cumberland County, usually boarding at the home of a wealthy planter and providing his and the neighbors' children with some rudimentary education.[1]

---

[1] Devereux Jarratt, *The Life of the Reverend Devereux Jarratt*, ed. John Coleman (New York: Arno Press, Inc., 1969) 20-28, 52. For a shrewd analysis of Jarratt, see David L. Holmes, "Devereux Jarratt: A Letter and a Reevaluation," *Historical Magazine of the Protestant Episcopal Church* 47 (March 1978): 37-49. Also on Jarratt see Henry G. Rabe, "The Reverend Devereux Jarratt and the Virginia Social Order," *Historical Magazine of the Protestant Episcopal Church* 33 (December 1964): 299-336. On education in colonial Virginia see Philip Alexander Bruce, *Institutional History of Virginia in the Seventeenth Century*, 2 vols. (New York: The Knickerbocker Press, 1910) 1:323; John C. Rainbolt, *From Prescription to Persuasion: Manipulation of Eighteenth [Seventeenth] Century Virginia Economy* (Port Washington NY: Kennikat Press, 1974) 23; George MacLaren Brydon, *Virginia's Mother Church and the Political Conditions Under Which it Grew*, 2 vols. (Richmond: The Virginia Historical Society, 1947) 1:388-91.

Although teaching may have spared Jarratt from the plow, he was not a very successful tutor. After a decade of dwindling enrollments and indifferent pay, the twenty-nine-year-old Jarratt chose to embark upon a new vocation: "It was in the spring, 1762, when I quit my school, and began to prepare for immediate entrance into Holy Orders." Jarratt's decision to become a minister in Virginia's Anglican Church began a journey that would take him through the colony's backcountry, to the "metropolis" of Williamsburg, then across the sea to London and back. It was the beginning of one trip and the culmination of another, for Jarratt's spiritual journey had begun years earlier while he was still teaching school.[2]

Different in its particulars, his story was nonetheless much like those of thousands of colonial lay people and of dozens of other ministers who served Virginia's colonial church in the seventeenth and eighteenth centuries, more archetype than aberration. Both his earliest exposure to religion and his first serious yearnings for greater relationship with the divine came outside the formal structures of the institutional church. During his second year as a tutor, Jarratt had boarded at the home of John Cannon of Albemarle County in the colony's piedmont region. Cannon's wife, a New Light Presbyterian who had been converted to the evangelical way of the Great Awakening, soon included Jarratt in her nightly routine of reading a sermon. While she read aloud, the young tutor, eager to please, listened to what she read and "affected a very close attention," sometimes even asking her to read a second sermon so as to impress her with his feigned piety. Their routine continued for nearly two months, one evening blending into the next "without any other effect on me, but fatigue and drowsiness." One night, however,

---

[2] *Life of Jarratt*, 55. For an account of the process of becoming an Anglican minister for Virginia during the colonial period, see Joan Rezner Gundersen, "The Anglican Ministry in Virginia, 1723-1776: A Study of a Social Class" (Ph.D. diss., University of Notre Dame, 1972) 35-68, esp. 52-57; and Joan R. Gundersen, "The Search for Good Men: Recruiting Ministers in Colonial Virginia," *Historical Magazine of the Protestant Episcopal Church* 48 (1979): 461-63.

while Mrs. Cannon read a sermon on the text "*Then opened he their understanding*," Jarratt perceived God acting upon him through her spoken words. "It pleased God," that evening, "to draw out my attention, and fix it on the subject, in a manner unknown to me before."[3]

The young teacher was not completely ignorant of religion. Although his family violated colonial laws and rarely attended the nearby parish church, Jarratt's parents had raised him and his brothers in the Church of England, teaching them the basic elements of the Christian faith at an early age. They had taught their children "short prayers," and, as Jarratt recounted, "made us perfect in repeating the *Church Catechism*." His mother and father had also read to their children stories from the Bible, encouraging the siblings to commit passages to memory: "Before I knew the letters of the alphabet, I could repeat a whole chapter in the Bible...especially if the subject of it struck my fancy," like the tale of Samson.[4]

It is not surprising that young Devereux received his early religious education from a book introduced to him by his parents rather than from the minister of the local parish. Virginia's institutional church was weak in Jarratt's day, as it had been throughout the colonial period, and there were rarely enough ministers to fill the colony's many cures. Colonists did not help matters by insisting on living on plantations or small farms widely separated from the residences of other Virginians. Roger Greene compared members of Virginia's Anglican Church to plants that "grow wilde in that Wildernesse," untended by a gardener. Alexander Forbes, the minister of Isle of Wight Parish on the south side of the James River, expressed similar concerns: "the distance of the way may hinder many at sometimes who cannot be prepared to come X. XII. or XV miles, tho' that they might and would if they had but V. or VI." With the shortage of clergy and the vastness of the colony, many Virginians were lucky

---

[3] *Life of Jarratt*, 33-34.

[4] *Life of Jarratt*, 16, 20, 35; Rhys Isaac, *The Transformation of Virginia, 1740-1790* (Chapel Hill: University of North Carolina Press, 1982) 58.

if a minister read divine service near their residences once every two or three weeks.[5]

These hindrances to the church's teaching ministry meant that much religious education became the responsibility of private families rather than the public church. Late in the seventeenth century, Governor William Berkeley responded to an inquiry from the Crown regarding the instruction of the colonists in the "christian religion" by explaining that Virginians followed "the same course that is taken in England out of towns; every man according to his ability instructing his children." Jarratt's parents were no different, and they provided for their children's spiritual welfare as best they could.[6] They could have chosen from any one of several catechectical works to provide their children's early religious instruction. The *Book of Common*

---

[5] Edmund S. Morgan, *American Slavery, American Freedom: The Ordeal of Colonial Virginia* (New York: W. W. Norton & Company, Inc., 1975) 374; "A Letter from Mr. John Clayton to the Royal Society," Peter Force, ed., *Tracts and Other Papers, Relating Principally to the Origin, Settlement, and Progress of the Colonies in North America*, 4 vols. (Gloucester MA: Peter Smith, 1963) 3:12:12, 21; R[oger] G[reene], *Virginia's Cure: or An Advisive Narrative Concerning Virginia* (London, 1662) Force, *Tracts and Other Papers*, 3:15:4-5, 6-8; Alexander Forbes to Bishop Edmund Gibson, 21 July 1724, in William Stevens Perry, ed., *Historical Collections Relating to the American Colonial Church*, 5 vols., (New York: AMS Press, 1969) 1:273, 284, 292, 299, 312, 327, 328 (quotation); Bruce, *Institutional History of Virginia in the Seventeenth Century*, 1:191-93; Richard Beeman, *The Evolution of the Southern Backcountry: A Case Study of Lunenburg County, Virginia, 1746-1832* (Philadelphia: University of Pennsylvania Press, 1984) 21; Warren M. Billings, John E. Selby, and Thad W. Tate, *Colonial Virginia: A History* (White Plains NY: KTO Press, 1986) 65, 134-36; Henry Hartwell, James Blair, and Edward Chilton, *The Present State of Virginia, and the College*, ed. Hunter Dickinson Farish (Williamsburg: Colonial Williamsburg, Inc., 1940) 65, 67; T. H. Breen, *Tobacco Culture: The Mentality of the Great Tidewater Planters on the Eve of Revolution* (Princeton: Princeton University Press, 1985) 41; John C. Rainbolt, "The Absence of Towns in Seventeenth-Century Virginia," *Journal of Southern History* 35 (1969): 347, 343.

[6] William Waller Hening, ed. *The Statutes at Large: Being a Collection of All the Laws of Virginia...*, 13 vols. (Richmond, 1809-1823) 2:517.

Prayer, Bishop Thomas Wilson's *The Knowledge and Practice of Christianity Made Easy to the Meanest Capacities: or, An Essay Towards an Instruction for the Indians*, and English minister John Lewis' popular *The Church Catechism Explain'd by Way of Question and Answer* were all widely available in the colony. In addition to dividing their time between the churches and chapels of ease in their parishes, ministers spread the teachings of the established church by distributing these and other religious books to those who wanted the volumes. John Talbot, a missionary for the Society for the Propagation of the Gospel in Foreign Parts (SPG), wrote from Virginia requesting prayer books "new or old, of all sorts & sizes," explaining that if he received these books, he would "carry them 100 miles about and disperse them abroad to all that desired 'em...'tis a comfort to the People in the Wilderness to see that some body takes care of them." For Alexander Forbes, books and tracts helped bring the Church's teachings to people in areas where the ministers could not travel frequently. In 1724 he asked Bishop Edmund Gibson to send him "such books and printed sermons according to the doctrine of the Church of England...to be dispersed and read among such remote Inhabitants of the parish as live at a great distance from all Churches and chapels, where Gods word is commonly taught and read." And William Dawson, the commissary or representative of the Bishop of London in Virginia, reported in 1743 that he had recently distributed 400 copies of Wilson's *Essay* throughout the colony. He later asked Virginia's ministers to put the bishop's essays "into the hands of every Schoolmaster, Scholar, and Person who can read, in your Parish." The Anglican Church did not lead the settlers into the Virginia wilderness. Rather, it followed behind them, trying to bring religion to a people who in theory were already Christians, but in fact were often unchurched, by circumstances if not by choice.[7]

---

[7] John Talbot to Richard Gillingham, 3 May 1703, SPG Archives, ser. A, vol. 1, f. 120. See also William Black to SPG Secretary, 7 April 1711, SPG Archives, ser. A, vol. 6, f. 101; Alexander Forbes to Bishop Edmund Gibson,

Books became substitutes for ministers who could not properly serve their parishes and for the general scarcity of clergymen. William Dawson admonished the clergy to be especially careful when they distributed books to their parishioners: "give some suitable Advice, and Instruction how to make use of this excellent Charity to the Purposes of a Christian Life. For...the best of Books, when lightly given, will be lightly valued, and as lightly made us of." Yet ministers were not alone in their estimation of religious books. People then commonly believed that men and women should find happiness in God and religion. Some Virginians felt the absence of the institutional church deeply in their lives and responded by turning to English devotional materials for religious instruction and guidance. Although ministers often distributed religious tracts to their poorer parishioners, more well to do colonists purchased the same materials from England, or, after 1732, from the printing office of William Parks in Williamsburg. Post-riders for William Hunter, who succeeded Parks as publisher of the *Virginia Gazette*, frequently carried religious titles alone to sell on their travels throughout the colony.[8]

---

21 July 1724, Fulham Palace Papers, vol.12, ff. 27-30; William Dawson to Henry Neuman, [?] 22, 1743, Dawson Papers, Library of Congress, vol. 1, f. 16; William Dawson to Dr. Bearcroft, 12 July 1744, Dawson Papers, vol. 1, f. 22.

[8] William Dawson to Henry Neuman, [?] 22, 1743, Dawson Papers, vol. 1, f. 16; Patricia U. Bonomi and Peter R. Eisenstadt, "Church Adherence in the Eighteenth-Century British American Colonies," *William and Mary Quarterly* 3rd ser. 39 (1982) 245; James Maury Sermons, Sermon no. 90, 13, John D. Rockefeller, Jr. Library Colonial Williamsburg Foundation; James Blair, *Our Saviour's Divine Sermon on the Mount, Contain'd in the Vth, VIth, and VIIth Chapters of St. Mathew's Gospel, Explained; and the Practice of it Recommended in Divers Sermons and Discourses*, 5 vols., (London, 1722) 1:202, 4:225; Robert Paxton Sermon Book, Sermon no. 20, "Of Man's Blessed End," 4, Houghton Library, Harvard University; Richard L. Morton, *Colonial Virginia*, 2 vols. (Chapel Hill: University of North Carolina Press, 1960) 2:515-16; Billings, Selby, and Tate, *Colonial Virginia*, 215; William Hunter Printing Office Journal, 1750-1752, passim, especially 3 and 17 June 1751.

Jarratt probably learned his catechism from either the edition included in the *Book of Common Prayer* or from Lewis' little volume, which was a favorite among Virginians, especially after the first stirrings of evangelical dissent. The work proved so popular, in fact, that in 1738 William Parks published an edition out of his Williamsburg press, advertising it as "being very proper for a New Year's Gift to Children." At no more than a shilling a copy, Lewis' *Catechism* was probably more affordable to middling folk like the Jarratt family than the more expensive *Book of Common Prayer*, which sold for anywhere from six to eighteen shillings.[9]

Whatever version Jarratt's parents used, the catechism their children learned had been written by an English author. Catechisms were formal works, designed to introduce individuals young and old to the basic tenets of the faith. They presented rudimentary elements of doctrine, theology, and duty in an alternating patter of questions and answers that could be easily memorized. Lewis' *Catechism* was much like others:

---

[9] *Virginia Gazette*, 15-22 December 1738; 9-16 February 16-23 February, 23 February-2 March, 2-9 March, 9-16 March 1738/39. England and the colonies did not adopt the Gregorian Calendar until 1752. Although the year did not change until 25 March, the Feast of the Annunciation of the Blessed Virgin Mary, New Year's Day was often celebrated on 1 January, the Feast of the Circumcision in the Church of England's liturgical calendar and a time when people exchanged presents in remembrance of the gifts brought by the magi to the Christ child at Epiphany. New Year's may also have been a traditional time for Virginians to pass along religious works to their children. The devotional work John Page wrote for his son was given as a New Year's gift, and the *Gazette* advertised Lewis's *Catechism* as a New Year's gift from mid-December through late March, aiming at both New Year's dates in the English calendar. See David Cressy, *Bonfires and Bells: National Memory and the Protestant Calendar in Elizabethan and Stuart England* (Los Angeles: University of California Press, 1989) 16. The prices for Lewis' *Catechism* and the *Book of Common Prayer* are from the William Hunter Printing Office Journal, 1750-1752, passim (typescript), John D. Rockefeller, Jr. Library, Colonial Williamsburg Foundation.

Q. Why do you stile God, *Almighty*?

A. Because he has Power to dispose of, and govern all Things as he pleaseth.

Q. What is it to honour God's name?

A. It is to use it with Reverence in our Oaths, Vows, Promises, Discourses, and Worship.

Edward Mashborne, a minister in Nansemond County, wrote back to England that the catechism given him by an SPG minister had proved very useful in his parish. "Thro' God's Assistance," he wrote, "I have fixt not only in Children but in those of Riper Years the Fundamentals of Religion, whereby they are able to give a Rational & well grounded Accott. of the Faith they were Baptized in." Back in the settled town of Williamsburg, Commissary Dawson held a somewhat more elevated understanding of the catechism. He believed it could help "prevent the Temptations of the Devil, by...imprinting on their tender Minds, the Im[age] of Virtue, & the Beauty of Holiness."[10] When Jarratt and his brothers set about memorizing the catechism, they engaged in a rational exercise in which they gave assent to, and gained understanding of, the doctrines and beliefs of England and Virginia's established church, thus participating in one facet of the colonists' ambiguous relationship with the mother country. Although English books and English ministers helped to spread English religion throughout the colony and Virginians eagerly sought these volumes, they nonetheless stubbornly insisted on their own ecclesiastical structures.

Yet books did more than instruct individuals in virtue and introduce them to the fundamental beliefs of the church; Virginia's clergy believed that books could have a powerful

---

[10] *Life of Jarratt*, 24; John Lewis, *The Church Catechism Explain'd by Way of Question and Answer* (London, 1712) 36, 78; Edward Mashborne to SPG Secretary, 25 April 1716, SPG Archives, ser. A, vol. 11, ff. 401-402; undated sermon notes, Dawson Papers, vol. 2, f. 301.

influence in the lives of individuals. James Craig's view was typical of that held by other ministers in colonial Virginia. Conditions in the backcountry shocked him when he took charge of Lunenburg County's Cumberland Parish in 1759. Nearly thirty years earlier, William Byrd II had also been struck by the area's rudeness, describing it as a place "quite out of Christendom." Place-names in the region testified to the hardships of life there: Wolf Trap, Difficult, Wild Cat, and Terrible. Existence was often coarse as well; several families had patented land along Fucking Creek and the Tickle Cunt Branch. Craig seemed to wonder how religion could possibly thrive in such a setting. "There were many Settlements of People," he wrote, "which by Reason of their Distance from any place of Divine Worship, had never or seldom, been at Church, since they were baptized." Many of those people who did attend divine service he learned were "ignorant of the very first Principles of Christianity."[11]

Life among Lunenburg's settlers was harsh, marked by drunkenness, debauchery, and profaneness. County justices rarely meddled with such delicate issues as religion or morality, and offenses such as bastardy, swearing, and violating the Sabbath usually went unpunished. Even in more settled and civilized York County, people who failed to attend church were rarely presented to the county court unless they had made themselves a nuisance in some other fashion beforehand. Craig turned to religious books to help reform his parishioners: "the putting proper Books in their Hands will, I conceive, be one very good Expedient for this Purpose." To Thomas Dawson, then Virginia's commissary, Craig sent requests for volumes on baptism and the Lord's Supper, for tracts explaining the duty of God-parents, for Bishop William Beveridge's frequently reprint-ed sermon on the excellency of the *Book of Common Prayer*, and for a series of

---

[11] Beeman, *Evolution of the Southern Backcountry*, 15, 18; James Craig to Thomas Dawson, 8 September 1759, Dawson Papers, vol. 2, ff. 217-18. Cumberland Parish was identical in size to Lunenburg County: 5,000 square miles; see Beeman, *Evolution of the Southern Backcountry*, 46, 52.

other texts. "I would freely give any Consideration," he wrote, "to have these & such other Books to distribute among the people NOW." It seemed as though religious books could help create a new world in the American wilderness. The ideas they conveyed might transform lives and lead people to act differently, to repent, and to reform. "To read," according to one historian, "was to feel," for "reading involved the affective self—the heart, the will." Books were capable of arousing strong emotions in and persuading individuals to act and think in ways that might please God.[12]

Like many other Virginians, Jarratt had derived most of his early spiritual learning from devotional works read in private. One of the many religious volumes available in the colony later changed his life. As he sat in the Cannon household listening to a sermon read aloud, Jarratt perceived God acting upon him, focusing his attention upon the discourse: "*Then opened he their understanding.*" This experience was much different from the rote memorization of a catechism, at once wonderful and terrifying, involving both invitation and damnation. The event opened to Jarratt the possibility of a personal relationship with the Christian deity. It called him to further discoveries of "spiritual illumination" and at the same time brought an understanding of condemnation for sin and the realization that "I was a stranger to that spiritual illumination and its consequent discoveries, and... was yet in a dark and dangerous state," unprepared "for death and judgment."[13]

Seventeenth- and eighteenth-century preachers called the sensation Jarratt experienced that evening the fear of God: a feeling of awe which attracted individuals to a deity of infinite

[12] James Craig to Thomas Dawson, 8 September 1759, Dawson Papers, vol. 2, ff. 217-18; Beeman, *Evolution of the Southern Backcountry,* 44-45, 206-207; Leslie M. Kesler, "'For Thus His Neglect,' Grand Jury Presentments for Failure to Attend Church, York County, Virginia, 1750-1775" (M.A. thesis, College of William and Mary, 1992) 77-81; David D. Hall, *Worlds of Wonder, Days of Judgment: Popular Religious Belief in Early New England* (New York: Alfred Knopf, 1989) 40.

[13] *Life of Jarratt,* 34-35.

power and at the same time made people aware of their own smallness and sinfulness, consuming them with unease. Early in the eighteenth century Robert Paxton had tried to explain the inner workings of this feeling to his Tidewater congregation at Kecoughtan: "Fear is a passion yt is most deeply rooted in our nature, & flows immediately from yt principle of self-preservatn qch God hath planted in every man." Man has a "natural dread" of all things that can destroy him, "& the greatest danger is from the greatest power, & yt is omnipotency." "The fear of God," he explained, "is an inward acknowledgment of a holy & just being qch is armed wt an Almighty & irresistible power, God having hid in every mans Conscience a secret awe, & dread of his infinite power & eternal justice."[14]

Anglicans in Virginia often spoke of this sensation within the context of the creation as John Clayton did when he saw evidence of God in the smallest flowers or as Thomas Ludwell did when he marveled at the power of a great tempest. Although less sensually dramatic than the forces of creation and the beauties of nature, the content of books too could arouse feelings of wonder and awe at the enormity of God's might. Far from the church or meeting house and in relative privacy, Jarratt was awakened to the deity's power. One minister explained such events as "a certain inward working of [God's] spirit, in & wt the minds of men." Several decades earlier a devotional work read in private had also stirred deep emotions in William Byrd II of Westover: "I read a sermon of Dr. Tillotson's which affected me very much and made me shed some tears of repentance." While Byrd responded to what he had read with an act of repentance, Jarratt soon turned to a series of religious "helps" to direct his growth in the faith. He attended sermons, read borrowed devotional volumes, and discussed religion with friends, all the while cooperating with God in his spiritual journey.[15]

---

[14] Paxton, Sermon no. 19, "On the Wisdom of Fearing God," 1.

[15] Edmund and Dorothy Berkeley, *John Clayton: Pioneer of American Botany* (Chapel Hill: University of North Carolina Press, 1963) 28; Morton, *Colonial Virginia*, 2:831; Thomas Ludwell to Lord Berkeley of Stretton, 7

Like Byrd, Jarratt also turned to books for religious edification, and they were a special delight as he struggled to understand his evolving relationship with God. In the evenings, he later recalled, "my custom...was to sit down flat on the heart, erect the volume on the end of a chest, which stood near, and, by the light of the fire, read till near midnight." He read numerous volumes, usually those written by dissenting authors such as Isaac Watts, Richard Baxter, and Philip Doddridge. He read Church of England authors as well—eclecticism typical of colonial Virginians—and a borrowed copy of the churchman William Burkitt's work on the New Testament offered him much "light and instruction." More than any other work, Burkitt opened the Bible to Jarratt's understanding. It also led the young teacher to question the criticism he had heard directed at Virginia's established church. Gradually, Jarratt changed his opinion of the Anglican Communion and its formal liturgy. He read the *Book of Common Prayer* and thought well of it, claiming: "it contained an excellent system of doctrine and public worship—equal to any other in the world." Although he had originally intended to seek Presbyterian orders, Jarratt decided to become a minister in the Church of England, despite the danger it necessitated of sailing to London for ordination.[16]

Having decided to enter the Anglican ministry, Jarratt needed to find a parish, for without title to a cure, Virginia's commissary would not send him to London to receive Holy Orders. Jarratt soon found a vacancy in Lunenburg County. By 1762, the Reverend James Craig had grown weary with conditions at Cumberland Parish and gave the vestry their notice that he intended to leave. Jarratt applied to the vestry, a colonial

---

November 1667, PRO CO 1/21, ff. 282-83; *Life of Jarratt*, 46-47; Paxton, Sermon no. 11, "Of Salvation," 1; Louis B. Wright and Marion Tinling, eds., *The Secret Diary of William Byrd of Westover, 1709-1712* (Richmond: The Dietz Press, 1941) 175. See also George Keith, *The Power of Gospel, in the Conversion of Sinners*, (Annapolis, 1702) 11.

[16] *Life of Jarratt*, 46, 40, 58. The title of Burkitt's volume, not given by Jarratt, is *Expository Notes, with Practical Observations on the New Testament.* See *Dictionary of National Biography*, 7:371-72.

custom, and probably met with them at the mother church located on Reedy Creek. They liked the young postulant, and in late May granted a title to "Mr. Deverix Jarratte, a Candidate for Holy Orders," and recommended him both to the governor and the commissary.[17]

From Lunenburg Jarratt traveled to King and Queen County on the Middle Peninsula between the York and Rappahannock Rivers to present his credentials to Commissary William Robinson. He arrived in early June, carrying with him title to Cumberland Parish and letters from three clergymen of the established church bearing testimony to his piety and moral character. As the commissaries did with other postulants, Robinson examined Jarratt in some matters of faith and doctrine. Satisfied that he possessed at least a "Moderate share of Learning," the commissary wrote and signed a letter to the bishop of London approving Jarratt's candidacy for orders. As part of his feud with Governor Francis Fauquier—but one in a series of disputes between commissaries and governors—Robinson sealed the letter so that the governor would have to write his own recommendation when Jarratt called upon him in Williamsburg. Jarratt completed the thirty-mile trip south to Williamsburg within a few days, and like Robinson, Fauquier also wrote a letter urging Bishop Richard Osbaldeston to ordain him. The necessary bureaucratic paperwork taken care of, Jarratt sailed for England a few months later.[18]

---

[17] Landon C. Bell, ed. *The Vestry Book of Cumberland Parish, Lunenburg County, Virginia, 1746-1816* (Richmond: The William Byrd Press, Inc., 1930) 383; Clive Raymond Hallman, Jr., "The Vestry as a Unit of Local Government in Colonial Virginia" (Ph.D. diss., University of Georgia, 1987) 223. See also Joan Rezner Gundersen, "The Myth of the Independent Virginia Vestry," *Historical Magazine of the Protestant Episcopal Church* 44 (1975): 133-41.

[18] *Life of Jarratt*, 55; Commissary William Robinson to Bishop Osbaldeston, 8 June 1762, Fulham Palace Papers, vol. 13, f. 54; Francis Fauquier to Bishop Osbaldeston, 12 June 1762, Fulham Palace Papers, vol. 13, f. 106.

The voyage to London caused Jarratt much anxiety, and he worried about the "peril and danger" of sailing to England and back. Although pirates were no longer the danger they had been in James Blair's day, any voyage across the Atlantic risked storms or privateers. Foul shipboard conditions discouraged some persons from making the journey. Nicholas Moreau, an Anglican minister in Virginia who despised the colony, wanted to return "home," but did not think he could endure the trip: "My weakness makes me afraid of not being capable to bear the ill smell of a ship, nor to digest the victuals wich commonly are afforded therein." Nor were ministers and postulants always treated well by their shipmates. The Reverend Richard Hewitt complained to Bishop Edmund Gibson of the treatment of one young man, a Mr. Ogilvie, who had taken passage on a military vessel. Sailors cut the ends of his hammock while he slept, causing Ogilvie to fall upon the ship's guns, repeatedly attempted to sodomize him, and finally, took the Bibles he intended to distribute among colonists and used them to beat the young man in the head.[19]

Jarratt's voyage to Great Britain was uneventful, at least until he reached the Irish coast. There he made land at Fair Foreland, the site where Roman Catholics had massacred Protestants during the reign of King Charles I. Jarratt had read of this event and believed the inflated estimate of 100,000 Protestant deaths. The sight of the town frightened him. This was a different world, and the European heritage of religious violence was foreign to Jarratt. Yet the denominational animosities of Europe's past lingered: "The sight of that place, with the recollection of that massacre made such a deep and awful impression on my heart, as

---

[19] *Life of Jarratt*, 58; Gundersen, "Recruiting Good Men," 462; Nicolas Moreau to Archbishop Thomas Tenison, 29 May 1700, Fulham Palace Papers, vol. 11, ff. 119-120; Richard Hewitt to Bishop Gibson, 29 July 1725, Fulham Palace Papers, vol. 12, ff. 95-96. See also Thomas Ludwell to Secretary Coventry, 3 April 1677, Coventry Papers, vol. 68, f. 28. For a travel journal noting conditions at sea during a voyage to Virginia, see Luther Anderson, ed., "Diary of Rev. Andrew Rudman, 25 July 1696-14 June 1697," *German American Annals* 9 (1907): 9-17.

is not easily described." His Virginia had never known such religious fury.[20]

The source of Jarratt's fears changed once his voyage continued. The ship's captain, who identified it as a French privateer, spotted a vessel in the distance. All hands were called to arms, Jarratt taking his place at a nine-pound cannon. Although alarmed by the prospect of defending the ship, "to do honor to America, [he] declared that a Virginian had steel to the back, and would never flinch." The vessel turned away, and Jarratt did not have to prove his courage. Yet his journey to England revealed that he thought of himself as a Virginian. After passing the canonical examinations, Jarratt boasted that he, a colonial, had exceeded the marks of ordinands from Cambridge and Oxford.[21]

By the time Jarratt reached London, Advent had begun, and Bishop Osbaldeston refused to ordain candidates during this semi-penitential season. Sometime during the following liturgical seasons celebrating the feasts of Christmas and the Epiphany the bishop ordained Jarratt to the priesthood of the Church of England. The colonial church in which he would serve, however, was far different from that of the mother country. Although English catechetical and devotional writings contributed to the religious development of colonial Virginians, for dissenters as well as for members of the established church, they did so in an ecclesiastical world structured differently from that of England. No Anglican bishop ever held a see in colonial North America. Thus, Jarratt had been forced to travel to London, for only a bishop could ordain a man to the ministry of the Anglican Church. But with the exception of conferring holy orders, Virginia's regular clergy performed many of a bishop's duties. They consecrated church buildings and admitted those who had reached the age for confirmation to the communion table, although they did not always make vigorous efforts to

---

[20] *Life of Jarratt*, 60; R. F. Foster, *The Oxford History of Ireland* (New York: Oxford University Press, 1992) 120-21.

[21] *Life of Jarratt*, 61; Holmes, "A Letter and a Reevaluation," 41.

catechize the young before allowing them to receive the sacrament.[22]

Jarratt returned to this New World syncretism, and learned first hand about one of the colony's other ecclesiastical peculiarities. In the summer of 1762, after Jarratt's departure for London, James Craig had changed his mind about leaving Cumberland Parish, and the vestry unanimously received him back as their minister, even agreeing to finish construction of his glebe house. When Jarratt landed in Yorktown in April 1763 and, as he phrased it, "had the pleasure of treading on my native soil," he soon discovered that as a result of the vestry's whims, he had no cure. He learned, however, of a vacancy at Bath Parish in Dinwiddie County, in the basin formed by the Appomattox and Roanoke Rivers on the Southside. In August, after hearing him preach three times, the vestry accepted Jarratt as their minister. He had returned to Virginia as a missionary—for that is how the Church of England saw its ministers in the colonies—to bring the Gospel to a people who earned their living through the "irksome" labor of harrowing the soil, to take part in the continuing drama of the bringing the Reformation to the English-speaking people, a process that as late as the mid-eighteenth century had yet to be completed. Jarratt's pastoral work was much like that of both contemporary English clergymen and his colonial predecessors such as Alexander Whitaker and James Blair. Even the *Book of Common Prayer* he read the Church's offices and rites from was largely like the version used by the first colonists and their ministers in the early seventeenth century. But Devereux Jarratt was a Virginian, and unlike those clergymen, he had come home to practice his ministry and to

---

[22] *Life of Jarratt*, 71-72; Brydon, *Virginia's Mother Church*, 1:407n.8; Bonomi and Eisenstadt, "Church Adherence in the Eighteenth-Century," 252. See also Graham Frank to Thomas, Lord Bishop of London, 11 November 1756, Public Records Office, High Court of Admiralty Papers, 30/258, f. 161.

serve God.[23] In many ways, Devereux Jarratt had returned to where he began. His life to that point—both in his sense of personal identity and in the established church he served—testified to the tensions inherent in being a Virginian and an Englishman.

---

[23] Morton, *Colonial Virginia*, 2:606; Bell, *Vestry Book of Cumberland Parish*, 383; Rabe, "The Reverend Devereux Jarrat and the Social Order," 314; *Life of Jarratt*, 7.

BIBLIOGRAPHY

Unpublished Primary Sources:
John D. Rockefeller, Jr. Library, Colonial Williamsburg
Foundation
   William Blathwayt Papers, 1631-1722
   Dawson Papers, Library of Congress, (microfilm)
   Sol Fienstone Collection of the American Revolution, David
   Library of the American Revolution, (microfilm)
   Peter Fontaine Sermon, 10 May 1727, (transcript)
   Fontaine-Maury Papers
   William Gooch typescripts
   William Hunter Printing Office Journal, 1750-1752,
   (typescript)
   Letter, John Catlett to Thomas Catlett, 1 April 1664
   Letter, Richard Lee to [?], 21-22 October 1652,
   Morristown National Historical Park (microfilm)
   James Maury Manuscript Sermons
   Francis Nicholson Papers
   York County, Deeds, Orders, and Wills, Books 1-13,
   (microfilm and transcripts)

Virginia Colonial Records Project (all microfilm)
   Coventry Papers, Marquess of Bath Deposit, Longleat
   House
   Dr. Bray's Associates, Papers, Lambeth Palace
   Ferrar Papers, Magdalene College
   Fulham Palace Papers, Lambeth Palace
   Library of the Society of Friends
   Public Records Office, Colonial Office, Class 1, Record
   Groups 1-64

Public Records Office, Colonial Office, Class 5, Record
Groups 1305-1319, 1337, 1339-1343, 1354-1359 S.P.G.
Archives

Houghton Library, Harvard University
Robert Paxton Manuscript Sermon Book

Virginia Historical Society
William Byrd Commonplace Book, ca. 1722-1732
William Byrd, "Religion: A History of the Jews Before the
Birth of Jesus," ca. 1725
Robert Carter, Letterbook, 1723-1730
Protestant Epsicopal Church, Virginia Diocese, Papers
John Robinson Commonplace Book, 1735-1747

Published Primary Sources:
[Allestree, Richard]. *The Whole Duty of Man*. London, 1658.
Ames, Susie M., editor. *County Records of Accomack-
Northampton, Virginia, 1632-1640*. Washington, DC:
American Historical Association, 1954.
_____, editor. *County Court Records of Accomack-Northampton,
Virginia, 1640-1645*. Charlottesville: University Press of
Virginia, 1973.
Arber, Edward, editor. *Works of Captain John Smith*.
Westminster: Archibald Constable & Co., 1895.
Barbour, Philip L., editor. *The Jamestown Voyages Under the First
Charter, 1606-1609*, 2 Volumes. London: Cambridge
University Press, 1969.
_____, editor. *The Complete Works of Captain John Smith*, 3
Volumes. Chapel Hill: University of North Carolina Press,
1986.
Bemiss, Samuel M., editor. *The Three Charters of the Virginia
Company of London With Seven Related Documents: 1606-
1621*. Williamsburg: Virginia 350th Anniversary Celebration
Corporation, 1957.

Benson, George. *A Sermon Preached at Paules Crosse*. London, 1609.

Berkeley, Edmund and Dorothy, editors. *John Clayton: Parson With a Scientific Mind*. Chapel Hill: University of North Carolina Press, 1965.

Berkeley, William. *A Discourse and View of Virginia*. London, 1663.

Beveridge, William. *A Sermon Concerning the Excellency and Usefulness of the Common Prayer*. London, 1681.

Billings, Warren M., editor. *The Old Dominion in the Seventeenth Century: A Documentary History of Virginia, 1606-1689*. Chapel Hill: University of North Carolina Press, 1975.

_____, editor. *The Papers of Francis Howard Baron Howard of Effingham, 1643-1695*. Richmond: Virginia State Library and Archives, 1989.

_____, editor. "A Quaker in Seventeenth-Century Virginia: Four Remonstrances by George Wilson." *William and Mary Quarterly* 3rd ser. 33 (1976): 127-40.

Blackstone, Bernard, editor. *The Ferrar Papers, Containing a Life of Nicholas Ferrar*. London: Cambridge University Press, 1938.

Blair, James. *Our Saviour's Divine Sermon on the Mount, Contain'd in the Vth, VIth, and VIIth Chapters of St. Matthew's Gospel, Explained; and the Practice of it Recommended in Divers Sermons and Discourses*, 5 Volumes. London, 1722.

Breen, T.H., James H. Lewis, and Keith Schlesinger, editors. "Motive for Murder: A Servant's Life in Virginia, 1678." *William and Mary Quarterly* 3rd ser. 40 (1983): 106-120.

Brown, Alexander, editor. *The Genesis of the United States*, 2 Volumes. New York: Russell & Russell, 1964.

Butler, Jon, editor. "Two 1642 Letters from Virginia Puritans." *Massachusetts Historical Society Proceedings*. 84 (1972): 99-109.

Byrd, William. *History of the Dividing Line betwixt Virginia and North Carolina Run in the Year of Our Lord 1728*. In *The*

Prose Works of William Byrd of Westover, edited by Louis B. Wright. Cambridge: Harvard University Press, 1966.

Camp, Ichabod. *Men have Freedom of Will and Power, and their Conduct, whether good or Evil, is of Choice.* New Haven, 1760.

Clayton, John. *Christ Crucified; the Power of the God, and the Wisdom of God.* London, 1706.

_____. *The Defence of a Sermon, Preach'd upon the Receiving into the Communion of the Church of England, the Honorable Sir Terence Mac-Mahon Baronet, and Christopher Dunn. Converts from the Church of Rome.* Dublin, 1701.

Copeland, Patrick. *Virginia's God be Thanked.* London, 1622.

Crashaw, William. *A Sermon Preached in London before the right honorable the Lord Laware, Lord Governour and Captaine Generall of Virginea.* London, 1610.

Davis, Richard Beale, editor. *William Fitzhugh and His Chesapeake World, 1676-1701.* Chapel Hill: University of North Carolina Press, 1963.

Donne, John. *A Sermon upon the viii. Verse of the i. chapter of the Acts of the Apostles. Preached to the Honourable Company of the Virginia Plantations.* London, 1622.

_____. *An Essay Upon the Government of the English Plantations on the Continent of America.* London, 1701. Edited by Louis B. Wright. San Marino: The Huntington Library, 1945.

Fausz, J. Frederick and Jon Kukla, editors. "A Letter of Advice to the Governor of Virginia, 1624." *William and Mary Quarterly* 3rd ser. 34 (1977): 104-129.

Force, Peter, editor. *Tracts and Other Papers, Relating Principally to the Origin, Settlement, And Progress of the Colonies in North America,* 4 Volumes. Gloucester MA: Peter Smith, 1963.

Frank, Joseph, editor. "News From Virginny, 1644." *Virginia Magazine of History and Biography* 65 (1957): 84-87.

Gatford, Lionel. *Publick good without private Interest. Or, A compendious remonstrance of the present sad state and condition of the English colonie in Virginea.* London, 1675.

Giberne, William. *The Duty of Living Peaceably with all Men.* Williamsburg, 1759.

Glover, Thomas. *An Account of Virginia, its Scituation, Temperature, Productions, Inhabitants And their manner of planting and ordering Tobacco*. London, Royal Society, 1676.

Godwyn, Morgan. *The Negro's and Indian's Advocate suing for their Admission into the Church*. London, 1680.

_____. *Trade Preferr'd before Religion, and Christ Made to Give Place to Mammon*. London, 1685.

Gray, Robert. *A Good Speed to Virginia*. London, 1609. Edited by Wesley Frank Craven. New York: Scholars' Facsimiles & Reprints, 1937.

G[reene], R[oger]. *Virginia's Cure: or an Advisive Narrative Concerning Virginia*. London, 1662.

Hammond, John. *Leah and Rachel, or, The Two Fruitfull Sisters Virginia and Maryland: Their Present Condition Impartially Stated and Related*. London, 1656.

Hamor, Ralph. *A True Discourse of the Present [E]state of Virginia*. London, 1615; reprint, Richmond: Virginia Historical Society, 1957.

Hartwell, Henry, James Blair, and Edward Chilton. *The Present State of Virginia, and the College*. London, 1727. Edited by Hunter Dickinson Farish. Williamsburg: Colonial Williamsburg, Inc., 1940.

Hening, William Waller, editor. *The Statutes at Large: Being a Collection of All the Laws of Virginia. . .*, 13 Volumes. Richmond, 1809-1823.

Hosmer, James Kendall, editor. *Winthrop's Journal: "History of New England," 1630-1649*, 2 Volumes. New York, 1908.

Jarratt, Devereux. *The Life of the Reverend Devereux Jarratt*. Edited by John Coleman. Baltimore, 1806; reprint, New York: Arno Press, 1969.

Johnson, Robert. *Nova Britannia. Offering Most Excellent Fruits By Planting in Virginia*. London, 1609; reprint, Rochester, 1897.

_____. *The New Life of Virginia*. London, 1612; reprint, Rochester, 1897.

Johnson, Robert C., editor. "The Indian Massacre of 1622: Some Correspondence of the Reverend Joseph Mead." *Virginia Magazine of History and Biography* 71 (1963): 408-410.

———, editor. "Virginia in 1632." *Virginia Magazine of History and Biography* 65 (1957): 458-466.

Jones, Hugh. *The Present State of Virginia, From Whence is Inferred a Short View of Maryland And North Carolina.* London, 1724. Edited by Richard L. Morton. Chapel Hill: University of North Carolina Press, 1956.

Keith, George. *The Doctrine of the Holy Apostles and Prophets the Foundation of the Church of Christ.* Boston, 1702.

———. *The Great Necessity & Use of the Holy Sacraments of Baptism & the Lords Supper.* New York, 1704.

———. *The Notes of the True Church With the Application of them to the Church of England, And the Great Sin of Seperation [sic] from Her.* New York, 1704.

———. *The Power of the Gospel, in the Conversion of Sinners.* Annapolis, 1703.

King, John. *A Sermon at Paules Crosse, on Behalfe of Paules Crosse.* London, 1620.

Kingsbury, Susan Myra, editor. *The Records of the Virginia Company of London,* 4 Volumes. Washington, DC: United States Government Printing Office, 1906-1935.

Lewis, John. *The Church Catechism Explain'd by Way of Question and Answer.* London, 1712.

McCulloch, Samuel Clyde, editor. "James Blair's Plan of 1699 to Reform the Clergy of Virginia." *William and Mary Quarterly* 3rd ser. 4 (1947): 70-86.

McIlwaine, H.R., editor. *Executive Journals of the Council of Colonial Virginia,* 6 Volumes. 2nd edition. Richmond: Virginia State Library, 1976.

———, editor. *Journals of the House of Burgesses of Colonial Virginia,* 13 Volumes. Richmond: Virginia State Library, 1905-1915.

———, editor. *Minutes of the Council and the General Court of Colonial Virginia.* 2d edition. Richmond: Virginia State Library, 1979.

More, Paul Elmer and Frank Leslie Cross, editors. *Anglicanism: The Thought and Practice of The Church of England, Illustrated From the Religious Literature of the Seventeenth Century*. London: S.P.C.K., 1962.

Page, John. *A Deed of Gift to My Dear Son, Captain Matt. Page, One of His Majesty's Justices for New Kent County, in Virginia*. N.P., 1687; reprint, Philadelphia: Henry B. Ashmead, 1856.

Pead, Deuel. *Jesus is God: or, The Deity of Jesus Christ Vindicated. Being an Abstract of some Sermons Preach'd in the Parish Church of St. James Clerkenwell*. London, 1694.

_____. *A Practical Discourse Upon the Death of Our Late Gracious Queen*. London, 1695.

_____. "A Sermon Preached at James City in Virginia, the 23rd of April 1686, Before the Loyal Society of Citizens born in and about London and inhabiting in Virginia." Edited by Richard Beale Davis. *William and Mary Quarterly* 3rd ser. 17 (1960): 371-94.

Pender, Thomas. *The Divinity of the Scriptures, From Reason & External Circumstances*. New York, 1728.

Percy, George. "A Trewe Relaycon of the Proceedeinges and Occurrentes of Momente which have hapned in Virginia from the Tyme Sir Thomas Gates was shippwrackte upon the Bermudas anno 1609 until my departure outt of the Country which was anno Domini 1612." *Tylers' Historical Quarterly and Geneological Magazine* 3 (1922): 260-82.

Perry, William Stevens, editor. *Historical Collections Relating to the American Colonial Church*, 5 Volumes. Hartford, 1870; reprint, New York: AMS Press, 1969.

Price, Daniel. *Sauls Prohibition Staid*. London, 1609.

Rolfe, John. *A True Relation of the State of Virginia lefte by Sir Thomas Dale Knight in May Last 1616*. New Haven: Yale University Press, 1951.

Story, Thomas. *A Journal of the Life of Thomas Story: Containing an Account of His Remarkable Convincement of and Embracing the Principles of Truth, as Held by the People Called Quakers*. Newcastle upon Tyme, 1747.

Strachey, William. *Historie of Travell into Virginia Britania*. London, 1612. Edited by Louis Wright. London: Hakluyt Society, 1953.

_____. *A Voyage to Virginia in 1609*. London, 1609. Edited by Louis B. Wright, Charlottesville: University Press of Virginia, 1967.

Symonds, William. *Virginia, A Sermon Preached at White-Chapel*. London, 1609; reprint, New York: Da Capo Press, 1964.

Tillotson, John. *The Works of Dr. John Tillotson, Late Archbishop of Canterbury*. 10 Volumes. London: J.F. Dove, 1820.

Tinling, Marion, editor. *The Correspondence of the Three William Byrds of Westover Virginia, 1684-1776*. 2 Volumes. Charlottesville: University Press of Virginia, 1977.

Tyler, Lyon Gardiner, editor. *Narratives of Early Virginia, 1606-1625*. New York: Barnes & Noble, 1952.

Tynley, Robert. *Two Learned Sermons Preached, the one at Paules Crosse, the other at the Spittle*. London, 1609.

The Vain Prodigal Life, and Tragical Penitent Death of Thomas Hellier Born at Whitchurch *Near Lyme in Dorsetshire: Who for Murdering his Master, Mistress, and a Maid, was Executed according to Law at Westover in Charles City, in the country of Virginia, near The Plantation called Hard Labour, where he perpetrated the said Murders*. London, 1680.

Warrington, Thomas. *The Love of God, Benevolence, and Self-Love, considered together. A Sermon Preached at Norfolk, Before a Society of Free and Accepted Masons, December 27ᵗʰ, 1752*. Williamsburg, 1753.

Whitaker, Alexander. *Good Newes From Virginia*. London, 1613. Reprint, Wesley Frank Craven, editor. New York: Scholars' Facsimiles & Reprints, 1937.

Wright, Louis B, editor. *The Letters of Robert Carter, 1720-1727: The Commercial Interests of a Virginia Gentleman*. San Marino: The Huntington Library, 1940.

_____, editor. "William Byrd's Defense of Sir Edmund Andros." *William and Mary Quarterly* 3rd ser. 2 (1945.

_____, and Marion Tinling, editors. *The Secret Diary of William Byrd of Westover, 1709-1712.* Richmond: The Dietz Press, 1941.

Secondary Sources:

Ames, Susie M. *Studies of the Virginia Eastern Shore in the Seventeenth Century.* Richmond: The Dietz Press, 1940.

Anesko, Michael. "So Discreet a Zeal: Slavery and the Anglican Church in Virginia, 1680-1730." *Virginia Magazine of History and Biography* 93 (1985): 247-78.

Avis, Paul. "What is 'Anglicanism.'" In *The Study of Anglicanism*, edited by Stephen Sykes and John Booty, 405-423. London: S.P.C.K., 1988.

Axtell, James. *The Invasion Within: The Contest of Cultures in Colonial North America.* New York: Oxford University Press, 1988.

Barbour Philip L. "The Riddle of the Powhatan 'Black Boyes.'" *Virginia Magazine of History and Biography.* 88 (1980): 148-54.

Barrie-Currie, Viviane. "The Clergy of the Diocese of London in the Eighteenth Century." In *The Church of England c.1689-c.1833: From Toleration to Tractarianism*, edited by John Walsh, Colin Haydon, and Stephen Taylor, editors, 86-109. New York: Cambridge University Press, 1993.

Beeman, Richard. *The Evolution of the Southern Backcountry: A Case Study of Lunenburg County, Virginia, 1746-1832.* Philadelphia: University of Pennsylvania Press, 1984.

Beeth, Howard. "Outside Agitators in Southern History: The Society of Friends, 1656-1800." Ph.D. dissertation, University of Houston, 1984.

Bertelson, David. *The Lazy South.* New York: Oxford University Press, 1967.

Billings, Warren M. "Berkeley and Effingham: Who Cares?" *Virginia Magazine of History and Biography* 97 (1989): 33-46.

_____. "The Cases of Fernando and Elizabeth Key: A Note on the Status of Blacks in Seventeenth-Century Virginia." *William and Mary Quarterly* 3rd ser. 30 (1973): 464-74.

_____. "English Legal Literature as a Source of Law and Legal Practice for Seventeenth-Century Virginia." *Virginia Magazine of History and Biography* 87 (1979): 409-416.

_____. "The Growth of Political Institutions in Virginia, 1634-1676." *William and Mary Quarterly* 3rd ser. 31 (1974): 225-42.

_____. "Pleading, Pleading, and Practice: The Meaning of Due Process of Law in Seventeenth-Century Virginia." *Journal of Southern History* 47 (1981): 569-84.

_____. "Sir William Berkeley and the Diversification of the Virginia Economy." *Virginia Magazine of History and Biography* 104 (1996): 433-54.

_____. *Virginia's Viceroy: Their Majesties' Governor General: Francis Howard, Lord Howard of Effingham.* Fairfax VA: George Mason University Press, 1991.

_____, John E. Selby, and Thad W. Tate, *Colonial Virginia: A History.* White Plains NY: KTO Press, 1986.

Bonomi, Patricia U. *Under the Cope of Heaven: Religion, Society, and Politics in Colonial America.* New York: Oxford University Press, 1986.

_____, and Peter R. Eisenstadt, "Church Adherence in the Eighteenth-Century British American Colonies." *William and Mary Quarterly* 3rd ser. 39 (1982): 245-86.

Bossy, John. *The English Catholic Community, 1570-1850.* New York: Oxford University Press, 1976.

Bouwsma, William J. *John Calvin: A Sixteenth-Century Portrait.* New York: Oxford University Press, 1988.

Bowler, Clara Ann. "The Litigious Career of William Cotton, Minister." *Virginia Magazine of History and Biography.* 86 (1978): 411-26.

Breen, T.H. *Puritans and Adventurers: Change and Persistence in Early America.* New York: Oxford University Press, 1980.

_____. *Tobacco Culture: The Mentality of the Great Tidewater Planters on the Eve of Revolution.* Princeton: Princeton University Press, 1985.

Brown, Alexander. *The First Republic in America.* Boston: Houghton, Mifflin and Company, 1898.

Brown, Kathleen M. *Good Wives, Nasty Wenches, and Anxious Patriarchs: Gender, Race, and Power in Colonial Virginia.* Chapel Hill: University of North Carolina Press, 1996.

Bruce, Philip Alexander. *Institutional History of Virginia in the Seventeenth Century: An Inquiry into the Religious, Moral, Educational, Legal, Military, and Political Condition of the People Based on Original and Contemporary Records.* New York: The Knickerbocker Press, 1910.

Brydon, George MacLaren. *Virginia's Mother Church and the Political Conditions Under Which it Grew,* 2 Volumes. Richmond: Virginia Historical Society, 1947-1952.

Butler, Jon. *Awash in a Sea of Faith: Christianizing the American People.* Cambridge: Harvard University Press, 1990.

_____. "Magic, Astrology, and the Early American Religious Heritage, 1600-1760." *American Historical Review* 84 (1979).

Carpenter, Edward. *The Protestant Bishop, Being the Life of Henry Compton, 1632-1713, Bishop of London.* New York: Longmans, Greene, and Company, 1956.

Collinson, Patrick. *The Religion of Protestants.* Oxford: Oxford University Press, 1982.

Craven, Wesley Frank. *The Dissolution of the Virginia Company: The Failure of a Colonial Experiment.* New York: Oxford University Press, 1932.

_____. "Indian Policy in Early Virginia." *William and Mary Quarterly* 3rd ser. 1 (1944): 65-82.

Cressy, David. *Bonfires and Bells: National Memory and the Protestant Calendar in Elizabethan and Stuart England.* Los Angeles: University of California Press, 1989.

Cross, Arthur Lyon. *The Anglican Episcopate and the American Colonies.* New York: Longmans, Green, and Company, 1902.

Crow, Stephen D. "'Your Majesty's Good Subjects': A Reconsideration of Royalism in Virginia, 1642-1652." *Virginia Magazine of History and Biography* 87 (1979): 158-73.

Cust, Richard, and Ann Hughes, editors. *Conflict in Early Stuart England: Studies in Religion and Politics, 1603-1642.* New York: Longman, 1989.

Davies, Horton. *Worship and Theology in England,* 5 Volumes. Princeton: Princeton University Press, 1961-1975.

Davis, Richard Beale. "The Devil in Virginia in the Seventeenth-Century." *Virginia Magazine of History and Biography* 65 (1957): 131-49.

_____. *Intellectual Life in the Colonial South, 1585-1763,* 3 Volumes. Knoxville: University of Tennessee Press, 1978.

de Grazia, Sebastian. *Machiavelli in Hell.* Princeton: Princeton University Press, 1989.

Diamond, Sigmund. "From Organization to Society: Virginia in the Seventeenth Century." In *Colonial America: Essays in Politics and Social Development,* editor, Stanley N. Katz, 3-31. Boston: Little, Brown, and Company, 1971.

Earle, Carville V. "Environment, Disease, and Mortality in Early Virginia." In Thad W. Tate and David L. Ammerman, editors, 96-125. *The Chesapeake in the Seventeenth Century: Essays on Anglo-American Society.* Chapel Hill: University of North Carolina Press, 1979.

Edmundson, William. *A Journal of the Life, Travels, Sufferings and Labour of Love in the Work of the Ministry, of that Worthy Elder and faithful servant of Jesus Christ, William Edmundson.* London, 1774.

Elmer, Paul. "Richard Allestree and *The Whole Duty of Man.*" *The Library* 5th ser. 6 (1951): 19-27.

Elton, G.R. *The Tudor Revolution in Government: Administrative Changes in the Reign of Henry VIII.* Cambridge: Cambridge University Press, 1969.

Fausz, J. Frederick. "Middlemen in Peace and War: Virginia's Earliest Indian Interpreters, 1609-1632." *Virginia Magazine of History and Biography* 95 (1987): 41-64.

Fiering, Norman. "The First American Enlightenment: Tillotson, Leverett, and Philosophical Anglicanism." *New England Quarterly* 54 (1981): 307-344.

Fincham, Kenneth and Peter Lake. "The Ecclesiastical Policies of James I and Charles I." In *The Early Stuart Church, 1603-164,* edited by Kenneth Fincham, 23-50. Stanford: University Press, 1993.

Fischer, David Hackett. *Albion's Seed: Four British Folkways in North America.* New York: Oxford University Press, 1989.

Goodwin, Edward Lewis. *The Colonial Church in Virginia.* Milwaukee: Morehouse, 1927.

Greenblatt, Stephen. *Marvelous Possessions: The Wonder of the New World.* Chicago: University of Chicago Press, 1991.

_____. *Renaissance Self-Fashioning: From More to Shakespeare.* Chicago: University of Chicago Press, 1980.

Gregory, Jeremy. "The Eighteenth-Century Reformation: The Pastoral Task of Anglican Clergy After 1689." In *The Church of England c.1689-c.1833: From Toleration to Tractarianism,* editors, John Walsh, Colin Haydon, and Stephen Taylor, 67-86. New York: Cambridge University Press, 1993.

Gundersen, Joan Rezner. "The Anglican Ministry in Virginia, 1723-1776: A Study of a Social Class." Ph.D. dissertation, University of Notre Dame, 1972.

_____. "The Myth of the Independent Virginia Vestry." *Historical Magazine of the Protestant Episcopal Church* 44 (1975): 133-41.

_____. "The Search for Good Men: Recruiting Ministers in Colonial Virginia." *Historical Magazine of the Protestant Episcopal Church* 47 (1979): 453-64.

Haigh, Christopher, editor. *The English Reformation Revisited.* Cambridge: Cambridge University Press, 1987.

Hall, David D. *Worlds of Wonder, Days of Judgment: Popular Religious Belief in Early New England.* New York: Alfred Knopf, 1989.

Hallman, Clive Raymond, Jr. "The Vestry as a Unit of Local Government in Colonial Virginia." Ph.D. dissertation, University of Georgia, 1987.

Hambrick-Stowe, Charles E. *The Practice of Piety: Puritan devotional Disciplines in Seventeenth-Century New England.* Chapel Hill: University of North Carolina Press, 1982.

Hatch, Charles E., Jr., and Thurlow Gates Gregory. "The First American Blast Furnace, 1619-1622: The Birth of a Mighty Industry on Falling Creek in Virginia." *Virginia Magazine of History and Biography* 70 (1962): 259-96.

Helgerson, Richard. *Forms of Nationhood: The Elizabethan Writing of England.* Chicago: University of Chicago Press, 1992.

Hill, Christopher. *The English Bible and the Seventeenth-Century Revolution.* New York: Penguin Books, 1994.

Holmes, Peter. *Resistance and Compromise: The Political Thought of the Elizabethan Catholics.* Cambridge: Cambridge University Press, 1982.

Horn, James. *Adapting to a New World: English Society in the Seventeenth-Century Chesapeake.* Chapel Hill: University of North Carolina Press, 1994.

Ingle, H. Larry. *First Among Friends: George Fox and the Creation of Quakerism.* New York: Oxford University Press, 1994.

Ingram, Martin. *Church Courts, Sex and Marriage in England, 1570-1640.* Cambridge: Cambridge University Press, 1987.

Isaac, Rhys. *The Transformation of Virginia, 1740-1790.* Chapel Hill: University of North Carolina Press, 1982.

Jones, Rufus Matthew. *The Quakers in the American Colonies.* London: MacMillan and Co., 1911.

Kocher, Paul H. *Science and Religion in Elizabethan England.* San Marino: Huntington Library, 1953.

Konig, David Thomas. "Dale's Laws and the Non-Common Law Origins of Criminal Justice in Virginia." *American Journal of Legal History* 26 (1982): 345-75.

Kukla, Jon. "Order and Chaos in Early America: Political and Social Stability in Pre-Restoration Virginia." *American Historical Review* 90 (1985): 275-98.

Kupperman, Karen Ordahl. *Roanoke: The Abandoned Colony.* Totawa NJ: Rowman & Allanheld, 1984.

_____. *Settling With the Indians: The Meeting of English and Indian Cultures in America, 1580-1640*. Totawa NJ: Rowman & Littlefield, 1980.

Lake, Peter. *Anglicans and Puritans? Presbyterian and English Conformist Thought from Whitgift to Hooker*. London: Unwin Hyman, 1988.

Levy, Babette M. "Early Puritanism in the Southern and Island Colonies." *American Antiquarian Society Proceedings* 70 (1960).

Lewis, Jan. *The Pursuit of Happiness: Family and Values in Jefferson's Virginia*. New York: Cambridge University Press, 1983.

Lockridge, Kenneth A. *The Diary, and Life, of William Byrd II of Virginia, 1674-1744.*   Chapel Hill: University of North Carolina Press, 1987.

Maltby, Judith. "'By This Book': Parishioners, the Prayer Book, and the Established Church." In *The Early Stuart Church, 1603-1642,* edited by Kenneth Fincham, 115-38.

McGregor, J.F., and Barry Reay, editors. *Radical Religion in the English Revolution*. New York: Oxford University Press, 1984.

Meade, William. *Old Churches, Ministers and Families of Virginia,* 2 Volumes. Philadelphia: J.B.Lipincott,& Co., 1878.

Middleton, Arthur Pierce. "The Colonial Virginia Parson." *William and Mary Quarterly* 3rd ser. 26 (1969): 425-40.

Miller, Perry. "Religion and Society in the Early Literature of Virginia." In *Errand Into the Wilderness,* 101-40. New York: Harvard University Press, 1956.

Morgan, Edmund S. *American Slavery, American Freedom: The Ordeal of Colonial Virginia*. New York: W.W. Norton, 1975.

_____. "The Labor Problem at Jamestown, 1607-1618," 595-611. *American Historical Review* 76 (1971).

Morton, Richard L. *Colonial Virginia,* 2 Volumes. Chapel Hill: University of North Carolina Press, 1960.

Muir, Edward. *Ritual in Early Modern Europe*. New York: Cambridge University Press, 1997.

Norman, Edward. *Roman Catholicism in England from the Elizabethan Settlement to the Second Vatican Council.* New York: Oxford University Press, 1985.

Notestein, Wallace. *The English People on the Eve of Colonization, 1603-1630.* New York: Harper & Row, 1954.

Parker, John. "Religion and the Virginia Colony, 1609-1610." In K.R. Andrews, N.P. Canny, And P.E. Hair, editors, *The Westward Enterprise: English Activities in Ireland, the Atlantic, and America, 1480-1650,* 245-70. Detroit: Wayne State University Press, 1979.

Parramore, Thomas C. *Southampton County, Virginia.* Charlottesville: University Press of Virginia, 1978.

Pearce, Roy Harvey. *Savagism and Civilization: A Study of the Indian and the American Mind.* Berkeley: University of California Press, 1984.

Pennington, Loren E. *"Hakluytas Posthumous*: Samuel Purchas and the Promotion of English Overseas Expansion." In *Emporia State Research Studies* 14 (1966): 5-39.

Perry, James R. *The Formation of a Society on Virginia's Eastern Shore, 1615-1655.* Chapel Hill: University of North Carolina Press, 1990.

Porter, Harry Culverwell. "Alexander Whitaker: Cambridge Apostle to Virginia." *William and Mary Quarterly* 3rd ser. 14 (1957): 317-43.

Powell, William S. "Books in the Virginia Colony Before 1624." *William and Mary Quarterly* 2d ser. 5 (1948): 177-84.

Prall, Stuart E. *Church and State in Tudor and Stuart England.* Arlington Heights IL: Harland Davidson, 1993.

Quinn, David Beers. *Set Fair For Roanoke: Voyages and Colonies, 1584-1606.* Chapel Hill: University of North Carolina Press, 1985.

Rabb, Theodore K. *Jacobean Gentleman: Sir Edwin Sandys, 1561-1629.* Princeton: Princeton University Press, 1998.

Rabe, Henry C. "The Reverend Devereux Jarratt and the Social Order." *Historical Magazine of The Protestant Episcopal Church* 33 (1964): 299-336.

Rainbolt, John C. "The Absence of Towns in Seventeenth-Century Virginia." *Journal of Southern History* 35 (1969): 343-60.

_____. *From Prescription to Persuasion: Manipulation of Eighteenth [Seventeenth] Century Virginia Economy.* Port Washington NY: Kennikat Press, 1974.

Reay, Barry, editor. *Popular Culture in Seventeenth-Century England.* New York: St. Martin's Press, 1985.

_____. *The Quakers and the English Revolution.* London: Temple Smith, 1985.

Robinson, W. Stitt, Jr. "Indian Education and Missions in Colonial Virginia." *Journal of Southern History* 18 (1952): 152-68.

Rouse, Parke, Jr. *James Blair of Virginia.* Chapel Hill: University of North Carolina Press, 1971.

Rutman, Darrett. "The Evolution of Religious Life in Early Virginia." *Lex et Scientia* 14 (1978): 190-214.

Seed, Patricia. *Ceremonies of Possession in Europe's Conquest of the New World, 1492-1640.* New York: Cambridge University Press, 1995.

_____. "Taking Possession and Reading Texts: Establishing the Authority of English Overseas Empires." *William and Mary Quarterly* 3rd series, 49 (1992): 183-209.

Seiler, William H. "The Anglican Parish in Virginia." In *Seventeenth-Century America: Essays.* In *Colonial History,* edited by James Morton Smith, 119-42. Chapel Hill: University of North Carolina Press, 1959.

_____. "The Church of England as the Established Church in Seventeenth-Century Virginia." *Journal of Southern History* 15 (1949): 478-508.

Sharpe, J.A. *Crime in Early Modern England, 1550-1750.* New York: Longman, 1084.

Sheehan, Bernard W. *Savigism and Civility: Indians and Englishmen in Colonial Virginia.* New York: Cambridge University Press, 1980.

Smith, Timothy L. "Congregation, State, and Denomination: The Forming of the American Religious Structure." *William and Mary Quarterly* 3rd ser. 25 (1968): 155-76.

Smits, David B. "'Abominable Mixture': Toward the Repudiation of Anglo-Indian Intermarriage in Seventeenth-Century Virginia." *Virginia Magazine of History and Biography.* 95 (1987): 157-92.

Sobel, Mechal. *The World They Made Together: Black and White Values in Eighteenth-Century Virginia.* Princeton: Princeton University Press, 1987.

Solt, Leo. F. *Church and State in Early Modern England, 1509-1640.* New York: Oxford University Press, 1990.

Spufford, Margaret. *Contrasting Communities: English Villages in the Sixteenth and Seventeenth Centuries.* New York: Cambridge University Press, 1979.

Spurr, John. "The Church, The Societies and the Moral Revolution of 1688." In *The Church of England c.1689-c.1833: From Toleration to Tractarianism,* edited by John Walsh, Colin Haydon, and Stephen Taylor, 127-42. New York: Cambridge University Press, 1993.

_____. *The Restoration Church of England, 1646-1689.* New Haven: Yale University Press, 1991.

_____. "'Virtue, Religion and Government': The Anglican Uses of Providence." In *The Politics of Religion in Restoration England,* edited by Tim Harris, Paul Seward, and Mark Goldie, Oxford: Basil Blackwell Ltd., 1990.

Steiner, Bruce. E. "The Catholic Brents of Colonial Virginia: An Instance of Practical Toleration." *Virginia Magazine of History and Biography* 70 (1962): 387-409.

Thomas, Keith. *Man and the Natural World: A History of the Modern Sensibility.* New York: Pantheon Books, 1983.

_____. *Religion and the Decline of Magic: Studies in Popular Beliefs in Sixteenth and Seventeenth Century England.* London: Wiedenfeld and Nicolson, 1971.

Underdown, David. *Fire From Heaven: Life in an English Town in the Seventeenth Century.* New Haven: Yale University Press, 1992.

_____. *Revel, Riot, and Rebellion: Popular Politics and Culture in England, 1603-1660*. New York: Oxford University Press, 1985.

Upton, Dell. *Holy Things and Profane: Anglican Parish Churches in Colonial Virginia*. New York: M.I.T. Press, 1986.

Walsh, James P. "'Black Cotted Raskolls': Anti-Anglican Criticism in Colonial Virginia." *Virginia Magazine of History and Biography* 88 (1980): 21-36.

Walter, Donna Joanne. "Imagery in the Sermons of James Blair." M.A. thesis, University of Tennessee, 1967.

Washburn, Wilcomb. *The Indian in America*. New York: Harper & Row, 1975.

Watts, Michael R. *The Dissenters: From the Reformation to the French Revolution*. New York: Oxford University Press, 1978.

Webb, Stephen Saunders. *Lord Churchill's Coup: The Anglo-American Empire and the Glorious Revolution Reconsidered*. New York: Alfred A. Knopf, 1995.

Whiting, Marvin Yeomans. "Religious Literature in Virginia, 1685-1786: A Preface to a Study of the History of Ideas." M.A. thesis, Emory University, 1975.

Woolverton, John F. *Colonial Anglicanism in North America*. Detroit: Wayne State University Press, 1984.

Worrall, Jay, Jr. *The Friendly Virginians: America's First Quakers*. Athens GA: Iberian Publishing Company, 1992.

Wright, Louis B. "Elizabethan Politics and Colonial Enterprise." *North Carolina Historical Review*. 32 (1955): 254-69.

_____. "Pious Reading in Colonial Virginia." *Journal of Southern History* 6 (1940): 383-92.

INDEX